ARABI

NERDS *one*

Fill The Gaps.

270 Questions About
Arabic Grammar

Upgraded First Edition – With Index

by
Gerald Drißner

Gerald Drißner (Drissner),

born 1977 in a mountain village in Austria, is an economist and award-winning journalist. He has been living in the Middle East and North Africa for ten years, where he has intensively studied Arabic.

He is the author of *Islam for Nerds* (500 Questions and Answers) and *Arabic for Nerds 2* (450 Questions and Answers).

IMPRINT/IMPRESSUM – Arabic for Nerds 1

1ˢᵗ edition, upgraded and fully revised, October 2015 (080919)

Copyright © 2015 by Gerald Drißner (Drissner)

Cover design, layout: © 2015 by Gerald Drißner

Publisher:	pochemuchka (Gerald Drißner)
Internet:	https://drissner.me
E-Mail:	mail@drissner.me
Address:	Postfach 35 03 30, D-10212 Berlin, Germany
ISBN-13:	978-3-9819848-7-3 (Paperback)
ISBN-13:	978-3-9819848-2-8 (Hardcover)

For my love
who hates grammar

ARABIC FOR NERDS ONE

Acknowledgements

This book consumed huge amount of work, research and dedication. I would like to express my gratitude to the many people who saw me through this book; to all those who taught me Arabic and allowed me to quote their remarks.

I would like to thank

Michael Guggenheimer
for his numerous comments which I am going to miss.

Judith Zepter, in Hamburg,
for her profound and helpful remarks.

Badrul Aini Sha'ari, in Kuala Lumpur,
for his valuable comments.

Kenan Kalajdzic, in Sarajevo,
for his thorough reading and insightful suggestions.

Above all, I want to thank
my wife
who supported and encouraged me
in spite of all the time it took me away from her.

Introduction

A: كَيْفَ الْحال؟

B: دائِمًا مَنْصُوب !

(A joke shared among Arabic grammar nerds.)

The cover picture was taken when I started to fall in love with Arabic. It happened in 2009 in Egypt after my first lesson with مصطفى حميدة, a highly esteemed professor at the University of Alexandria. When I showed it to my friends at home in Austria, they thought of mathematics or physics – as there are a lot of arrows and arithmetic signs.

This is what Arabic is all about, patterns and structures. If you want to feel the beauty and strength of the Arabic language, you have to understand its inner logic. I used to play chess at a young age and grandmasters told me that you have to study pawn structures and patterns – and not opening moves. I guess it is quite the same with Arabic.

I have been collecting interesting facts about grammar, vocabulary and expressions, hints and traps for almost ten years. Now, I have compiled them to a book: *Arabic for Nerds*.

This book should fill a gap. There are plenty of books about Arabic for beginners and some for intermediate students but it is difficult to find good material on the advanced level.

Which leads us to the question: What is advanced?

If your mother tongue is English, it is said that you need 700 hours (of instruction) to become fluent in French, German, Spanish, Danish or Swahili. You need 1400 hours for Greek, Hindi, Russian or Urdu. And you need 2800 hours if you want to reach the level *advanced high* in Japanese, Korean, Chinese – and Arabic.

This book is suitable for you if you have been studying Arabic intensively for at least two years. You have a sound knowledge of vocabulary (around 3000 words) and know about tenses, verb moods and plurals.

During my studies in the Middle East and North Africa, I met students from Europe and the USA. They all shared a similar experience: They studied Arabic the same way they had learned German, English, French or Spanish – by using the grammar terms and syntax they knew from their native language. This only works in some cases. However, it will definitely make it difficult to achieve an advanced level in Arabic – because you won't get the feeling how this fascinating Semitic language works.

When I decided to study Arabic, I wanted to study it the Arab way. I realized that Arabic grammar is actually much easier than German grammar – but only if you use the Arabic terms. If you read German books on Arabic grammar, you need a Latin dictionary and eventually get frustrated.

I was happy to find an old Arabic teacher who couldn't speak English. I avoided translating words. English has a word for nearly everything. In Arabic, a single word can mean dozens of things depending on the context. Arabic is a poetic language but have you ever felt its poetic core?

Let us look at the word دُنْيا: It is translated in books as *world*. The meaning is correct but if you have a closer look, you will understand that it is not a good idea to focus on translations too much (see *question #147*).

This book doesn't teach you vocabulary, nor are there exercises. This book explains how Arabic works and gives you hints in using and understanding the language better. Since most of the Arabic words are given in translation, you should be able to read this book without a dictionary.

I used تَشْكِيل, diacritical marks, for the correct pronunciation wherever it is necessary – especially when dealing with cases and moods. Before the feminine ending ة ـَ, I do not write the short vowel "a" because by definition it must be either the vowel "a" (فَتْحَةٌ) or Aleph (آ), a so-called أَلِفٌ ساكِنة, like in the words فَتاةٌ (young girl), مُجاراةٌ (conformity) or قُضاةٌ (judges). I also mix English and Arabic. I hope you don't mind the strange combination sometimes. Many Arabic grammar terms can't be translated precisely. For this reason, I use as many options as possible now and then. I usually give the indefinite, singular form of Arabic grammar terms, though I may use different forms in the English text.

Since there are already a lot of points in the Arabic alphabet I sometimes don't follow the correct English punctuation (e.g., full stops or commas) to make it easier for the reader.

This book isn't scientific, nor academic. This book is a working paper and will constantly be updated and upgraded. I am sure there are inaccuracies as I have a mere practical view.

If you spot mistakes, have ideas or corrections, please kindly let me know by e-mail: mail@drissner.me

Berlin, October 2015

1. What is the secret of Arabic vowels?

Even if you don't have a clue about the meaning of a word, you will actually know a lot – simply by looking at its final vowel.

Arabic is like a mathematical game. You take the root of a word, which normally consists of three letters, and you start playing. Your tools are pre- and suffixes, three vowels and a mark of silence or anti-vowel.

The vowels at the end of words are essential for understanding the inner meaning and logic of Arabic. If you think about the pronunciation and how this influences the rhythm, you will improve your understanding of a sentence. You will also get a better feeling for the الْإِعْرابُ, i.e., putting case markers.

Let us have a closer look at the **main (final) sounds** in Arabic. Note that we use the term *mood* **for verbs** and *case* **for nouns**.

u	ضَمَّة	This is the regular ending. Endings in *"u"* mark normal situations. They are used for primacy and for action. It represents complete meanings and essential things.
		In grammar, we use the word مَرْفُوعٌ. It comes from the root-verb رَفَعَ which denotes: *to raise; to place; to take off/to start; to pronounce the final consonant with "u"*.
		It occurs in **nouns** (اِسْمٌ) and **verbs** (فِعْلٌ). Closest meaning in English grammar: *nominative* (nouns) or *indicative* (verbs).

a	فَتْحة	The word فَتْحة comes from the root *to open*. The vowel *"a"* is an open vowel and it is used for situations of installing, setting up or appointing things (تَصْبُ).
		In grammar, we use the word مَنْصُوبٌ. It literally means *set up, installed*. Generally speaking, the فَتْحة at the end of a word enriches a sentence with additional in-

formation, it unfolds the action. It is like a supplement of information (e.g., the object of a verb).

The مَنْصُوب- mood indicates that a verb is used in the context of intention (German: *Absichtssätze*), permission, purpose, expectation, necessity, or possibility.

Technically (semantically) speaking, you have to use a verb in the مَنْصُوب-mood after particles such as أَنْ (indicating an action not yet realized) or لَنْ (*I won't*).

It occurs in **nouns** and **verbs**. Closest meaning in English: *accusative* (nouns) or *subjunctive* (verbs).

| i | كَسْرَةٌ | The vowel "*i*" requires the lips to be stretched way out to the sides. At the end of a noun it marks situations of reduction, dragging and causing (جَرٌّ) and sets up a dependency in meaning (e.g., after a preposition or the second part of a إِضافة-construction).

In grammar, we use the word مَجْرُورٌ. It literally means *dragged* or *pulled*. The كَسْرَة specifies and coordinates information.

You can <u>only</u> find it at the end of **nouns** (اِسْمٌ). Closest English term: *genitive*.

| - | سُكُونٌ | Quiescence: mark of silence or anti-vowel (سُكُونٌ).

At the end of a verb it evokes the action of cutting, clipping or decision (جَزْمٌ). If there is a weak letter (و or ي) in the verb (حَرْفُ الْعِلّةِ), the weak letter will usually drop if you have to put a سُكُون at the end.

In grammar, we use the word مَجْزُومٌ. It literally means *cut short; clipped*. In English, you may use the term *jussive mood* (verbs) or *apocopate*. The word *jussive* relates to the Latin word *jubeō*: to order, to command.

It occurs in **verbs** <u>only</u>.

Some remarks: I strongly recommend using the Arabic grammar terms. In this book, I occasionally use the Latin terms just to give readers (who aren't familiar with the Arabic terms yet) a hint. There is one big advantage: Most people have no clue what the Latin grammar terms actually mean.

However, Arabic grammar terms are Arabic words with a meaning (see *question #154*). Thus, always try to translate the grammar term literally.

It will help you to remember the terms. You will also develop a better idea of the grammar concept. If you use the Arabic terms, Arabic grammar will eventually become a lot easier. For example: verbs or nouns can be مَنْصُوب in Arabic.

- If a **noun** has the مَنْصُوب-ending *"a"*, then it might be the *direct object*. Thus, the noun takes the *accusative case*. See example 1 in the table below.

- If a **verb** has the مَنْصُوب-ending, we may deal with an *interpreted infinitive* (مَصْدَر مُؤَوَّل) molded by أَنْ plus verb. The Latin grammar term for this situation is *subjunctive mood*. See example 2.

Forget these complicated Latin terms! There is a reason why Arabic uses the same term (مَنْصُوب) for both ideas (verbs and nouns). Remember: A فَتْحة at the end of a word enriches a sentence with **additional information, it unfolds the action.**

I want a book. (*A book* is what **I want**.)	أُرِيدُ كِتَابًا. 1
I want to read a book. (*To read a book* is what **I want**.)	أُرِيدُ أَنْ أَقْرَأَ كِتَابًا. 2

2. How many roots does the Arabic language have?

Mathematically: 21,952 roots. Practically, you get 6,332 roots.

There are many Arabic dictionaries. *Hans Wehr's Arabisches Wörterbuch für die Schriftsprache der Gegenwart* (named after a German scholar, published in 1952) is the most complete dictionary of <u>Standard Arabic</u> ever published in the West. It contains **2967** roots (جِذْر) with 3 letters and 362 with 4 letters.

The most famous dictionary of <u>Classical Arabic</u> is *Lisān al-ʿArab* (لِسان الْعَرَب), compiled by Ibn Manzūr (اِبْن مَنْظُور) in the early 14ᵗʰ century (711 AH). It contains around 80,000 entries and in total (3 + 4 letters + foreign words) **9273** roots.

Since the Arabic alphabet consists of 28 letters (consonant phonemes) there are **21,952** theoretical combinations ($=28^3$) of roots with <u>three</u> radicals. However, certain combinations are considered to be impossible (with few exceptions):

- There is <u>no</u> Arabic root which consists of **three identical** consonants.

- There are <u>no</u> Arabic roots with **identical** consonants in the **first** and **second** position.

- There are (almost) <u>no</u> Arabic roots with identical consonants in the **first** and **third** position. (An exception would be قَلِق – *to be troubled*.)

- However, there <u>are</u> roots whose **second** and **third** letter are **identical**, for example, *to pass* (م-ر-ر).

Taking into account all possible restrictions, the theoretical number of all possible combinations of roots (morphemes) with three letters is **6332**[1].

---

1   *Gustav Herdan* (1962): "The Patterning of Semitic Verbal Roots Subjected to Combinatory Analysis"

Remark: What are the most common root letters?

In *Hans Wehr*, the most common root letter is ر (722 times). The ظ is the least common: only 42 times (1.4 %). The ن is the most common first radical (235 times).

3. Which letters can you add to a root?

There are only ten.

Almost every Arabic word (except proper nouns and foreign words) has a root that consists of three or four letters, so-called radicals. In Arabic, a radical is called حَرْفٌ أَصْلِيٌّ. The word أَصْلِيّ means *original* or *authentic*.

It is easy to identify a root (جِذْر) as there are **only ten letters** in Arabic which can be added to a root. These letters are:

Hamza (ء-أ-ئ-ؤ), *Mīm* (م), *Aleph* (ا-ى), *Nūn* (ن),
Wāw (و), *Tā'* (ت), *Sīn* (س), *Hā'* (ـه), *Yā'* (ي), *Lām* (ل)

They are called حُرُوفُ الزِّيادةِ.

Talking about **verbs**, you can only add **five** extra letters:

أ - ت - س - ن - ا

You can remember them easily because they can be summed up in phrases. For example:

- سَأَلْتُمُونيهَا – literally: *"you (pl.) asked me it (that)."*

- أَمانٌ وتَسْهِيلٌ - *safety and convenience.*

Remark: سَأَلْتُمُونيهَا is a weird phrase. Let's do a quick analysis:

هـا	ي	ن	و	سَأَلْتُم
2nd direct object (مَفْعُـولٌ) (بِهِ ثانٍ)	1st direct object (مَفْعُـولٌ) (بِهِ أَوَّل)	*Guarding or preventive Nūn* (النُّونُ لِلْوِقاية). It prevents the final vowel of the verb from being absorbed by the long vowel *"ee/ii"*.	So-called واوُ لِلإِشْـبَاع (*Wāw of satiation*). It helps to lengthen the ضَمّة (*"u"*) to be a و. Such extra و is added to تُم or كُم when they are followed by another pronoun, resulting in تُمُو.	Verb, past tense

4. Letters without dots - Does it work?

It did, a long time ago.

At first Arabic was written without vowel-signs above or under letters.

Furthermore, letters were written **without dots** which makes reading pretty difficult – because the letters ف and ق as well as the letters ب and ن and ي might look the same in certain situations. Try to read the following sentence without the dots:

فـل اں فـل فـل فـل فـل الـهر

This sentence can have several meanings. It depends on where and how you add the dots, e.g., the first word can mean:

killed	قَتَّل		before	قَبْلَ		elephant	فِيل

This is how you could read the sentence:

It was said that the elephant killed an elephant in front of the river.	قيل إن فيل قتل فيل قبل النهر.
This is the sentence with all the vowels.	قِيلَ إِنَّ فِيلًا قَتَلَ فِيلًا قَبْلَ النَّهرِ.

5. Who was the first Arabic grammar expert?

The first grammar expert was أَبُو الْأَسْوَد الدُّؤَلِيّ, *in transliteration: Abū al-'Aswad al-Du'alī (603 – 688).*

He converted to Islam during the time of the prophet Muhammad and later migrated to Basra (which is in present-day Iraq) where a mosque is named after him. When more and more people converted to Islam, many of them couldn't read the Qur'an without making mistakes which led to a misunderstanding of words.

Historians also say that it was أَبُـو الْأَسْـوَد الـدُّؤَلِيّ who marked the letters with points approximately in the year 664 (42 هـ), at a time when the vowel signs (تَشْكِيلْ), which we use now, had not existed.

Remark: In the 8th century, a grammarian from present-day Oman invented a writing system which we basically use in standard Arabic until today. His name is Al-Khalīl ibn 'Ahmad al-Farāhīdī (الْخَلِيل بن أَحْمَد الْقَراهِيدِيّ), a grammarian who was born in 718 (100 AH) in present-day Oman. It is said that he started using a small س for the الشَّدّة (*Shadda*) : ّ

6. What does the word نَحْوُ mean?

It has many meanings: direction; side; way; manner, fashion; corresponding to; similar to; like – and it means: <u>grammar</u>!

The original meaning of the root ن-ح-و is *direction*. In old grammar books, the word نَحْوُ was used to express the meaning of *to show someone the direction*. Later, it also acquired the meaning of *for example*. So, what we call *grammar* (syntax) was in old times just a way to show people how Arabic works.

نَحْوُ is a very tricky word. It is a noun (اِسْمٌ) and can be used in several ways expressing *direction* (الْمِقْدارُ or الْإِقْتِرابُ).

A) It can serve as an **adverbial accusative of place** (ظَرْفُ الْمَكانِ). Now it is getting complicated: In Arabic, we don't have the word **type** "adverb" like in English. Words can only have the **function** of an adverb. In Arabic an adverb of place is an <u>object</u> (مَفْعُولٌ فِيهِ). This is the reason for the accusative marker "a" (فَتْحَةٌ) which such words receive. So we get نَحْوَ. It only gets one فَتْحَةٌ because it serves as the first part of a إِضافةٌ. The second part gets the genitive case and tells you the actual place. نَحْوَ has the meaning of *towards, in the direction of; approximately*. Note that نَحْوَ is often synonymous with the word صَوْبَ.

B) If you connect نَحْو with a **true preposition** (حَرْفُ الْجَرِّ) like in the expression بِنَحْوِ, the word is treated as a normal, <u>declinable</u> اِسْمٌ which implies that نَحْو takes regular case endings. Since there is a preposition involved, the word نَحْو is in the genitive case (مَجْرُورٌ).

C) نَحْو can also be used **with numbers**. Then it conveys the meaning of *about, approximately*.

He came to (towards) us.	أَتى نَحْوَنا.	A

نَحْوَ is in the position of a ظَرْفُ (*adverb of place*). It gives us information about the direction that is related to the action of *to come*.

around five o'clock...	...فِي نَحْوِ السَّاعَةِ الْخَامِسةِ	B
in this way...	...عَلَى هٰذا النَّحْوِ	

Here we have a preposition (فِي) involved. نَحْوَ gets the treatment of a noun (اِسْمُ) in such positions. It is dragged into the genitive by the preposition and is مَجْرُورٌ as you can see by the "i" (كَسْرةٌ).

approximately eleven years...	...نَحْوُ أَحَدَ عَشَرَ عَامًا	C
about four thousand men...	...نَحْوُ أَرْبَعةِ آلافِ رَجُلٍ	
I read about ten books.	قَرَأْتُ نَحْوَ عَشَرَةِ كُتُبٍ.	

In the last example, نَحْوَ is the **direct** object (مَفْعُولٌ بِهِ) of *to read*.

7. Are there long vowels in Arabic?

In Arabic, precisely speaking, there aren't. The term long vowel is used to make things easier to understand, also in this book.

So-called **long vowels** are described in Arabic by the term حُرُوفُ الْمَدِّ. The word مَدّ has the meaning of *lengthening*. So what we describe as a long vowel is, in fact, just a lengthening of the preceding sound, i.e., "*a*", "*i*", or "*u*".

Arabic doesn't have real long vowels. It has **only three short vowels** (a, i, u). The letters و and ي are treated as (semi-) **consonants**. The letter ا (Aleph) is a special case – see *question #9*.

The long vowel ī ("*ii*" or "*ee*"), for example, is composed of a كَسْرة under the preceding letter plus the silent consonant يْ

– which all together results in the lengthening or prolongation of the preceding sound. This is what we are talking about:

long a (أَلِفُ مَدَّ)	"aa"	ـَا
long I (يَاءُ مَدَّ)	iy = "ii"	ـِي
long u (وَاوُ مَدَّ)	uw = "uu"	ـُوْ

8. Can a word start with a vowel?

No, it can't.

This brings us to a golden rule in Arabic: <u>Every Arabic utterance or sentence has to start with a **consonant** followed by a **vowel**</u>. Standard Arabic forbids initial consonant clusters and more than two consecutive consonants in other positions.

If you see ...

- the definite article اَل like in the word اَلْكِتَابُ

- an imperative - for example: اُكْتُبْ!

- the Arabic word for *son* (اِبْنٌ) or *name* (اِسْمٌ)

... at the beginning of an utterance or in isolation, then the first sound coming out of your mouth has to be a هَمْزَة, a so-called glottal stop.

The sound of a هَمْزَة exists in English or German in speech too, but it is not written. It is phonetically a catch in the throat by holding one's breath and suddenly releasing it. The word *little* is an example in colloquial English. If you don't pronounce the *"tt"*, then you will get a word like *"li'le"*. *Spiegel-Ei* is an example of a German word with a glottal stop; the glottal stop is pronounced where the dash is.

9. Why is the letter ‌ا (Aleph) so special?

Because it can never be part of the root.

There are three letters in Arabic that often cause difficulties:

ا - و - ي

Especially the Aleph (اَلِفٌ) is a tricky letter. We will now examine three rules which will help us to deal with it:

RULE I: An Aleph can never be part of the root.

The three (weak) letters ‌ا - ي - و are called حُرُوفُ الْعِلّةِ. The word عِلّةٌ means *defect, deficiency.*

But only two of them - و and ي - can be part of the root. If you spot an Aleph (ا) in a word, it will never be a root letter. The Aleph is, in fact, originally either و or ي which has changed its form to ‌ا.

Watch out: Notice the difference between the ‌ا (long vowel) and the Hamza (هَمْزَةٌ), i.e., glottal stop, in the shape of an Aleph (أ). Let's take, for example, the verb *to point at*: أَدّى إِلَى.

Here, the Aleph is a real هَمْزَةٌ, written in the shape of an Aleph with a هَمْزَةٌ on top, because the following vowel has an "*a*"-sound. However, the root of the word is: ‌ء - د - و.

RULE II: The special letter آ is called *extended Aleph* (الْأَلِفُ الْمَمْدُودَةُ) – in grammar, you will often just hear: الْمَدّةُ.

Watch out: Don't mix it up with the Aleph that simply works as long "a" (أَلِفُ مَدّ) and which is written as ‌ا + ٰ .

The letter آ is a combination of two letters. There are several possibilities and positions in which it may occur:

meaning	example		construction	
traces, effects	آثارٌ	أَاثارٌ	ا + آ	1
rewards; compensation	مُكافآتٌ	مُكافأةٌ	ا + آ	2
Qur'an	قُرآنٌ	قُرْأَانٌ	ا + آ	3
to believe	آمَنَ	أَأمَنَ	أ + آ	4

This is a IV-verb (أَفْعَلَ) of the I-verb أَمُنَ (*to be faithful; reliable*). Watch out: The I-verb (أَمِنَ) with كَسْرة means *to be safe*.

- In example 1, two letters were merged (آ plus أ). This is the standard situation as آ usually occurs at the **beginning**.
- In example 2, we got the letter آ as we moved **from singular to plural**.
- In example 3, we can see that the letter آ may also occur in the **middle of a word**.
- In example 4, we had two Hamzas that collided.

Now what about the pronunciation of the letter آ? You have to pronounce the letter آ (all together) as a <u>glottal stop plus a long "a"</u>. And the correct pronunciation matters! Notice the difference in the following two examples:

meaning	explanation	root	example
tragedies	This is the plural of the word مَأساةٌ (*tragedy*).	ء - س - و	مَآسٍ
diamonds	This is a collective noun. If you want to say a *single diamond*, you need to add a ة resulting in: ماسةٌ.	proper noun	ماسٌ

RULE III: An Aleph can't start an utterance.

This might sound strange but as we have seen above, no sentence in Arabic can start with a vowel. The Aleph at the beginning of a word is never pronounced – unless it marks the beginning of a sentence (= glottal stop). It is only there to facilitate the pronunciation.

The letter I at the beginning might get mixed up with a regular هَمْزة – the so-called هَمْزةُ الْقَطْعِ – which is written as أ and is pronounced as a glottal stop. It is therefore important to understand the function of the Aleph when it starts a word.

There are two different types of the Aleph that don't function as a long vowel:

هَمْزةُ الْوَصْلِ	هَمْزةُ الْقَطْعِ
The Hamza of liaison; the connecting Hamza	*The Hamza of rupture; the cutting Hamza*
Written as ٱ or آ or أ. Although it looks like an Aleph, it is in fact a special type of the هَمْزة.	Always written with a small هَمْزة on top = أ.
This letter is **only** treated as a **consonant** (هَمْزة) when it marks the **beginning** of an utterance.	Always treated as a **consonant** (هَمْزة).
This هَمْزة is **only** pronounced as a glottal stop if it marks the **beginning** of a sentence. Apart from that, it is **not pronounced at all.** You need a helping vowel in the preceding word to connect the word with the هَمْزةُ الْوَصْلِ.	This هَمْــزة is **always pronounced as a glottal stop.**

Examples

هَمْزَةُ الْوَصْلِ		هَمْزَةُ الْقَطْعِ	
The ا is found in some verb patterns, for example, pattern VIII and X.	اِفْتَعَلَ, اِسْتَفْعَلَ	The أ here marks the first person singular *I* or the comparative form.	أَفْعَلُ
Definite article	ال	Personal pronoun *you*	أَنْتَ
		مَصْدَر of a IV-verb	إِفْعالٌ

The هَمْزَةُ الْوَصْلِ could be translated into English as *joining* or *elidable* Aleph.

The following verb patterns in the *imperative* (أَمْر), *past tense* (ماضٍ) as well as their respective *infinitives* (مَصْدَر) all have a هَمْزَةُ الْوَصْلِ at the beginning which is (depending on the position of the word) pronounced as a glottal stop, as a vowel – or it is even unpronounced.

verb form	مَصْدَر	past tense
VII	اِنْفِعالٌ	اِنْفَعَلَ
VIII	اِفْتِعالٌ	اِفْتَعَلَ
IX	اِفْعِلالٌ	اِفْعَلَّ
X	اِسْتِفْعالٌ	اِسْتَفْعَلَ

When the هَمْزَةُ الْوَصْلِ is preceded by a وَ or فَ, then the ا is not pronounced at all. Let's take, for example, the verb *to get away* (اِنْصَرَفَ) and let's place a وَ or فَ before. How do you pronounce it then? You say: *"wansarafa"* and *"fansarafa"*.

10. What is a weak letter?

The letters و and ي – which may get dropped or changed into another letter.

If there is a و or a ي in the root, we call it a root with a weak letter (حَرْفُ الْعِلّةِ). These letters complicate Arabic grammar as they sometimes have to be elided or even change into a different letter. A verb containing a weak letter is called فِعْلٌ مُعْتَلٌّ (*defective* verb).

There are several types of weak verbs:

1	**Quasi-sound verb:** This verb has a و or ي as a first root-letter. Often translated as *assimilated verb.*	فِعْلٌ مِثالٌ
	Watch out: Verbs with initial ي are not really *assimilated*. In I-verbs, the ي usually stays, e.g., the (past tense) verb يَئِسَ (*to give up all hope*). The present tense is: هُوَ يَيْأَسُ	
	Whereas in the I-verb وَأَدَ (*to bury alive*), the و drops in the present tense: هُوَ يَئِدُ	
	to arrive (وَصَلَ)	

2	**Hollow verb:** This verb has a و or a ي in the middle of the root.	فِعْلٌ أَجْوَفُ
	to say (قالَ)	

3	**Defective verb**: This verb has a و or a ي as the last letter of the root.	فِعْلٌ ناقِصٌ
	Note: The term فِعْلٌ ناقِصٌ may denote also something else. A verb that necessarily needs a predicate to express a complete meaning. For example: *to be* (كانَ).	
	to call (دَعا)	

| 4 | **Doubly weak verb**: Has two weak letters in its root. | فِعْلٌ لَفِيفٌ |

| to grill (شَوَى) |

| to carry out (وَقَى) |

A special form is the verb *to seek refuge* (أَوَى). It not only has two weak root letters – the third one is also special as it is هَمْزَةٌ.

11. When does ‍ا or ى or ي cause trouble?

If one of them is the last letter of a word.

You should always be careful if you spot a weak letter or a هَمْزَة in a word – but especially if **a word ends** in:

- a ا (Aleph)
- a ى – no matter if pronounced ي or ا ("*i*"- or "*a*"-sound)
- ءا

Here is an overview of all three different possibilities and how they are called in Arabic:

الْاِسْمُ الْمَمْدُودُ	الْاِسْمُ الْمَنْقُوصُ	الْاِسْمُ الْمَقْصُورُ
ءا at the end	ي at the end	ا or ى at the end
Lit.: *the extended*	Lit.: *the reduced*	Lit.: *the shortened*
Noun with **extended ending**; *prolonged noun.*	Noun with **curtailed ending**; *defective, deficient noun.*	Noun with **shortened ending**; *abbreviated, indeclinable noun.*
desert صَحْرَاءُ	*the* judge الْقَاضِي	*stick* عَصًا
red حَمْرَاءُ	*the* club النَّادِي	*young man* فَتًى

Now, what should we make out of that?

It is important to identify the correct type of word...

- if you want to إعْرَاب words (put case and mood endings according to the position of words in the sentence);
- if you need to form a <u>dual</u> (الْمُثَنَّى) or <u>plural</u> (الْجَمْعُ).

We will get back to all this in the following *questions*. Notice: In all three groups above, we are talking about a اسْم. The grammar of all this has nothing to do with verbs (e.g., قَضَى – *to perform*) or prepositions (إِلَى).

12. How do you say *his colleagues?* زُمَلاءهُ or زُمَلاؤُهُ, زُمَلائِهِ؟

All of them are correct.

How is that possible? Well, it depends on the function and position of the word in the sentence, in short: on the necessary **case ending**. Grammatically speaking, the word زُمَلاءُ is a so-called noun with an extended ending (اِسْمٌ مَمْدُودٌ) which is important to keep in mind. Let us look at all three forms:

1	his colleagues		زُمَلاؤُهُ
	Used as a subject (مُبْتَدَأٌ or فَاعِلٌ).	مَرْفُوعٌ	زُمَلاؤُهُ
	His colleagues came.		جَاءَ زُمَلاؤُهُ.

2	his colleagues		زُمَلاءَهُ
	Used as a direct object (مَفْعُولٌ بِهِ).	مَنْصُوبٌ	زُمَلاءَهُ
	I met his colleagues.		قَابَلْتُ زُمَلاءَهُ.

3	his colleagues	زُمَلائِهِ
	Used after a preposition (ex. 1) or as the 2nd part of a إِضافة-construction.	مَجْرُورٌ زُمَلائِهِ
	I took the books from his colleagues.	أَخَذْتُ الْكُتُبَ مِن زُمَلائِهِ.
	his colleagues' house (the house of his colleagues)	بَيْتُ زُمَلائِهِ

13. أَلِفٌ مَقْصُورةٌ - What is so special about this Aleph?

It's an Aleph at the end of a word - written in the shape of ى. In other words, you write ى without dots and pronounce it as "a".

You find this **hybrid Aleph** in many words, e.g., *to come* (أَتَى). In general, you get such an Aleph when the Aleph is found **as the final letter**, and when the Aleph belongs to the root.

Wait! We said that the Aleph cannot be part of the root. Yes, this is true. The Aleph was originally a و or ي which was changed into l (Aleph). What we mean here is that the Aleph is not additional – but simply disguises its real character.

The أَلِفٌ مَقْصُورةٌ is sometimes also called *permanent Aleph* (أَلِفٌ لازِمةٌ). Why? Placed at the end of a word, it does not change because it is not a sign of declension. There are **two situations** in which we get such an Aleph (أَلِفٌ مَقْصُورةٌ):

1	It occurs as the **third root** letter and its origin is ي.	*to come* (أَتَى), *boy* (فَتَّى)
2	It occurs as a **fourth letter** or more.	*to finish* (إِنْتَهَى), *hospital* (مُسْتَشْفَى)

Now, watch out:

1. Sometimes the Aleph is **just a case marker** and is not part of the root. Let us take, for example, the word أَبٌ which means *father*. In the following sentence, the Aleph of أَبا is not part of the root – it simply marks the مَنْصُوب-case (*direct object, accusative case*):

I met Abu Bakr.	قَابَلْتُ أَبا بَكْرٍ.

2. The ا is a *fixed, invariable letter* and stays the same in all cases. We call such words indeclinable (مَبْنِيٌّ). For more information about that see *question #59*.

Let's examine the أَلِفٌ مَقْصُورَةٌ that is found in nouns (اِسْمٌ):

أَلِفٌ at the third position?	explanation	sound feminine plural جَمْعُ الْمُؤَنَّثِ السّالِمُ	dual (الْمُثَنَّى)	word	root
yes	و is part of the root: the أَلِف changes into و.	عَصَوَاتٌ _sticks_	عَصَوانِ _two sticks_	عَصًا _"asan"_ _stick_	ع-ص-و
		Note: The feminine plural is a common option for the plural of عَصًا. But there are other plural forms too such as أَعْصٍ or عُصِيٌّ or عِصِيٌّ.			
yes	ي is part of the root.	فَتَياتٌ _girls_	فَتَيانِ _two boys_	فَتًى _"fatan"_ _boy_	ف-ت-ي
		فَتَياتٌ is the plural of _girl_ (فَتاةٌ).			
no	---	كُبْرَياتٌ _bigger things_	كُبْرَيانِ _two bigger_	كُبْرَى _"kubrā"_ _bigger_	ك-ب-ر

What happened? In the dual, the ى changes into its original form (i.e., ي or و) and in the sound feminine plural, the ى becomes ي before the suffix ـات.

Question: Would it be possible that the Aleph in our examples is an *extended Aleph* (أَلِفٌ مَمْدُودَةٌ)?

No! Because an *extended Aleph* is extra (أَلِفٌ زَائِدَةٌ) and doesn't belong to the root. It is followed by a Hamza (هَمْزَةٌ). Let's take, for example, the word *friends* (أَصْدِقَاءُ). The root is ص-د-ق. The أَلِفٌ مَقْصُورَةٌ, however, is part of the root.

Extended, **long** Aleph.	أَلِفٌ مَمْدُودَةٌ
Shortened, "imprisoned", "confined" Aleph.	أَلِفٌ مَقْصُورَةٌ

Regarding case endings, a اِسْمٌ مَقْصُورٌ gets **virtual** (estimated, assumed) **case markers**. We call that الْإِعْرَابُ الْمُقَدَّرُ. That is perhaps also the reason for how that type of Aleph got its name: مَقْصُورٌ. The case markers are estimated in all three cases. The root ق-ص-ر means *to be* or *become short*; however, it may also convey the meaning of *to lock up; to confine* - like in the word for *castle* (قَصْرٌ).

Some scholars, e.g., Ibn Mālik (اِبْن مَالِك), have suggested that this may be the reason for the grammar term: Because of their **inner confinement**, words with a أَلِفٌ مَقْصُورَةٌ cannot get case endings (لِأَنَّهُ مَحْبُوسٌ عَنِ الْمَدِّ أَوْ عَنْ ظُهُورِ الْإِعْرَابِ).

Let us check the **sound masculine plural** (جَمْـعُ الْمُـذَكَّرِ السَّالِمُ). For example, the word أَعْلَى. It is a comparative (اِسْمُ التَّفْضِيلِ) and means *higher (highest)*.

	root	masculine plural	explanation
أَعْلَى	ع-ل-و	أَعْلَوْنَ	You have to delete the أَلِف and add a سُكُون on top of the و. Notice the correct pronuncia-
		أَعْلَيْنَ	tion of أَعْلَـوْنَ. It is not: "a3lūna" -> it is "a3lawna".
		→ genitive (مَجْرُورٌ) or accusative (مَنْصُوبٌ)	

Now, what about the تَنْوِينٌ (nunation)? In other words, which case markers should we use if the word is **indefinite** (نَكِرَةٌ)? Nothing changes in any case!

In the following examples the case marker of the word الْفَتَى is not written. We say that we use a *hidden, estimated marker*, also called *presumptive vowel* (مُقَدَّرَةٌ).

Therefore, the word ends in ى (or let's say: it stays the same) <u>in all three cases</u>! Furthermore, the pronunciation doesn't change either. It is *"al-Fatā"* in all three cases. This is because the last letter is actually an Aleph (أَلِفٌ) and not a ي!

The young boy came.	جَاءَ الْفَتَى.	1
I met the young boy.	قَابَلْتُ الْفَتَى.	2
I greeted the young boy.	سَلَّمْتُ عَلَى الْفَتَى.	3

الْفَتَى		
Subject (فَاعِلٌ) of the verbal sentence. Thus, it needs the nominative case (مَرْفُوعٌ). However, we can only marked by a virtual, assumed case marker (مَرْفُوعٌ بِضَمَّةٍ مُقَدَّرَةٍ),	1	
Direct object (مَفْعُولٌ بِهِ) of the verb *to meet*. It would need the marker of the accusative case (مَنْصُوبٌ). But we can't put the appropriate marker. We can only use virtual markers (مَنْصُوبٌ بِفَتْحَةٍ مُقَدَّرَةٍ).	2	
Prepositional phrase (الْجَارُّ وَالْمَجْرُورُ). The word fol-	3	

> lows a preposition and thus has to be in the genitive case (مَجْرُور). Regarding its place value, this is true. However, visually, we cannot mark it as such. We can only apply a virtual marker (مَجْرُور بِكَسْرةٍ مُقَدَّرةٍ).

14. رَأْي and الْقاضِي - Same ending, same problem?

No, we have to deal with different grammatical problems.

Let us first check the meaning of both words: رَأْي denotes *(an) opinion;* الْقاضِي expresses *the judge.*

As a general rule we could say that if you see the letter ي (the original ي with two dots underneath) at the end of a word, you have to watch out. There are several reasons and all of them have an impact on three things: case endings (تَنْوِينٌ), the dual form and plural form.

Before we continue our analysis, we should introduce an important grammar term: اِسْمٌ مَنْقُوصٌ. We could translate it as *noun with curtailed ending.* The word مَنْقُوص is the passive participle (اِسْمُ الْمَفْعُولِ) of the I-verb نَقَصَ (*to curtail; to diminish*) and thus means: *reduced; deficient; insufficient.*

So, how can we identify the اِسْمٌ مَنْقُوصٌ? It is pretty easy.

A اِسْمٌ مَنْقُوصٌ **ends in a permanent** ي – preceded by the vowel "i" (كَسْرةٌ). For example: الْقاضِي

In Arabic, we would say: يُخْتَمُ بِياءٍ لازِمةٍ قَبْلُها كَسْرةٌ

You shouldn't make the mistake and think that every word ending in ي is a اِسْمٌ مَنْقُوصٌ. We will see why.

In the following table the numbers on the left side correspond to the conditions listed further below.

	grammar term	اِسْمٌ مَنْقُوصٌ؟	example, meaning	
4	It is a regular noun (اِسْمٌ).	NO	*opinion*	رَأْيٌ
3;2	This is a so-called *Nisba* adjective (نِسْبَةٌ).	NO	*Egyptian*	مِصْرِيٌّ
	Note: Any noun (اِسْمٌ) in Arabic can easily be turned into an adjective (صِفَةٌ) by adding the so-called ي *of relation* (also called نِسْبَةٌ). The word نِسْبَةٌ means *relation*. Notice the شَدّة on the ي! A *Nisba* is used to indicate the affiliation of something to this noun, e.g., *Egyptian*. Grammarians call such words also اِسْمٌ مَنْسُوبٌ (literally, *relative noun*).			
	This a اِسْمٌ مَنْقُوصٌ. Notice the كَسْرة ("*i*") before the ي which is typical for such words.	**YES**	*the judge*	الْقَاضِي
3	Passive participle (اِسْمـــٌ الْمَفْعُولِ) of the root بَنَى.	NO	*built*	مَبْنِيٌّ

Let us sum up the conditions for a اِسْمٌ مَنْقُوصٌ:

1. The word must be capable of taking visible **case endings**. We say that it is a *declinable* noun (اِسْمٌ مُعْرَبٌ). Therefore, words like الَّذِي (relative pronoun meaning *which*) cannot be a اِسْمٌ مَنْقُوصٌ. We call words like الَّذِي *indeclinable/with a fixed building* (مَبْنِيٌّ).

2. The ي must be **part of the root** – يَاءُ لَازِمَةٌ.

3. There is **no** شَدّة above the ي.

4. The **vowel** before the ي has to be كَسْرةٌ – **not** a سُكُونٌ.

This brings us to an important question: What's the problem with the إِسْمٌ مَنْقُوصٌ? Answer: It is not always necessary to write the ي! Let us see why and check all possible situations.

1. **Keep** the ي – in the <u>dual</u> and the <u>feminine</u> plural.

a messenger; delivery boy	ساعٍ	indefinite
the messenger; the delivery boy	السَّاعِي	definite
the two delivery boys	السَّاعِيانِ	**dual**
	السَّاعِيَيْنِ	
the delivery boys	السَّاعِياتُ	**feminine plural**

2. **Delete** the ي – if it is a sound <u>masculine</u> plural.

a lawyer	مُحامٍ	indefinite
the lawyer	الْمُحامِي	definite
the lawyers	الْمُحامُونَ	**masculine plural**
	الْمُحامِينَ	

Notice the difference between the pronunciation of the last letter in the dual and the masculine plural:

السَّاعِيانِ ("i"-sound; dual) and الْمُحامُونَ ("a"-sound; plural).

Now, what about the correct case endings? Let's see.

A. The word functions as the **subject** (فاعِلٌ or مُبْتَدَأٌ). This means that it needs to be in the nominative case (مَرْفُوعٌ).

explanation	case marker	example	
The judge came.	We can't put the appropriate case marker. We can only assign virtual case endings (مَرْفُــوعٌ بِضَمّةٍ مُقَدَّرةٍ).	جَاءَ الْقَاضِي.	1
The judge of the city came.		جَاءَ قَاضِي الْمَدِينةِ.	
A judge came.	Since we can't visibly put a ضَمّة on قَاضٍ, we say that it has an implied, imaginary ضَمّة. Fine, but put on which letter?	جَاءَ قَاضٍ.	2

Well, it is (picture that in your mind) on the <u>deleted</u> ي! In Arabic, we say: ضَمّةٌ مُقَدَّرةٌ عَلَى الْيَاءِ الْمَحْذُوفةِ. You pronounce the ending as "-*in*" since there are two كَسْرة-signs (nunation) under the ض. Nevertheless, **according to its place and function** in the sentence, قَاضٍ is **nominative** although you cannot see that.

B. The word functions as the **direct object** (مَفْعُولٌ بِهِ). This means that it needs to be in the accusative case (مَنْصُوبٌ). In this situation, **you have to apply the regular rules.**

explanation	case marker	example	
I met **the** judge.	Here you <u>can</u> put the appropriate case marker. (مَنْصُوبٌ بِفَتْحةٍ ظاهِرةٍ)	قَابَلْتُ الْقَاضِيَ.	1
I met **the** judge of the city.		قَابَلْتُ قَاضِيَ الْمَدِينةِ.	

If you mark the word according to its position in the sentence, you put the ending "*a*" (فَتْحة). This is possible here. That is why *the judge* is pronounced with final "*a*" ("-*ya*").

| I met **a** judge. | If the word is **indefinite** (in the accusative case), you also | قَابَلْتُ قَاضِيًا. | 2 |

| | put the standard (visible) case markers (مَنْصُوبٌ بِفَتْحةٍ ظاهِرةٍ): "*an*". | |

C. The word comes **after a preposition** (حَرْفُ جَرٍّ). This means that it needs to be in the genitive case (مَجْرُورٌ).

explanation	case marker	example	
I greeted the judge.	We cannot place the appropriate case marker. We can only assign virtual case endings (مَجْـرُورٌ بِكَسْرةٍ مُقَدَّرةٍ).	سَلَّمْتُ عَلَى الْقاضِي.	1
I greeted the judge of the city.		سَلَّمْتُ عَلَى قاضِي الْمَدِينةِ.	

The ending of *the judge* is pronounced as "*i*" as there is a ي.

Watch out: The ي has no case marker! (no كَسْرة under the ي).

| I greeted a judge. | Same as above: We use estimated case markers for the genitive (مَجْـرُورٌ بِكَسْرةٍ مُقَدَّرةٍ). | سَلَّمْتُ عَلَى قاضٍ. | 2 |

Stop! Why do we use virtual markers when we pronounce the ending as "-*in*" which looks like the usual ending for an indefinite word in the genitive case? Well, the ending is pronounced "in" – but this is **not the real** and **actual case marker**! Don't be confused: Yes, there are two كَسْرة-signs (nunation). But don't forget that the ي was elided! Thus, the ending is actually not under the last letter. What do we make out of that? We say that the virtual case marker is under the deleted letter ي!

Note: For a detailed discussion about the nature of the اِسْمٌ مَنْقُوصٌ and why you can't use certain case markers and why the ي may get dropped, see *Arabic for Nerds 2, question #40*.

To sum it up:

You only pronounce the real and appropriate case marker...

... if the اِسْمٌ مَنْقُوصٌ is in the accusative case (مَنْصُوبٌ)!

indefinite, مَنْصُوبٌ	"qaadiyan"	قاضِيًا
definite, مَنْصُوبٌ	"qaadiya"	الْقاضِيَ

15. Are there words that look the same in all cases?

Yes, there are.

Let us take a root that contains a weak letter (و or ي) at the position of the last radical, e.g., the verb عَنَى (root: ع-ن-ي) which means *to concern; to regard; to mean*. From this root, we can form the word for *meaning*: مَعْنًى.

Words like this are called اِسْمٌ مَقْصُورٌ. There is something special about them: These words are **indeclinable** in all three cases. This is also the reason why you call the اِسْمٌ مَقْصُورٌ also the *indeclinable noun* - see question #13. Let's examine the word for *meaning*: مَعْنًى

case	indefinite	definite
nominative (مَرْفُوعٌ)	مَعْنًى	الْمَعْنَى
genitive (مَجْرُورٌ)	مَعْنًى	الْمَعْنَى
accusative (مَنْصُوبٌ)	مَعْنًى	الْمَعْنَى

Some other examples:

meaning	example	root
(a) level; *(indefinite)*	مُسْتَوًى *to be equal*	س-و-ي
villages *(plural)*	قُرًى *to receive hospitably*	ق-ر-ي
given *(passive participle* (اِسْمُ الْمَفْعُول) *of* أَعْطَى.)	مُعْطًى Verb form IV means *to give* (أَعْطَى). Form I and II isn't used.	ع-ط-و

Remark: Which pattern did we use to form the word مَعْنًى?

Well, the *regular infinitive* (الْمَصْدَرُ الْأَصْلِيُّ) would be عَنْيٌ (or عِنايَةٌ). The word مَعْنًى follows the pattern مَفْعَلٌ. This pattern is used for several forms, e.g., for the *noun of place* (اِسْمُ الْمَكانِ) or *time* (اِسْمُ الزَّمانِ) to denote the place or time where the action of the root occurs. But that is not what we need here. The pattern مَفْعَلٌ is also used for a special type of the مَصْدَر, the so-called مَصْدَرٌ مِيمِيٌّ, which is what we need to explain the form of مَعْنًى. For more details see *question #76*.

Note: The plural of مَعْنًى is مَعَانٍ or مَعَانِي.

16. سَماءٌ - How did the هَمْزة get into this word?

It has to do with the last root letter, i.e., the و.

سَماءٌ means *sky*. If we want to answer our question, we need to have a look at the root of this word – which is س-م-و.

It is a very ancient Semitic root that is found in Aramaic, Ugaritic, and Hebrew and finally also entered Arabic. Its original meaning is probably *high place, height*.

Some scholars assume that the verbal root was deducted from the noun, as the noun came before the verbal meaning – which is *to be high, elevated; to be above*. In grammar, we call them *denominal verbs* - verbs derived from nouns (*see qu. #42*).

Let's start our analysis by applying the root letters to our word. If we do that, we will get the word سَمَأْوُ for *sky*. Such a word would be difficult to pronounce. And for exactly that reason, the و turned into a ء resulting in سَماءُ.

But that is actually the exception.

- In the *Nisba*-form (نِسْبة), which is used to form adjectives (صِفة), the weak root letter و suddenly appears again: سَماوِيٌّ. It means *heavenly*.

- This is also true in the correct form of the plural which will be dealt in *question #17*.

What about the <u>gender</u> of the word سَماءُ? Both genders - masculine and feminine - are theoretically possible. However, most scholars treat سَماءُ as feminine (مُؤَنَّثٌ).

Remark: What we said here applies to many roots which have a weak letter (ي or و) in position 3, i.e., the last root letter. Some examples:

- The word بِناءُ which means *building*. It is the مَصْدَر of the root ب-ن-ي. Therefore, the word should be spelled like that: بِنَأْيٌ. But this would be hard to pronounce.

- The word لِقاءُ which means *meeting*. It is the مَصْدَر of لَقِيَ. It has the plural form لِقَاءاتٌ.

Watch out: Of course it isn't always like that. There are plenty of Arabic words that do not substitute the و or ي after an Aleph by the Hamza – despite that the pronunciation is a bit difficult, e.g., مُتَساوٍ (*equal, similar*).

17. What is the plural of the word *sky* (سَماءُ)?

You have two options: سَماوَاتٌ *and* سَماءَاتٌ. *In the Qur'an you find* سَماوَاتٌ *more often. But both are correct.*

If we want to understand the logic behind these two plural forms, we need to look at the ending ءا of the singular form of the Arabic word for *sky* (سَماءُ).

In other words, we need to examine the so-called *extended Aleph* (أَلِفٌ مَمْدُودَةٌ) and need to talk about the اِسْمٌ مَمْدُودٌ. The word مَمْدُودٌ literally means *lengthened* or *extended*.

We can safely say that words ending with ءا are usually a اِسْمٌ مَمْدُودٌ.

We have to look at three possible situations:

Situation 1: The Hamza - i.e., ء - is part of the root – هَمْزَةٌ أَصْلِيَّةٌ. In this situation, the ء remains.

meaning	masculine plural*	feminine plural	dual*	root	word
construction	---	إِنْشاءات	إِنْشاءَانِ إِنْشاءَيْنِ	ن-ش-ء	إِنْشاءُ
somebody who reads a lot	قَرَّاءُون قَرَّائِين	---	قَرَّاءَانِ قَرَّاءَيْنِ	ق-ر-ء	قَرَّاءُ

* nominative (مَرْفُوعٌ) and accusative (مَنْصُوبٌ)/genitive (مَجْرُورٌ).

Situation 2: The ء is extra – هَمْزَةٌ زائِدَةٌ.
- There is <u>no masculine</u> plural.

- All words of this pattern are **feminine**.
- The ء turns into a و.

meaning	feminine plural	dual*	root	word
desert	صَحْرَاوَاتٌ	صَحْرَاوَانِ صَحْرَاوَيْنِ	ص-ح-ر	صَحْرَاءُ

* nominative (مَرْفُوعٌ) and accusative (مَنْصُوبٌ)/genitive (مَجْرُورٌ).

Note: صَحْرَاءُ is a so-called *diptote* (مَمْنُوعٌ مِن الصَّرْفِ) and doesn't get *nunation* (تَنْوِينٌ) → You only put one ضَمّة - "*u*" instead of "*-un*".

Situation 3: The ء was originally a و or ي. In this situation, the ء **remains** or, alternatively, it **turns into** و. The latter is used in the Qur'an more often.

meaning	masculine plural*	feminine plural	dual*	root	word
building	---	بِنَاءَاتٌ	بِنَاءَانِ بِنَاءَيْنِ	ب-ن-ي	بِنَاءٌ
	---	بِنَاوَاتٌ	بِنَاوَانِ بِنَاوَيْنِ		
runner	عَدَّاءُونَ عَدَّائِينَ	---	عَدَّاءَانِ عَدَّاءَيْنِ	ع-د-و	عَدَّاءٌ
	عَدَّاوُونَ عَدَّاوِينَ	---	عَدَّاوَانِ عَدَّاوَيْنِ		

* nominative (مَرْفُوعٌ) and accusative (مَنْصُوبٌ)/genitive (مَجْرُورٌ).

Notice the spelling of the ء in the <u>dual form</u> of the مَجْرُورٌ- and مَنْصُوبٌ-case of عَدَّاءَيْنِ. Since there is a سُكُونٌ on the letter ي of the dual ending (يْنِ), you should write a <u>lone</u> ء and not a ئ (which is, by the way, also called "yā' chair").

Let' see some action now.

The tallest building was built in front of the club.	١ أُقِيمَ الْبِنَاءُ الْأَعْلَى أَمَامَ النَّادِي.
The (two) tallest buildings were built in front of the (two) clubs.	أُقِيمَ الْبِنَاءَانِ= الْبِنَاوَانِ الْأَعْلَيَانِ أَمَامَ النَّادِيَيْنِ.

Promote virtue and prevent vice.	٢ كُنْ دَاعِيًا إِلَى الْمَعْرُوفِ, نَاهِيًا عَنِ الْمُنْكَرِ.
dual form	كُونَا دَاعِيَيْنِ إِلَى الْمَعْرُوفِ, نَاهِيَيْنِ عَنِ الْمُنْكَرِ.
masculine plural	كُونُوا دَاعِينَ إِلَى الْمَعْرُوفِ, نَاهِينَ عَنِ الْمُنْكَرِ.

Note that in the second sentence, we use the verb كَانَ in the imperative form, so the predicate (خَبَرُ كَانَ) - which is the word دَاعِيًا - has to be in the accusative case (مَنْصُوبٌ).

Remark: In ancient spelling, for example in the Qur'an, the أَلِفٌ مَمْدُودَةٌ - the letter آ - is used to illustrate the sound sequence **long vowel plus Hamza.**

Thus, the Qur'an uses the following spelling for *sky*: سَمَآءُ. For the verb *to come* the Qur'an uses جَآءَ. The same is true for all terminations: ءَآ-. By the way, this type of spelling is not only applied to the sequence "a" plus Hamza. It is also used for "u" and "i" plus Hamza.

18. حَرْفُ عَطْفٍ - What is so special about it?

Such words "copy" the case of the preceding word and pass it on.

The word عَطْفٌ means *sympathy* in Arabic. In grammar, a so-called *letter of attraction* (حَرْفُ عَطْفٍ) stands in the middle of two words which have the same case. In English grammar, we usually use the term *conjunction*.

Arabic knows <u>ten</u> words that fall into that category:

but	لَكِنْ	6	and	وَ	1
but rather; in fact	بَلْ	7	even; even though	حَتَّى	2
or	أَمْ	8	or	أَوْ	3
then, thereupon	ثُمَّ	9	so, and	فَ	4
not	لا	10	except	إِلَّا	5

Zayd didn't come, it was rather Khālid.	مَا جَاءَ زَيْدٌ بَلْ خَالِدٌ.	7

Note that both زَيْدٌ and خَالِدٌ take the same case, i.e., the *nominative case* (مَرْفُوعٌ). Zayd is the *subject* (فَاعِلٌ) of the verbal sentence. The word بَلْ is a *conjunction* (حَرْفُ عَطْفٍ) which means that it will pass on the case of the preceding word. Therefore, the word *Khalid* is the so-called *attracted* (مَعْطُوفٌ) in the grammatical analysis. In Arabic, we would say: مَعْطُوفٌ عَلَى "خَالِدٌ" تَابِعٌ لَهُ فِي الرَّفْعِ.

I ate all the fish, even its head.	أَكَلْتُ السَّمَكَةَ حَتَّى رَأْسَها.	2

Both words which are "coupled" by the word حَتَّى and stand in between it take the same case, i.e., the *accusative case* (مَنْصُوبٌ) since the word fish serves as the direct object (مَفْعُولٌ بِهِ).

Watch out for the difference!

With a شَدّة on top of the final ن, this word means *but* as well. You have to use this form when you place a full sentence after it. This sentence has to follow the rules of إنَّ: • The "subject" (اِسْمُ إنَّ) is in the accusative (مَنْصُوبٌ). • The predicate (خَبَرُ إنَّ) is in the nominative (مَرْفُوعٌ).	لٰكِنَّ

Let's see an example now. In the following sentence, the word *Mustafā* starts a new sentence.

My two sisters are dark skinned, but **Mustafā's** two sisters are fair skinned.	أُخْتايَ سَمْراوَانِ وَلٰكِنَّ أُخْتَيْ مُصْطَفَى شَقْراوَانِ.

- Note 1: The pronunciation of *"ukhtāya"* (long "aa").

  The first word is the dual-form of *sister* أُخْتٌ with the possessive pronoun *my* – this is the reason for the Aleph: أُخْتايَ.

- Note 2: the pronunciation after لٰكِنَّ.

  It is *"ukhtay"*: A dual in the 1st part of a إضافة merely loses the final ن. Nothing else happens. If the 2nd part of a إضافة is a word beginning with ٱل, then you need a helping vowel on the ي. But the helping vowel is always كَسْرة – not فَتْحة. For example: أُخْتَي الطَّالِبِ.

19. شُنُونٌ or شُؤُونٌ - What is correct?

Both are correct.

Both words are the plural (جَمْع) of شَأْنٌ which means *affair* or *matter*. In Egypt, the form شُنُونٌ is more common whereas in most other parts of the Arab world, the form شُؤُونٌ - with the ء over the و - is more often found.

20. What is the definite article اَل made of?

This is not entirely clear.

The Arabic grammarians call the definite article اَل the *instrument of definition* (أَداةُ التَّعْريفِ). It consists of...

- the Aleph (ا). This prefixed letter is a helping letter. It is a *Hamza of liaison* (هَمْزةُ وَصْلٍ). Depending on the position in the sentence (beginning or not), it is pronounced as a Hamza (glottal stop) or neglected.

- the letter لام. Grammarians call this type the *Lām of definition* (حَرْفُ التَّعْريفِ). It is only there to lighten the pronunciation. Note that the ل here is not a preposition; it is the ل that is also found in الَّذِي. In fact, it is the demonstrative letter ل.

The resulting definite article is always joined with the following word. What is interesting:

Though it has become *determinative* (making the expression definite), it was originally denoting a direction (*demonstrative* use) which still appears in words like الْيَوْمَ, expressing *to-day* (more of *this* day and not *the* day), **having the accusative case** (مَنْصُوبٌ).

Remark: Some scholars regard the Aleph as an integral part of the definite article. They say that it was originally أَل – with a pronounced Hamza (أَلِفُ الْقَطِعِ) sharing the same pattern as هَلْ or بَلْ. Over time, it was gradually weakened to اَل.

21. Why does the definite article sometimes have a ribbon?

Because the ا *in the definite article* ال *is not pronounced if you find a word before it.*

In Arabic, the definite article consists of two parts: ا and the letter ل. The first part ا in the definite article ال is a so-called *Hamza of liaison* (هَمْزَةُ وَصْلٍ).

It is never pronounced unless it marks the beginning of a sentence/utterance – then, it must be pronounced as a **glottal stop**. But as soon as the definite article is preceded by a word, the ا in the definite article is elided and gets a special form:

This Aleph is treated as if it wasn't there.	ٱ

That is why you mark it with a وَصْلَة or صِلة which looks like a ribbon above the ا. The sign probably reflects the letter ص which is included in صِلة. It is rarely used in books or newspapers.

Let us examine it.

explanation; translation	example	
"al-kitābu" - the book	أَلْكِتَابُ	1
The هَمْزَةُ وَصْلٍ turns into a *(cutting) Hamza of rupture* (هَمْزَة قَطْع) if it marks the beginning of a sentence. Then, you write it as أ and start with (and pronounce) a glottal stop! The ل is pronounced like the following letter if that following letter is a so-called *sun letter* (حَرْفٌ شَمْسِيٌّ) - see below. The phonetic characteristic of sun letters is that in all of them, the tongue is raised towards the front part of the upper palate.		
"Hādhal-kitaābu" – this book	هٰذا أَلْكِتَابُ	2
Here, you don't pronounce a glottal stop! You take the preceding vowel "a" of the word هٰذا and connect it with the ل.		

Remark: Purist grammarians never write the definite article as أَلْ with a هَمْزَةُ قَطْعٍ. Instead, they prefer the writing of a simple dash (plain Aleph: ا) with a vowel on the top or at the bottom of the letter – even at the beginning of a sentence or in isolation when it has to be pronounced as هَمْزة.

<u>Excursus:</u> **sun letters** and **moon/lunar letters**.

In Arabic, there are two different kinds of consonants: *sun letters* (حَرْفٌ شَمْسِيٌّ) and *moon letters* (حَرْفٌ قَمَرِيٌّ).

- Sun letters take the attention and make the ل of the definite article disappearing. In other words, sun letters assimilate the letter ل in a definite article – this eventually results in doubling the sun letter (شَدّةٌ).

- Moon letters keep the pronunciation of the ل of definition as it is.

- The names are no coincidence: The word for *the sun* - الشَّمْسُ - is pronounced *"ash-shams"* and assimilates the ل whereas the word for *the moon* (الْقَمَرُ) - *"al-Qamar"* - doesn't.

The sun letters are:

ت	ث	د	ذ	ر	ز	س	ش	ص	ض	ط	ظ	ل	ن
t	th	d	dh	r	z	s	sh	ṣ	ḍ	ṭ	ẓ	l	n

The moon letters are:

ء	ب	ج	ح	خ	ع	غ	ف	ق	ك	م	و	ي	ه
ʼ	b	j	ḥ	kh	ʽ	gh	f	q	k	m	w	y	h

22. The word *but* - How do you write it?

You need a dagger Aleph resulting in لٰكِنْ.

It is pronounced with a long "ā"-sound after the ل although the "long Aleph" is usually not written. This has to do with a specialty: the writing of the Aleph. It should be: لٰكِنْ.

Such Aleph is called *dagger Aleph* (أَلِفٌ خَنْجَرِيّةٌ) as خَنْجَرٌ means *dagger*. It has to do with the history of the script. The original Semitic alphabet had no vowel signs. Eventually some vowels came to be marked with letters, but in the Qur'an you still have many words in which the vowels are not marked.

Usually people don't notice that because the Qur'an is fully vocalized, but, for example, if you read the first sura (الْفَاتِحةُ) you will see that the word الْعَالَمِين in the second verse has no Aleph. Nor does the word مالِك in the fourth verse.

Today they have *daggers* instead.

translation	example in the Qur'an, sura الْفَاتِحة	verse (Ayah)
(All) praise is (due) to Allah, Lord of the worlds;	الْحَمْدُ لِلّٰهِ رَبِّ الْعَلَمِينَ.	2
The Entirely Merciful, the Especially Merciful;	الرَّحْمٰنِ الرَّحِيمِ	3
Sovereign of the Day of Recompense.	مٰلِكِ يَوْمِ الدِينِ.	4

Eventually the script became more orderly and today we have absolute rules. However, some words - including *this* (هٰذا) and religious words like *the merciful* (الرَّحْمٰن) - are still spelled in the old way and vocalized with daggers.

23. *This* and *that* - Why are they special in Arabic?

They are both combinations of words.

If we want to understand the words *this* or *that* in Arabic, the so-called *demonstrative nouns/pronouns* (اِسْمُ إِشارَةٍ), we need to take a closer look at their origin.

In Arabic, هٰذا (*hādhā*) means *this* and ذٰلِكَ (*dhālika*) means *that*. Both have a long "a"-vowel after the first letter (which is usually written with a vertical dash, i.e., *the dagger Aleph* – see *question #22*). Why is that? In order to get closer to the answer, we should first check the **main body** of both words:

feminine, singular (several options)	ذِي، ذِهْ تا، تَهْ
feminine, dual	تان
feminine, plural	أُولاءِ

<->

masculine singular	ذا
masculine, dual	ذان
masculine, plural	أولاءِ
for places	هُنا

If you want to talk about something that is close to you, you will have to combine these words with the so-called *H of attention* (هاءُ التَّنْبِيهِ) - the letter ه which usually goes along with an Aleph: ها. The word تَنْبِيهٌ means *warning* or *alarm*.

The هاءُ التَّنْبِيهِ, i.e., the word ها, conveys the meaning of *look!* or *there!* In fact, the ها works as an amplifier and indicator of distance. Some examples:

Look, there he is!	ها هُوَ !
Hey, you!	ها أَنْتُم !
Here I am! (Notice that the final Aleph of أَنا is omitted.)	ها أَنَذا !

Let's continue with the expression *this*. It is used if the speaker points to something **near** him. Thus, we call such words in Arabic أَسْمَاءُ الإِشارةِ إلَى الْقَرِيبِ.

A hint: Since you talk about something that is **close** to you, you put the amplifier ها at the **beginning**.

fem. singular	هٰذِهٖ		masc. singular	هٰذا
* feminine, dual; *these two*	هَاتانِ		masculine, dual; *these two*	هٰذانِ
feminine, plural; *these*	هٰؤُلاءِ	<->	masculine, plural; *these*	هٰؤُلاءِ
			* for (near) places	هَهُنا or هاهُنا

* Remark: Check the spelling of the Aleph. If the consonant after the هاءُ التَّنْبِيهِ is a ت or a ه, you don't write the *dagger Aleph* (see *question #22*). This is just a convention. The pronunciation is the same.

Now, let's see how it works for something that is **far from the speaker** – the expression *that*. In Arabic, we call such words أَسْمَاءُ الإِشارةِ إلَى الْبَعِيدِ. Here, we need a different *amplifier* and *indicator of distance*.

A hint: Since you talk about something that is **far** from you, you put the additional letter(s) – a ك or a combination of ك+ل – at the **end**!

feminine, singular	تِلْكَ		masculine singular; *those*	ذاكَ or ذٰلِكَ
feminine, dual	ناكِ or تَيْنِكَ	<->	masculine dual; *those two; both of those*	ذانِكَ or ذَيْنِكَ

feminine, plural	أُولَئِكَ	<->	masculine plural; *these*	أُولَئِكَ
			for places	هُنَاكَ or هُنَالَكَ

Some remarks:

- The ل is a long-distance indicator and usually signals that something is *far away*; it is called لَامُ الْبُعْدِ.

- When you address another person, you add a ك. What precedes the ك relates to the person or thing indicated. The letter ك is the so-called كَافُ الْخِطَابِ (*letter of allocution*). This ك agrees in case, number, and gender with the addressee! (see *question #178*)

masculine plural	كُمْ
feminine plural	كُنَّ

singular	كَ or كِ
dual	كُمَا

- If there is لَكَ or لِكِ after ذا, the long Aleph is written as a vertical dash. After the letter ت, the long Aleph is omitted (you just pronounce a short vowel "a").

- You can never combine both ها and ل because the ها denotes nearness and the ل remoteness.

Let's play with these words.

explanation		construction
ذا is the اِسْم الْإِشارة. It is combined with the word ما. See *question #24*.	*what*	ذا + ما = ماذا	1
The ها is only used to give attention - to give notice to the addressed person. Watch out: Only ذا is the demonstrative	*this*	ها + ذا = هذا	2

noun (اِسْمُ الْإِشارةِ).		
For things that are further away.	*that*	3 ذا + ل + ك = ذٰلِكَ
Combined with a personal pronoun, it means: *that one*; *look at that one!*		4 هُوَ ذا، هِيَ ذي

Let's analyze a sentence. If there is a **definite noun after the demonstrative pronoun**, the analysis is tricky!

This student is diligent.	هٰذا الطَّالِبُ مُجْتَهِدٌ.

Demonstrative noun (اِسْمُ الْإِشارةِ). It is placed as the **subject** (مُبْتَدَأ) of the nominal sentence (جُمْلةٌ اِسْميّةٌ). It is **indeclinable** and has a fixed shape cemented on the "i"-vowel (مَبْنِيٌّ عَلَى الْكَسْرِ). Therefore, we can't put case markers. Since it is the subject, it would need the nominative case. However, we can only **assign a place value** and say that it is located in the **position (place) of a nominative case** (فِي مَحَلِّ رَفْعٍ).	هٰذا
The student is the expression to which the demonstrative noun (also called "pronoun") *this* **points to** (الْمُشارُ إِلَيْهِ). If we look at its function, it is an **apposition** (بَدَلٌ لِاسْمِ الْإِشارةِ) for the subject (i.e., the demonstrative noun *this*). In grammar, an apposition describes the situation when you have two words next to each other which refer to the same person/thing. For example, *my friend Peter...* An apposition is a follower (تابِع) in Arabic and takes the same case as the word it refers to. Therefore, the expression *the student* also takes the nominative case (مَرْفُوعٌ بِالضَّمّةِ). See *question #209 for the apposition.*	الطَّالِبُ
Predicate (خَبَر); in the nominative case (مَرْفُوعٌ بِالضَّمّةِ).	مُجْتَهِدْ

Summary: Words like هٰذا or هٰؤُلاءِ are actually a construction of two or three words.

24. ذا - Does it only mean *this*?

No, it doesn't. It may indicate possession.

Let's check why and start with the characteristics of ذا.

- ذا is a *demonstrative noun* (in English grammar, we call it *demonstrative pronoun*) – a so-called اِسْمُ إِشارةٍ.

- ذا basically denotes *this one; this;* in combinations: *that.*

- The feminine form of ذا is ذِي (also written as: ذِهِ).

- The plural is أُولاءِ.

But that is not all. Sometimes, the word ذا is mistaken with another word: ذُو – which means *master of; a possessor; an owner of.* Why is that? Well, it has to do with cases. ذُو in the accusative case (مَنْصُوبٌ) turns into ذا and in the genitive case (مَجْرُورٌ), we will get ذِي. Let's check that in detail:

nominative case (مَرْفُوعٌ)		1
The man with a hat...	...الرَّجُلُ ذُو قُبْعةٍ	
genitive case (مَجْرُورٌ)		2
Next to the man with the hat...	...إِلَى جِوارِ الرَّجُلِ ذِي الْقُبْعةِ	
accusative case (مَنْصُوبٌ)		3
I saw a man with a hat.	رَأَيْتُ رَجُلًا ذا قُبْعةٍ.	

Remark: In Egyptian Arabic, instead of هٰذا and هٰذِهِ, you say: دَه ("*da*") and دِي ("*di*") – so don't get confused.

25. ماذا and ما ذا (with space) – What is the difference?

The grammar is totally different.

Let's analyze the **word ذا step by step:**

1. You can combine the word ذا with two other words: *what* (ما) or *who* (مَنْ). Regarding the grammar, this type of ذا is a *relative pronoun* or *conjunctive noun* (اِسْمٌ مَوْصُولٌ).

2. Such type of ذا has the meaning of الَّذِي – *which, that.*

3. The words مَنْ and ما are both questions words, so-called interrogative nouns (اِسْمُ اِسْتِفْهامٍ). The word مَنْ is only used for human beings. (Remark: For the different applications of ما, see *question #134*.)

4. However, ذا is only a relative pronoun if it is **unconnected** with the preceding word ما – resulting in ما ذا (with space).

5. If it is connected (i.e., merged), then we treat it as a single entity and count it as a question word: ماذا

Okay, but what does that practically mean? Is there a difference in meaning? Let's see.

> **1.** ذا is a *demonstrative noun/pronoun* (اِسْمُ إِشارةٍ). Both words, ما and ذا, are written **separately.**

meaning	example
What is this book?	ما ذا الْكِتابُ؟ = ما هٰذا الْكِتابُ؟

- ما is the *subject* (مُبْتَدَأٌ) of the nominal sentence (جُمْلةٌ اِسْمِيّةٌ).

- ذا is the *predicate* (خَبَرٌ).

2. ذا is a *relative pronoun* (اِسْمٌ مَوْصُولٌ). Both words, ما and ذا, are written separately (notice the space). It is translated as *that which*, or simply *that* or *what* or *which*.

meaning	example	
What brings you here? (Lit.: What is it that brings you here?)	ما الَّذِي أَتَى بِكَ؟ =	ما ذا أَتَى بِكَ هُنا؟

- ما is the *subject* (مُبْتَدَأٌ) of the nominal sentence (جُمْلةٌ اِسْمِيّةٌ).
- ذا is the *predicate* (خَبَرٌ).

3. ذا merges with ما and becomes one entity (a single word). In Arabic, we would say: مُرَكَّبةٌ مَعَ ما.

- There is **no** space between the first two words.
- ماذا has the meaning of أَيُّ شَيْءٍ.
- ماذا can function as a direct object (مَفْعُولٌ بِهِ) or a prepositional phrase (شِبْهُ الْجُمْلةِ).
- The grammatical function of ماذا depends on the position in the sentence.

grammatical function	example	
ماذا is the direct object (مَفْعُولٌ بِهِ).	What did you write?	ماذا كَتَبْتَ؟
ماذا is an indeclinable question word (اِسْمُ اِسْتِفْهامٍ مَبْنِيٌّ) that is located in the position (place) of a genitive case	Why did you come?	لِماذا جِئْتَ؟

(فِي مَحَلّ جَرٍّ) since it is preceded by a preposition (حَرْفُ جَرٍّ). We thus have a prepositional phrase (جَارٌّ وَمَجْرُورٌ).	

Watch out for the difference:

What does he exactly want?	ماذا يُرِيدُ بِالضَّبْطِ؟	1
What is it <u>that</u> he wants?	ما ذا يُرِيدُ بِالضَّبْطِ؟	
	= ما الَّذِي يُرِيدُ بِالضَّبْطِ؟	
Who is <u>that</u> is in the office?	مَنْ ذا فِي الْمَكْتَبِ؟	2
Who is <u>this who</u> is in the office?	مَنْ ذا الَّذِي فِي الْمَكْتَبِ؟	

Some additional remarks:

1. The question word ماذا (without space) – *what*?

- ماذا is normally used in verbal sentences (جُمْلةٌ فِعْلِيَّةٌ).
- ماذا can serve as a subject (فاعِلٌ) or object (مَفْعُولٌ بِهِ) of a verb.

subject	<u>What</u> happened after that?	ماذا حَدَثَ بَعْدَ ذَلِكَ؟
object	<u>What</u> do you want?	ماذا تُرِيدُ؟

2. ما ذا (with space; ذا used as a relative pronoun).

After a relative pronoun many kinds of information (words) can follow:

جُمْلَةٌ فِعْلِيَّةٌ – verbal sentence	1
I read the book that you bought.	قَرَأْتُ الْكِتَابَ الَّذِي اِشْتَرَيْتَهُ.

جُمْلَةٌ اِسْمِيَّةٌ – nominal sentence	2
Those who are my friends came.	حَضَرَ الَّذِينَ هُمْ أَصْدِقَائِي.

شِبْهُ جُمْلَةٍ – prepositional (3.1; جَارٌّ وَمَجْرُورٌ) or adverbial phrase (3.2; ظَرْفُ مَكَانٍ)	3
Give me the pen that is in the office.	أَعْطِينِي الْقَلَمَ الَّذِي فِي الْمَكْتَبِ.	3.1
Give me the pen that is in front of you.	أَعْطِينِي الْقَلَمَ الَّذِي أَمَامَكَ.	3.2

26. Are there biliteral roots (only two letters)?

Yes, very few Arabic roots consist of two consonants only.

Some scholars have tried to count them, for example *Theodor Nöldeke* from Germany (1836-1930). He stated that there are **37 Arabic roots with only two radicals**. Most of these roots go back to the early beginnings of the Semitic languages. It is difficult to give a date, but many experts say that this may happened between 3700 and 2400 BC.

Words with only two radicals are part of the very basic vocabulary which people needed in ancient times. *Georges Bohas* (University of Paris) has done quite some research about this subject. He basically says that Arabic roots are derived from what he calls *etymons* – a combination of two letters to which a third letter is added. The added letter can precede the *etymons*, follow them, or it can be put in between.

From my own experience, I can tell that it is definitely worth thinking about the meaning of roots which look similar. Let us take the roots: ح-م-د and م-د-ح and م-ح-د.

They all share two root letters - م and د - although in different positions. And somehow they denote similar things.

- حَمِدَ basically means *to praise* in the meaning of *to thank*. It is mainly used with the word *God/Allah*.

- مَدَحَ also means *to praise* – but more in the meaning of *to commend, to say good things about something or someone*.

- مَجُدَ too has meanings that are related to *being glorious, exalted, praised*.

However, this kind of relationship is not universal in Arabic. Many other verbs have the same letters in different positions, but express totally different things. For example: نَقَشَ (*to paint*) versus شَنَقَ (*to hang; to execute*).

Note: In colloquial Arabic, root letters are sometimes twisted. For example, the word for *husband* is زَوْج in Standard Arabic – but جُوز in Egyptian Arabic.

Now, what is the answer: Are there biliteral roots? Andrzej Zaborski, a professor from Poland, writes in his article *Biradicalism* (2006) that there are 37 nominal roots in Arabic consisting of only two consonants. They belong to the basic vocabulary going back to Proto-Semitic and even Proto-Hamito-Semitic/Afro-Asiatic and describe mainly basic things human beings needed to survive. Some grammarians say that most of the following words have only two radicals:

water	ماءٌ	father-in-law	حَمٌ	hand	يَدٌ
father	أَبٌ	blood	دَمٌ	mouth	فَمٌ
				vulva	حِرٌ

Also the following words (as most grammarians agree) have only two root letters:

son	اِبْنٌ	tongue	لِسانٌ	name	اِسْمٌ
root	ب-ن	(with lexicalized suffix)		root	س-م

Note: The Aleph in the words اِسْمٌ and اِبْنٌ is **not** part of the root. It disappears in speech. The Aleph in these words *is the connecting Hamza* or *Hamza of liaison* (هَمْزةُ الْوَصْلِ). Western grammarians call it *prothetic Aleph*: "i-".

How do you find a biliteral root in the dictionary? Usually, you find them as a triliteral root which is sometimes based on the plural form:

root	plural	word
ف-و-ه	أَفْواهٌ	فَمٌ
ب-ن-و	أَبْناءٌ	اِبْنٌ
ل-س-ن	أَلْسُنٌ	لِسانٌ
ح-م-و	أَحْماءٌ	حَمٌ

root	plural	word
د-م-و	دِماءٌ	دَمٌ
م-و-ه	مِياهٌ	ماءٌ
س-م-ي	أَسْماءٌ	اِسْمٌ
ء-ب-و	آباءٌ	أَبٌ
ح-ر-ح	أَحْراحٌ	حِرٌ

Notice: The word حِر is an exception to the rule. Some say that the origin is حِرْحٌ.

What about roots with four consonants? They are rare. Many of them are "artificially" built by the reduplication of original root consonants, e.g., *to shake, to upset* (خَصْخَصَ). In the Qur'an, only 15 roots with four consonants are used against 1160 roots with three root consonants.

27. Are there Arabic roots which are related to each other?

Yes, there are.

As seen in the previous *question #26*, some scholars have suggested that Semitic words, in the very beginning, consisted of only two root letters.

No one knows, but it is interesting to check the meaning of roots with three consonants which share two of three radicals.

Let's see some examples. Notice that every verb in the following table starts with the same two root consonants: قط.

to cut	قَطَعَ
to cut off	قَطَلَ
to cut off; to break off	قَطَمَ
to knit; to stitch; to concentrate	قَطَبَ
to skim off; to harvest (to cut off a fruit)	قَطَفَ
to trim; to sharpen	قَطَّ
to trickle; to drip	قَطَرَ

28. Does the word order matter in Arabic?

Not really.

In Arabic, the word-order usually doesn't change the meaning of a sentence. However, changing the position of a word may have the effect of an amplifier – and give emphasis.

The standard word order in **English** is: subject + verb + object. Before we move on to the system in Arabic, let us quickly define the terms:

subject	Usually a noun or pronoun (a person, thing or place).
verb	The action. It tells you what the subject actually does.
object	Any word that is influenced by the verb. For example: I read **a book**.

In English, since there are no case markers, your options of playing with the word-order are limited. For example: *The dog crossed the street.* If you change the sequence, the sentence would be rubbish: *The street crossed the dog.*

In Arabic, this is different – mainly because you have case markers. Arabic has a relatively free word order. The standard word-order in Arabic depends on the type of sentence:

verbal sentence (جُمْلَةٌ فِعْلِيّةٌ)

(1) verb (فِعْلٌ) + (2) subject (فَاعِلٌ) + (3) object (مَفْعُولٌ بِهِ)

nominal sentence (جُمْلَةٌ اِسْمِيّةٌ)

(1) subject (مُبْتَدَأٌ) + (2) predicate (خَبَرٌ)

Inversion happens when we reverse (invert) the standard word order of a sentence.

In other words, we disrupt the most common subject-verb word-order. Let's play with that. The following sentences roughly mean the same: *The students read the books.* However, there are some fine points regarding the emphasis (تَأْكِيدْ).

read (past) + *the students* + *the books*	.قَرَأَ الطُّلَّابُ الْكُتُبَ	1
read (past) + *the books* + *the students*	.قَرَأَ الْكُتُبَ الطُّلَّابُ	2
the books + *read* (past) + *the students*	.الْكُتُبَ قَرَأَ الطُّلَّابُ	3
the students + *read* (past tense, 3rd person plural - they) + *the books*	.الطُّلَّابُ قَرَؤُوا الْكُتُبَ	4
Here, we have a nominal sentence! If you put the subject before the verb, there are two effects: • the **subject** gets more **emphasis**; • the **object** is <u>un</u>stressed;		
the books (nominative case!) - *to read* (them) - *the students*	.الْكُتُبُ قَرَأَها الطُّلَّابُ	5
Here, the natural subject (the last word: *students*) is <u>un</u>stressed.		

Let's stop for a moment. If your native language is English or German, it is quite tricky to understand the nuances. Both sentences below mean: *Zayd hit.*

verbal sentence	Here we assume that the action has happened. Of course, we want to know you performed the action – thus, the logical emphasis is on **Zayd**.	.ضَرَبَ زَيْدٌ
nominal sentence	Here we know that Zayd did something – thus we want to know what he did. The sen-	.زَيْدٌ ضَرَبَ

> tence answers the question of what Zayd did. Since it was the action of *to hit*, the logical emphasis is on the verb.

In general, we can say that the dominant thing or person stands at the beginning of the sentence. However, usually the second (latter) part of the sentence is where the main emphasis is put on. Eventually, it will also depend on the intonation.

In grammar, we use two terms to describe that we changed the usual word order: You may **forward** a word (تَقْدِيمٌ) or **delay** it (تَأْخِيرٌ).

Remark: There is a grammatical trick called *anacoluthon*. It means that you isolate the natural subject - with the effect that you emphasize the subject. In most cases you use a personal pronoun suffix or a solo pronoun to achieve that.

The income of Karim is big.	دَخْلُ كَرِيمٍ كَبِيرٌ.
Karim's income is big.	كَرِيمٌ دَخْلُهُ كَبِيرٌ.
Here, we isolate the word كَرِمٌ.	

Zayd – I killed him.	زَيْدٌ قَتَلْتُهُ.
Zayd – his father died.	زَيْدٌ مَاتَ أَبُوهُ.
In both examples, we have isolated the word زَيْدٌ. Instead of زَيْدٌ, you could use the expression: ...إِنَّ زَيْدًا	
For a deep analysis of this construction, see *Arabic for Nerds 2*, *question #112, #113, #216, and #222.*	

29. Why is the Arabic word for *son* special?

There are two reasons.

The Arabic word for *son* is اِبْن.

First of all, it is one of the so-called *five nouns* (أَسْماءٌ خَمْسةٌ). This has an impact on how we mark the cases. But that is not our topic now. We will deal with that in *question #220*.

Secondly, it belongs to another **special group of words.** They stand out due to two special features:

- Some of them have only two root letters.

- And all of them start with an Aleph.

two, masculine	اِثْنانِ
two, feminine	اِثْنَتانِ
name	اِسْمٌ
I swear by God	آيْمُ اللهِ

son	اِبْنٌ
daughter	اِبْنةٌ
man	اِمْرُؤٌ

The letter ا in the above words is a *connecting Hamza*, also called *Hamza of liaison* (هَمْزةُ وَصْلٍ). What is its purpose here? Classical Arabic does not know the **occurrence of two consonants at the beginning of a word** – which means that no Arabic word can begin with a سُكُون on top, like the original word for *son*: بن. We fix that with a هَمْزةُ وَصْلٍ.

But what happens if the word اِبْن marks the start of the utterance or sentence? Then the Aleph is pronounced as a هَمْزة – as **no Arabic sentence/utterance can start with a vowel.** We need a consonant followed by a vowel. You pronounce a هَمْزة and a كَسْرة resulting in: **'ibn.**

The first letter ‍ا, i.e., the هَمْزَةُ وَصْلٍ, brings along more complications regarding the correct pronunciation. If the letter ‍ا in words like اِبْنٌ or اِسْمٌ isn't the first letter of the utterance, you need to <u>neglect</u> it! Thus, the correct spelling would be اَبْنُ

meaning	pronunciation	expression
And his name	*"wasmuhu"*	وَاسْمُهُ
O son of a dog!	*"yabnalkalbi"*	يا ابْنَ الْكَلْبِ !
	Note: This expression is an insult (شَتِيمَةٌ).	
What's your name?	*"masmuka?"*	ما اسْمُكَ؟

There are three special situations:

1. The *Basmalah* (بَسْمَلَةٌ) - the expression بِسْمِ اللهِ. It literally means *in the name of God/Allah*. In this special sentence, the هَمْزَةُ وَصْلٍ is omitted.

2. If you start a question with the particle اَ (similar to هَلْ), then the هَمْزَةُ وَصْلٍ is omitted too. For example: *Is your son present?* In Arabic, you write: أَبْنُكَ مَوْجُودٌ؟

3. If you add the particle لَ or لِ before the definite article الْ, then the letter ‍ا also drops. For example: لِلْبَيْتِ and not: لِالْبَيْتِ

30. Osama *bin* Laden or Osama *ibn* Laden - What is correct?

Even if you tried hard, in Arabic, you would never arrive at bin.

In English and other foreign languages, you will hear and read the name *Osama bin Laden*. He was the former head of the terrorist organization *al-Qāʿida*. His name is the transliterated form of أُسَامَةُ بْنُ لاِدِن – literally meaning: *Osama, son of Laden*. The entire second part of the name – *son of Laden* – stands in apposition to the first name, i.e., *Osama*.

Before we move on: If you are wondering why there is the feminine ending ة although Osama was a man, jump to *question #57*. Note that **masculine proper names** ending in ة are *diptotes* (مَمْنُوعٌ مِن الصَّرْفِ).

In Hebrew, the word for *son* is *ben* (בֵּן). In ancient times, when the Semitic languages emerged, the word only consisted of these two letters. In Arabic, however, the word for *son* has another type of skeleton. A third letter comes into the game: the letter ا, a so-called *Hamza of liaison* (هَمْزَةُ وَصْلٍ).

The letter ا makes it impossible to arrive at *bin* in Arabic. Why? In Classical Arabic, when the word does not start an utterance, the letter ا is neglected. Therefore, we have to deal with the letter-combination بن. It is pronounced as follows:

The sequence is: "u/a/i" plus "bn" plus "u/a/i".

Let me explain this:

- Since the word ابن does not stand at the beginning, there must be a vowel before it: **a case ending, a mood marker,** or a **helping vowel.**

- Then we add ابن. Since it is not the start of an utterance/ sentence, the ا is neglected.

- What do we have then? If the preceding word is in the nominative case (مَرْفُوعٌ), we will get *"ubn"*. If it needs the accusative case (مَنْصُوبٌ), we will have *"abn"*. This is the first part of the expression.

- The word ابن gets a **case marker** as well. The case marker depends on the position and function in the sentence. Theoretically, it could be "*u*", "*a*", or "*i*".

- Therefore, the second half of the expression is "*bnu*", "*bna*", or "*bni*".

The son of Karim came.	جاءَ ابْنُ كَرِيمٍ.
Pronunciation: "*jā'abnukarīm*".	

Arabic newspapers often write the name *Bin Laden* with quotation marks: "بن لادن". So what is the **correct spelling** of اِبْن?

The important point is the letter ا – the so-called هَمْزَةُ وَصْلٍ. The word اِبْن behaves exactly in the same way as اِسْمٌ, except that in the word اِسْمٌ, - despite the fact that you don't pronounce it, you don't drop the letter ا in writing. For example: What's your name? (مَا اسْمُكَ؟). However, there are exceptions – see *question #29*.

These are the spelling rules for اِبْن:

- Usually you write اِبْن with the هَمْزَةُ وَصْلٍ if it marks the beginning of a sentence or utterance.

- In genealogical phrases, however, you don't write the هَمْزَةُ وَصْلٍ in the words for *son* (اِبْن) and *daughter* (اِبْنَة) - if they stand in apposition (بَدَل) to the first word. What does that mean? For example:

Muhammad, son of Abdallah (= his father).	مُحَمَّدُ بْنُ عَبْدِ اللهِ
The pronunciation of this sequence is "*muhammadubnu 'abdi...*" Why? Well, personal names that get the standard case endings	

> (*triptotes*) **lose the sign of indefiniteness** (*nunation*) in **genealogical citations** before the word بِن (*son of*)!
>
> If you use nunation, the sentence would mean: Muhammad **is** the son of Abdallah (مُحَمَّدٌ اِبْنُ عَبْدِ اللهِ). That is why I highlighted the comma in the translation.

Let's see the difference:

1	Khālid **is** the son of Muhammad.	خَالِدٌ اِبْنُ مُحَمَّدٍ.
	Here, the part *son of Muhammad* is the **predicate** (خَبَر) of the subject (مُبْتَدَأ), i.e., Khālid. You have to write the هَمْزَةُ وَصْلٍ! You can't write بِن.	
2	Khālid, son of Muhammad	خَالِدُ بْنُ مُحَمَّدٍ
	Here, the part *son of Muhammad* (a إِضافة-construction) stands in **apposition** (بَدَل) to *Khālid*. This is not a complete sentence. In this situation, the هَمْزَةُ وَصْلٍ is not written.	

Note: You will find a detailed discussion about the word اِبْن in *Arabic for Nerds 2, question #102.*

To sum it up:

- If you express *Bin Laden* in Arabic, you should pronounce the هَمْزَةُ وَصْلٍ at the beginning and write: اِبْنُ لادِن

- If you cite his entire name, you should say and write: أسامةُ بْنُ لادِن

31. How are family names constructed in Arabic?

The system is entirely different compared to Western names.

In Europe or the USA we have a first name (given name), maybe a middle name, and a surname (family name). How is it in the Arab world? Let us examine, for example, this name:

Al-Farūq 'Abū Karīm Muhammad 'Ibn Khālid al-Baghdādīy

الْفارُوقُ أَبُو كَرِيمٍ مُحَمَّدُ اِبْنُ خالِدٍ الْبَغْدَادِيُّ

In general, Arabic names consist of **five parts** which don't necessarily have to follow a particular order. However, you will often find the following order:

1 لَقَبٌ	2 كُنْيَةٌ	3 اِسْمٌ	4 نَسَبٌ	5 نِسْبَةٌ

(Ibn... Ibn... Ibn...)

Epithet	الْفارُوقُ لَقَبٌ	1

The لَقَب is defined as an epithet, usually a religious, honorific, or descriptive title. The لَقَب can precede the اِسْم and sometimes comes to replace it. There are mainly three possibilities:

- physical qualities: الطَّوِيلُ - *the tall*
- virtues: الْفارُوقُ - *he who distinguishes truth from falsehood* or الرَّاشِدُ - *the rightly guided.*
- compounds with الدِّين (*religion*): *light of the religion* (نُورُ الدِّينِ)

Honorific name (street name) – to identify a person by his first-born child.	أَبُو كَرِيمٍ كُنْيَةٌ	2

Name under which people call somebody on the street; mostly named after the first child: *father of; mother of.*

The كُنْيَة is a **honorific name**. It is not part of a person's formal name and is usually not printed in documents. The كُنْية is very important in Arabic culture – even a person who has no child might have a كُنْية which makes him (or her) symbolically the parent of a special quality, such as *father of good deeds*.

(First) name	مُحَمَّد	اِسْمٌ	3

This could be a traditional Arab name that is found in the Qur'an, a (nice) attribute, a foreign name, or a compound with the most famous prefix: عَبْد – which means *servant of* and is followed by one of the 99 names (attributes) of Allah.

Genealogy (family origin): **son of… son of… son of...**	اِبْنُ خالِدٍ	نَسَبٌ	4

The نَسَب is the patronymic. It is more or less a list of ancestors, each introduced with *son of* (اِبْن) or *daughter of* (بِنْت).

It often relates back to two or three generations. That's why Arabic names can be very long: أَبَنُّ بْنُ عَبَّاسٍ بْنِ سَهْلِ بْنِ سَعْدٍ

In this example, 'Abbās is the father and Sahl the grandfather and Sa'd the grand-grandfather.

Indication of origin. The *Nisba* is usually preceded by the definite article اَل.	الْبَغْدادِيٌّ	نِسْبة	5

The نِسْبة is similar to what people in the West may call the surname. It is rarely used in Egypt and in Lebanon where the لَقَب incorporates its meaning. A person may have several نِسْبة

It is usually an adjective (نِسْبة) derived from:

• the place of birth, origin: الْبَغْدادِيٌّ (*from Baghdad*);

• the name of a religious sect or tribe or family: التَّمِيمِيٌّ (*belonging to the Tamīm tribe*);

• a profession: الْعَطّارِيٌّ (*the perfume vendor*);

Watch out: In the Arab world women don't take their husband's surname when they get married. They keep their names they were given at birth.

Children, however, do take their father's name – which is expressed in the نَسَب: *daughter of* (name of the father).

32. الْبَرادِعِيُّ - What is the meaning of this name?

It denotes a person who makes a piece of cloth for saddles.

You may have heard of the Egyptian Nobel Peace Prize winner and one-time presidential-hopeful Mohamed ElBaradei (مُحَمَّد الْبَرادِعِيّ).

The word الْبَرادِعِيُّ goes back to بَرْذَعة (alternative spelling: بَرْدَعة) which denotes a piece of cloth which is put under the saddle of a donkey, mule or camel (رَحْل). The plural form of this word is بَرادِعُ (alternative spelling: بَرادِعُ).

If we form a *noun of relation* (نِسْبة) of the plural form – which is done by adding the letter ي plus شَدّة -, then we can say that el-Baradei's name denotes a person who makes these pieces of cloth for the saddle. A kind of *saddle-maker*.

Arab names sometimes relate to professions and are expressed by a نِسْبة or a *form of exaggeration* (صِيغةُ الْمُبالَغةِ) - see *questions #51 and #86*. Some examples:

weaver	نَسّاج	tiler	بَلّاط	perfume vendor	عَطّار

33. Are there pet names in Arabic?

Yes, they are very common.

The word for *pet name* is اِسْمُ الدَّلْعِ. The root د-ل-ع means *to loll; to let the tongue hang out.* There are many pet names in Arabic and you will hear them quite often. Some of them have tricky endings. Although the person is masculine, the nickname may look feminine.

pet name	meaning of the name	proper name	
حَمادة	'Ahmad: *more praiseworthy*; 'Ahmad can be used as a synonym for Muhammad (which means *praised*).	'Ahmad, Muhammad	أَحْمَدُ مُحَمَّدُ
دَرْش	*Chosen; selected; the chosen one*; Mustafā is also a synonym for Muhammad.	Mustafā	مُصْطَفَى
	دَرْش means *black leather*. But that is not the origin of the pet name. Legend has it that دَرْش relates back to an Ottoman Sultan called Mustafa, who became a *Dervish* (دَرْويِشُ). Over time, دَرْويِشُ was reduced to دَرْش.		
زَنُّوبة	*an aromatic tree*	Zaynab	زَيْنَبُ

You also find many pet names that are less formal:

pet name	meaning of the name	proper name	
أَبُو تُوت	Literal meaning: *success* (granted by God), *happy outcome; adjustment.*	Tawfīq	تَوْفِيقُ
سُوسُو	Name of a prophet.	Ismā'īl	إِسْماعِيلُ

كَوْكَبُ الشَّرْقِ	كُلْثُومٌ means *elephant* or, said of a person, *someone with a chubby face.*	Umm Kulthūm	أُمُّ كُلْثُومٍ
The expression كَوْكَبُ الشَّرْقِ means *star of the Orient* is the pet name of the famous Egyptian singer 'Umm Kulthūm. Note that the third daughter of the Islamic prophet Muhammad was also named 'Umm Kulthūm.			

34. What are the main plural forms in Arabic?

In Arabic there are sound (intact) and broken plural forms.

The plural in Arabic is a noun indicating **more** than two units. The so-called **sound plural forms** are mostly used for human beings. Let's have a look at the three major types:

Sound masculine plural (جَمْعُ الْمُذَكَّرِ السّالِمُ) - regular
It is easily formed by adding ونَ in the nominative case (مَرْفُوعٌ) and ينَ in the genitive (مَجْرُورٌ) and accusative (مَنْصُوبٌ) case.
Note that the final letter ن always takes a فَتْحة, i.e, the vowel *"a"*.

translation	plural مَجْرُورٌ/ مَنْصُوبٌ	plural مَرْفُوعٌ	singular
engineer/s (m)	مُهَنْدِسِينَ	مُهَنْدِسُونَ	مُهَنْدِسٌ

Sound feminine plural (جَمْعُ الْمُؤَنَّثِ السّالِمُ) - regular
It is easily formed by adding اتٌ in the nominative case (مَرْفُوعٌ) or اتٍ in the genitive (مَجْرُورٌ) **and** accusative (مَنْصُوبٌ) case.

Note: A singular noun can be masculine, but the plural is built like a sound feminine plural. For example, the Arabic word for *hospital* (مُسْتَشْفَى) which is a *noun of place* (اِسْمُ الْمكانِ).

I saw big hospitals. (شاهَدْتُ مُسْتَشْفَياتٍ كَبيرَةً.)

translation	plural مَجرُورٌ/ مَنْصُوبٌ	plural مَرْفُوعٌ	singular
engineer/s (f.)	مُهْنْدِساتٍ	مُهْنْدِساتٌ	مُهَنْدِسةٌ

GOLDEN RULE #1:

In **sound <u>feminine</u> plurals**, you can **<u>never</u>** find a فَتْحة – the vowel "a" – on the final letter ت!

Why? Because the sound feminine plural has **only two vowel endings** for the three cases – whether they are definite or indefinite: ضَمّةٌ and كَسْرةٌ.

Broken plural (جَمْعُ التَّكْسِيرِ) - irregular		
There are many patterns; some of them produce *diptotes* (مَمْنُوعٌ مِن الصَّرْفِ).		
translation	plural مَجرُورٌ/ مَنْصُوبٌ	plural مَرْفُوعٌ	singular
man/men	رِجالٍ - رِجالاً	رِجالٌ	رَجُلٌ
book/books	كُتُبٍ - كُتُبًا	كُتُبٌ	كِتابٌ

The broken plural brings us to another very important principle in Arabic. The main rule of agreement.

GOLDEN RULE #2:

Anything that has to **agree** in some way with a <u>**non-human plural**</u> will always be **feminine singular!**

In other words, we treat plural non-human nouns as grammatically <u>feminine singular</u>! This is important for the correct agreement: An adjective or verb that goes along with such a noun has to be in the feminine singular as well! But there are rare exceptions – a famous example of the Qur'an: آيَاتٌ بَيِّنَاتٌ

I saw beautiful cars in many places.	رَأَيْتُ سَيَاراتٍ جَمِيلةً فِي أَماكِنَ كَثِيرةٍ.

Direct object (بِهِ مَفْعُولٌ), indefinite; it should take فَتْحة (nunation: "-an") on the final letter to mark the **accusative** case. But since we have a **sound feminine plural**, it is مَنْصُوب by كَسْرة (nunation: "-in")	سَياراتٍ
Adjective (صِفةٌ) for the direct object *cars*. It has to agree with the noun it refers to (*cars*) – thus it takes the accusative case (مَنْصُوبٌ) - the regular مَنْصُوب-ending "-an". However, all words that are in agreement with a feminine sound plural need to be in the **singular** (feminine) form!	جَمِيلةً
Noun in the genitive case (مَجْرُورٌ) as it follows the preposition فِي. Since it is indefinite, it should normally take كَسْرة and nunation resulting in the ending "-in". However, since it is the **broken plural** of the singular form مَكان, we need to deal with a pattern that does <u>not</u> get nunation (مَمْنُوعٌ مِن الصَّرْفِ) and instead takes a single فَتْحة to mark the genitive case. See *question #240*.	أَماكِنَ
Adjective (صِفةٌ) for *places,* which is grammatically (but not visibly) in the genitive case. Therefore, the word كَثِيرةٍ takes two كَسْرة. And it has to be feminine, singular!	كَثِيرةٍ

35. What is a preposition in Arabic?

One of only 17 words in total.

Prepositions in English are words like *in, at, on, above, with*. In Arabic, we only call the following words *prepositions* (حَرْفُ جَرٍّ). Note that a one-letter-word can be a preposition:

مُنْذُ	13	عَنْ	7	بِ	1
مُذْ	14	فِي	8	تَ	2
عَدَا	15	عَلَى	9	لِ	3
حاشا	16	مِن	10	كَ	4
خَلا	17	إِلَى	11	تاءُ الْقَسَمِ	5
		حَتَّى	12	واوُ الْقَسَمِ	6

But what about words such as بَعْدَ (*after*) or تَحْتَ (*under*) which we call prepositions in English and German?

In Arabic, they are **nouns** (اِسْمٌ) and get case markers. They serve in the position of an **adverb of time** or **place**. We call them *circumstantial of place* (ظَرْفُ مَكَانٍ) or *time* (ظَرْفُ زَمَانٍ). The word ظَرْف means *circumstance; vessel, container*.

An adverb is a word that qualifies the meaning of a verb. An adverb indicates manner, time, place, cause or degree and gives answers to questions such as when, where, how, or how much. Especially adverbs of place or time can theoretically appear anywhere in the sentence.

adverb of time	ظَرْفُ الزَّمانِ 1
You traveled on the day off.	سافَرْتَ يَومَ الْعُطْلةِ.

2 ظَرْفُ الْمَكانِ	adverb of place
جَلَسَتْ النَّحْلةُ فَوْقَ الشَّجَرةِ.	The bee sat on the tree.

Notice the فَتْحة at the end of يَوْمَ and فَوْقَ.

In the grammatical analysis (الْإِعْرابُ), when we determine the function of such words in a sentence, we call them *local* or *temporal* **objects** (مَفْعُولٌ فيهِ). It is just another way of saying *adverbs of time* or *place*.

Since they are treated as objects, we have an explanation for the فَتْحة at the end. They serve as the first part of a إِضافةٌ. If they are **not followed** by another word, they get **nunation**!

جِئْتُ بَعْدَ الْمَغْرِبِ.	I came after sunset.
جِئْتُ بَعْدًا.	I came after.

Let's see some **adverbs of place**. In English, most of them would be called prepositions. In Arabic they are nouns (اِسْمٌ).

above	فَوْقَ	towards	ناحِيةَ
under	تَحْتَ	during; through	خِلالَ
behind	خَلْفَ	beside	جانِبَ
near	قُرْبَ	right	يَمينَ
around	حَوْلَ	left	يَسارَ
towards	تُجاهَ	north	شَمالَ
in front of	أَمامَ	south	جَنُوبَ
between; among	بَيْنَ	east	شَرْقَ
middle; amongst	وَسْطَ	west	غَرْبَ

36. Is مَع (*with*) a noun (إِسْمٌ) or preposition (حَرْفُ جَرٍّ)؟

Most grammarians say that مَع (with) is a noun (إِسْمٌ).

There is a debate going on but most grammarians think that مَعَ, which means *with,* is a إِسْمٌ and not a حَرْفٌ. But why is the word *with* rather a noun than a preposition? Because مَع can sometimes have *nunation* (تَنْوِينٌ)!

They came together.	جاؤُوا مَعًا.

This is crucial. A حَرْفٌ is by definition *indeclinable* (مَبْنِيٌّ), which means that it always looks the same – no matter what the position in the sentence may be. It has a **cemented shape**. For example, the Arabic word for *in* (فِي).

Okay, but how can we describe the function of مَع in a sentence? Basically, there are three jobs for مَع:

grammatical term	meaning	example	
adverb of time/place (ظَرْفُ زَمانٍ/مَكانٍ)	You played with the children.	لَعِبْتَ مَعَ الْأَطْفالِ.	1
مَعَ has to end with the vowel "a" (فَتْحة) because it serves as a circumstantial object (مَفْعُولٌ فِيهِ) to define place or time. It is the first part of a إِضافةٌ. It is treated as a noun (إِسْمٌ).			

declined noun (إِسْمٌ مُعْرَبٌ). Usually after a preposition.	I went together with him.	ذَهَبْتُ مِنْ مَعِهِ.	2
Here, مَع receives case endings. The word مَع in the expression with him مَعِهِ has the vowel "i" under the letter ع. Why? Because the preceding preposition مِنْ dragged مَع into the genitive case (مَجْرُورٌ).			

circumstantial description (حالٌ). مَعًا is in the accusative case (مَنْصُوبٌ)	They came together.	جاؤُوا مَعًا.	3

- What is a حالٌ? It describes the aspect of a certain noun during the occurrence of the action of the verb. For example: *he came, smiling.* (جاءَ مُبْتَسِمًا). *Smiling* is a حالٌ – see *questions #245 and #246.*

- We say that مَعًا is a **inert noun interpreted as if it were derived** (اِسْمٌ جامِدٌ مُؤَوَّلٌ بِمُشْتَقٍّ). Thus, it gets nunation.

So why do people say that مَع is a preposition?

Because it works as the first part of a إضافة-construction. This means that the second part (مُضافٌ إِلَيْهِ) – the annexed noun – has to be in the genitive case (مَجْرُورٌ).

If we only looked at the result, we could assume that the genitive case was not induced by the إضافة, but by a preposition. Let us look at two examples:

Karim **sat** with Muhammad.	جَلَسَ كَرِيمٌ مَعَ مُحَمَّدٍ.

Adverb of **place** (ظَرْفُ مَكانٍ). Why? Because the action of *to sit* is more associated with a place and not with time. It also works as the first part of the إضافة-construction.	مَعَ

Karim **came** with Muhammad.	جاءَ كَرِيمٌ مَعَ مُحَمَّدٍ.

Adverb of **time** (ظَرْف زَمان) - because the action of *to come* is more associated with time. It also works as the first part of the إضافة-construction.	مَعَ

What about the word *Muhammad* in both examples?

Second part of the إِضافة-construction (مُضافٌ إِلَيْهِ مَجْرُورٌ) (بِالْكَسْرِةِ).	مُضافٌ إِلَيْهِ مَجْرُورٌ	مُحَمَّدٍ

37. Why is it important to count syllables in Arabic?

It will tell you more about word stress.

Arabic has two kinds of syllables (C = consonant; V = vowel):

1. **Open syllables:** CV and CVV (VV = long vowel)

2. **Closed syllables:** CVC

Furthermore, Arabic has some special features:

- **Every syllable begins with a consonant** and never with a vowel! Note that the Hamza (e.g., أ) is a consonant.

- The سُكُونْ is the sign of **quiescence**. It is the anti-vowel. It tells us that a consonant does not have a vowel. The word literally means *tranquillity* or *quietude*.

- The سُكُونْ is the absence of sound and **cuts the word into syllables**. There are light and heavy syllables.

light syllable	C V	open
heavy syllable	C V V	open
	C V C	closed

Remark: Verbs such as ظَنَّ (*to think*) actually follow the sequence ظَنَنَ. The first ن takes a سُكُونْ. Therefore, grammatically speaking, it has two syllables: **C V C - C V**, although they are usually not pronounced as such (ظَنْ+نَ).

So, how can we find the right stress? In general *word stress* (German: *Betonung*) means that one syllable in a word is more prominent than other syllables.

Word stress in Arabic does not really matter.

Linguists say that word stress is not distinctive in Arabic. In other words, word stress in Arabic does not change the meaning of words.

In Classical Arabic, word stress is not a big issue. The ancient grammarians did not cover the topic at all. Only when the readings of the Qu'ran were developed, people started to think about accentuation. However, most of these rules are based on stress patterns of modern dialects. Many scholars have tried to set up rules for the correct accentuation of Classical Arabic. **Before we go into the details, two hints:**

- The ultimate (last) syllable is <u>never</u> stressed.

- The stress <u>can't</u> be put on the definite article ال, nor on a preposition, or conjunction.

Let's analyze the three main rules for Classical Arabic and Modern Standard Arabic.

RULE 1: **Stress a <u>superheavy</u> last syllable** - but only, if you use the pausal form which means that you don't pronounce the last vowel (case or mood marker).

| ya-**qūl** | light-→superheavy | he says | يَقُول |

RULE 2: **Stress the rightmost <u>non-final heavy</u> syllable.**

| mu-dar-ri-**sū**-na | light-heavy-light-→heavy-light | teachers | مُدَرِّسُونَ |

mas-'a-la-tu-ha	→heavy-light-light-light-light	her problem	مَسْأَلَتُها

RULE 3: Otherwise, **stress the antepenult** (=the third-to-last syllable of a word).

This rule applies also to the standard verb form, for example, *he wrote/to write* (كَتَبَ).

ka-ta-ba	→light-light-light	he wrote	كَتَبَ
ka-**ta**-ba-tā	light-→light-light-heavy	they both wrote (fem. dual)	كَتَبَتا

In modern Arabic dialects, stress is very important because it is one of the distinguishing features and ingredients of the sounds and melody of a dialect.

In **Egyptian Arabic**, the stress is put on the penultimate syllable (= second from end). This is different to **Eastern Arabic** dialects where we stress the third from the end like in formal Arabic.

Regarding word stress, Classical Arabic and the dialects of Palestine and Damascus follow almost the same rules.

Eastern dialects	Egyptian Arabic	syllable structure	example/ meaning
mad-ra-sa	mad-**ra**-sa	CV - CV - CV	مَدْرسة
→light-light-light	light-→light-light	light-light-light	*school*
mu-**dar**-ri-sa	mu-dar-**ri**-sa	CV - CVC - CV - CV	مُدَرِّسة

| light-→light-light-light | light-light-→light-light | light-light-light-light | *teacher (f.)* |

38. Why do you need helping vowels?

You need helping vowels to avoid consonant clusters.

In Arabic, most words end with a vowel (case marker, mood marker for verbs, hidden/implied pronoun, etc.). We use this vowel as a connector. E.g.: *You are the teacher* (أَنْتَ الْمُدَرِّسُ).

explanation	pronunciation
This is, precisely speaking, wrong. Beginners who are still reading sentences word by word are likely to pronounce it like that – and make a pause after the word أَنْتَ.	ʾanta ʾal-Mudarrisu
This is how a native speaker would pronounce the sentence. The sentence is pronounced as it would only be one entity, without a pause.	ʾantalmudarrisu

The هَمْزَةُ وَصْلٍ of the definite article الـ is not pronounced; it basically disappears. It would only remain if it would be the first letter of an utterance or sentence – in such a situation, you have to pronounce it as a glottal stop.

But what happens if the preceding word ends with سُكُون? What should we do if the preceding word is, for e.g., مِنْ, هَلْ, or مَنْ? Let's put our sentence into a question.

| Is the teacher present? | هَلْ الْمُدَرِّسُ مَوْجُودٌ؟ |

You can't pronounce this sentence because two consonants would collide: The لْ of هَلْ and the لْ of the definite article. We have to get rid of the first سُكُون and replace it with a helping vowel.

In most situations, we use the vowel "i" (كَسْرَةٌ) as a helping vowel. This is how the above sentence would be pronounced then: هَلِ الْمُدَرِّسُ مَوْجُودٌ؟

The particle هَلْ which originally ends in a سُكُون is now connected to the following word by the vowel "i". We basically have added a vowel.	halilmudarrisu mawjūdun?

But there are exceptions:

- The preposition مِنْ often takes فَتْحة as a helping vowel. But strictly speaking, the helping vowel of مِن is فَتْحة only if the word is followed by the definite article: مِنَ الْ. Otherwise, it is كَسْرة. For example: مِنِ امْتِحان.

- If the last vowel (not the case-marker!) of a word is ضَمّة ("u"), the helping vowel will be a ضَمّة. But watch out: The helping vowel is ضَمّة only at the end of pronouns or pronominal endings that end in ضَمّة, e.g.,: هُم, كُم, تُم.

- Otherwise, the helping vowel is كَسْرة – even when a word ends in ضَمّة, e.g.: لَمْ يَعُدِ الرَّجُلِ

39. فَ plus اِسْمَعُوا - How do you pronounce that?

You say: "fasma'ū!"

The sentence فَاسْمَعُوا means: *and listen.*

- If you say the entire expression, you should not stop after فَ and should ignore the letter ا, which is a *Hamza of liaison* (هَمْزَةُ وَصْلٍ).

- Therefore, you will end up saying "*fasma'ū*" and not "*fa-'isma'ū*", because you don't pronounce the letter ا.

- Without فَ, however, when the word اِسْمَعُوا is the start of your utterance or sentence, it would be pronounced *'isma'ū!* – with a glottal stop and "i".

40. Can you study Arabic grammar in verses?

Yes, you can.

If you want to study Arabic in the most cultivated way, there is a book for you: *ʾAlfiya* (اَلْفِيّة). It contains most of the Arabic grammar – in **1000 verses**.

The famous grammarian Ibn Mālik (اِبْن مالِك), an Andalusian scholar who lived in the 13th century, summarized almost the entire Arabic grammar in this book. It contains the essential things about نَحْوٌ (*grammar*) and صَرْفٌ (*morphology*).

But I have to warn you: It is only for very proficient readers.

Ibn Mālik died in Damascus in 1274 (672هـ).

41. What is essential to know about verb forms?

Many Arabs don't know what a I-verb or X-verb is. They only know patterns.

Grammarians use the term وَزْن (or plural أَوْزان) which literally means *measure; weight* to describe a **model**.

The word *weight* is a good description for what we actually do in Arabic. Imagine a pair of scales and weights in form of vowels and extra letters. On the left side, we place what we want to get: the pattern. On the right side, we only throw in the root letters, In order to keep the balance, we have to add weights (vowels and/or extra letters) to the root.

The Roman numerals which are widely used in the West to describe the different verb forms were invented by Western scholars. If you want to increase your understanding of Arabic, it is important to switch from numbers to patterns as this will automatically give you a better feeling for the language.

Theoretically, each triliteral Arabic root could be transformed into one of **15 possible (and documented) verb forms**. Forms 11 through 15 (as well as 9) are very rare.

There are basically two groups of verbs:

unaugmented – *the pure root.* The verb consists only of its three or four root letters.	مُجَرَّدٌ	1
augmented (enhanced root) Used for the verb-patterns from II to X.	مَزيدٌ	2

Grammarians use the term مُجَرَّدٌ ثُلاثِيٌّ if a verb consists of its 3 root letters only and مُجَرَّدٌ رُباعِيٌّ if it is based on 4 root letters.

If I use the term ثُلاثِيٌّ in this book, you know that we talk about a form I-verb. All other forms are called مَزِيدٌ.

Let's check the most common verb patterns. The capital letters next to the examples refer to the capital letters in the list:

Only **one** Arabic letter is added to the root:	مَزِيدٌ بِحَرْفٍ	2.1
A) تَضْعِيفٌ (doubling of a letter)		
B) an *Aleph* (أَلِفٌ)		
C) a "real" Hamza (you pronounce it)		
D) the letter ت		

		to teach	عَلَّمَ	II	فَعَّلَ	A
root has 3 radicals		to meet	قابَلَ	III	فاعَلَ	B
		to take out	أَخْرَجَ	IV	أَفْعَلَ	C
root has 4 radicals		to quake	تَزَلْزَلَ	II	تَفَعْلَلَ	D

Two Arabic letters are added to the root.	مَزِيدٌ بِحَرْفَيْنِ	2.2
A) ت plus تَضْعِيفٌ		
B) ت plus أَلِفٌ		
C) *Hamza of liaison* (هَمْزَةُ وَصْلٍ) plus ن		
D) *Hamza of liaison* (هَمْزَةُ وَصْلٍ) plus ت		
E) *Hamza of liaison* plus تَضْعِيفٌ		

root has 3 radicals	to study	تَعَلَّمَ	V	تَفَعَّلَ	A
	to cooperate	تَعاوَنَ	VI	تَفاعَلَ	B
	to be broken	إِنْكَسَرَ	VII	إِنْفَعَلَ	C

	to take part in	اِشْتَرَكَ	VIII	اِفْتَعَلَ D
	to become green	اِخْضَرَّ	IX	اِفْعَلَّ E
root has 4 radicals	to be reassured	اِطْمَأَنَّ	IV	اِفْعَلَلَّ E

Three letters are added to the root.	مَزِيدٌ بِثَلاثةِ أَحْرُفٍ 2.3

This is a combination of:
- a *Hamza of liaison* (هَمْزةُ وَصْلٍ)
- The letter س
- The letter ت

root has 3 radicals	to import	اِسْتَوْرَدَ	X اِسْتَفْعَلَ

42. Does every verb pattern convey a different meaning?

Yes – but there are exceptions.

Some verb patterns (forms/أَوْزانٌ) convey a similar meaning. Even if you don't know a verb, you may be able to derive an idea just by looking at its pattern.

In the following tables, the capital letters next to the examples refer to the capital letters in the list.

يُفَعِّلُ	فَعَّلَ	fa''ala	II - 2
A) Can strengthen the meaning of a I-verb (often an **intensive version** of the I-verb).			
B) Can make a I-verb **transitive** (فِعْلٌ مُتَعَدٍّ). Transitive verbs can have a direct object.			

C) Can make a I-verb **causative**. Causative verbs are verbs that show the reason that something happened. Usually the express the following action: to make (someone) doing (something); to let (someone) doing (something).

	II-verb			I-verb	
A	to teach	دَرَّسَ		to study	دَرَسَ
B	to clean something	طَهَّرَ	◄	to be clean	طَهَرَ
C	to remind somebody	ذَكَّرَ		to remember	ذَكَرَ

يُفاعِلُ	فاعَلَ	fā'ala	III - 3

A) Shows the **attempt** to do something – *try to...*

B) *To do to* (someone); **to involve someone**. Describes someone doing the action in question to or with someone else.

Watch out: I-verbs need a preposition in Arabic to connect the action with the other part – <u>III-verbs don't</u>. In Arabic, III-verbs go along with a direct object (مَفْعُولٌ بِهِ).

In English, however, the meaning of III-verbs is often translated with an <u>**in**direct object</u> – so you will need the English words *with* or *against* to get a meaningful sentence.

	III-verb			I-verb	
A	to try to kill (to fight)	قاتَلَ		to kill	قَتَلَ
B	to do business with	عامَلَ	◄	to work	عَمِلَ
B	to correspond	كاتَبَ		to write	كَتَبَ

to dance	رَقَّصَ	فَعَلَ	I-verb

| to dance **with** | راقَصَ | فاعَلَ | III-verb |

| He danced at the party. | رَقَصَ فِي الْحَفْلةِ. | I |
| He danced **with her** at the party. | راقَصَها فِي الْحَفْلةِ. | III |

In Arabic, III-verbs often take a direct object (مَفْعُولٌ بِهِ). They are transitive (فِعْلٌ مُتَعَدٍّ). In English, the meaning of Arabic III-verbs are often <u>in</u>transitive (فِعْلٌ لازِمٌ) which means that they are translated with a preposition.

| يُفْعِلُ | أَفْعَلَ | 'af'ala | IV - 4 |

A) Makes a I-verb **transitive** (having a direct object);

B) Makes a I-verb **causative** – *to make or cause someone or something to do or be.* This is the pattern's most common application. This form has the strongest causative meaning.

C) It can also **strengthen** the meaning of a I-verb.

	IV-verb				I-verb	
A	to make happy	أَسْعَدَ			to be happy	سَعِدَ
B	to inform somebody	أَعْلَمَ	◄		to know	عَلِمَ
C	to lock	أَغْلَقَ			to close	غَلَقَ

| يَتَفَعَّلُ | تَفَعَّلَ | tafaʿʿala | V - 5 |

A) **Reflexive meaning** of the II-verb (فَعَّلَ). It may also convey a light passive meaning. What does reflexive mean? Reflexive words show that the person who does the action is also the person who is affected by it.

B) Sometimes it is an **intensive** version of a **I-verb**.

C) Occasionally, it has the meaning of **pretending something**.

	V-verb		**I- or II-verb**	
A	to be separated	تَفَرَّقَ	to separate	فَرَّقَ
A	to be frightened	تَرَوَّعَ	to scare	رَوَّعَ
B	to track	تَتَبَّعَ	to follow	تَبِعَ
B	to congregate	تَجَمَّعَ	to gather, to join	جَمَعَ
C	to pretend/claim to be a prophet; to foretell	تَنَبَّأَ بِـ	to inform, to tell	نَبَّأَ بِـ
C	to force oneself; to pretend to do something; to take upon over something	تَكَلَّفَ بِـ	to charge, to assign	كَلَّفَ بِـ

يَتَفَاعَلُ	تَفَاعَلَ	tafāʻla	VI -6

A) **Reflexive** form of a **III-verb** (فَاعَلَ). It often has a **reciprocal** meaning: *to do something together; to do something between or among each other.*

A reciprocal verb expresses the idea of an action that is done by two or more people or things to each other.

B) May convey (similar to stem V) the meaning of **pretending**.

	VI-verb		**I- or III-verb**	
A	to share with one another	تَشارَكَ	to share	شارَكَ

A	to reveal (secrets, thoughts, feelings) to each other	تَكاشَفَ	to reveal	كاشَفَ (بِ)
B	to feign sleep; to pretend to be asleep	تَناوَمَ	to sleep	نامَ

يَنْفَعِلُ	اِنْفَعَلَ	'infa'ala	VII - 7

A) **Passive** meaning of the **I-verb** (the basic stem). Watch out: This form is not the real passive tense. Why? If we use a VII-verb, the action happens to the subject (فاعِلٌ) without knowing the actual doer of the action (agent).

B) **Reflexive meaning** – showing that the person who does the action is the one who is targeted/affected by it. However, in most situations, a VII-verb indicates both: passive and reflexive meaning.

	VII-verb			I-verb	
A	to be/become broken	اِنْكَسَرَ		to break sth.	كَسَرَ
A	to be wrung out	اِنْعَصَرَ		to squeeze	عَصَرَ
B	to be uncovered	اِنْكَشَفَ	◄	to uncover	كَشَفَ
B	to be put to flight	اِنْهَزَمَ		to put to flight	هَزَمَ

يَفْتَعِلُ	اِفْتَعَلَ	'ifta'ala	VIII - 8

A) **Reflexive** or **passive** meaning of a **I-verb** (similar to VII);

B) It may express the meaning of: *to do something for oneself*;

C) It may express: *to do something with someone else.*

	VIII-verb			I-verb	
A	to take fire; to be burned	اِحْتَرَقَ		to burn sth.	حَرَقَ
A	to be occupied (with)	اِشْتَغَلَ بِ		to occupy	شَغَلَ
B	to be far from homeland	اِغْتَرَبَ	◄	to go away	غَرَبَ
B	to take for oneself; take up	اِتَّخَذَ		to take	أَخَذَ
C	to be associated (with)	اِقْتَرَنَ		to associate	قَرَنَ

يَفْعَلُّ	اِفْعَلَّ	'if'alla	IX - 9

A) **Reflexive** meaning of a II-verb (referring to colors or physical deficiencies).

	XI-verb			II-verb	
A	to blush; to become red	اِحْمَرَّ		to make red	حَمَّرَ
A	to be crooked	اِعْوَجَّ	◄	to bend, crook sth.	عَوَّجَ

يَسْتَفْعِلُ	اِسْتَفْعَلَ	'istaf'ala	X - 10

A) It expresses **to regard/find/consider** something as...

B) Derived verbal meaning of a noun (اِسْمٌ) - *denominal verbs*;

C) Expresses a **wish or a desire** (*to let sb. do sth. for you; to demand sth. for yourself*) → *to seek, ask for, require an action;*

D) **Reflexive** meaning of أَفْعَلَ (form IV);

E) X-verbs may make **I-verbs causative**;

	X-verb		I- or IV-verb; noun	
A	to find ugly	اِسْتَقْبَحَ	to be ugly	قَبُحَ
C	to ask for permission	اِسْتَأْذَنَ	to allow	أَذِنَ
B	to invest; to profit	اِسْتَثْمَرَ	fruit (noun)	ثَمَرٌ
B	to adopt oriental manners; to study the Orient	اِسْتَشْرَقَ ◄	the Orient	شَرْقٌ
C	to inquire	اِسْتَعْلَمَ	to know	عَلِمَ
D	to prepare oneself	اِسْتَعَدَّ	to prepare	أَعَدَّ
D	to consider oneself great	اِسْتَكْبَرَ	to deem great	أَكْبَرَ
E	to cause to serve; to use	اِسْتَخْدَمَ	to serve	خَدَمَ
E	to cause (call) to witness	اِسْتَشْهَدَ	to witness	شَهِدَ

Remark: Form X is not the only stem that produces so-called *denominal verbs*. The root of such verbs is based on a **concrete noun** (اِسْمٌ) - especially, when the noun is one of the very first and essential words used by people.

Especially verb forms II (فَعَّلَ), IV (أَفْعَلَ), and X (اِسْتَفْعَلَ) have such roots. Some examples:

meaning	stem	verb	meaning	noun
to shine; to blossom	IV - 4	أَزْهَرَ	blossoms	زَهْرٌ
to greet	II – 2	سَلَّمَ	greeting, peace	سَلامٌ
to appoint as successor	X – 10	اِسْتَخْلَفَ	successor	خَلَفٌ

43. How do you say *both* in Arabic?

You use the dual form of a special word.

In Arabic, there is a special way to express the English word *both*. Two words are essential to express the idea in Arabic:

both; masc. sing.	Both are exclusively used in a إِضافة-construction and thus lost their final نْ. Originally they were كِلَانِ an كِلْتانِ.	كِلَا	1
both; fem. sing.		كِلْتا	2

They both express the dual (مُثَنَّى) – however, grammatically, they are **singular** (مُفْرَدٌ)! The only difference between كِلَا and كِلْتا is the gender. كِلَا is masculine and كِلْتا is feminine.

So far, so good – but where should we put them in a sentence? There are two possibilities.

1st part of the إِضافة. The 2nd part must be a <u>definite</u>, <u>dual</u> noun.	both men	كِلَا الرَّجُلَيْنِ	1
	both times	كِلْتا الْمَرَّتَيْنِ	
In this application, both words – كِلَا and كِلْتا – are **proper nouns** of genus (اِسْمُ عَلَمٍ جِنْسِيٌّ).			

Apposition (بَدَلٌ). Placed after a dual noun. You have to add a <u>dual pronoun suffix</u> (ضَمِيرُ الْمُؤَكِّدِ) to كِلَا and كِلْتا respectively.	both men	الرَّجُلانِ كِلاهُما	2
	both times	الْمَرَّتانِ كِلْتاهُما	
In this application, we treat كِلَا and كِلْتا as **followers** (تابِعٌ). They convey **emphasis** (أَلْفاظُ التَّوْكِيدِ الْمَعْنَوِيِّ لِلشُّمُولِ).			

Both options express the same meaning, although the literal translation is slightly different.

Your **both** (two) sisters have traveled.	سافَرَتْ كِلْتا أُخْتَيْكَ.	1

Your two sisters have traveled, **both of** them.	٢ سافَرَتْ أُخْتاكَ كِلتاهُما.

Let's focus on the interesting part: the grammar. Both words must agree in gender with the noun or pronoun they refer to. So we match كِلْتا and كِلَا either with...

- the gender of the second part of the إضافة-construction, i.e., مُضافٌ إِلَيْهِ;

- the gender of the word to which كِلَا or كِلْتا refer. It is the word before them, i.e., مُبْدَلٌ مِنْهُ.

What you need to keep in mind if you use option 1, the إضافة-construction:

- كِلَا (and كِلْتا respectively) agrees in gender with the noun it modifies – but **not** in case! What does that practically mean? Well, ...

- ...when they serve as the first part of the إضافة and when they are followed by an *apparent noun* (اِسْمٌ ظاهِرٌ), then they are not inflected for cases.

- However, if they are followed by a pronoun suffix in the إضافة-construction, they do get inflected!

- كِلَا and كِلْتا are grammatically treated as singular. Thus, a verb, adjective, or noun that relates to them, is either masculine or feminine <u>singular</u>.

What you need to keep in mind if you use option 2 (placed after the word they relate to – in apposition):

- When كِلَا or كِلْتا are combined with a pronoun suffix, you have to mark the case visibly. In the nominative (مَرْفُوعٌ), they stay as they are. However, in the accusative (مَنْصُوبٌ)

or genitive case (مَجْرُور), they will get a visible marker. How can we do that? We change the ا into ي.

- This is similar to the dual of nouns or verbs which also have ا in the nominative case (مَرْفُوعٌ) and a ي in the مَجْرُور and -مَنْصُوب-case.

- So we get كِلَيْهِما ("kilayhima") and كِلْتَيْهِما ("kiltayhima"). Note: The ضَمَّة of the suffix هُما or هُمْ or هُنَّ is changed into كَسْرة ُ after ـِ or يْ or ـَيْ resulting in هِما or هِمْ.

Let's put all that input into sentences. We start with **option 1** – the إِضافة-construction.

Both of them are teachers.	1 | كِلَاهُما مُدَرِّسٌ.

Both were nice.	1 | كانَ كِلاهُما لَطيفًا.
Since كِلا is the "subject" (اِسْمُ كانَ) here and needs the **nominative** case (مَرْفُوعٌ), the Aleph stays.	

Both men saw her.	1 | كِلا الرَّجُلَيْنِ رَآها.
The verb is used in the third person, masculine, **singular** – and not in its dual form although we are referring to a dual.	

I saw both young men.	1 | رَأَيْتُ كِلا الْفَتَيَيْنِ.
Since كِلا is followed by a noun (and not a pronoun!), it does not undergo a visible change – although it is in the position of an accusative case! The same is true for the genitive case, for example: *I passed by two young men* (مَرَرْتُ بِكِلا الْفَتَيَيْنِ).	

In both times...	1 | فِي كِلْتا الْمَرَّتَيْنِ
Although كِلْتا is preceded by a preposition, it is not inflected for case. Why? Because it is the **first part** of a إِضافة.	

with both of us	بِكِلَيْنا	1

Since it is not connected to a اِسْم but to a personal pronoun, we have to use the مَجْرُور-case! (The Aleph turns into a ي.)

Everything that happened to both of us...	كُلُّ ما حَدَثَ لِكِلَيْنا.	1

Let's continue with **option 2** – the apposition.

It belongs to both of you (plural).	هُوَ لَكُما كِلَيْكُما.	2
	هِيَ لَكُما كِلْتَيْكُما.	

These are quite tricky sentences. The expression كِلَيْكُما (or كِلْتَيْكُما respectively) is placed as an apposition. It has to agree in case and gender with the word to which it refers.

The ل in the expression لَكُما is a preposition (حَرْفُ جَرٍّ) which drags the suffix كُما into the genitive case(مَجْرُور). However, the suffix is indeclinable and cannot get case markers – we can only assign a place value. Since the apposition gets the same case as the word it refers to, كِلَيْكُما has to be genitive (مَجْرُورٌ) too.

I saw young men, both of them.	رَأَيْتُ الْفَتَيَيْنِ كِلَيْهِما.	2

Young men is the **direct object** (مَفْعُولٌ بِهِ) and has to be in the accusative case (مَنْصُوب) – and so does the apposition.

44. My two colleagues - How do you say that?

Answer: زَمِيلاي (nominative) *and* زَمِيلَيَّ (genitive/accusative).

My two colleagues in Arabic – sounds easy, but it is actually quite tricky. There are **three things** *we have to solve:*

1. We need to form the dual (مُثَنَّى) of *colleague*. It is زَمِيلانِ
   in the nominative (مَرْفُوعٌ) and زَمِيلَيْنِ in the other cases;

2. We need the correct possessive marker for the first person (*my*): ي;

3. We have to solve how to add that pronoun because the
   possessive pronoun is the second part of a إِضافة-con-
   struction.

Here is a step-by-step-guide:

1. First take the dual: زَمِيلَيْنِ or زَمِيلانِ.

2. Delete the ن of the dual. So we get زَمِيلا and زَمِيلَي.

3. Add the possessive pronoun: ي. So we get زَمِيلاْي and
   زَمِيلَيْيْ which merges to زَمِيلَيّ.

4. Add a فَتْحة on top of the last letter ي. Why? By definition, the possessive suffix ي needs the vowel "i" (كَسْرة)
   before it. When the preceding letter can't carry a كَسْرة,
   because it is already occupied with a vowel, then we fix
   and build the least letter ي on a vowel, i.e., the "*a*" (مَبْنِيّ
   عَلَى الْفَتْحِ). This is done to harmonize the sounds and is
   exactly the situation if we have a dual.

5. So we get زَمِيلايَ and زَمِيلَيَّ.

case	pronuncia-tion	*my two colleagues*	*two colleagues*	*(one) col-league*
مَرْفُوعٌ	zamīlā-ya	زَمِيلايَ	زَمِيلانِ	زَمِيلٌ
مَجْرُورٌ / مَنْصُوبٌ	zamīlayya	زَمِيلَيَّ	زَمِيلَيْنِ	

For a detailed discussion, see *Arabic for Nerds 2, question #105*

45. وَالِدَيَّ - **What does this word mean?**

It means: my (two) parents – in the accusative or genitive case.

Let us first check the pronunciation of وَالِدَيَّ. It is *"wālidayya"*.

The interesting part is the last letter and its vocalization, i.e., يَّ, which tells us that we deal with a dual word in the accusative (مَنْصُوبٌ) or genitive (مَجْرُورٌ) case. If you are not sure why, have a look at the previous *question #44*.

Let's see how the expression is used.

translation	remarks	word
father		وَالِدٌ
(two) parents	nominative case (مَرْفُوعٌ); you use this form, for example, if the word serves as the subject (مُبْتَدَأٌ or فَاعِلٌ).	وَالِدانِ
(two) parents	accusative (مَنْصُوبٌ) or genitive (مَجْرُورٌ)	وَالِدَيْنِ
my (two) parents	nominative (مَرْفُوعٌ). Notice: There is **no** شَدّة at the end!	وَالِدايَ
my (two) parents	مَجْرُورٌ or مَنْصُوبٌ; notice the شَدّة!	وَالِدَيَّ

Let's check another example.

translation	remarks	word
brother		أَخٌ
my two brothers	nominative (مَرْفُوعٌ) → **no** شَدّة.	أَخَوايَ
my two brothers	accusative (مَنْصُوبٌ) or genitive (مَجْرُورٌ) → with شَدّة	أَخَوَيَّ

Some remarks:

- The ن of the dual is omitted in a إضافة-construction or if a possessive pronoun is added (which is a إضافة).

- If we add the possessive pronoun *my* to a dual, and if this expression needs to take the genitive (مَجْرُورٌ) or accusative (مَنْصُوبٌ) case, we need some fixing. Why? Because we have two colliding letters at the end: ي+ي. This is expressed by a شَدّة over the يّ.

- Last step: We need to add a فَتْحة on top of the يّ. For the reasons, see *question #44*.

Excursus: Brother or stepbrother?

In Arabic, there is another word for *brother* (شَقِيقٌ). The root is ش-ق-ق and means *to split; to cut* or *divide it lengthwise*. The word شِقٌّ denotes *the half of a thing of any kind*. When a thing is divided in halves, each of the halves is called the شَقِيقٌ. Hence, the *counterpart* of a person or thing.

شَقِيقٌ describes that you have the same mother and father as your brother (الأَخُ مِن الأَبِ وَالأُمِّ); i.e., he is a brother on the paternal and maternal side - whereas أَخ can also be used if either the mother or father is different or if you want to use *brother* figuratively. The same is true for شَقِيقةٌ (*full sister*).

شَقِيقٌ and شَقِيقةٌ are both also frequently used by politicians when talking about Arab nations. Both words may be used to denote *brother-, sister-*. Then, they are placed after a noun and work as adjectives (نَعْت) or may precede the noun functioning as an apposition (بَدَل).

brothers (plural of شَقِيقٌ)	أَشِقّاءُ
sisters (شَقِيقةٌ)	شَقائِقُ or شَقيقاتٌ

the brother country	الْقُطْرُ الشَّقِيقُ
the sister states (reference to Arab countries)	الدُّوَلُ الشَّقِيقَةُ
two sister nations	شَعْبانِ شَقِيقانِ
the sister-country Iraq	الشَّقِيقَةُ الْعِراقُ

46. *This car is mine* - How do you express that?

We need a trick.

Arabic has no words for *mine; yours; his* or *hers.* In English, these words are a form of the possessive case of the pronoun *I* used as a predicate adjective.

In order to express the same meaning in Arabic, we need a work-around:

1. **Repeat** the thing that is possessed.

2. Then, add the appropriate **possessive marker**, a pronoun suffix.

Two examples:

| This car is **mine**. | هٰذِهِ السَّيّارةُ سَيّارتي. |
| The book is **hers**. | الْكِتابُ كِتابُها. |

47. شِبْهُ الْجُمْلةِ - What is that?

It is a quasi-sentence: a prepositional or adverbial phrase which could not stand alone as it does not provide a full meaning.

The word شِبْه means *like; quasi or semi*. جُمْلة means *sentence*. The literal translation is *quasi/semi sentence*.

If we want to understand the logic behind such phrases, we should first have a look at a "full" sentence. In Arabic, we call such a sentence جُمْلة مُفِيدة because it provides a meaningful sentence.

It is either a nominal sentence (جُمْلة اِسْمِيّة) which usually starts with a noun or it is a verbal sentence (جُمْلة فِعْلِيّة) which starts with a verb.

Now, what about the شِبْه الْجُمْلةِ? It does not form a full and meaningful sentence. It usually gives us additional information that is related to the verb.

There are two possibilities:

Adverb of time or **place** plus **noun** (genitive). We get a إضافة-construction.	ظَرْفٌ + مُضافٌ إلَيْهِ	1
above the tree	فَوْقَ الشَّجَرةِ	
afternoon	بَعْدَ الظُّهْرِ	

Preposition plus **noun** (genitive).	حَرْف الْجَرّ plus مَجْرُور	2
in the house	فِي الْبَيْتِ	
on the desk	عَلَى الْمَكْتَبِ	

48. How many types of words are there in Arabic?

Three.

The grammar terms we use in German or English, e.g., adverb, adjective, preposition, pronoun, etc., don't really work in Arabic. This has to do with the core of the language body. In Arabic, there are **only three main types of words**:

اِسْمٌ ● فِعْلٌ ● حَرْفٌ

- A اِسْم (*noun*) refers to a place, time, person, thing, condition, adverb, adjective, etc. It is <u>not</u> affected by time. Only a اِسْم can get **case markers** (nunation).

- A فِعْل (*verb*) is a word that is stuck in time. It indicates an action or occurrence. Arabic tenses do not really express time – but rather an aspect: either an action is completed (الْماضِي) or not (الْمُضارِعُ). See *Arabic for Nerds 2, questions #24, #61.* A verb can only get mood markers: jussive (مَجْزُومٌ), subjunctive (مَنْصُوبٌ).

- A حَرْف (*particle*) is a word that (usually) does <u>not</u> convey a meaning on its own. It needs to be connected to other words. A حَرْف **never** gets case endings. They all have an **indeclinable** (مَبْنِيٌّ) shape.

Here is a list of some common types of a حَرْف:

translation	grammatical term	
preposition; particle of subordination	حَرْفُ جَرٍّ	فِي
letter of negation; negation particle	حَرْفُ نَفْيِ	لا, لَمْ
particle of digression, retraction	حَرْفُ إِضْرابٍ	بَلْ
conjunction; copulative particle	حَرْفُ عَطْفٍ	وَ

interrogative particle	حَرْفُ اِسْتِفْهامٍ	هَلْ
conditional particle	حَرْفُ شَرْطٍ	لَوْ

In German, for example, students learn that there are ten types of words: nouns, articles, verbs, adjectives, pronouns, numerals (which are all irregular) and adverbs, prepositions, conjunctions and interjections (which are all regular).

In Arabic, a اِسْمٌ may serve in different functions. This varies from sentence to sentence. It may be placed **in the position** of a *subject* (فاعِلٌ/مُبْتَدَأٌ), an *adjective* (نَعْتٌ/صِفَةٌ), or an *adverb* (ظَرْفٌ), but it is still a اِسْمٌ. In Arabic, we name the function in the sentence – but not the type.

49. How do you recognize a اِسْم in a text?

There are three features that only nouns (اِسْمٌ) can have.

It is easy to detect and identify a noun (اِسْمٌ) in an Arabic sentence. There are **three grammatical features** which can only occur with nouns in Arabic.

If you see one of them, you can be sure that you are dealing with a noun. Let's check them and use the noun كِتابٌ (*book*):

	feature	explanation	example
1	تَنْوِينٌ	Only a اِسْم can receive *nunation* (تَنْوِينٌ).	هذا كِتابٌ. This is a book.
2	تَعْرِيفٌ بِأل	Only a اِسْم can take the definite article.	قَرَأْتُ الكِتابَ. I read the book.

3	إضافة	Only a اِسْم can be part of a إِضافة-construction.	قَرَأْتُ كِتابَ النَّحوِ.
			I read the grammar book (book of the grammar).

50. What can be used as adjectives in Arabic?

You have mainly four options.

This is something complicated and confusing for native speakers of English, German, or French – because Arabic does not know a specific word *class* called *adjective*. If we use the term adjective in Arabic, we denote a function and not a form.

But that is the only difference. Like in English, an adjective in Arabic is a word (or phrase) that describes or clarifies a noun or pronoun. Adjectives tell us more about size, shape, age, color, origin, or material of a person, thing, a place, or time. In Arabic, adjectives are called صِفةٌ or نَعْتٌ. Both terms mean *description, characterization*.

Note: If you want to know more about the difference between the terms صِفةٌ and نَعْتٌ, check out *Arabic for Nerds 2, question #171*.

What are the main forms that can serve as adjectives or attributes in Arabic?

4	3	2	1
صِيغةُ الْمُبالَغةِ	الصِّفةُ الْمُشَبَّهةُ	اِسْمُ الْمَفْعُولِ	اِسْمُ الْفاعِلِ
form of exaggeration	adjectives similar to active (and passive) participles	passive participle	active participle

In order to **qualify** as an adjective in Arabic, the above mentioned forms need to be in **agreement** with the word to which
they relate.

Hence, they have to "mirror" the following grammatical features: **number** (singular, plural), **gender** (masculine, feminine), **determination** (definite or indefinite), and **case** (nomi-
native/مَرْفُوع, genitive/مَجْرُور, accusative/مَنْصُوب).

Let us check them in detail:

1. The ***active participle*** (اِسْمُ الْفاعِلِ) is a description of an
action. In Arabic, we would call this صِفةٌ بِالْحَدَثِ. This is
pretty much the same in English or German. The active participle for *to go* is *going* (*gehend* in German).

2. The ***passive participle*** (اِسْمُ الْمَفْعُولِ) refers to something
having undergone the action of the verb. For example: *to break*
– *broken* (*gebrochen* in German).

3. The ***quasi participle*** (الصِّفةُ الْمُشَبَّهةُ), literal meaning: *similar quality*, is a noun that indicates a meaning of firmness. It
indicates persistence and permanence. It usually denotes a
quality inherent in people or thing. This explains why the root
of a صِفةٌ مُشَبَّهةٌ can't build an active participle (اِسْمُ فاعِلٍ). A
صِفةٌ مُشَبَّهةٌ like *noble* (كَرِيمٌ) denotes not something that happens on one occasion only but something that is inherent in
the character.

We could say that the الصِّفة الْمُشَبَّهةُ functions like a repre-
sentative or substitute for the non-existent اِسْمُ الْفاعِلِ. The II-
verb شَبَّه means *to make it to be like* or *to resemble*. Regarding
its form, it is a derived noun (اِسْمُ مُشْتَقٌّ) of the root. Purist
grammarians thus say that you should use the مَصْدَر for ana-

lyzing and forming derived nouns – and not the past tense verb.

4. The ***form of exaggeration*** (صِيغة الْمُبالَغة) is built from a root which is capable of forming the active participle (اِسْمُ الْفاعِلِ.) Now, can every verb build an active participle? As we have already indicated above, the answer is **no**! We will analyze that in *question #143*.

The صِيغةُ الْمُبالَغةِ is actually just a way to say that someone is performing the active participle (i.e., an action) often, many times, intensively (يَحْدُثُ كَثيرًا لَهُ اِسْمُ الْفاعِلِ).

51. Why do adjectives need agreement?

Full agreement is necessary to charge a word with the function of an adjective (نَعْت). Otherwise, it may be a predicate (خَبَر).

You will often hear that an adjective has to agree with a noun. But what does ***agreement*** (الْمُطابَقةُ) actually mean?

When we use this term, we want to express that words need to share **four grammatical features**:

1. Gender: masculine or feminine (التَّذْكيرُ وَالتَّأْنيثُ)
2. Definiteness or indefiniteness (التَّعْريفُ وَالتَّنْكيرُ)
3. Number: singular, dual, or plural (الْإِفْرادُ وَالتَّثْنِيَةُ وَالْجَمْعُ)
4. Case (الْإِعْرابُ)

Let's see an example:

| The honorable man came. | جاءَ الرَّجُلُ الْفاضِلُ. |

We say that *honorable* (الْفاضِلُ) is a *true description* (نَعْتٌ
حَقيقيٌّ). This is because the adjective grammatically (fully)
agrees with the preceding اِسْمُ, i.e., *the man* (الرَّجُلُ).

This brings us to the three main forms of a نَعْتٌ حَقيقيٌّ.
Don't forget that the adjective is placed after the noun which
should be further described (مَنْعُوتٌ).

1	noun (اِسْمٌ ظاهِرٌ)
Cairo is a great city.	الْقاهِرةُ مَدِينةٌ عَظِيمةٌ.
adjective (نَعْتٌ)	عَظِيمةٌ

2	quasi-sentence (شِبْهُ الْجُمْلةِ): adverb (ظَرْفٌ) or preposition (حَرْفُ جَرٍّ)
I listened to a professor on the platform.	اِسْتَمَعْتُ إِلَى أُسْتاذٍ فَوْقَ الْمِنْبَرِ.

Is فَوْقَ الْمِنْبَرِ an adjective for the word *professor*? This is a debate.
Some say yes.

Others say that the prepositional phrase is not an adjective – but
linked to a deleted predicate (خَبَرٌ مَحْذُوفٌ) which could be, e.g.,
the word *found* (مَوْجُودٌ). See *Arabic for Nerds 2*, quest. #140 to
know more about the nature of such sentences.

3.1	nominal sentence (جُمْلةٌ اِسْمِيّةٌ)
A very cold day passed.	مَضَى يَوْمٌ بَرْدُهُ قارِصٌ.

The entire nominal sentence بَرْدُهُ قارِصٌ is placed as an adjective
for *day* (نَعْتٌ لِيَوْم).

3.2	verbal sentence (جُمْلَةٌ فِعْلِيّةٌ)

This is a work which is useful. (meaning: This is a useful work.)	هٰذا عَمَلٌ يُفِيدُ.

The verb يُفِيدُ is placed as an adjective for *work* (نَعْتٌ لِعَمَل). Instead of the verb you could also use مُفِيدٌ - which is the active participle (أَسْمُ فاعِلٍ) of the verb أفادَ (*to be of help*).

Watch out: If you want to use an entire sentence (3.1 and 3.2), then the مَنْعُوتٌ must be **in**definite (نَكِرَةٌ).

Remark: Did you know that there is a so-called *causative description* (نَعْتٌ سَبَبِيٌّ)? If not, jump to *question #144*.

52. How do you say *would* in Arabic?

There is no single word in Arabic that could be translated to "would" in English.

What is the nature of the English word *would*? Technically, *would* is the past tense of *will*. It is an *auxiliary modal verb* that is used to form tenses, questions, or the passive voice.

The *mood* (or ***purpose***) of a sentence is related to its form. *Tense* is a **form** as well as an **idea**. The past tense, e.g., can express time or an idea (e.g., the conditional mood). When a sentence makes a statement, it is in the indicative mood (فِعْلٌ مَرْفُوعٌ) - the normal mood. When it indicates possibility, a verb is in the ***conditional*** mood – this is what we talk about.

Now, what is a *modal verb*? We use such verbs to indicate that you believe something is certain, probable, or possible (or not). In English, we use such words to make sentences conditional – for example, by adding a word like *may, should, could, would*, or *must*.

Do not use modal verbs for things which happen definitely.

In English, you use *would* all the time – mainly, because you want to be polite or to express a hypothetical situation. In Arabic, we don't have a single word for *would*. Instead, you need to learn some phrases which can be used in certain situations. Let's check some workarounds.

A. You use the **future time** in Arabic – but by looking at the circumstances, it is clear that the meaning is conditional. Usually, a past tense verb is involved earlier in the sentence – which helps to clarify the meaning.

They said the weather would be clear.	قالُوا إِنَّ الْجَوَّ سَيَكُونُ صافِيًا.
He promised he would go.	وَعَدَ بِأَنَّهُ سَيَذْهَبُ.

B. You can use كانَ plus a verb in the present tense (الْمُضارِعُ).

he would have done it	كانَ سَيَفْعَلُ
he would not have done it	لَمْ يَكُنْ سَيَفْعَلُ

Who would have thought that?	تُرى مَنْ كانَ يُمْكِنُ أَن يَتَصَوَّرَ ذَلِكَ؟
I wondered if you would come.	تَساءَلْتُ عَمّا إِذا كُنْتَ سَتَجِيءُ.

C. You use *would* to express a wish, command, or suggestion.

In Arabic, you can use the verb *to want* (أرادَ) or *to want/*

would like (وَدَّ) or any other polite expression. Note that it doesn't sound rude to say "I want" - but don't forget to add an appropriate form of address, for example, حَضْرَتُكَ.

I wish I could spend the summer in the mountains.	وَدِدْتُ لَوْ أَقْضِي الصَّيْفَ فِي الْجَبَلِ
I said I would do it. Note: مُسْتَعِدٌّ لِ means *to be ready for*.	قُلْتُ إِنِّي مُسْتَعِدٌّ لِعَمَلِهِ.
Would you be so kind to tell him? Note: The V-verb تَفَضَّلَ means *to be kind enough to*.	هَلَا تَفَضَّلْتَ بِإِخْبَارِهِ؟
Would you mind closing the door? Note: مَانِعٌ literally means *obstacle, something preventing*.	هَلْ لَدَيْكَ مَانِعٌ مِن غَلْقِ الْبَابِ؟
You would! (Literally: *This is what was expected of you!*)	هٰذَا مَا كَانَ مُتَوَقَّعًا مِن أَمْثَالِكَ!

D. You use a conditional construction (جُمْلَةُ الشَّرْطِ) to express a hypothetical situation.

You achieve that by the particle لَوْ plus past tense verb in the first part (الشَّرْطُ - *apodosis*) and by adding the particle لَ at the beginning of the second part (جَوَابُ الشَّرْطِ - *protasis*).

I would do it if I were you. Note: لَوْ كُنْتُ مَكَانَكَ is a quite common expression for *If I were you…*	لَوْ كُنْتُ مَكَانَكَ لَفَعَلْتُ...
I wouldn't do it if not…	مَا كُنْتُ لِأَفْعَلَ لَوْ لا...

53. Do all English tenses exist in Arabic?

No, they don't.

Tenses are usually among the most difficult things in any language – but not in Arabic. In French, for example, there are five past tense forms: *l'imparfait, le passé simple, le passé composé, le plus-que-parfait, le passé antérieur.*

We need to introduce two linguistic terms in order to understand the concept of tenses in Arabic:

- **Tense:** a form of the verb which shows the *time* at which an action happened – in relation to the speaker.

- **Aspect:** deals with the degree of *completeness* of an action or state. Is the action completed, ongoing, or yet to happen?

Arabic does not have accurate time-points as English or French. The *imparfait* in French, for example, clearly describes a continuing state or action in the past. If you want to translate an Arabic sentence, you have to understand the overall situation of an event in order find an appropriate tense for the English translation.

I use the term *tense* in this book only because I don't want to confuse readers. In Arabic, there are two main "tenses":

- the **past tense** or perfect tense (الْماضِي). It denotes that the action is completed at the time to which reference is being made.

- the **present tense** or imperfect (الْمُضارِع). It is used for incomplete or yet to happen actions.

Now, what should we do if we want to express the past perfect tense, a verb tense which is used to talk about actions that were completed before some point in the past? We use a combination of verbs or devices that help us to express the idea.

Here is a list of the most important English tenses and how they may be expressed in Arabic. Watch out for the mood markers! Note that there are other solutions as well.

1. Present tense (الْمُضارِعُ الْبَسِيطُ).

he does	يَفْعَلُ
he does indeed	لَيَفْعَلَنَّ

he doesn't	لا يَفْعَلُ
he doesn't; rarely used	ما يَفْعَلُ

2. Present progressive tense (الْمُضارِعُ الْمُسْتَمِرُّ). In English: *to be* plus *-ing*.

The present continuous expresses what is happening now by one's will – whereas in the present simple tense it happens without one's will. The present progressive is used when we want to speak about things that are happening during speaking. How do we translate it?

It mainly depends on the context. In most situations, you can use an *active participle* (اِسْمُ فاعِلٍ). Sometimes, the *simple present tense* (الْمُضارِعُ) would do the job as well.

She is studying now.	إِنَّها تُذاكِرُ الْآنَ.
He is coming	هُوَ قادِمٌ.

3. Past tense (الْماضِي الْبَسِيطُ).

he did/he has done	فَعَلَ
he has already done; he had done	قَدْ فَعَلَ
he (indeed) did; he (indeed) has done	لَقَدْ فَعَلَ

he did not do; he has not done	لَمْ يَفْعَلْ
he did not do; he has not done	ما فَعَلَ
he has not done yet	لَمْ يَفْعَلْ بَعْدُ

4. Past tense progressive (الْماضِي الْمُسْتَمِرُّ). In English: *was* or *were* plus -*ing*.

It is used to express an action that was going on during a certain time in the past or when another action took place.

he was doing	كانَ يَفْعَلُ
he was (still) doing	ظَلَّ يَفْعَلُ

he was not doing* (negation of فَعَلَ)	كانَ لا يَفْعَلُ
he was not doing (negation of كانَ)	لَمْ يَكُنْ يَفْعَلُ
* The negation of فَعَلَ is more common than the negation of كانَ	

He was traveling.	كانَ مُسافِرًا.
I was going to say that...	كُنْتُ سَأَقُولُ إِنَّ...
I was writing the letter when the telephone rang.	كُنْتُ أَكْتُبُ الْخِطابَ عِنْدَما دَقَّ جَرَسُ التِّلِيفُون.
While I was walking, I fell down.	بَيْنَما كُنْتُ أَسِيرُ وَقَعْتُ عَلَى

	الْأَرْضِ.

5. Past perfect tense/pluperfect (الْماضِي الْبَعِيدُ).

This tense is not really common in Arabic. It is mainly used to express two actions: one has happened before the other. Oftentimes, you connect both actions with *after* or *before* – you then may just use the simple past tense as the notion of time is understood from the context.

he had done it	كانَ قَدْ فَعَلَ

he had not done it* (negation of كانَ)	ما كانَ قَدْ فَعَلَ
	لَمْ يَكُنْ قَدْ فَعَلَ
he had not done it (negation of فَعَلَ)	كانَ ما فَعَلَ
	كانَ لَمْ يَفْعَلْ
* The negation of كانَ is more common than the negation of فَعَلَ.	

After I had studied my lesson, I played soccer.	بَعْدَما ذاكَرْتُ دَرْسِي لَعِبْتُ كُرةَ الْقَدَمِ.
She had told him.	كانَتْ قَدْ أَبْلَغَتْهُ.

6. Past perfect continuous (الْماضِي التّامُّ الْمُسْتَمِرُّ). In English: *had* + *been* + participle

This tense is used to express the duration of an action up to a certain time in the past. In Arabic, you often just use the past tense progressive (4). The notion of time is often understood from the context.

Su'ād told me that she had been trying to get me on the phone three times.	أَخْبَرَتْنِي سُعادُ أَنَّها حاوَلَتْ أَنْ تَتَّصِلَ بِي ثَلاثَ مَرّاتٍ بِالتِّلِيفُون.

7. Future tense I (الْمُسْتَقْبَلُ).

he will do (in near future)	سَيَفْعَلُ
he will do (distant future)	سَوْفَ يَفْعَلُ

he will not do (near future)	لَنْ يَفْعَلَ
he will not do (distant future)	سَوْفَ لا يَفْعَلُ

Remark: In English, the *immediate future* is expressed by the present progressive (*to be* + -ing). In Arabic, we use the simple future tense with the prefix س.

She is coming here next month.	إِنَّها سَتَأْتِي هُنا الشَّهْرَ الْقادِمَ.
We are going out at five.	سَنَخْرُجُ السَّاعَةَ الْخامِسَةَ.

8. Future tense progressive (الْمُسْتَقْبَلُ الْمُسْتَمِرُّ).

he will be doing	سَيَظَلُّ يَفْعَلُ
	يَكُونُ + active participle
	يَكُونُ + فِي + ال + مَصْدَر

Okay, I will be waiting.	حَسَنًا, سَأَكُونُ فِي الاْنْتِظارِ.
He will be traveling.	يَكُونُ مُسافِرًا.

In English, you often express the *definite future* with the future continuous tense. In Arabic, you just use the simple future (7). It is understood from the context.

Hurry up! The bus will be leaving in a few minutes!	إِسْرَعْ! سَيَرْحَلُ الْأُوتُوبِيسُ خِلالَ بَعْضِ دَقائِقَ.

9. Future perfect/future II (الْمُسْتَقْبَلُ التّامُّ).

This is very rare in Arabic.

he will have done it	كانَ سَوْفَ يَفْعَلُ
he will have done it	سَيَكُونُ (قَدْ) فَعَلَ

he will not have done it* (negation of كانَ)	سَوْفَ لا يَكُونُ (قَدْ) فَعَلَ
	لَنْ يَكُونَ (قَدْ) فَعَلَ
he will not have done it (negation of فَعَلَ)	كانَ سَوْفَ لا يَفْعَلُ
	كانَ لَنْ يَفْعَلَ
* The negation of كانَ is more common than the negation of فَعَلَ.	

He will have contacted us tomorrow.	سَيَكُونُ قَدْ إِتَّصَلَ بِنا غَدًا.
She will have finished the job.	تَكُونَ قَدْ إِنْتَهَت الْعَمَلَ.

Watch out: You may use the particle قَدْ plus a past tense verb (الْماضِي) to distinguish the future perfect (*will have done it*) from the subjunctive (*would have done it*).

10. The German *Konjunktiv I*.

In German, it is mainly used for reporting indirect speech and old-fashioned or polite commands and requests (*er möge bitte warten*). There is no real equivalent to that in Arabic. Besides, you don't need that mood form if you convert a direct speech into the reported speech – see *Arabic for Nerds 2, quest. #267*.

11. Past subjunctive (Konjunktiv II) - *should, would, could*.

The past subjunctive mood of *I want* is *I would*; of *I can* is *I could*. By using this mood in English or German, you describe hypothetical situations, express doubt, or wishes. You use it in situations in which the standard mood (indicative) - *I want* - would sound rude or boring.

There is no single word for *would* in Arabic. You have to be creative and express the meaning of *would* indirectly – *see question #52*.

In many situations, you use a conditional sentence (جُمْلةُ الشَّرْطِ). If you want to express something impossible, you usually have two ingredients: لَوْ and لَ – see *questions #126* and *#253*. You have many options regarding the appropriate tense as the meaning mostly depends on the context.

12. Imperative (الْأَمْرُ).

	sing. m.	sing. f.	dual m./f.	plural m.	plural f.
do!	اِفْعَلْ	اِفْعَلِي	اِفْعَلا	اِفْعَلُوا	اِفْعَلْنَ
don't do!	لا تَفْعَلْ	لا تَفْعَلِي	لا تَفْعَلا	لا تَفْعَلُوا	لا تَفْعَلْنَ

54. *"Prayer is better than sleep"* - Is it really *"better"*?

Yes, at least regarding the grammar.

In Sunni Islam, the Muezzin uses a special phrase to call people to come and pray during dawn (الْفَجْرُ). It goes like this:

$$ الصَّلاةُ خَيْرٌ مِن النَّوْمِ . $$

Prayer is better than sleep.

This is an interesting grammatical construction. We do not use the regular *comparative form* (اِسْمُ التَّفْضِيلِ) here, following the pattern أَفْعَلُ.

But then why do we have a comparative meaning?

The word خَيْرٌ is usually translated as *good*, which is correct. But it also has another meaning – that of a اِسْمُ تَفْضِيلٍ.

The word خَيْر has pretty much the same meaning as أَحْسَنُ which means *better*. Let us check some examples:

Prayer is **better** than sleep.	الصَّلاةُ خَيْرٌ مِن النَّوْمِ.
Work is **better** than laziness.	الْعَمَلُ خَيْرٌ مِن الْكَسَلِ.
He is **better** than...	هُوَ خَيْرٌ مِنْ...ـ
I am not **better** than the student.	لَسْتُ خَيْرًا مِن الطَّالِبِ.

The word for *better* was originally أَخْيَرُ and later became خَيْر. This happened a long time ago. In the Qur'an, خَيْر is already used in the meaning of *better*. The word comes from the root خ-ي-ر. The corresponding I-verb is خَارَ. Watch out for the correct plural form:

meaning	plural	singular	
good; excellent/better; best	خِيارٌ or أَخْيارٌ	خَيْرٌ	1
blessing; good thing	خُيُورٌ	خَيْرٌ	2

There are other words which behave like خَيْرٌ, for example, the word شَرٌّ (*bad, evil*; or: *worse*), but it is less common.

She is **worse** than... Note that there is no feminine form of شَرٌّ.	هِيَ شَرٌّ مِنْ...

Watch out: If you use خَيْرٌ or شَرٌّ in a إِضافة-construction, they will have the meaning of the **superlative**.

(the) best student	خَيْرُ طَالِبٍ

* In Arabic you don't use the definite article although it has a definite meaning in English.

* As it is a إِضافة-construction, the word خَيْرٌ doesn't get nunation.

Remark: What kind of noun is صَلَاةٌ? Its old spelling is صَلوةٌ. It is the so-called *noun of origin* (اِسْمُ مَصْدَرٍ). The original, standard مَصْدَرٌ of the II-verb *to pray* (صَلَّى) would be تَصْلِيةٌ - but this word is not used by Muslims at all. The plural form of صَلَاةٌ is صَلَوَاتٌ. Note that the root ص-ل-و is almost only used for the stem II (صَلَّى). This may indicate that the verbal root is actually derived from a noun.

If you want to know more about the اِسْمُ مَصْدَرٍ, see *Arabic for Nerds 2, question #110.*

55. What does the name *Husayn* (حُسَيْن) mean?

It literally means: small beauty.

Husayn (often also spelled *Hussein*) is a common name for Muslims. It is a diminutive of the name Hasan (حَسَنٌ) whose meaning is *good, handsome,* or *beautiful.* The literal meaning of حُسَيْنٌ, however, is that of a diminutive (تَصْغِيرٌ). They are often difficult to translate because oftentimes, you won't find them in dictionaries. You need to know the form.

Let's check some of the most common patterns:

1	Derived from a اِسْمٌ consisting of **three letters**. I don't mean 3 root letters – but to total number of letters.	فُعَيْلٌ

door	بابٌ		small door	بُوَيْبٌ
child	وَلَدٌ	→	small child	وُلَيْدٌ
river	نَهْرٌ		small river	نُهَيْرٌ

Note: Also *adverbs of place/time* (ظَرْفٌ) use this pattern: - قَبْلَ قُبَيْلَ (*shortly before*) or بَعْدَ - بُعَيْدَ (*shortly after*).

2	When the original noun consists of **four letters** in total. Again, we don't mean 4 root letters!	فُعَيْلِلٌ

friend	صاحِبٌ	→	small friend	صُوَيْحِبٌ

3	**Feminine nouns**. They have a ة and follow the rules of number 2. Note: If the original noun is feminine but does not end in ة, the diminutive will get a ة. For example, the word for *market* (سُوقٌ) is treated as feminine.	فُعَيْلِلٌ

tree	شَجَرَةٌ		bush	شُجَيْرَةٌ
drop	نُقْطَةٌ	→	droplet	نُقَيْطَةٌ
market	سُوقٌ		small market	سُوَيْقَةٌ

4	This pattern is used when the original اِسْم shares the following pattern: the second letter of the اِسْم is followed by a long vowel.	فُعَيِّل

book	كِتابٌ		small book	كُتَيِّبٌ
small	صَغِيرٌ	→	tiny	صُغَيِّرٌ

56. Is حَرْبٌ (*war*) masculine or feminine?

Strangely, the word for war (حَرْبٌ) is feminine in Arabic.

The same is true in French where *la guerre* is also feminine. The problem in Arabic is that you cannot see the gender because unlike French, the definite article is the same for masculine (مُذَكَّرٌ) and feminine (مُؤَنَّثٌ) words.

Let us first check the regular feminine endings. In Arabic, there are **three indicators** to define the feminine gender:

Tā' of feminiza-tion (تاءُ تَأْنِيثٍ)	Aleph of feminization (أَلِفُ تَأْنِيثٍ)			
	extended (مَمْدُودة)		shortened (مَقْصُورة)	
1	ة	**2**	ءُ	**3**	يَا or ى
طالِبةٌ (*a female student*)	صَحْراءُ (*desert*), سَوْداءُ (*black*, fem.*)		عُلْيَا (*higher/highest*), كُبْرَى (*bigger/biggest*) – feminine comparative/superlative	

Some remarks about the Aleph of feminization (2 and 3):

- The ending اء is also part of the pattern for colors and physical deficiencies (صِفَةٌ) in the singular feminine form.

- The letter ى is the pattern for the feminine form of a comparative (اِسْمُ تَفْضِيلٍ).

Some more examples:

desert	صَحْراءُ
color red	حَمْراءُ

smaller	صُغْرَى
memory	ذِكْرَى

Now what about حَرْبٌ? It doesn't look feminine – but it is! Like in other languages there are words that look masculine by shape but are treated as feminine. Here is a list of common exceptions:

war	حَرْبٌ
land	أَرْضٌ
soul	نَفْسٌ
market	سُوقٌ

fire	نارٌ
house	دارٌ
cup	كَأْسٌ
well	بِئْرٌ

sun	شَمْسٌ
wind	رِيحٌ
paradise	الْفِرْدَوْسُ
Ghoul; ghost	غُولٌ

Now, if you want to add an **adjective** (صِفَةٌ), which form should you take? You need the feminine form!

a central market	سُوقٌ مَرْكَزِيّةٌ

Watch out if you deal with body parts:

- When you have <u>two parts</u> of one (mostly pairs) like the words for *leg* (رِجْلٌ), *eye* (عَيْنٌ), *ear* (أُذُنٌ / أُذْنٌ), *tooth* (سِنٌّ), or *hand* (يَدٌ), then these words are treated as <u>feminine</u>.

- In contrast, the words for *nose* (أَنْفٌ), *mouth* (فَمٌ), etc. are <u>masculine</u> as you only have one!

- Some parts of the body can either be masculine or feminine, e.g., *head* (رَأْسٌ), *liver* (كَبِدٌ), *upper arm* (عَضُدٌ).

Also of feminine gender are:

- names of newspapers and magazines: *al-Ahram* (الْأَهْرامُ).

- names of countries, cities, and towns – except for: *Morocco* (الْمَغْرِبُ), *Jordan* (الْأُرْدُنُّ), *Lebanon* (لُبْنانُ), *Iraq* (الْعِراقُ) and *Sudan* (السُّودانُ).

Watch out: Some nouns can be treated as masculine or feminine – you will encounter both versions.

country	بَلَدٌ	way	سَبِيلٌ	wine	خَمْرٌ
situation	حالٌ	road	طَرِيقٌ	salt	مِلْحٌ
sky	سَماءٌ	alley	زُقاقٌ	gold	ذَهَبٌ
soul	رُوحٌ	hell(fire)	جَحِيمٌ		

57. Are there words with ة that are masculine?

Yes, there are – but only a few.

Usually they refer to masculine human beings – to people. For native-speakers, the ة doesn't sound wrong. There are no rules, you have to know it. The most important are:

successor, caliph	خَلِيفَةٌ	tyrant	طاغِيَةٌ

explorer	رَحَّالةٌ	Mu'āwiya (name of a Caliph)	مُعاوِيةُ
very learned man	عَلَّامةٌ	Hamuda (man's name)	حَمُودةُ
eminent scholar	بَحَّاثةٌ	Osama, it is one of the names for *lion* (عَلَمُ لِلْأَسَدِ)	أُسامةُ
distinguished man	نابِغةٌ		

Now, what happens if we want to use an adjective with such words? The **adjective** (صِفةٌ) has to be **masculine**!

A great explorer	رَحَّالةٌ عَظيمٌ
The great scholar	الْعَلَّامةُ الْكَبِيرُ

Excursus: What can a feminine ending indicate in Arabic?

Some scholars suggested that the ة may express some kind of emphasis. But there are many ideas about the origin of the feminine endings. Let's check some.

- The original idea is probably to indicate something inferior [disclaimer: this may sound misogynistic but it is the original idea of the feminine signification in old Semitic languages]. The first idea was not to denote sex or gender.

- In the very beginning, the feminine ending indicated a diminutive or was used to downgrade a thing or person.

- But over the years, this has often changed even into the opposite. Thus, the feminine ending may work as an amplifier and is used for augmentation, i.e., they reinforce the idea of the original word (see examples above!)

- The feminine ending may be used to indicate abundance.

58. Can you use a masculine adjective for a feminine noun?

Yes, this is possible.

When you say that a woman is *pregnant*, you use the Arabic word حامِلٌ.

a pregnant woman	اِمْرَأَةٌ حامِلٌ

The word حامِلٌ is, grammatically speaking, the active participle (اِسْمُ الْفاعِلِ) of the root *to carry*. But why do we use the masculine form to say that a woman is pregnant?

When we talk about something that can only happen to women or is applied to women – like being *pregnant* –, then we don't have to write a ة at the end. Here is a list of words that follow this rule. Remark: Some of them are not really exclusively attributed to women – but maybe were in ancient times.

pregnant	حامِلٌ
menstruating	حائِضٌ
barren, sterile	عاقِرٌ

divorced	طالِقٌ
unmarried and of middle age	عانِسٌ

Notice the difference!

She is pregnant.	هِيَ حامِلٌ.
She is carrying luggage.	هِيَ حامِلةٌ مَتاعًا.

However, sometimes these special adjectives (صِفةٌ) can be used for men and women:

an old woman	اِمْرَأَةٌ عَجُوزٌ
an old man	رَجُلٌ عَجُوزٌ = شَيْخٌ

59. أَمْسِ - حَيْثُ - الآنَ - What do they have in common?

They are indeclinable (مَبْنِيٌّ) and never change their form.

The words mean *now* (الآنَ), *yesterday* (أَمْسِ), *where* (حَيْثُ). No matter what their position in the sentence may be, they always stay the same.

They never change their final vowel. We say that they have a fixed (structured, cemented) shape.

Some examples:

meaning	fixed vowel at the end	example
this	"a" - ا	هٰذا
yesterday	"i" - كَسْرَةٌ	أَمْسِ
where	"u" - ضَمَّةٌ	حَيْثُ
now	"a" - فَتْحَةٌ	الآنَ

60. Why is there a و in the proper name عَمْرُو (Amr)?

It is an old way of spelling the proper name Amr.

By adding the letter و, people can distinguish between *Amr* and the proper name *Omar* – which is written in the same way: عُمَرُ.

Note that *Amr* takes *nunation* (تَنْوِينٌ) – but *Omar* not. *Omar* is a diptote (مَمْنُوعٌ مِنَ الصَّرْفِ). It doesn't take *nunation* like all proper names which follow the pattern فُعَلُ. For example, Omar (عُمَرُ), Zuhal (زُحَلُ), Hubal (هُبَلُ), Juha (جُحا).

Let's see how *Amr* and *Omar* behave:

accusative	genitive	nominative	
عَمْرًا	عَمْرٍو	عَمْرُو	Amr
عُمَرَ		عُمَرُ	Omar

Amr gets *nunation* (تَنْوِينٌ); rarely, you may see it spelled with و. Also in إضافة-constructions, the و is usually written.	*I saw Amr.*	رَأَيْتُ عَمْرًا.
No Aleph, no nunation – it is a diptote.	*I saw Omar.*	رَأَيْتُ عُمَرَ.

61. How do you build the imperative of قَالَ in the dual?

It is قُولا – "you both say".

This is a rather unusual form as in most Arabic dialects, the dual (الْمُثَنَّى) is very rare – in colloquial Arabic, you use the plural of the imperative (أَمْرٌ) to express the dual.

Let us recall how we build the imperative in Arabic:

1. Form the present tense. For example, *you write* (تَكْتُبُ).

2. Put the verb into the jussive mood (مَجْزُومٌ): تَكْتُبْ

3. Delete the prefix – which is the ت. So we get: كْتُبْ

4. If you now have a word that starts with a consonant plus vowel, you are already done. This would be the situation in all verb forms other than I (فَعَلَ). For example: *you speak* (تَتَكَلَّمُ) → تَتَكَلَّمْ → تَكَلَّمْ (*speak!*)

5. If you end up with a word beginning with a consonant plus سُكُون, you need to add a prefix based on the stem vowel. This would be the situation for I-verb كَتَبَ.

6. If the stem vowel is "u" (ضَمَّةٌ), your prefix is اُ. This would the situation for يَكْتُبُ - كَتَبَ. So our final result for *write!* is اُكْتُبْ

7. If the stem vowel is "a" (فَتْحةٌ) or "i" (كَسْرةٌ), then your prefix is اِ. For examples, *to sit*: يَجْلِسُ - جَلَسَ. So eventually, we get *sit!* (اِجْلِسْ)

The verb *to say* (قَالَ) has a weak letter (حَرْفُ عِلّةٍ) in the middle. Let's follow the above steps to form the imperative. Note that we only need the first three steps!

step 1	step 2	**step 3 = imperative**
تَقُولُ	تَقُلْ	قُلْ!

But what about the other forms? What happens if we have to add a suffix after قُلْ?

say!	قُلْ!	you; masculine
	قُولِي!	you; feminine
	قُولُوا!	you; masculine plural
	قُلْنَ!	you; feminine plural

We see that the vowel found on the last root letter ل is crucial for the form of the imperative. Let's have a closer look.

impact	vowel on ل	imperative
the weak letter disappears	no vowel (سُكُونٌ)	قُلْ ; قُلْنَ
the weak letter is written	"i" (كَسْرةٌ) or "u" (ضَمّةٌ)	قُولِي ; قُولُوا

This has to do with a very important rule in Arabic:

- It is impossible to have two consecutive سُكُون. For example: قُوْلُ or قُوْلْنَ – so the weak letter is omitted!

Now, let's move on to the dual of *to say*.

meaning	dual	present tense	past tense verb
(you both) say!	قُولا	يَقُولُ	قالَ
(you both) be!	كُونا	يَكُونُ	كانَ

Let us check some examples now for the dual form of the imperative for all verb forms (with or without a weak letter):

meaning	imperative dual	imperative - singular masculine and fem.	past tense verb	form
write!	أُكْتُبا	أُكْتُبْ, أُكْتُبِي	كَتَبَ	I
stop!	قِفا	قِفْ, قِفِي	وَقَفَ	
want!	وَدّا	وَدَّ, وَدِّي	وَدَّ	
follow!	لِيا	لِ, لِي	وَلِيَ	II
agree!	وَافِقا	وَافِقْ, وَافِقِي	وَافَقَ	III
arrest!	أَوْقِفا	أَوْقِفْ, أَوْقِفِي	أَوْقَفَ	IV
stop!	تَوَقَّفا	تَوَقَّفْ, تَوَقَّفِي	تَوَقَّفَ	V
be modest!	تَواضَعا	تَواضَعْ, تَواضَعِي	تَواضَعَ	VI
leave!	اِنْطَلِقا	اِنْطَلِقْ, اِنْطَلِقِي	اِنْطَلَقَ	VII
connect!	اِتَّصِلا	اِتَّصِلْ, اِتَّصِلِي	اِتَّصَلَ	VIII
blush!	اِحْمَرّا	اِحْمَرَّ, اِحْمَرِّي	اِحْمَرَّ	IX
stop (sb.)!	اِسْتَوْقِفا	اِسْتَوْقِفْ, اِسْتَوْقِفِي	اِسْتَوْقَفَ	X

62. اِزْدَحَمَ - What is the root of this word?

The verb means "to be crowded". The root is ز-ح-م.

The word اِزْدَحَمَ is a VIII-verb following the pattern اِفْتَعَلَ.

We said that the root is ز-ح-م, so why does the د come into the game? Well, the د takes the place of the letter ت in the pattern اِفْتَعَلَ. The letter ت in the VIII-stem always turns into د if the first root letter is ز (زاي). Hence, the pattern اِفْتَعَلَ will change into اِفْدَعَلَ. It facilitates the pronunciation.

meaning	root	verb
to be crowded	ز-ح-م	اِزْدَحَمَ
to swallow; to gulp	ز-ق-م	اِزْدَقَمَ
to increase	ز-ي-د	اِزْدَادَ

63. Are there abbreviations in Arabic?

Yes, there are.

But they are less common than in English. Some examples:

translation and meaning	full text	abbr.
Upon him be peace.	عَلَيْهِ السَّلَامُ	عم
Muslims say this phrase when they mention the name of the Islamic prophet Muhammad. Meaning: *Allah bless him and grant him salvation* (i.e., eulogy for Muhammad).	صَلَّى اللهُ عَلَيْهِ وَسَلَّمَ	صلعم صَلَّى اللهُ عَلَيْهِ وَسَلَّم
Muslims say this when they say the name of a	رَضِيَ اللهُ	رضه

companion (الصَّحابَةُ) of Muhammad. Literal meaning: *May Allah be pleased with him.*	عَنْهُ (تَعالَى)	
Said if a person died (eulogy for the dead). Lit.: *May Allah have mercy upon him.*	رَحِمَهُ اللهُ	رحه
et cetera (etc.) Used at the end of a list to indicate that further, similar items are included. Literal meaning in Arabic: *to its end.*	إلى آخِرِه	الخ

64. The letter ء - How do you spell it correctly?

You need to know which vowels are stronger than others.

The glottal stop, the letter هَمْزة, is often misspelled, even in Arabic newspapers or books.

The correct spelling is actually not difficult at all. The key to all this is that you need to know that the three **Arabic vowels have different strengths.**

- The stronger vowel (usually) decides which letter becomes the bearer of the هَمْزة. The letters ا, و, and ى serve as carriers or seats for the Hamza. However, in certain situations, none of the three letters works, and we have to rely on ء - the solo version which has no seat.
- The vowel "*i*" is stronger than the "*u*".
- The vowel "*u*" is stronger than the vowel "*a*".

In short: i → u → a

Let's throw all this into the following table. Note that we are looking at the **diacritical mark (vowel)** on the letter **before** the Hamza and **on the Hamza**.

	explanation	spelling of ء	vowel before
1	كَسْرة is the strongest vowel. If there's a كَسْرة **before** or **after** the Hamza (ء), it becomes ئ.	ئ ← ئِ or ئُ	◌ِ
	You also use this spelling if the letter Hamza is preceded by ي. The letter ي (with سُكُون) is considered to be as strong as كَسْرة.		يْ
	Note: The ي loses its diacritical marks (the two dots underneath) when it serves as a seat for the Hamza.		
2	The second strongest vowel is ضَمّة. If there is **no** كَسْرة before or after Hamza, but if there is a ضَمّة, the Hamza will be spelled like ؤ.	ؤ	◌ُ
3	The weakest vowel is فَتْحة. If there is no other vowel involved but only "a", ء becomes أ.	أ	◌َ
4	As a **first** letter, Hamza (ء) is written in the shape of Aleph – no matter what the vowel is.	إ - أ - آ	
5	At the **end of the word,** after a long vowel or after سُكُون (end of syllable), it is written as a solo letter: ء.	ء	
	The سُكُون is not a vowel and therefore does not have a related letter. It marks the absence of a vowel. It is treated as the weakest of all sounds, except for the situation in which it goes along with ي resulting in ئ (see no. 1).		◌ْ

Let us look at some examples. Note that the numbers on the left correspond to the numbers in the table above.

	explanation	meaning	e.g.	spelling of ع
1	There is a سُكُونْ on top of the ي which has the same value of strength as كَسْرَةٌ. Therefore, the "a" afterwards doesn't count.	environ-ment	بِيْئَة	(ئ) ـئـ
5	Hamza is the final letter of the word. We have a preceding سُكُونْ, however, it is not written on the ي but on زْ → we use the solo-version.	portion	جُزْءًا	ء
5	This is different to the first example. We have سُكُونْ before, followed by the vowel "a". However, the سُكُونْ is not on the letter ي but on ا, so we need to the solo-version of ء.	two buildings (nomi-native)	بِنَاءَانِ	ء
4	It is placed at the beginning.	daughter	أُخْتٌ	أ
		fee	أُجْرَةٌ	
3	There is no كَسْرَةٌ and neither ضَمَّةٌ before, but the vowel "a".	head	رَأْسٌ	أ
		to ask	سَأَلَ	
2	The ضَمَّة is stronger than the فَتْحة. Note: The singular is رَئِيسٌ.	presi-dents	رُؤَساءُ	ؤ
1	كَسْرة is stronger than فَتْحة.	presi-dency	رِئَاسةٌ	(ئ) ـئـ
		to be thirsty	ظَمِئَ	ئ
5	As a final letter after سُكُون, it is ء.		شَيْءٌ	ء
1	Here, we have شَيْءٌ in the accusa-tive case (مَنْصُوبٌ). It is written in	thing	شَيْئًا	(ئ) ـئـ

	this form because it comes after ي.		
5	As a final letter after a long vowel, it gets its standalone form: ء.	sky	سَماءُ	ء

Watch out: In the **middle of a word** – after a سُكُون or a long vowel – هَمْزة (in Classical Arabic) used to be written as ء.

meaning	Modern Standard Arabic	Classical Arabic
issue, matter	مَسْأَلةٌ or مَسْئَلةٌ	مَسْءَلةٌ

Question: How do you write the *nunation* (تَنْوِين) on top of a final Hamza (الْهَمْزةُ الْمُنَوَّنةُ)؟

example		result		What letter / vowel is before Hamza?
thing	شَيْئًا	ئًا		يْ
sky	سَماءً	ءً		ا
subject	مُبْتَدَأً		ءً +	فَتْحةٌ
	جُزْءًا		أً	سُكُونٌ (any other letter than ي)
pearl	لُؤْلُؤًا			ضَمّةٌ
alike	مُتَكافِئًا			كَسْرةٌ

65. What is *syntax*, what is *form*?

These are two linguistic concepts we need to analyze if we want to understand a sentence.

If you have to translate a sentence, you need to check every word from two perspectives:

1. We have to deal with a word's form: صَرْفٌ.
2. We have to check its function in the sentence: إِعْرَابٌ.

In the following three sentences the word *reader* (الْقَارِئ) is charged with different grammatical functions.

The reader sat in the library.	جَلَسَ الْقَارِئُ فِي الْمَكْتَبِةِ.	1
I saw the reader.	شَاهَدْتُ الْقَارِئَ.	2
I greeted the reader.	سَلَّمْتُ عَلَى الْقَارِئِ.	3

What does الْقَارِئ have in common in all three sentences? The word الْقَارِئ has the same form in all three examples. It is an *active participle* (اِسْمُ الْفَاعِلِ), a noun expressing that someone is carrying out the action of a verb (*to read - the reader*).

- If we want to analyze the <u>form</u> (صِيغَةٌ) of word, we have to isolate it and enter the area of *morphology* (صَرْفٌ).

- In order to identify the function of the word *reader*, we have to identify its <u>position</u> in a sentence.

The function of the اِسْمُ الْفَاعِلِ in the examples is different.

- In the first sentence, *reader* is the subject of the verbal sentence (فَاعِلٌ). Note that the grammatical term فَاعِلٌ is the active participle (اِسْمُ فَاعِلٍ) of the verb *to do* (فَعَلَ), as the grammatical term *subject* describes *the do-er*.

- In the second sentence, *reader* is the direct object (مَفْعُولٌ
  بِهِ). Note that the term مَفْعُولٌ بِهِ is the passive participle
  (اِسْمُ مَفْعُولٍ) of *to do*, so the direct object can never describe the person or thing which is doing the action – but
  the one to whom or which the action is being done.

- In the third sentence, *reader* takes the *genitive* (مَجْرُورٌ)
  case. The term مَجْرُور literally means *drawn* or *dragged*.
  Grammatically speaking, it describes a word which is
  governed by a preposition or the first part of a إِضافة-con-
  struction. The second part, the so-called مُضافٌ إِلَيْهِ, has
  to be genitive.

Watch out: In the third example, *reader* would be the direct
object in English (*I saw him*) and in German (*Ich sah ihn*). But
since the Arabic verb for *to greet* demands a preposition (سَلَّمَ
عَلَى), it can't be the direct object (مَفْعُولٌ بِهِ) because the direct object always follows the verb without a preposition. Note:
There are some verbs in Arabic that can have two or three direct objects! See *questions #109 and #110.*

Excursus: What does a إِضافة-construction consist of?

First part of the إِضافة	"*the possessed thing*". <u>Never</u> takes the definite article. Can get all cases – but never *nunation* (تَنْوِينٌ). The case markers are only "*u*", "*a*", *or* "*i*" (and never: "*un*", "*an*", *or* "*in*") and depend on the function of this word in the sentence.	الْمُضافُ
	A mnemonic: The grammatical term consists of <u>one</u> word (one = first).	
Second part of the إِضافة	"*the possessor*". Definite or indefinite. Always in the genitive case (مَجْرُورٌ).	الْمُضافُ إِلَيْهِ

| | A mnemonic: The grammatical term consists of <u>two</u> words (two = second). | |

Note that the **last part** defines if we treat the entire construction as definite or indefinite:

- If the last term is definite (مَعْرِفة), the entire construction is definite (every word of it): **the** *house of* **the** *teacher* = **the** *teacher's house* (بَيْتُ الْمُدَرِّسِ).

- If the last term is indefinite (نَكِرة), the entire construction is indefinite: *A house of* **a** *teacher* = **a** *teacher's house* (بَيْتُ مُدَرِّسٍ).

66. الدَّرْسُ مَفْهُومٌ and فُهِمَ الدَّرْسُ - Any difference?

Both sentences mean the same (The lesson is understood.) - but there is a finesse.

Let us look deeper into the structure of both sentences:

جُمْلَةٌ فِعْلِيَّةٌ	verbal sentence	فُهِمَ الدَّرْسُ.

We have a verb. Every verb contains three things:

- an indicator of time
- a هَدَفٌ (*goal*; what are you actually doing = the action)
- the actor (subject - فاعِلٌ)

If there is a verb, we will get some hints about the time of the action; when it happened – **now, in the future,** or in the **past.**

Since the past tense in Arabic does not really tell us much about the time but more about whether the action has been completed or not, we do get a feeling that in this sentence, the action has already happened.

جُمْلَةٌ اِسْمِيَّةٌ	nominal sentence	الدَّرْسُ مَفْهُومٌ.

There is no verb! We use a passive participle (اِسْمُ مَفْعُولٍ), which is a noun in Arabic.

This means there is <u>no indicator of time at all</u>. We don't know, when the action happened: now, in the past, or in the future.

67. Can a verbal sentence serve as the predicate (خَبَرٌ)?

Yes, it can.

In fact, it is very common that the ***predicate*** (خَبَرٌ) of a *nominal sentence* (جُمْلَةٌ اِسْمِيَّةٌ) is a ***verbal sentence*** (جُمْلَةٌ فِعْلِيَّةٌ). Let us look at two sentences which both mean the same:

	يَجْلِسُ الْوَلَدُ.	verbal sentence	1
The child sits.	الْوَلَدُ يَجْلِسُ.	nominal sentence	2

The first sentence is a جُمْلَةٌ فِعْلِيَّةٌ since the sentence starts with a verb. A verbal sentence consists of a verb (فِعْلٌ) and a subject (فَاعِلٌ). It may carry a direct object (مَفْعُولٌ بِهِ) as well as other additional information – all governed by the verb.

The second sentence is a جُمْلَةٌ اِسْمِيَّةٌ. A nominal sentence consists of a subject (مُبْتَدَأٌ) and a predicate (خَبَرٌ). In our examples, الْوَلَدُ is the subject and يَجْلِسُ is the predicate.

Now comes the interesting part: The predicate يَجْلِسُ itself is a verbal sentence (جُمْلَةٌ فِعْلِيَّةٌ).

The verb يَجْلِسُ has a hidden/implied pronoun (*he*). If we only look at the verb, it means: *he sits*. Thus, the sentence literally means:

The child, he sits.	الْوَلَدُ يَجْلِسُ.

Therefore, in our analysis, the predicate (خَبَر) is a complete verbal sentence (جُمْلَةٌ فِعْلِيّةٌ).

يَجْلِسُ		الْوَلَدُ	
predicate (خَبَر)	+	subject (مُبْتَدَأ)	1ˢᵗ layer: nominal sentence
Verb; present tense, indicative mood (فِعْلٌ مُضارِعٌ مَرْفُوعٌ). The **subject** (فاعِلٌ) is a hidden pronoun (ضَمِيرٌ مُسْتَتِرٌ) with the implied meaning of *he* (هُوَ).			2ⁿᵈ layer: verbal sentence

Remark: See *Arabic for Nerds 2, question #56,* if you want to know whether there is a difference between a nominal and verbal sentence.

68. أَوْ or أَمْ - What is the correct word for *or*?

It depends on the question.

In English, there is only one word to express doubt or equalization (in your preference) – the word *or*. In Arabic, we have two words, أَمْ and أَوْ. So when do you use which one?

The word أَوْ.

	Used if there is doubt.	الشّكُّ
1	Muhammad may come in the evening or at night.	قَدْ يَصِلُ مُحَمَّدٌ مَساءً أَوْ لَيْلاً.

2	Letting choose	التَّخْيِيرُ
I advise you to join the literature faculty or law faculty.		أَنْصَحُكَ بِأَنْ تَلْتَحِقَ بِكُلِّيَّةِ الْآدَابِ أَوْ كُلِّيَّةِ الْحُقُوقِ.

The word أَمْ.

1	Used to separate a single pair of choices – you have to choose one.	طَلَبُ تَعْيِينِ أَحَدِ الشَّيْئَينِ
أَمْ is often used after the non-translated question word أ which is similar to the French *est-ce que*.		
Do you want coffee or tea?		أَقَهْوَةً تُرِيدُ أَمْ شَايًا؟
Two things are important here: • Word order! • The words *coffee* and *tea* are direct objects. • You need the letter أ before you introduce the two possibilities!		

2	Equalization	التَّسْوِيةُ
It doesn't make any difference to me if you travel or stay here.		سَوَاءٌ عَلَيَّ أَسَافَرْتَ أَمْ بَقِيْتَ هُنا.
You could also use أَوْ in the example above but if you do so, you will have to delete the أ before the word سَافَرْتَ.		= سَوَاءٌ عَلَيَّ سَافَرْتَ أَوْ بَقِيْتَ هُنا.

Note: Both أَمْ and أَوْ are *conjunctions* (حَرْفُ عَطْفٍ). The word which comes <u>after</u> *or* takes the same case as the word <u>before</u>.

69. Why is *lesson* (دِراسةٌ) a مَصْدَرٌ but *river* (نَهْرٌ) not?

Because river is not linked to any action.

The word دِراسةٌ means *lesson*. The word نَهْرٌ *river*.

Any مَصْدَرٌ in Arabic is a so-called اِسْمُ مَعْنًى – an *abstract noun*; something that has no color, no size, something that is not connected to the five senses – but to an action. For example, *writing, swimming*. Such words don't give us information about the actor nor an indication of time – they only tells us about the action.

All other nouns are called اِسْمُ ذاتٍ - *concrete nouns* – and can be recognized with your senses – you can see, smell, taste, or hear them.

That is why نَهْرٌ (*river*), جَبَلٌ (*mountain*), or كُرْسِيٌّ (*chair*) cannot be a مَصْدَر. A مَصْدَر doesn't have a body, nor a concrete shape or form. How can you describe the word *reading*? You can't say it is big, blue, or loud.

Note: Every مَصْدَر - like every verb – needs a **goal** (هَدَفٌ) and you can only grasp it with your mind.

70. How do you build the مَصْدَر of a root?

Except for I-verbs, this is easy – because there are patterns.

There are actually rules for building the مَصْدَر (*original noun*) of the main I-verb (فَعَل), however, there are many exceptions. You have to learn them by heart.

Let's check the **stems II to X:**

example		verb	مَصْدَر	stem
training	تَدْرِيبًا	دَرَّبَ	تَفْعِيل	II
congratulations	تَهْنِئَةً	هَنَّأَ	تَفْعِلة	
Pattern تَفْعِلة is used if the last letter is a weak letter (و or ي) or Hamza (ء).				
struggle	جِهادًا	جاهَدَ	فِعال	III
observation	مُشاهَدَةً	شاهَدَ	مُفاعَلة	
transmission	إِرْسالًا	أَرْسَلَ	إِفْعال	أَفْعَلَ	IV
coming forward	تَقَدُّمًا	تَقَدَّمَ	تَفَعُّل	تَفَعَّلَ	V
cooperation	تَعاوُنًا	تَعاوَنَ	تَفاعُل	تَفاعَلَ	VI
discontinuation	اِنْقِطاعًا	اِنْقَطَعَ	اِنْفِعال	اِنْفَعَلَ	VII
gathering	اِجْتِماعًا	اِجْتَمَعَ	اِفْتِعال	اِفْتَعَلَ	VIII
yellowing	اِصْفِرارًا	اِصْفَرَّ	اِفْعِلال	اِفْعَلَّ	IX
plea for pardon	اِسْتِغْفارًا	اِسْتَغْفَرَ	اِسْتِفْعال	اِسْتَفْعَلَ	X

- The مَصْدَر of a IV-verb always starts with a أ = ء.

- The Aleph in all the other forms is only pronounced as هَمْزة, if the مَصْدَر is the beginning of an utterance/sentence. See *question #8*.

- You will often find the مَصْدَر given in the accusative case (مَنْصُوبٌ). What you see is the form of the *absolute infinitive* – to **emphasize the idea of the verb in the abstract**, i.e., it speaks of an action (or state) without any regard to the agent (subject; doer of the action) or to the circumstances of time and mood under which it takes place.

This idea is also found in the *absolute object* (مَفْعُولٌ مُطْلَقٌ) which will be dealt with in *question #122*.

71. How do you express *already*?

You need to be creative – Arabic has no word for already.

Already is a tricky word even in English. In Arabic, similar to the word *still*, there is no single word for it. In spoken Arabic, especially people from the upper class use foreign words to express the idea.

- In Algeria, the French *déja* is used;

- in Egypt, you may hear *already* (the English word itself), خَلاص or لِسّا;

- in Saudi-Arabia, you may hear أَصْلًا (*originally*);

- in Palestine and Lebanon, you may encounter صار (*to become*).

But how should we deal with it in formal Arabic?

already (*by now*; German: *schon jetzt*): مُنْذُ الْآنَ	
You can already see the house.	تَسْتَطِيعُ أَنْ تَرَى الْبَيْتَ مُنْذُ الْآنَ.

already (*previously*): سَبَقَ لَهُ or by سابِقًا or مِنْ قَبْلُ	
I have already been to Cairo. (Literally: *I visited Cairo before.*)	زُرْتُ الْقَاهِرَةَ سابِقًا.
He had already done it before.	لَقَدْ سَبَقَ لَهُ أَنْ فَعَلَهُ.
Note: After أَنْ we use the past tense here – in order to paraphrase	

the pluperfect! See *question #108.*	
He had met him before.	سَبَقَ لَهُ أَنْ قَابَلَهُ.
We have already said that...	سَبَقَ لَنا الْقَوْلُ بِأَنَّ... ـ
I have already talked to him.	سَبَقَ أَنْ تَحَدَّثْتُ مَعَهُ

already (by that time) – expressed by an emphasis, e.g., قَدْ, إِنَّ	
She was already there when I arrived.	إِنَّها كانَتْ مَوْجُودَةً عِنْدَما وَصَلْتُ.
Have you eaten your dinner already?	هَلْ قَدْ تَناوَلْتَ عَشاءَكَ؟

already – expressed by the verb اِبْتَدَأَ *(to begin, to start)*	
I am already doing it.	قَد اِبْتَدَأْتُ فِي ذَلِكَ.

72. What is a hidden (implied) pronoun?

A pronoun which is not there (not written, not pronounced) – but implicitly understood.

In Arabic, the verb usually starts a sentence and not the noun like in English or German. Furthermore, in Arabic you don't put the respective personal pronoun before the verb. The verb includes the pronoun – which is symbolized by letters.

Which personal pronouns does Arabic know?

Let's check the two main forms.

A. The separated (solo) personal pronoun (ضَمِيرٌ مُنْفَصِلٌ).

It is a separate noun with a fixed shape (اِسْمٌ مَبْنِيٌّ) - and it is separated from other words. We have two types of the separated pronoun – for the nominative case (when it functions as the subject – *I, he, she*) and for the accusative case (when it functions as the object – *me, him, her*).

	pronoun is found in the (gram.) position of a...	
...accusative case (فِي مَحَلِ نَصْبٍ)	...nominative case (فِي مَحَلِ رَفْعٍ)	
إِيَّاهُ, إِيَّاهُما, إِيَّاهُمْ, إِيَّاها, إِيَّاهُما, إِيَّاهُنَّ	هُوَ, هُما, هُمْ, هِيَ, هُما, هُنَّ	3rd person (غَائِبٌ - *absent*)
إِيَّاكَ, إِيَّاكُما, إِيَّاكُمْ, إِيَّاكِ, إِيَّاكُما, إِيَّاكُنَّ	أَنْتَ, أَنْتُما, أَنْتُمْ, أَنْتِ, أَنْتُما, أَنْتُنَّ	2nd person (مُخاطَبٌ - *spoken-to*)
إِيَّايَ, إِيَّانا	أنا, نَحْنُ	1st person (مُتَكَلِّمٌ - *speaker*)

B. The attached pronoun (ضَمِيرٌ مُتَّصِلٌ).

It only occurs at the end of words. When do you use it?

- Attached to the **past tense verb** and serving as the **subject**. For example: *I wrote* (كَتَبْتُ) - the تُ is the pronoun.

- Attached to a **verb** – it may serve as the **object** then. For example: *He wrote it* (كَتَبَهُ).

- Serving as the **second part** of a إِضافة-construction – what we know as *possessive pronouns* (*my, yours, hers*). For example: *his book* (كِتابُهُ).

- After a **preposition**. For example: *on us* (عَلَيْنا).

accusative (نَصْب) / genitive (جَرّ)					nominative (رَفْع)			
his book	كِتابُهُ	he promised him	وَعَدَهُ	هُ	-	-	-	هُوَ
their (b.) book	كِتابُهُما	he promised them (b.)	وَعَدَهُما	هُما	they (b.) do	يَفْعَلانِ	انِ	هُما
their book	كِتابُهُمْ	he promised them	وَعَدَهُمْ	هُمْ	they do	يَفْعَلُونَ	ونَ	هُمْ
her book	كِتابُها	he promised her	وَعَدَها	ها	-	-	-	هِيَ
their (b.) book	كِتابُهُما	he promised them (b.)	وَعَدَهُما	هُما	they (b.) do	تَفْعَلانِ	انِ	هُما
their (f. pl.) book	كِتابُهُنَّ	he promised them (f. pl.)	وَعَدَهُنَّ	هُنَّ	they (f. pl.) do	يَفْعَلْنَ	نَ	هُنَّ
your (m.) book	كِتابُكَ	he promised you	وَعَدَكَ	كَ	you did	فَعَلْتَ	تَ	أَنْتَ
your (b.) book	كِتابُكُما	he promised you (both)	وَعَدَكُما	كُما	you (b.) did	فَعَلْتُما	تُما	أَنْتُما
your book	كِتابُكُمْ	he promised you (pl.)	وَعَدَكُمْ	كُمْ	you (pl.) did	فَعَلْتُمْ	تُمْ	أَنْتُمْ
your (f.) book	كِتابُكِ	he promised you (f.)	وَعَدَكِ	كِ	do! (f.)	افْعَلِي	ي	أَنْتِ
your (b.) book	كِتابُكُما	he promised you (both)	وَعَدَكُما	كُما	do! (dual)	افْعَلا	ا	أَنْتُما
your (f. pl.) book	كِتابُكُنَّ	he promised you (f. pl.)	وَعَدَكُنَّ	كُنَّ	do! (f. pl.)	افْعَلْنَ	نَ	أَنْتُنَّ
my book	كِتابِي	he promised me	وَعَدَنِي	ي (نِي)	I did	فَعَلْتُ	تُ	أَنا
our book	كِتابُنا	he promised us	وَعَدَنا	نا	we did	فَعَلْنا	نا	نَحْنُ

A ضَمِيرٌ مُتَّصِلٌ can never stand alone. As a pronoun suffix it is not independent of its regent (عامِلٌ), i.e., the verb, which governs the subject (= the connected pronoun) in the nominative case. This is similar to the conjunction و which has to be connected to the word which comes after it. It would be wrong to use a space (فاصِلٌ).

Now, let's get back to our question: What is a *hidden (understood, implied, inferred) pronoun* (ضَمِيرٌ مُسْتَتِرٌ)? First of all, all pronoun suffixes that are listed in the table above are **not** hidden pronouns. But then what is a hidden pronoun?

Let's take the past tense verbs كَتَبَ (*he wrote*) and كَتَبَتْ (*she wrote*). In the third person singular, we say that the subject of the verb is a *hidden pronoun*. It has the virtual, estimated meaning of *he* (هُوَ) or *she* (هِيَ). What is the logic behind this concept?

In Arabic, there are two kinds of personal pronouns: *apparent* (بارِزٌ) – which are all pronouns listed in the above table – and *hidden, concealed* (مُسْتَتِرٌ) pronouns. The latter is hidden in speech and writing. For example:

1	كَتَبَتْ الْبِنْتُ الدَّرسَ.	The girl wrote the lesson.
	Here, the position of the subject (فاعِلٌ) is filled by an *apparent noun* (اِسْمٌ ظاهِرٌ). This is only possible if we have a verb in the 3rd person singular. We don't necessarily need a hidden pronoun here since we have a given subject in the sentence.	
2	كَتَبَتْ [هِيَ] الدَّرسَ.	She wrote the lesson.
	Here, we need to find a subject for the verb كَتَبَتْ. Why? The ت here is **not** a pronoun – but simply a marker for femininity! Thus, we say that the subject (فاعِلٌ) is a *hidden pronoun* (ضَمِيرٌ مُسْتَتِرٌ) having the virtual, estimated meaning of *she* (هِيَ).	

In Arabic, we can only use the singular form of a verb to start a sentence.

Only if we use the **verb** in the **third person singular** (*he; she* - الْغَائِبُ), we could also use an *apparent noun* (اِسْمٌ ظَاهِرٌ) as the subject (فَاعِلٌ) in the nominative case (example 1). That is why we say that we may hide the pronoun (ضَمِيرٌ مُسْتَتِرٌ جَوَازًا). In all the other forms, we cannot do that.

Let's check some examples to illustrate the issue.

- If we used the (solo) personal pronoun (ضَمِيرٌ مُنْفَصِلٌ), we would change the meaning – and get an **emphasis**.

I am happy.	أَفْرَحُ.	1
It's me who is happy.	أَفْرَحُ أَنا.	2
This sentence has a **different meaning**! The word أَنا here serves as an *amplifier* (تَأْكِيدٌ) and emphasizes the subject (which is the hidden pronoun included in the verb). So if we want to express *I am happy* (أَفْرَحُ), we need to hide the pronoun.		
I am happy. Literal meaning: *I, I am happy.*	أَنا أَفْرَحُ.	3
That is a different story. We have a **nominal sentence** (جُمْلَةٌ اِسْمِيَّةٌ). The entire verbal sentence – which has an implied, hidden subject (فَاعِلٌ with virtual meaning of أَنا – serves as the predicate (خَبَرٌ).		

- If we used an apparent noun (اِسْمٌ ظَاهِرٌ), the sentence **wouldn't make sense** anymore - except for the 3rd person singular (*he, she*).

I write.	أَكْتُبُ.	1
??? (The sentence doesn't make sense.)	أَكْتُبُ مُحَمَّدٌ.	2

> The combination *I write* plus *Muhammad* as the subject of the
> verb – that's a mismatch. We can't place an apparent noun after
> the verb as the subject (فَاعِل) instead of the hidden pronoun.

All this is sophisticated and part of the core of Arabic grammar. Let's dig deeper and examine what is actually happening
inside verbal sentences.

meaning	example	
The river overflows.	يَتَدَفَّقُ النَّهْرُ.	1
This is a verbal sentence (جُمْلَةٌ فِعْلِيّةٌ). We place an apparent noun as the subject (النَّهْرُ) after the verb which is possible since we have the verb in the third person singular.		

The river overflows. Lit. meaning: The river, [he/it] overflows.	النَّهْرُ يَتَدَفَّقُ [هُوَ].	2
Here we have **two sentences** (a compound): A primary nomi-nal sentence (جُمْلَةٌ اِسْمِيّةٌ) starting with النَّهْرُ (which is the subject/مُبْتَدَأ), and an entire verbal sentence (جُمْلَةٌ فِعْلِيّةٌ) con-sisting of يَتَدَفَّقُ and serving as the predicate (خَبَر).		
The interesting thing here is that you need to connect both sentences. The virtual pronoun هُوَ is already contained in the verb itself which is why we call it *concealed pronoun* (ضَمِير مُسْتَتِر) – and it is this hidden pronoun which takes the place of the noun which stands before the verb. We can say that it falls back upon it.		

The river's water is overflowing. Literal meaning: The river, his water is overflowing.	النَّهْرُ يَتَدَفَّقُ ماؤُهُ.	3

The word ‫مَاءٌ‬ is the subject (‫فَاعِلٌ‬) of the verb ‫يَتَدَفَّقُ‬. That is why it is in the nominative case (‫مَرْفُوعٌ‬) Now what about the pronoun at the very end? Such a pronoun is called a *binder* or *connector* (‫رَابِط‬). It represents (falls back upon) the noun at the very beginning (‫مُبْتَدَأ‬), in our example, the word ‫النَّهْرُ‬.

Remark: If the sense is pretty clear, you can go without a binder. For example: *The one who I like arrived* (‫جَاءَتْ الَّتِي‬ ‫أُحِبُّ‬). The syntactical (virtual) meaning is: ‫جَاءَتْ الَّتِي أُحِبُّهَا‬

Note: If you want to know how the subject is expressed in the past and present tense verbs, see *Arabic for Nerds 2, question #36*.

73. Can you use an active participle (‫إِسْمُ فَاعِلٍ‬) instead of a verb (‫فِعْلٌ‬)?

Yes, the meaning is basically the same. But there is a difference.

- A *verb* (‫فِعْلٌ‬) can carry more information. You will know about the subject in detail. It is also capable of forming both tenses. A verb does not take case endings. It can only express different *moods*.

- The *active participle* is not a verb. It is a noun (‫إِسْمُ‬) as its name says already: ‫إِسْمُ الْفَاعِلِ‬. Since it is a ‫إِسْمُ‬, it gets case endings and can be charged with various functions in a sentence.

- However, both express more or less the same meaning.

- Regarding the grammatical (syntactical) power, the ‫إِسْمُ‬ ‫الْفَاعِلِ‬ is treated like a verb – and may be responsible to guard a word, for example, as the direct object (and thus induce case endings in other words).

Some examples:

We use the active participle instead of the verb.	كُنْتُ فَاهِمًا الدَّرْسَ.	1.1
	I understood the lesson.	
We use the verb.	كُنْتُ أَفْهَمُ الدَّرْسَ.	1.2
	I understood the lesson.	
I turned on the lamp to light up the room.	أَنَوَّرْتُ الْمِصْبَاحَ مُنيرًا الْغُرْفةَ.	2
Room is a **direct object** (مَفْعُولٌ بِهِ). Its regent (i.e., the reason why *room* is in the accusative) is مُنيرًا which is a اِسْمُ فَاعِلٍ.		

74. Is every noun (اِسْمٌ) derived from a root?

No, it is not.

Let us check why. If we want to understand how the Arabic noun (اِسْمٌ) works, we need to check its foundations.

A اِسْمٌ can occur in **two forms**:

1. Inert noun (اِسْمٌ جَامِدٌ).

The word جَامِدٌ literally means *frozen* or *in a solid state*. Such nouns are <u>not</u> taken from another word. They do not have a root to refer to or derive from. Such words describe either the **core meaning of the root** (مَصْدَر) or describe things which you can grasp with your **five senses** like *mountain* (جَبَلٌ), *man* (رَجُلٌ), or *Egypt* (مِصْرُ).

The term مَصْدَر in grammar denotes <u>*original noun*</u>. A مَصْدَر is a word which...

- describes the action without giving you information about the one who is performing the action;

- does **not** give you information about the <u>time</u>.

For example, the word drinking (شُرْبٌ). This word is describing the action, but we don't have information about the person who drinks.

2.   Derived noun (اِسْمٌ مُشْتَقٌّ).

The word مُشْتَقٌّ means *derived* and that is why we call these nouns *derived nouns*. Such nouns are taken from another word. They have a root to refer to and to derive from.

Watch out: Such nouns are built from the *core past tense verb* (الْماضِي الْمُجَرَّدُ) which in turn is built from the *bare original noun* (مَصْدَرٌ مُجَرَّدٌ) - for example, *drinking* (شُرْبٌ).

So how do we get a مُشْتَقٌّ? We take a root, for example *to write* (ك-ت-ب). If we want to form the word for the place where the process of *writing* is done - *the desk* -, you can use a special pattern and eventually get the word مَكْتَبٌ (*desk* or *office*). It is the place where the action of *to write* is done.

The most common مُشْتَقَّاتٌ are:

meaning	example	formula	type	
liar	كاذِبٌ	رَجُلٌ + كَذَبَ person + verb	اِسْمُ فاعِلٍ	1
Active participle. It may describe • a state of being: *understanding* (فاهِمٌ);				

- what a person is doing right now: *sleeping* (نَائِمٌ);
- that someone/something is in a state of having done something: *having put something somewhere* (حَاطِطٌ).

somebody who lies a lot	كَذَّابٌ	رَجُلٌ + كَذَبَ كَثِيرًا person + verb	صِيغَةُ الْمُبَالَغةِ	2

Such a form doesn't exist in English. It is a noun of exaggeration or superlativeness. It denotes that a person is doing the action many times. It I similar to the active participle (اِسْمُ فاعِلٍ) - but emphasizes the intensity of the action.

factory	مَصْنَعٌ	مَكَانٌ + صِناعةٌ place + مَصْدَرٌ	اِسْمُ مَكانٍ	3

A اِسْمُ مَكانٍ denotes the place where the action takes place.

Since the person is not important for the place, the مَصْدَر is meant here and not the verb itself (as the verb always gives you information about the subject/the doer).

appointment	مَوْعِدٌ	زَمانٌ + وَعَدَ time + مَصْدَرٌ	اِسْمُ زَمانٍ	4

Denoting the time when the action takes place.

Since the person is not important for the time of the action, the مَصْدَر is used and not the verb.

known	مَعْرُوفٌ	رَجُلٌ + مَعْرِفةٌ person + مَصْدَرٌ	اِسْمُ مَفْعُولٍ	5

Passive participle. The action was done but the word doesn't give us information who had done it. As the person isn't important in the passive, we use the مَصْدَر and not the verb.

stronger	أَقْوَى	رَجُلٌ + قُوَّةٌ + أَكْثَرُ person + مَصْدَرٌ + comparison	اِسْمُ تَفْضِيلٍ	6

Comparative or superlative of an adjective in English.

great	عَظِيمٌ	رَجُلٌ + عُظْمَةٌ person + مَصْدَرٌ	صِفَةٌ مُشَبَّهَةٌ	7

The مَصْدَر we use here usually has an abstract meaning which is not always easy to translate. What we eventually get is a noun which has a similar quality as the active participle. Such words usually have the meaning of adjectives in English. See *question #50.*

key	مِفْتَاحٌ	أَدَاةٌ + فَتْحٌ tool/thing + مَصْدَرٌ	اِسْمُ آلَةٍ	8

This kind of اِسْم has several patterns which are used to build words for all kinds of tools and instruments. *See quest. #175.*

75. A مَصْدَرٌ can never be indefinite - Is that true?

Yes, this is true – but <u>only</u> in the nominative case (مَرْفُوعٌ).

Any مَصْدَر has to be definite, either by the article الـ or by a إِضافة-construction, if it is in the **nominative** case (مَرْفُوعٌ).

This can help you to identify a مَصْدَر in a sentence, especially if you don't understand the structure or the meaning of the words.

76. Why is there a مَصْدَرٌ مِيمِيٌّ in Arabic?

The مَصْدَرٌ مِيمِيٌّ is a special form of a مَصْدَر. It is called مِيمِيّ because it always starts with the additional letter م.

A مَصْدَرٌ مِيمِيٌّ usually does not differ in meaning from the original مَصْدَر. So, what is it good for?

Well, the poets needed it. It has more rhythm and melody as the original مَصْدَر. Sometimes, however, it indicates a stronger meaning (regarding the action/event of happening) than the original مَصْدَر – *see question #77*.

How do we build a مَصْدَرٌ مِيمِيٌّ? Here are the patterns:

A. The standard I-verb (الثُّلاثِيُّ).

There are two patterns:

- مَفْعَلٌ
- مَفْعِلٌ - especially for verbs starting with و. For example, the verb *to promise* (وَعَدَ) → مَوْعِدٌ
- مَفْعَلَةٌ - making the word feminine by the تاءُ التَّأْنِيثِ

Watch out: The same patterns are used for the اِسْمُ الْمَكانِ and the اِسْمُ الزَّمانِ.

B. All other verb forms: stem II to X (غَيْرُ الثُّلاثِيّ). You rarely see the مَصْدَر مِيمِيّ of them.

You use the same pattern as for the اِسْمُ الْمَفْعُولِ.

Some examples:

translation	الْمَصْدَر الْمِيمِيُّ singular and plural		original infinitive (الْمَصْدَر الأَصْلِيُّ)	verb
question	مَسائِلُ	مَسْأَلةٌ	سُؤالٌ	سَأَلَ
existence, life	مَعايِشُ	مَعيشةٌ	عِيشةٌ or عِيشٌ	عاشَ
benefit, utility	مَنافِعُ	مَنْفَعةٌ	نَفْعٌ	نَفَعَ
demand, request	مَطالِبُ	مَطْلَبٌ	طَلَبٌ	طَلَبَ
killing, murder	مَقاتِلُ	مَقْتَلٌ	قَتْلٌ	قَتَلَ
food	مَآكِلُ	مَأْكَلٌ	أَكْلٌ	أَكَلَ
drink	مَشارِبُ	مَشْرَبٌ	شُرْبٌ	شَرِبَ
descent, decline	مُنْحَدَراتٌ	مُنْحَدَرٌ	اِنْحِدارٌ	اِنْحَدَرَ

And finally, there is another reason for the مَصْدَر مِيمِيٌّ. The **plural form** is usually easier to build – because you can often avoid broken plural forms. Let's see why.

plural	الْمَصْدَر الْمِيمِيُّ	plural	الْمَصْدَر الأَصْلِيُّ	meaning	root
مَضَرَّاتٌ or مَضارُّ	مَضَرَّةٌ	أَضْرارٌ	ضَرَرٌ	*damage*	ض-ر-ر
مَنْفَعاتٌ or مَنافِعُ	مَنْفَعةٌ	نَوافِعُ	نَفْعٌ	*benefit*	ن-ف-ع

Watch out if you have to identify a مَصْدَرٌ مِيمِيٌّ. In the following table, you will find the word مُسْتَخْرَج in every sentence in with a different meaning and function!

translation	example	type
The well is the place of extraction for petroleum.	الْبِئْرُ مُسْتَخْرَجُ النَّفْطِ.	اِسْمُ الْمَكانِ
Petroleum is extracted from the well.	النَّفْطُ مُسْتَخْرَجٌ مِن الْبِئْرِ.	اِسْمُ الْمَفْعُولِ
The extraction of the oil is in the morning.	مُسْتَخْرَجُ النَّفْطِ صَباحًا.	اِسْمُ الزَّمانِ
I extracted petroleum quickly.	اِسْتَخْرَجْتُ النَّفْطَ مُسْتَخْرَجًا عَجِيلًا.	الْمَصْدَرُ الْمِيمِيُّ

77. Do سُؤَالٌ and مَسْأَلَةٌ both mean the same?

Basically there's no difference in meaning. Both mean question.

But there is a difference regarding the form.

- سُؤَالٌ is the original مَصْدَر of the verb سَأَل. It is the so-called الْمَصْدَرُ الْأَصْلِيُّ.
- مَسْأَلَةٌ is the so-called الْمَصْدَرُ الْمِيمِيُّ.

The مَصْدَرٌ مِيمِيٌّ is used because it is easier to pronounce. However, it may indicate a stronger meaning and reinforce the original مَصْدَر, regarding the action/event of happening.

If you find a ة at the end of a مَصْدَرٌ مِيمِيٌّ, it may indicate an exaggeration of the action or a special focus on the abundance/frequency of the action.

Furthermore, مَسْأَلةٌ does not only mean *question*. It also denotes *issue, problem; matter, affair*.

78. Freedom (حُرِّيّةٌ) - What kind of word is that in Arabic?

It is an artificial infinitive noun (مَصْدَرٌ صِناعِيٌّ).

What does this ending remind you of? A word that ends in يّة is usually the feminine form of a noun that is describing a person. We call it نِسْبةٌ. You just add the letter ي to any اِسْمٌ and get a word that can be used as *adjectives* (صِفة) – often to denote that someone is from a certain country or has a special profession. For example, *Egyptian* (مِصْريٌّ/مِصْريّةٌ).

However, the ending يّة can also indicate that the word in question is a مَصْدَرٌ صِناعِيٌّ, which could be translated as artificial مَصْدَر. In fact, the مَصْدَرٌ صِناعِيٌّ is related to the نِسْبةٌ because it follows the same logic. Therefore, we could also call it اِسْمٌ مَنْسُوبٌ.

Many مَصْدَرٌ صِناعِيٌّ denote **abstract meanings** which they didn't have before they were enhanced by the يّة. You will notice that most of these words describe a political system.

meaning	مَصْدَرٌ صِناعِيٌّ (اِسْمٌ مَنْسُوبٌ)		source	
humanity	إِنْسانِيّةٌ	◄	human	إِنْسانٌ
progressiveness	تَقَدُّمِيّةٌ		progression	تَقَدُّمٌ
socialism	اِشْتِراكِيّةٌ		partnership	اِشْتِراكٌ
freedom	حُرِّيّةٌ		independent	حُرٌّ

democracy	دِيُموقراطِيّة
communism	شُيُوعِيّة
capitalism	رَأْسُمالِيّة

-	-
spreading, circulation	شُيُوعٌ
capital	رَأْسُمالٍ (رَأْسُ مالٍ)
Note: The plural of رَأْسُمالٍ is رُؤُوسُ الْأَمْوالٍ.	

79. *To raise* (رَبَّى) – What is the مَصْدَرُ of this verb?

It is تَرْبِيةٌ *and means: upbringing.*

The verb رَبَّى means *to raise; to grow*. It is a II-verb and follows the pattern فَعَّلَ. But there is an issue here which we need to solve. The last root letter is not a ي. It is an Aleph which is spelled as ى! We said in *question #9* that an Aleph can never be part of the root – but was converted into that shape from either و or ي.

Since we said that our root letter in question is not ي, there is only one option left. The root of this verb is ر-ب-و.

The مَصْدَرُ of a II-verb is built by using the pattern تَفْعِيلُ – see *question #41*. However, when the last root letter is weak letter (حَرْفُ عِلّةٍ), then the pattern is تَفْعِلةٌ.

Thus, the correct مَصْدَرُ of رَبَّى is تَرْبِيةٌ.

Watch out: The word تَرْبِيةٌ is often mispronounced. There is no شَدّة on top of the ي! The stress is on the first letter ت.

80. *To have* - How can you express that in Arabic?

Unfortunately, there is no universal Arabic verb for: to have.

So what should we do then? We need a few detours. We can use adverbial expressions, prepositions, or express it by verbs.

عِنْدَ ● لِ ● لَدَى + pronoun	عِنْدَ and لَدَى literally mean *at* or *by*. لِ literally denotes *for* and is especially used to express ownership.

Watch out: The sentence is turned over in English. The direct object in English becomes the subject (مُبْتَدَأ) in Arabic – and therefore is مَرْفُوع! Notice the case endings in the following examples.

He has...	عِنْدَهُ [شَيْءٌ] or لَدَيْهِ [شَيْءٌ] or لَهُ [شَيْءٌ]

He doesn't have...	لَيْسَ	عِنْدَهُ [شَيْءٌ]
He had...	كانَ	عِنْدَهُ [شَيْءٌ]
He didn't have...	ما كانَ	عِنْدَهُ [شَيْءٌ]
	لَمْ يَكُنْ	
He had no time for...	لَمْ يَكُنْ لَدَيْهِ الْوَقْتُ الْكافِي لِ	

The focus is on **belonging - by right**.	لِ

لِ denotes the strongest notion of owning. It can also be used for abstract or possible actions (e.g.: *a book is reserved for you in the library*). Also for relatives (e.g.: *I have a brother*).

Do we know **where** the thing is now? **No**; we guess from the context.

The focus is on **having a thing physically with you**.	عِنْدَ

عِنْدَ may be used for possessing or owning in general as well. It may be used for temporary possession. E.g.: *You have a book which you borrowed from your friend.*

Do we know **where** the thing is? **Yes.** عِنْدَ usually indicates that you have a thing in your possession at your place – at your office, flat, etc.

Do we know who **owns** the book? We could say **yes.** It implies that the thing belongs to you/the person (unless stated differently).

Indicates having a thing in **possession physically** - which is either at a **certain place** or **with you.**	لَدَى

Do we know who **owns** it? **Not really.** If you say لَدَيَّ كِتابٌ (*I have a book*), it could also mean that it is someone else's book.

لَدَى and عِنْدَ often denote the same idea and can be used inter-changeably. لَدَى is more stylish – but not used in spoken language.

to have something with one	مَعَ
I don't have money with me.	لَيْسَ مَعِي مالٌ.

The focus is on having something physically with you. Do we know if I own the thing? No, not really; we can only assume it form the context.	مَعَ

Watch out: مَعَ and عِنْدَ and لَدَى can **only be used with <u>human</u> be-ings.** Never use them if the "subject" is an animal, plant, or any kind of inanimate. In such cases, you should use لِ.

meaning of: to own something	مَلَكَ، يَمْلِكُ
He has a house.	يَمْلِكُ بَيْتًا.

to have to do	pronoun plus عَلَى
She has to go.	عَلَيْها الذَّهابُ.

English expressions with *to have* that are expressed by special verbs.	
to have fear	خافَ, يَخافُ
to have patience	صَبَرَ, يَصْبِرُ
I got it! (German: *Ich hab's!*)	وَجَدْتُهُ!
to have a cold	يُصابُ بِالْبَرْدِ
to have the chance	تَسْنَحُ لَهُ الْفُرْصةُ
to have a crush	يَنْجَذِبُ لِ
to have it in mind	(كانَ) ذَلِكَ عَلَى بِلِهِ
to have a good knowledge of	يَعْرِفُ جَيِّدًا
to have a good time	يُمَتِّعُ نَفْسه
Have a good weekend!	أَتَمَنَّى لَكَ نِهاية أُسْبُوعٍ سَعِيدةٍ
to have a hangover	يُعانِي مِن تَأْثِيرِ الْكُحُولِ
to have a hard time doing sth.	يُواجِهُ صُعُوبَةً فِي
to have a heart attack	يُصابُ بِأَزْمةٍ قَلْبِيّةٍ
to have a look at	يَفْحَصُ
to have a piece of	يَتَشارَكُ فِي
to have lunch	تَناوَلَ الْغداءَ
to have a baby	أَنْجَبَتْ طِفْلًا

81. Do أُرِيدُ الذَّهابَ and أُرِيدُ أَنْ أَذْهَبَ *mean the same?*

Yes, they do! Both mean the same: I want to go.

The word ذَهابٌ is the مَصْدَر of the verb ذَهَبَ (to go).

The construction أَنْ plus present tense verb (فِعْلٌ مُضارِعٌ) has the same meaning as the pure مَصْدَر. It is even called a مَصْدَر, namely مَصْدَرٌ مُؤَوَّلٌ or interpreted مَصْدَر because مُؤَوَّل means interpreted. مُؤَوَّلٌ is the passive participle of to explain; interpret (أَوَّلَ). The original مَصْدَر is called مَصْدَرٌ صَرِيحٌ.

You can build the مَصْدَرٌ مُؤَوَّلٌ by using the particles أَنْ or ما. Thus, grammarians call them letter of the infinitive/original noun (حَرْفُ مَصْدَرِيّةٍ).

أَنْ يَذْهَبَ	=	ذَهابٌ
الْمَصْدَرُ الْمُؤَوَّلُ	=	الْمَصْدَرُ (الصَّرِيحُ)
going; go	=	going; go

Watch out: The verb يَذْهَبَ has a فَتْحة at the end because it is preceded by أَنْ. Therefore, the verb has to be in the *subjunctive mood* (مَنْصُوبٌ).

Let us check the details. You will see how to change a مَصْدَر مُؤَوَّلٌ into a مَصْدَرٌ صَرِيحٌ and vice versa:

type of مَصْدَر	example	A
مَصْدَرٌ مُؤَوَّلٌ	أَنْ تَصُومُوا خَيْرٌ لَكُمْ.	1
مَصْدَرٌ صَرِيحٌ	صِيامُكُمْ خَيْرٌ لَكُمْ.	2
Both sentences mean the same: *(Your) fasting is good for you.*		

grammatical explanation	مَصْدَر	A
The interpreted infinitive is located in the posi-tion of the **subject** of the **nominal sentence**; thus	أَنْ تَصُومُوا	1

it is in the position of a nominative case (مَصْدَرٌ مُؤَوَّلٌ فِي مَحَلِّ رَفْعِ مُبْتَدَأٌ).		
Subject of the **nominal** sentence (مُبْتَدَأٌ مَرْفُوعٌ)	صِيامُكُمْ	2

In short: The grammatical job of both types is exactly the same – because they are located in the same spot. Thus, an interpreted infinitive can be located as a subject, direct object, etc.

type of مَصْدَر	example	B
مَصْدَرٌ مُؤَوَّلٌ	أَسْعَدَنِي ما عَمِلْتَ.	1
مَصْدَرٌ صَرِيحٌ	أَسْعَدَنِي عَمَلُكَ.	2

The meaning is the same: *Your work (what you did) made me happy.*

grammatical explanation	مَصْدَر	B
The interpreted infinitive is located in the position of the **subject** of the **verbal sentence**; thus, it is in the position of a nominative case (مَصْدَرٌ مُؤَوَّلٌ فِي مَحَلِّ رَفْعِ فاعِلٌ).	ما عَمِلْتَ	1
Subject of the **verbal** sentence (فاعِلٌ مَرْفُوعٌ)	عَمَلُكَ	2

82. غِناءُ and تَغْنِيَةٌ - Do they mean the same?

Yes, they mean the same. Both words mean: singing or song.

They are both the مَصْدَر of the II-verb to sing (غَنَّى).

But why do they look different? You might know that the مَصْدَر of a II-verb (فَعَّلَ) is built by applying the pattern تَفْعِيلٌ. For example: *to teach* (دَرَّسَ) → *teaching* (تَدْرِيسٌ).

This is correct for regular verbs. But the pattern looks different if the last letter of the root is weak letter (حَرْفُ عِلَّةٍ) – one of the tricky letters و or ي. The pattern then changes to تَفْعِلةُ.

This is why the مَصْدَر of the verb غَنَّى is تَغْنِيةُ.

Now, what about غِناءُ? For native speakers, the pronunciation of the regular مَصْدَر is a little hard. Thus, a simplified pronunciation became popular following the pattern of I-verb (فَعَل).

To sum it up:

- The original مَصْدَر is تَغْنِيةُ and is called مَصْدَرٌ أَصْلِيٌّ.

- Native speakers prefer غِناءُ instead. Grammarians call such words *noun of origin* (اِسْمُ مَصْدَرٍ). Normally a اِسْمُ مَصْدَرٍ is shorter than the original مَصْدَر. It often denotes the same meaning as the original مَصْدَر.

Such forms occur quite often in Arabic and exist for almost all verb patterns. But before we deal with them, let us quickly check the correct pronunciation of the word: غِناء.

غَناءُ with a فَتْحة over the غ is the مَصْدَر of the verb غَنِيَ. This is a I-verb and means: *to be rich.* The مَصْدَر can be translated as _wealth._	غَناءُ 1
Notice the "*i*"-sound (كَسْرة) at the beginning of the word under the letter غ. This is an alternative for the regular مَصْدَر of the II-verb غَنَّى as explained above. غِناءُ means _singing_ or _song._	غِناءُ 2
Without vowels, you need to understand the context because both words for *song* and *wealth* look exactly the same!	

Now let's see some examples of the اِسْمُ مَصْدَرٍ.

meaning	verb	pat-tern	stem	مَصْدَرٌ أَصْلِيٌّ	اِسْمُ مَصْدَرٍ
to sing	غَنَّى	فَعَّلَ	II	تَغْنِيَةٌ	غِناءُ
to make a mistake	أَخْطَأَ	أَفْعَلَ	IV	إِخْطاءُ	خَطَأٌ
to travel	سافَرَ	فاعَلَ	V	مُسافَرَةٌ	سَفَرٌ
to buy things	اِشْتَرَى	اِفْتَعَلَ	VIII	اِشْتِراءُ	شِراءُ
to marry	تَزَوَّجَ	تَفَعَّلَ	V	تَزَوُّجٌ	زَواجٌ
to speak	تَكَلَّمَ	تَفَعَّلَ	V	تَكَلُّمٌ	كَلامٌ
to talk	تَحَدَّثَ	تَفَعَّلَ	V	تَحَدُّثٌ	حَديثٌ
to pray	صَلَّى	فَعَّلَ	II	تَصْلِيَةٌ	صَلاةٌ

For a special application of the اِسْمُ مَصْدَرٍ see *question #204*.

83. What are the so-called *five verbs* (أَفْعالٌ خَمْسةٌ)?

They contain a pronoun which will tell you more about the mood of the verb.

Before we talk about the *five verbs* (أَفْعالٌ خَمْسةٌ), let us check how to put a verb into the *jussive mood* (مَجْزُومٌ) - the one with the elided ending. The word *jussive* relates to the Latin word *jubeō*: to order, to command. The building of the *jussive* will be necessary to understand the logic behind the *five verbs*.

We need the imperative (أَمْرٌ) for the jussive mood, but for practical reasons, it is usually easier to form it from the present tense (الْمُضارِعُ). The particle لَمْ induces this mood and together with the verb, it conveys the meaning of the negation of the past tense.

1	**Regular verb – no weak letter.** If the conjugated verb in the present tense has no extra letter attached, put a سُكُون on the last letter.	*He did not go.*	لَمْ يَذْهَبْ.
		I did not write.	لَمْ أَكْتُبْ.
	This happens in the conjugation of *I* (أَنَا), *we* (نَحْنُ); *he* (هُوَ), *she* (هِيَ); *you* m. sing. (أَنْتَ).	*We did not open.*	لَمْ نَفْتَحْ.

| 2 | If you have a verb conjugation that ends in long vowel plus ن, then delete the ن. This is true for both regular verbs and roots with weak letters. |
| | This happens in the conjugation of *they* (هُمْ), *they both* (هُمَا); *you f. sing.* (أَنْتِ), *you both* (أَنْتُمَا), *you m. pl.* (أَنْتُمْ). |

example jussive (مَجْزُومٌ)		example present tense		verb
They did not go.	لَمْ يَذْهَبُوا.	*they go*	يَذْهَبُونَ	ذَهَبَ
You did not say.	لَمْ تَقُولِي.	*you (f.) say*	تَقُولِينَ	قَالَ
You (b.) didn't buy.	لَمْ تَبِيعَا.	*you both buy*	تَبِيعَانِ	بَاعَ
They (b.) didn't call.	لَمْ يَدْعُوَا.	*they both call*	يَدْعُوَانِ	دَعَا
You did not keep.	لَمْ تَفُوا.	*you (pl.) keep (a promise)*	تَفُونَ	وَفَى

| 3 | If the verb does not have any suffix in the present tense conjuga-tion – but has a weak letter (حَرْفُ عِلَّةٍ), delete the weak letter. |
| | a) If the weak letter was in the middle, then put a سُكُون on the final letter. |

b) Otherwise, just use the third person singular in the present tense and cut the last letter.

example jussive (مَجْزُومٌ)		example present tense		verb
He did not say.	لَمْ يَقُلْ.	*he says*	يَقُولُ	قالَ
He did not buy.	لَمْ يَبِعْ.	*he buys*	يَبِيعُ	باعَ
He did not meet.	لَمْ يَلْقَ.	*he meets*	يَلْقَى	لَقِيَ
He did not invite.	لَمْ يَدْعُ.	*he invites; calls*	يَدْعُو	دَعَا
He did not keep.	لَمْ يَفِ.	*he keeps (a promise)*	يَفِي	وَفَى

The only difficult form of the jussive is that of the **feminine plural forms**: *they* (هُنَّ) and *you* (أَنْتُنَّ). The trick here is that the indicative (مَرْفُوعٌ) and jussive (مَجْزُومٌ) as well as the subjunctive (مَنْصُوبٌ) all look the same:

	jussive	subjunctive	indicative	past tense	
You (pl. f.) didn't write.	لَمْ تَكْتُبْنَ.	أَنْ تَكْتُبْنَ	تَكْتُبْنَ	كَتَبْتُنَّ	أَنْتُنَّ
They (pl. f.) didn't write.	لَمْ يَكْتُبْنَ.	أَنْ يَكْتُبْنَ	يَكْتُبْنَ	كَتَبْنَ	هُنَّ

Now let's return to our topic. The *five verbs* (أَفْعالٌ خَمْسة). Why did we start our discussion with the مَجْزُوم-mood? You will see now.

In the <u>present tense</u> (and future since this is expressed by the suffix سَ or سَوْفَ + verb in the present tense), there are **only three different suffixes** which can be added to the verb with regard to the doer (pronoun) of the verb.

These three suffixes are:

- plural Wāw (و) for هُمْ and أَنْتُمْ;
- dual Aleph (I) for هُما and أَنْتُما;
- feminine yā' (ي) for أَنْتِ (second person feminine);

In the regular present tense (الْمُضَارِعُ), the letter ن is added to these suffixes. The three suffixes finally make up <u>five</u> forms which is the reason why we call them *five verbs*.

Watch out: Don't mix it up with the *five nouns* (أَسْماءٌ خَمْسَةُ) – *see question #220.*

They (both) go.	يَذْهَبانِ هُما	1
You (both) go.	تَذْهَبانِ أَنْتُما	2
They go.	يَذْهَبُونَ هُمْ	3
You (plural) go.	تَذْهَبُونَ أَنْتُمْ	4
You (feminine, singular) go.	تَذْهَبِينَ أَنْتِ	5

The crucial point: What happens if we put these verb forms into the مَجْزُوم-mood? Answer: The ن **disappears!**

They (two) did not go.	لَمْ يَذْهَبا هُما	1
You (two) did not go.	لَمْ تَذْهَبا أَنْتُما	2
They did not go.	لَمْ يَذْهَبوا هُمْ	3
You did not go.	لَمْ تَذْهَبوا أَنْتُمْ	4
You (feminine, singular) did not go.	لَمْ تَذْهَبي أَنْتِ	5

Some remarks:

- After the negation لَمْ and the *prohibitive* لا (لا النّاهِيةُ), we have to use the مَجْزُوم-mood. The *prohibitive* لا is used to warn or discourage people: usually translated as *don't...!*

- What we have seen above is also applied to the *subjunctive mood* (مَنْصُوبٌ). This mood weakens the clear meaning of the verb by giving it a hint of intent, hope, ability, necessity, doubt, purpose, or expectation. It is used after the particles أَنْ • لَنْ • حَتَّى.

- → In both moods, we elide the ن to mark the mood.

84. سَوْفَ يَذْهَبُ and سَيَذْهَبُ - Same meaning?

Almost.

They both mean *I will go*. But there is a small difference:

which future?		grammar term	example
سَ	near future	الْمُسْتَقْبَلُ الْقَرِيبُ	سَيَذْهَبُ غَدًا.
		He will go tomorrow.	
سَوْفَ	far future	الْمُسْتَقْبَلُ الْبَعِيدُ	سَوْفَ يَذْهَبُ بَعْدَ شَهْرَيْنِ.
		He will go in two months.	

How do you **negate** the future? You have two options. The best solution is to use the particle لَنْ plus verb in the subjunctive mood (مَنْصوبٌ). But you may also use لا and put it after سَوْفَ.

She won't write you a letter.	(هِيَ) لَنْ تَكْتُبَ لَكَ رِسالةً. 1
	(هِيَ) سَوْفَ لا تَكْتُبُ لَكَ رِسالةً. 2

85. If someone died, why do you use the passive voice?

It has to do with God/Allah.

In Arabic, there are several possibilities to express that a person has died. The most common uses the verb تَوَفَّى. It is a V-verb (تَفَعَّلَ) of the root وَفَى.

The basic root means *to be perfect; to satisfy; to fulfil.* The V-verb *to exact fully; to take one's full share of; to receive in full.* So why is this form used when somebody has died?

The **active voice** (مَعْلُومٌ فاعِلُهُ) of تَوَفَّى can only be used if God/Allah is the subject (فاعِلٌ).

Allah has taken him unto Him.	تَوَفَّاهُ اللهُ.
This expression has the meaning of أَخَذَ رُوحَهُ (*he took his soul*) or أَماتَهُ (IV-verb: *to make sb. die; to cause the death of somebody*).	
God/Allah takes the people to Him.	اللهُ يَتَوَفَّى النَّاسَ.

In religious beliefs, only God knows and decides when death will happen. This is the reason why you should only use the active voice when God/Allah is the subject (the doer).

In all other situations, the verb should be used in the **passive voice** (مَجْهُولٌ فاعِلُهُ) **to express that someone has died**: تُوُفِّيَ. The passive can be translated as *to die; to pass away.*

Someone died/passed away.	تُوُفِّيَ إِلَى رَحْمَةِ اللهِ تَعالَى.
Professor *xy* has died.	تُوُفِّيَ إِلَى رَحْمَةِ اللهِ تَعالَى الأُسْتاذُ xy.

What about the word for *the deceased*? Often people use the expression الرَّاحِلُ. But you can also use الفَقِيدُ. Furthermore,

you can use the **passive participle** (اِسْمُ مَفْعُولٍ) of the V-verb
(تَوَفَّى) which is مُتَوَفَّى - plural: مُتَوَفَّوْنَ.

86. كَذَّابٌ - What kind of liar is he?

A notorious liar.

In Arabic, you can distinguish by a single word if somebody
just lied to you once (كاذِبٌ) or is a *notorious liar* (كَذَّابٌ). The
latter form is called صِيغةُ الْمُبالَغةِ (*form of exaggeration*).

Such forms are pretty common in Arabic. They are also used
for job names. For example, a *butcher* (جَزَّارٌ) is someone *who
slaughters a lot*. The صِيغةُ الْمُبالَغةِ expresses that something is
very... or *notorious...* or *strong...* or just *often done*.

translation	plural form	صِيغةُ الْمُبالَغةِ	verb		pat-tern
notorious liar	كَذَّابُونَ	كَذَّابٌ	to lie	كَذَبَ	فَعّالٌ
notorious liar	كُذُبٌ	كَذُوبٌ			فَعُولٌ
merciful	رَحِيمُونَ / رُحَمَاءُ	رَحِيمٌ	to be merciful	رَحِمَ	فَعِيلٌ
courageous	مَقَادِيمُ	مِقْدامٌ	to lead the way	قَدَّمَ	مِفْعالٌ
cautious, wary	حَذِرُونَ / حَذِراتٌ	حَذِرٌ	to be cautious	حَذِرَ	فَعِلٌ

The صِيغة الْمُبالَغة can be built from ثُلاثِيّ-verbs (**I-verb**; مُجَرَّدٌ;
which means that no letter is added to the root) – with the exception of the pattern مِفْعالٌ.

As seen above, the صِيغَةُ الْمُبالَغةِ of the **II-verb** قَدَّمَ (*to lead the way; to make precede*) is مِقْدامُ. Another example is the IV-verb أَغازَ (*to invade*) which becomes in the exaggeration-form مِغْوارُ (*being notorious aggressive*).

Some remarks:

- The forms فَعّالٌ and فَعُولٌ denote exactly the same.
- For the feminine form, just add a ة.
- Watch out: Only فَعُولٌ is used for both gender. Thus, the masculine and the feminine form share the same pattern!

She is a (notorious) liar.	هِيَ كَذُوبٌ.
She is a (notorious) liar.	هِيَ كَذَّابةٌ.

Remark: The correct pronunciation matters! The word كُذَّاب (with "*u*" on the first letter) is one possible plural form of the active participle كاذِبٌ.

87. To respect each other - How do you say that in Arabic?

There are several ways. It mainly depends on the verb you use.

Each other is indicating a reciprocity. This means that the verb indicates an action or state which is directed from multiple subjects to each other. There are several ways to express such a meaning in Arabic.

An elegant way is to play with verb forms (stems). You may use a **III-verb** of the pattern فاعَلَ and simply add a ت to the beginning. By doing that, you convert it to a **VI-verb** (تَفاعَلَ).

The VI-verb often expresses association (مُشَارَكَة) which can be interpreted as expressing a reflexive meaning.

to fight one another	تَقَاتَل			to fight	قَاتَل	
to share with one another; to be partners	تَشَارَك	VI ◄		to share	شَارَك	III
to argue with one another; to quarrel	تَجَادَل			to argue	جَادَل	

But what can we do if the verb does not share the pattern فَاعَل? Let us take the verb *to respect* (إِحْتَرَمَ). It uses the pattern of a VIII-verb (إِفْتَعَل).

In such a situation, you cannot build a reflexive verb just by changing the pattern.

You need an **additional expression**: بَعْضُنا بَعْضًا (for *we*) or بَعْضُهُمْ بَعْضًا (for *they*) or بَعْضُها بَعْضًا (*she*; or if it relates to a non-human plural). You can use this expression also with any other verb. It may be rendered as *mutually; each other; one another*. See *question #216*.

We respect each other.	نَحْتَرِمُ بَعْضُنا بَعْضًا.
We understand each other.	نَفْهَمُ بَعْضُنا بَعْضًا.
A believer is like a brick for another believer, the one supporting the other. *(Hadith; Sahīh Muslim 2585)*	الْمُؤْمِنُ لِلْمُؤْمِنِ كَالْبُنْيَانِ يَشُدُّ بَعْضُهُ بَعْضًا.
Business and economic development reinforce one another.	إِنَّ الْأَعْمالَ التِّجارِيَّةَ وَالتَّنْمِيَةَ الْاِقْتِصادِيَّةَ تُعَزِّزُ بَعْضُها بَعْضًا.

88. How do you express probability with only one word?

You use the particle قَدْ.

In Arabic, there is a fine way of expressing probability:

قَدْ **plus** verb in the <u>present</u> tense (الْمُضارِعُ)

It describes an action that might happen (but is not certain).

For example, قَدْ تَكْتُبُ can mean:

- *You might write.*

- *Sometimes you write.*

- *It could be that you write.*

- *It happens that you write.*

The liar may tell the truth.	قَدْ يَصْدُقُ الْكَذُوبُ.	قَدْ + **present** tense verb
She might come.	قَدْ تَأْتِي.	
I might not see him.	قَدْ لا أَراهُ.	

Watch out: قَدْ **plus** <u>past</u> tense (الْماضِي) does the opposite! It gives the meaning that something has already happened → it indicates the termination of an action. Regarding the notion of time, it may indicate that something had happened further in the past (*pluperfect* = **had** + a past participle).

He already left.	قَدْ ذَهَبَ.	قَدْ + **past** tense verb
She said that he had (already) done it.	قَالَتْ إِنَّهُ قَدْ فَعَلَهُ.	
[Allah] said, "You have been granted your request, O Moses." *(Sura 20:36)*	قَالَ قَدْ أُوتِيتَ سُؤْلَكَ يَا مُوسَى.	

89. Can, should, must - Does Arabic have "modals"?

Yes, there are – but they work differently in Arabic.

In English, *can, may, might, must, should,* and *would* are modal verbs – verbs that are not conjugated or negated in the same way as regular verbs. Modal verbs allow the speaker to express the possibility, ability, necessity, obligation, or certainty of an action (verb). **How do they work in Arabic?**

1. In Arabic, you conjugate the modal verb.

2. Regarding the second part, you have to options:

    a) you use أَنْ and use the second verb in the subjunctive mood (مَنْصُوبٌ).

    b) You use the مَصْدَر of the second verb.

He has to pay.	يَجِبُ (عَلَيْهِ) أَنْ يَدْفَعَ.	a)
	يَجِبُ (عَلَيْهِ) الدَّفْعُ.	b)

He wanted to go.	أَرادَ أَنْ يَذْهَبَ.	a)
	أَرادَ الذَّهابَ.	b)

Here are some Arabic verbs that can be used as modal verbs.

	English	present tense	past tense
1	*want; would*	يُرِيدُ	أَرادَ
2	*can; could*	يَسْتَطِيعُ	إسْتَطاعَ
		pronoun + يُمْكِنُ	pronoun + أَمْكَنَ
		The verb يُمْكِنُ is tricky. You need a pronoun suffix to indicate the person. For example: *He can*	

English	present tense	past tense

	go with you (يُمْكِنُهُ = يُمْكِنُهُ أَنْ يَذْهَبَ مَعَكَ (الذَهابُ مَعَكَ). Furthermore, instead of the past tense (أَمْكَنَ), the present tense يُمْكِنُ is used with كانَ instead. In the translation of such a construction, you may use the word *actually*. For example: *He could have gone with you actually* (كانَ يُمْكِنُهُ أَنْ يَذْهَبَ مَعَكَ).		
3	*must*	يَجِبُ (عَلَيْهِ)	وَجَبَ (عَلَيْهِ)
	This verb is always used in the 3rd person singular (*he*). If you want to express *I must*, you have to add a personal pronoun to the preposition عَلَى. The result will be: يَجِبُ عَلَيَّ.		
4	*should; to be necessary*	يَنْبَغِي (عَلَيْهِ)	إِنْبَغَى (عَلَيْهِ)
		يَلْزَمُ (عَلَيْهِ)	لَزِمَ (عَلَيْهِ)
	These two verbs are always used in the 3rd person singular (*he*). If you want to express, for example, *you should*, you have to add a personal pronoun to the preposition عَلَى – so you get: يَنْبَغِي عَلَيْكَ.		
	should	عَلَى الْمَرْءِ أَنْ = يَنْبَغِي عَلَى الْمَرْءِ أَنْ	
5	*may; to be allowed*	يَجُوزُ لِ	جازَ لِ
	This verb is always used in the 3rd person singular (*he*). If you want to express, e.g., *you were allowed*, you have to add a personal pronoun to the preposition لِ – and will get: جازَ لَكَ.		
6	*to like to*	وَدَّ + مَصْدَرٌ مَنْصُوبٌ <u>or</u> أَنْ + فِعْلٌ مَنْصُوبٌ	
	Remark: This expression is often used to express a wish that can't be fulfilled anymore. Note that you		

	English	present tense	past tense
		have to use the word لَوْ after وَدَّ.	
		She likes to go with him.	تَوَدُّ أَنْ تَذْهَبَ مَعَهُ.
		He <u>would like</u> to travel with you.	يَوَدُّ لَوْ يُسافِرُ مَعَكَ.
		He <u>would have liked</u> to travel with you.	وَدَّ لَوْ سافَرَ مَعَكَ.

<u>Remark:</u> You may use كانَ plus present tense to express an **unreal situation** (conditional II; Konjunktiv II).

He would have wished to see you today.	كانَ يَوَدُّ لِأَنْ يَراكَ الْيَوْمَ.
You could have asked him.	كانَ يُمْكِنُكَ أَنْ تَسْأَلَهُ.
You should have written her a letter.	كانَ يَنْبَغِي عَلَيْكَ أَنْ تَكْتُبَ لَها رِسالَةً.

90. Can you use a present tense verb to describe the past?

Yes, this is possible.

But it must be clear that you are talking about a situation in the past. In Arabic, it is useful to look at the verb in two ways:

TENSE: It is a grammatical category.

Tense is marked by the concrete form of the verb (*what is written*; German: *Bezeichnetes*). Frankly, it's nothing but a term because a certain tense may refer to a different time than that expressed by its name. For example, the past tense may express an event in the future (in English and Arabic).

TIME: It describes the situation outside the grammatical sphere (*what is intended*; German: *Gemeintes*). Time is a concept which is related to the overall context.

Thus, always try to put yourself in the role of the narrator to check what *time* he had in mind.

So, how can a present tense verb describe the past tense?

Usually you use a verb in the <u>past tense at the beginning</u> of the sentence and later switch to the present tense to describe what has happened (despite that the action is already over from the time now).

What is important: The (second) action – expressed by the present tense – occurs at the same time as the (first) action which is expressed by the past tense.

Let us look at examples:

I thought that the house <u>was</u> collapsing.	اِعْتَقَدْتُ أَنَّ الْبَيْتَ يَنْهارُ.
She instructed me what I <u>had</u> to do.	شَرَحَتْ لِي ما يَجِبُ أَنْ أَفْعَلَ.

91. Past and future tense together - Does that work?

Yes, it does.

There are some constructions in Modern Standard Arabic that look a bit weird – but are correct. You may find them in Arabic newspapers. They are used in conditional sentences in order to express *would* or *would have*.

إِذا + past tense (الْماضِي) + future "tense" (الْمُسْتَقْبَلُ)
= إِذا + كانَ + سَوْفَ + (مُضارِعٌ مَرْفُوعٌ) + verb in the present tense
This construction expresses the future or conditional II.

إِذا كانَ سَوْفَ يَتَنَحّى...	If he resigned... = If he would resign...
وَقَدْ دَخَلَ الْمُهَنْدِسُونَ الْمَبْنَى فِي الْوَقْتِ الَّذي اِنْتَظَرَ فِيهِ سُكّانُ الْبُرْجِ وَسُكّانُ الْمَباني الْمُجاوِرَةِ، وَهُمْ لا يَعْلَمُونَ ما إِذا كانَ سَوْفَ يُتَمُّ السَّماحُ لَهُمْ بِالْعَوْدةِ لِمَنازِلِهِمْ فِي وَقْتِ الْاِحْتِفالِ بِعيدِ الْميلادِ.	The engineers entered the building as the residents of the tower and residents of nearby buildings waited, unaware whether they would be allowed to return home at the time of Christmas. *(source: shorouknews.com)*

92. How do you attract someone's attention in Arabic?

In Arabic, unlike in English or German, you use a tiny word if you want to address a person (such as يا).

The whole concept is called *vocative* (الْمُنادَى). The term مُنادَى is the passive participle (اِسْمُ مَفْعُولٍ) of the III-verb *to summon* (نادَى). Thus, مُنادَى doesn't refer to the particle itself – but to the following noun (the addressee). In other words, مُنادَى is the *spoken-to*, to whom an invitation or warning is sent.

Let us look at the different particles that are used to address people (حَرْفُ نِداءٍ).

1	**Used in literature**	to call a person who is <u>close/near</u>	أَيْ • أَ
	O little son!	أَيْ بُنَيَّ!	
	O Zainab!	أَ زَيْنَبُ!	

2	**Used in literature**	to call a person who is <u>far away</u>	أَيْ • ا • هَيَا
	O Karim!	أَيا كَرِيمُ!	

3	**Used in general speech and writing**	to call a person who is <u>near or far</u>	يا
	O Muhammad!	يا مُحَمَّدُ!	
	O Aisha!	يا عائِشَةُ!	

Now, let us focus on the most common particle يا. It is quite tricky to find the correct ending for the addressee. If you want to understand the reason and logic behind the case endings, see *Arabic for Nerds 2, question #412 and #413.*

A. Uninflected (you don't put the case marker). The addressee is fixed on the vowel "u" (مَبْنِيٌّ عَلَى ما يُرْفَعُ بِهِ).

1	always "u" (ُ)	يا + عَلَمُ مُفْرَدٌ
	You address a **person with his or her name** (proper noun). In this situation, the proper noun (addressee) is fixed and cemented on the last <u>vowel "u"</u> (ضَمّة) – which is the original vowel of the word before the vocative came into the game.		
	Watch out: Grammatically speaking, the addressee is located in the position of an accusative case (فِي مَحَلِّ نَصْبٍ). Why? Because we assume that it is a direct object of a deleted verb. Just imagine a sentence like: *I call Muhammad* (أُنادِي مُحَمَّدًا).		

O Aisha!	يا عائِشَةُ!
O Khalid!	يا خالِدُ!

2	always "u" (ـُ)	يا + نَكِرةٌ مَقْصُودةٌ
	Specifically intended vocative: a particular person is addressed, but **not** with his or her **name**! The same as in number 1. In such a construction, the word is fixed/built on the <u>vowel "u"</u> (مَبْنِيٌّ عَلَى ما يُرْفَعُ بِهِ). Thus, it does not get case inflection.	
	O (female) student!	يا طالِبَةُ!
	O man!	يا رَجُلُ!

B. The addressee has to be in the accusative case (مَنْصُوبٌ).

1	ending: "a" (ـَ)	يا +إضافةٌ
	The first part of the إضافةٌ is the so-called مُضافٌ. It gets the normal case endings (inflection) according to its position in the sentence – which is the location of a direct object (for the deleted, implicitly understood verb: I call). Thus, the addressee has to be in the <u>accusative</u> case (مَنْصُوبٌ). Watch out: Since it is the first part of the إضافة, it only takes one فَتْحة.	
	O employees of the company!	يا مُوَظَّفِي الشَّرِكَةِ!
	Notice: The word was originally مُوَظَّفِينَ. In a genitive construction, the ن disappears!	
	O students of the center!	يا طُلّابَ الْمَركَزِ!
	O Abdallah (Note that "'Abdullāhi" is a إضافة literally meaning servant of Allah)	يا عَبْدَ اللهِ!

2	ending: "an" (ً)	يا + شِبْهُ بالْمُضافِ

A construction **similar to a** إضافة. The addressee is not a proper name (A1) or the first part of a إضافة (B1). Instead, it is a word which gets described by additional information.

The word after يا is <u>indefinite</u> (نَكِرةٌ) and has to be مَنْصُوبٌ because according to its location, it is the direct object of a deleted, virtual verb (e.g., أُنادِي). So it gets a فَتْحة plus <u>nunation</u>: "-an".

What about the word which follows? It completes the meaning and is connected to the word before. It may be serving as a subject (فاعِلٌ), a direct object (مَفْعُولٌ بِهِ), a prepositional (جارٌّ وَمَجْرُورٌ) or adverbial phrase (ظَرْفٌ).

O you, who reads the book!	يا قارِئًا الْكِتابَ!
O you (people), who love reading books!	يا مُحِبِّينَ الْقِراءَةَ!
O you, who are living in this house!	يا مُقيمًا فِي البيتِ!
O you, who are sitting in the car!	يا جالِسًا فِي السَّيّارَةِ!
O you, who drinks the water of the Nile!	يا شارِبًا مِنْ ماءِ النِّيلِ!

3	ending: "an" (ً)	يا + نَكِرةٌ غَيْرُ مَقْصُودةٍ

If you don't address a particular person but want to address a **group** or **people in general** (e.g., in a speech), you use an abstract, <u>indefinite</u> word after the vocative particle. It is in the accusative case (مَنْصُوبٌ) and takes regular nunation (تَنْوِينٌ).

O Arab!	يا عَرَبِيًّا!
O intellectual!	يا مُثَقَّفًا!

How is the situation if we don't want to address a person by his or her proper name? Or if we want to use just a single word to address a person – which would mean that we have to use the definite article?

Then, we need something in-between. This can be...

- a *demonstrative noun* (اِسْمُ إِشارَةٍ). Actually, this is similar to what we have seen in *A1* (proper name).

- the expression أَيُّها for masculine and أَيَّتُها for feminine. That is a different type of construction. For example:

O respected viewers!	يا أَيُّها الْمُشاهِدُونَ الأَعِزّاءُ!

Let us put both type of constructions under the microscope.

O (this) girl!	يا هٰذِهِ الْفَتاةُ!	1

Vocative particle (حَرْفُ نِداءٍ)	يا
The *spoken-to, addressee* (مُنادّى). It has a fixed shape (مَبْنِيٌّ) which never changes. However, we say that هٰذِهِ is located in the position of an accusative case (فِي مَحَلِّ نَصْبٍ) - but you cannot mark nor see that.	هٰذِهِ
This word is an *apposition* (بَدَلٌ) to هٰذِهِ, in other words, it refers to the same person. Now, why is it in the nominative case then? It's complicated. If we used *Muhammad* instead of هٰذِهِ, Muhammad would be fixed on the "u" resulting in يا مُحَمَّدُ. We assume that hypothetically, the same happened to هٰذِهِ. Since the word الْفَتاةُ stands in apposition, and since an apposition has to mirror the case ending of the word to which it refers, it also gets a "u" (ضَمّة).	الْفَتاةُ

O citizens!	يَأَيُّها الْمُواطِنُونَ!	2

The addressee (مُنادّى). Imagine this word as a proper	أَيُّها

| This is a derived noun (إِسْمُ فَاعِلٍ) of the root ن-ط-و. Why is this important? Not for the case ending, but to properly identify its position and function. | الْمُواطِنُونَ |

noun – which is also the reason why it is cemented on this shape with vowel "u" (مَبْنِيٌّ عَلَى الضَّمِّ).

If the word after أَيُّها is a...

- ... **inert noun** (not taken from a root), for example, *man* (رَجُلٌ), then it is an **apposition** (بَدَلٌ);
- ... **derived noun** (إِسْمٌ مُشْتَقٌّ), then it takes the position of an **adjective** (نَعْتٌ). So الْمُواطِنُونَ is a نَعْتٌ.

In grammar, both the بَدَلٌ and نَعْتٌ are *followers* (تابِعٌ) and mirror the case of the preceding word.

Some more remarks on أَيُّها and أَيَّتُها (أَيُّ and أَيَّةُ):

- Both always take the same vowel: a single ضَمّة.
- The ها is just there to underline the attention.
- They can merge with يا to يَاأَيُّها but don't have to. It is also possible to write يا أَيُّها – for greater emphasis. E.g.:

| O friend! | يا أَيُّها الصَّدِيقُ! |
| O mother! | يا أَيَّتُها الأُمُّ! |

Watch out: Sometimes you can delete the vocative-particle, but even then, it will take the same vowel as if it was there!

| *O Muhammad, o student!* Notice that Muhammad takes only one ضَمّة. | مُحَمَّدُ! أَيُّها الطَّالِبُ! |
| *O my friend!* It was originally: يا صَدِيقِي
This shortening is called تَرْخِيم – *see q. #93)* | صَدِيقِ! |

O lord!	رَبِّ!

93. يا فاطِمَةُ or يا فاطِمَ - What is correct for: *O Fatima?*

Both are correct.

Fatima (فاطِمة) is a feminine proper noun. So logically, if you want to address Fatima, it should be: يا فاطِمةُ - which is also correct. However, يا فاطِمَ is also fine.

In Arabic, this style is called تَرْخِيمُ which literally means *shortening*. What is the purpose of it? We achieve *euphony*.

Linguists understand by this term the alteration of speech sounds, so as to make them easier to pronounce and pleasing to the ear. In Arabic, it denotes the process of cutting the last letter of the name which is addressed. The name is usually a feminine word.

You usually see it with proper nouns that have a final letter ة as a sign of feminization; rarely also with feminine proper nouns ending in ى (which is also a sign of feminization).

When you delete the ة, the word ends with the vowel that was already on top of the letter that preceded the ة - which is in almost all situations a فَتْحة. But you could also add a single ضَمّة ("u") as if in the standard vocative. Both are correct.

meaning	التَّرْخِيم	regular form
O Hamza!	يا حَمْزَ! = يا حَمْزُ!	يا حَمْزَةُ!
O Fatima!	يا فاطِمَ! = يا فاطِمُ!	يا فاطِمَةُ!
O Marwa!	يا مَرْوَ!	يا مَرْوَى!

Even proper nouns with four or more letters can be shortened in order to address people. You simply **cut the last letter.** But this is very rare.

O Ja'far!	يا جَعْفَ! = يا جَعْفُ!	يا جَعْفَرُ!
O Mālik!	يا مالِ! = يا مالُ!	يا مالِكُ!
O Su'ād!	يا سُعا!	يا سُعادُ!

94. The letter ج - Which pronunciation is correct?

There are no rules. It depends on the country.

In Egypt, the letter ج is pronounced as *"g"* like in the English word *"girl"*. In other countries, it is pronounced *"j"* (like in English *"job"*), sometimes hard (like in English *"jerry"*), sometimes very soft and close to *"sh"*.

	جِيمٌ قُرَيْشِيّةٌ	جِيمٌ قاهِرِيّةٌ	جِيمٌ شامِيّةٌ
Where?	rest of the Arab world	Egypt, Yemen, Oman, Sudan	Palestine, Syria, Jordan, Lebanon
Pronunciation of ج	"t-sha"	"g"	"d-sha"
English sound	Jennifer	girl	germ

About a hundred years ago, people in Egypt were pronouncing the ج as a جِيمٌ قُرَيْشِيّةٌ. Interestingly, the جِيمٌ قاهِرِيّةٌ comes originally from Yemen.

95. *Followed by...* - How do you say that in Arabic?

There are several possibilities.

I will show how you could use the word إِثْر to express *followed by*. إِثْر means *immediately after; right after*.

The word إِثْر is, grammatically speaking, a noun (اِسْم) that serves in the location of an adverb (ظَرْفُ مَكانٍ). This is the reason for the vowel *"a"* on which it is fixed (مَبْنِيٌّ عَلَى الْفَتْحِ).

What about the word after إِثْر؟ Well, إِثْر serves as the first part of the إِضافة, so it has to be in the genitive case (مَجْرُورٌ).

Now comes the tricky part. Since the base (إِثْر) is a اِسْم you can also use it together with a preposition: عَلَى الإِثِر. Since it is placed after a preposition, it gets a كَسْرة. Let us look at an example.

The nuclear plant exploded **after/followed** by an earthquake in Japan.	اِنْفَجَرَتْ مَحَطَّةٌ نَوَوِيَّةٌ إِثْر زِلْزالٍ كَبِيرٍ فِي الْيابان.

Here are some other words with a similar meaning:

as soon as; right after; immediately upon. The word حالَ a temporal meaning. Don't put a verb after it. If you want to express *as soon as we arrive*, you should use the مَصْدَر with a personal pronoun: حالَ وُصُولِنا	حالَ
after; one after another	تِلْوَ
as soon as; immediately after	فَوْرَ
immediately after	عَقِبَ

However, إِثْر can also denote *thereupon, as a result of*. It can express consequence, like the expression *one after another*.

She began to hand me book after book.	أَخَذَتْ تُعْطِينِي الْكِتَابَ إِثْرَ الْكِتَابِ.
The students left the university, one after the other (one by one).	إِنْصَرَفَ الطُّلَّابُ مِن الْجَامِعةِ وَاحِدًا إِثْرَ الْآخَرِ.

96. The direction *right* - Should you use يَمِينَ or أَيْمَنُ؟

It depends on what you want to express: adjective or adverb.

But how do you know whether you should use يَمِينَ or أَيْمَنُ؟ It is easy. You just have to know the difference between an adjective (صِفةٌ) and an adverb (ظَرْفٌ).

right	used when you need it as an adverb (German: *rechts*).	ظَرْفُ مَكَانٍ	يَمِين	1
	used when you need it as an adjective (German: *rechte*). In Arabic, it needs to agree with the noun to which it refers (gender, number, definite or indefinite, case).	صِفةٌ	أَيْمَنُ	2

She looked neither right nor left.	لَمْ تَلْتَفِتْ يَمِينًا وَلا يَسارًا.	1a
I walked on the right.	مَشَيْتُ يَمِينًا.	1a
I walked at the right of the street.	مَشَيْتُ يَمِينَ الطَّرِيقِ.	1b
I walked at the right.	مَشَيْتُ يَمِينٌ.	1c

to the right (nach rechts)	إِلَى الْيَمِينِ	1
right from (German: rechts von)	إِلَى يَمِينِهِ	1

the right hand	الْيَدُ الْيُمْنَى	2
the right side	الْجَانِبُ الْيَمِينُ	2

What should we do about the case endings in number 1?

يَمِين is usually the first part of a إِضافة-construction.

1a	If it is cut off from the إِضافة by pronunciation and by meaning, then it gets the ending "-an" (ـً).
1b	If it serves as the first part of a إِضافة, it gets the usual case ending of an adverb of place (مَفْعُولٌ فِيهِ) which is the accusative (مَنْصُوب). In other words, the vowel "a" (ـَ).
1c	There is a third option: You can fix it on the vowel "u" (مَبْنِيٌّ عَلَى الضَّمِّ) resulting in ـُ. This happens if it is cut off from the annexation – but not by meaning in fact, we delete the second part with the intention of the survival of its meaning). Regarding the grammar, the word is located in the position of an accusative (فِي مَحَلِّ نَصْبٍ), but you can't see that. You may know that from the expressions *previously* (مِنْ قَبْلُ).

Now, what about the nature of the word أَيْمَنُ؟ What form is it?

There are two possibilities – and you can only tell the difference by looking at the feminine form.

plural f.	singular f.	plural m.	singular. m.	type	
يُمْنَيَاتٌ	يُمْنَى	أَيَامِنُ	أَيْمَنُ	إِسْمُ تَفْضِيلٍ	1
يَمْناوَاتٌ	يَمْنَاءُ	يُمْنٌ		صِفَةٌ مُشَبَّهَةٌ	2

Some remarks about number 1 (إِسْمُ تَفْضِيلٍ):

- Number 1 is similar to *bigger* (أَكْبَرُ - كُبْرَى).

- If you talk about <u>directions</u>, you usually use number 2 – which only matter ins the feminine form يُمْنَى - and in the respective plural form!

- أَيْمَنُ is the opposite of أَيْسَرُ and يُسْرَى (f.) which means *left-handed, left*. Note that أَيْسَرُ which usually denotes *left* could be a real comparative (اِسْمُ تَفْضِيلٍ) which would then denote *easier* in the meaning of أَسْهَلُ.

- Number 1 is used as an **adjective** (صِفَةٌ) in Arabic.

Some remarks about number 2 (صِفَةٌ مُشَبَّهَةٌ):

- Here, the word أَيْمَنُ is the *quasi* active participle (صِفَةٌ مُشَبَّهَةٌ) of the I-verb *to be fortunate about* (يَمُنُ عَلَى). You have several options for the translation: as *that which is to the right-hand side*; *somebody who does or enjoys good things*. It is used as an **adjective** (صِفَةٌ) in Arabic.

- The صِفَةٌ مُشَبَّهَةٌ has many patterns (صِيغَةٌ). One is أَفْعَلُ for the masculine and فَعْلَاءُ for the feminine gender. This pattern is also used for colors (لَوْنٌ) and permanent characteristics (حِلْيَةٌ) like *lame* (أَعْرَجُ) or *stupid* (أَحْمَقُ).

- You use this type if you describe people. But you can only see the difference to number 1 if the word is feminine.

Now, where is the relation between being fortunate and a direction? This has to do with the Islamic tradition that **right is good and left is bad**. For example: You should eat with your right hand – as you use your left hand in the toilet. In ancient times, the term *left hand* was expressed by الْيَدُ الشُّؤْمَى.

The masculine form of it would be أَشْأَمُ which denotes *more/most unlucky, unfortunate, unprosperous*. It is pretty much the opposite of أَيْمَنُ and يُمْنَى. The word أَشْأَمُ is used in the sense of شُؤْم (*unluckiness*) similar to the word أَيْمَن which is used in the sense of يُمْن (*prosperity, blessing*). **Remark:** It is also interesting that in English, the word *right* is used to denote both *right* (direction) and *correct*, whereas *left* is also used in the sense of *not included; abandoned*.

What about **directions** (of the compass)? For example, the expression شامًا وَيَمَنًا means *to the north and south (northward and southward)*. In the beginning of Islam, people used the **prayer direction** (قِبْلَة) to name directions. All directions were seen as if one was standing in front of the door of the Kaaba in Mecca. This may explain the meaning of the country name *Yemen* (الْيَمَنُ) because Yemen lies on the right side of the Kaaba in Mecca in Saudi-Arabia (سُمِّيَتْ الْيَمَنَ لِأَنَّها عَنْ يَمِينِ الْكَعْبَةِ). However, other scholars suggested that the name may simply denote the core meaning of the root: *felicity* or *blessing* as much of the country back then was fertile.

a fortunate man	رَجُلٌ أَيْمَنُ
In the meaning of enjoying prosperity (good fortune) and good tidings (ذُو يُمْنٍ وَبَرَكَةٍ).	
the guided ones; (lit. *the people of the right-hand-side*); epithet for *the saved*.	أَصْحابُ الْيَمِينِ
the street on the right side.	الشَّارِعُ الْأَيْمَنُ
right side	الْجِهَةُ الْيُمْنَى
He is right-handed and his brother is left-handed.	هُوَ أَيْمَنُ وَأَخُوهُ أَيْسَرُ.
He looked to the right.	نَظَرَ أَيْمَنَ.
We called to him **from the right-hand side** of the mountain... *(Sura 19:52)*	وَنادَيْناهُ مِن جانِبِ الطُّورِ الْأَيْمَنِ...

Note: The word يَمِينٌ can also denote *oath* and in this application, is treated as a <u>feminine</u> noun. The usual plural form then is أَيْمانٌ (which could, theoretically, also denote *right hands*).

Excursus: The necessity of a second part in the إضافة.

<u>In Arabic, there are four special types of nouns:</u>

a) Nouns that can <u>never</u> serve as the first part of a إضافة – such as the pronouns أنا or the word هٰذا.

b) Nouns that can <u>never stand alone</u> (ما يَلْزَمُ الْإِضافَةَ لَفْظًا وَمَعْنًى) but must be followed by an annexed word (the 2nd part of a إضافة) – like the word *at* (عِنْدَ). Why? Because such words can't express a meaning by themselves.

c) Nouns that usually serve as the first part of a إضافة but <u>may do without it</u> (ما يَلْزَمُ الْإِضافَةَ مَعْنًى دُونَ لَفْظٍ) – such as the word *all* (كُلّ) or *some* (بَعْض). You can use them also as single, unconnected words (بلا إِضافَةٍ). They get the case according to their position in the sentence.

Everybody is laughing.	كلُّ ضاحِكٌ.	1
We say that the إضافة-construction is understood by meaning, but without pronouncing it, because the second part of the إضافة is deleted (الْمُضافُ إِلَيْهِ مَحْذُوفٌ). We are allowed to use the word كُلّ as a singular noun (مُفْرَدٌ). We compensate the deleted part by using nunation (تَنْوِينٌ) for كُلّ.		
All of the students are laughing.	كلُّ الطُّلّابِ ضاحِكٌ.	2
The standard situation: We use كُلّ in a إضافة which means that it gets followed by a second part (مُضافٌ إِلَيْهِ). Why did we use the singular form ضاحِكٌ although we talk about *students*? Because *students* is not the subject – it is كُلّ, which is singular. But you could use the *logical subject* and use ضاحِكُونَ – see q. #259.		

d) Words such as قَبْل or بَعْد or غَيْر or أَوَّل or دُون may be used as the first part of the إِضافة and then get the case ending (إِعْرابٌ) according to the function and position in the sentence.

However, they may do without a إِضافة and stand alone. → Then they are fixed/cemented on the vowel "u" (مَبْنِيٌّ عَلَى الضَّمِّ). Although we delete the second part, we assume that the meaning still survives. See *question #221*.

97. Which verbs have a predicate?

Every verb that is a sister of كانَ or كادَ (including verbs of approximation and verbs of hope) has a predicate.

And what about the other sentences? Well, regular verbal sentences may have <u>objects</u>.

Here, we deal with verbs denoting *almost; just about to* or *to begin* or *to hope.* Such sentences have a predicate (خَبَر). Practically speaking, it gives us more information about the subject.

Soon the winter will be over.	كادَ الشِّتاءُ يَنْتَهِي. 1
Here, *winter* is not the (verbal) subject (فاعِلٌ). It is called اِسْمُ كادَ (noun of *to be about to*). We could still roughly translate it as "subject" but you should also give the Arabic term to avoid confusion. The اِسْمُ كادَ takes the nominative case (مَرْفُوعٌ). The verbal sentence يَنْتَهِي is the predicate (خَبَرُ كادَ).	
The students started studying.	بَدَأَ الطُّلَّابُ يَدْرُسُونَ. 2
The word *students* is the اِسْمُ بَدَأَ. The verbal sentence يَدْرُسُونَ is the predicate (خَبَرُ بَدَأَ).	

Watch out:

The students took the book.	أَخَذَ الطُّلَّابُ الْكِتابَ.

The word *students* in this sentence is the subject (فاعِلٌ) – as the verb conveys its original meaning of *to take*!

Both sentences have the same meaning: *Khalid started to write/writing the letter.*	بَدَأَ خالِدٌ كِتابَةَ الرِّسالةِ.
	بَدَأَ خالِدٌ يَكْتُبُ الرِّسالةَ.

However, there is a grammatical difference:

- In the first sentence, we use a مَصْدَر instead of a present tense verb (فِعْلٌ). Therefore, *Khalid* is the regular subject (فاعِلٌ) of بَدَأَ and كِتابَةَ is the direct object.

- In the second sentence, *Khalid* is the so-called اِسْمُ بَدَأ because we have a verb in the present tense serving as the predicate (خَبَرُ بَدَأ). See *question #103*.

98. فِعْلٌ ناقِصٌ - **What is that?**

An incomplete verb.

The word فِعْلٌ means *verb* and ناقِصٌ *incomplete*. We have already encountered the term فِعْلٌ ناقِصٌ in *question #10* where we talked about verbs that have a weak letter (حَرْفُ عِلّةٍ). But there is also another application of the term.

In order to understand this, we have to distinguish between two main concepts:

- صَرْفٌ which means **inflection; forming of nouns, conjugation of verbs**. We look at a word in an isolated way.

- نَحْوُ which means **grammar.** We analyze the function and application of a word in a sentence.

A	نَحْوُ	فِعْلُ ناقِصٌ

When we analyze a sentence and use the term *incomplete, deficient verb*, we mean the following: A verb which does not give you a sufficient, complete (تامٌّ) meaning if you only use it with the subject. For example: *You were* (كُنْتَ). *You become* (تُصْبِحُ).

Therefore, you must add another word – a predicate (خَبَرٌ) – to complete the meaning. Now comes the fun part. The standard grammar rules don't work here. That's why these verbs are also called أَفْعالُ ناسِخةٌ – *abrogators* – as the root ن-س-خ means *to abrogate; to revoke.*

You must put the "subject" into the nominative (رَفْعُ الْإِسْمِ) and the predicate into the **accusative** case (نَصْبُ الْخَبَرِ).

There are two main groups:

- كانَ and its sisters
- كادَ and its sisters

What is the idea behind the *sisters*?

- These verbs intervene in the nominal sentence as the grammarians say (يَدْخُلُ عَلَى الْجُمْلةِ الإسْمِيّةِ).
- These verbs are called ناقِصٌ because they **only point to time** (يَدُلُّ عَلَى الزَّمانِ فَقَطْ), but not to the action (لَا يَدُلُّ عَلَى الْحَدَثِ) as regular verbs (فِعْلٌ تامٌّ). We could say that since they do not point to the action, they don't need a subject (فاعِلٌ).

Let us see the difference:

The weather is nice.	الْجَوُّ جَمِيلٌ.	1
This is a nominal sentence (جُمْلَةٌ اِسْمِيَّةٌ).		
The weather became nice.	أَصْبَحَ الْجَوُّ جَمِيلًا.	2
Most scholars say that this is a verbal sentence (جُمْلَةٌ فِعْلِيَّةٌ).		

Incomplete verb in the past tense (فِعْلٌ ماضٍ ناسِخٌ)	أَصْبَحَ
"Subject" which is called _noun_ of to become (اِسْمُ أَصْبَحَ). It must be in the nominative case (مَرْفُوعٌ).	الْجَوُّ
This is the _predicate_ of to become (خَبَرُ أَصْبَحَ). It must be in the nominative case (مَرْفُوعٌ).	جَمِيلًا

B	صَرْفٌ	فِعْلٌ ناقِصٌ - مُعْتَلٌّ

In the area of morphology, a _deficient verb_ is a verb that contains a final weak root letter (حَرْف الْعِلّة). See _question #10_.

Watch out: If you spot فِعْلٌ ناقِصٌ التَّصْريفِ, it means that a verb cannot be conjugated in all tenses. For example, the expression _still_ (ما زالَ). See _question #100_.

99. _To be_ (كانَ) - What is so tricky about its predicate?

The predicate (خَبَرُ كانَ) has to be in the accusative (مَنْصُوبٌ).

The verb _to be_ (كانَ) is a special verb in Arabic that follows specific rules. It governs its **predicate** (خَبَرُ كانَ) in the **accusative** case (مَنْصُوبٌ). Sometimes, however, you don't see that the predicate takes that case (examples 2 and 3).

So what would be suitable to serve as the predicate of كان؟

1	The predicate consists of <u>one word</u> (مُفْرَدٌ).	
	The weather was nice.	كان الْجَوُّ جَمِيلًا.

2	The predicate is a <u>verbal sentence</u> (جُمْلَةٌ فِعْلِيَّةٌ).	
	The professor was talking.	كان الْأُسْتاذُ يَتَكَلَّمُ.
	The predicate is an entire verbal sentence (يَتَكَلَّمُ) with a hidden/implied pronoun! Notice that the verb has a ضَمّة on top of the last letter – however, grammatically, the verbal sentence is located in the position of an accusative (فِي مَحَلِّ نَصْبٍ).	

3	The predicate is a <u>nominal sentence</u> (جُمْلَةٌ اِسْمِيَّةٌ).	
	The story was boring. (Lit.: The events of the story were boring.)	كانَتْ الْقِصَّةُ أَحْداثُها مُمِلَّةً.
	Notice the two ضَمّة: the first one on *events* (أَحْداثُها - "*u*") and the second one on the predicate of *events*, i.e. *boring*! ("un"). We say that the entire nominal sentence (أَحْداثُها مُمِلَّةٌ) is located in the position of an accusative case (فِي مَحَلِّ نَصْبٍ) because it serves as the predicate of كان. What about the pronoun suffix ها in the word أَحْداث؟ It links the nominal sentence with the "subject" (*story*).	

4	The predicate is a (A) <u>prepositional</u> (جارٌ وَمَجْرُورٌ) or (B) <u>adverbial</u> phrase (ظَرْفٌ) - so called شِبْهُ الْجُمْلةِ.		
A	The car was in its parking lot.	كانَتْ السَّيارةُ فِي الْمَوْقِفِ.	
B	The car was in front of the house.	كانَتْ السَّيارةُ أَمامَ الْبَيْتِ.	

100. What are the sisters of كانَ (*to be*)?

There are many.

كانَ (*to be*) is one of the very special and interesting verbs in Arabic. It is a so-called *deficient, incomplete verb* (فِعْلٌ ناقِصٌ) - see *question #97* - and has many *sisters* (أَخَواتُ كانَ) which means that these verbs behave grammatically in the same way: **They link a subject with a predicate.**

Like كانَ, also its *sisters* have usually an auxiliary function governing a subordinate verb. These are the sisters of كانَ:

to be (past tense).	كانَ

to become; *to come to be*; original: *to be in the morning.* If it is followed by **a present tense verb** (فِعْلٌ مُضارِعٌ), it usually conveys the meaning of *to begin.* Only in the present (فِعْلٌ مُضارِعٌ), it may have the original meaning of *to begin a new day*; *to wake up in the morning.* For example: If you wish *good night* in Arabic, you literally say: "*Wake up well!*" (تُصْبِحْ عَلَى خِيرٍ)	أَصْبَحَ

to become; *to begin*; literal meaning: *between morning and midday*, e.g., 9 o'clock in the morning.	أَضْحَى

to become (in the meaning of *to remain;* German *bleiben*); *to continue.*	ظَلَّ

to become; *to develop to the point of*; *to come to be.* Only in the present tense (فِعْلٌ مُضارِعٌ), it may denote the original meaning of *to be in the evening* or *when it is getting dark.*	أَمْسَى

to become (in the meaning of *to remain;* German *bleiben*); *time of the night;* literal meaning: *to stay overnight.* Note: This verb is frequently used also in spoken Arabic the express *to stay overnight.*	بَاتَ

to become; to come to be; to begin.	صَارَ

not to be; used to **negate** a nominal sentence (جُمْلةٌ اِسْمِيّةٌ).	لَيْسَ

still; not to cease to be	Watch out: These verbs are **NEGATED.** Only in the negation, they convey the meaning on the left.	ما زالَ
still; not to cease; not to stop		ما فَتِئَ
still; not to go away		ما بَرِحَ
still		ما اِنْفَكَّ

to continue, to last; as long as	This verb is **not** negated! The ما here is used to produce a circumstantial **interpreted infinitive** (مَصْدَرٌ مُؤَوَّلٌ).	ما دَامَ

Such ما is called ما الْمَصْدَرِيّةُ الظَّرْفِيّة since it has the power to mold an infinitive. It **replaces** the *adverb of time* (ظَرْفُ الزَّمان) which was eliminated and was placed as the first part of the إِضافة. For example: I will fight **as long as** I live (سَأُكافِحُ ما دُمْتُ حَيًّا).

Some examples:

I won't go to the market as long as it is still raining. (*raining* is مَنْصُوبٌ.)	لَنْ أَذْهَبَ إِلَى السُّوقِ مادامَ المَطَرُ مُتَساقِطًا.
The weather became nice.	أَضْحَى الْجَوُّ جَمِيلًا.

101. *Almost, just about to - How do you say that in Arabic?*

In Arabic, you use verbs to express "almost".

These verbs are called *verbs of approximation* (فِعْلُ مُقارَبةٍ). The best-known example is the verb كادَ - يَكادُ which may be translated as *to be about to; he (would have) almost*. All these verbs follow the rules of كانَ – but with some differences:

- The predicate of a *verb of approximation* is a **verbal sentence** (جُمْلةٌ فِعْلِيّةٌ) in the present tense (فِعْلٌ مُضارِعٌ) which follows directly after the *verb of approximation*.

- However, sometimes you may insert the particle أَنْ by which you produce an **interpreted infinitive** (مَصْـدَرٌ مُؤَوَّلٌ) following the formula: أَنْ + verb in the present tense subjunctive (فِعْلُ مُضارِعٌ مَنْصُوبٌ).

When should we use أَنْ?

1. أَنْ is **always** used with *verbs of hope* (فِعْلُ رَجاءٍ).

2. أَنْ is used with **some** *verbs of approximation* (فِعْـلُ مُقارَبةٍ).

3. أَنْ is **never** used with *verbs of beginning/initiative* (فِعْلُ شُرُوعٍ).

All of these verbs above are called *sisters* of كادَ (أَخَواتُ كادَ). Although the predicate consists of a verbal sentence, we need to think about the appropriate case – despite the fact that only nouns in Arabic can take case endings. Thus, we apply a place value and say that the predicate (the verbal sentence) is located in the position of an accusative case (فِي مَحَلِّ نَصْبٍ).

If this is all too sophisticated, you can't do anything wrong if you just mark the endings by using the standard rules for regular sentence (although the logic is entirely different).

The following verbs describe a situation or an event that is very likely and that will take place very soon. They all denote *be on the verge of; to be about to.*

usually used	explanation	verb
<u>without</u> أَنْ	The choice of the tense (past or present) depends on the view of the narrator (if he wants to tell something in the past or present).	كَادَ, يَكَادُ
<u>with</u> أَنْ		أَوْشَكَ, يُوشِكُ
<u>without</u> أَنْ	Only used in literature.	كَرَبَ

Let us look at an example:

Soon the winter will be over.	كَادَ الشِّتَاءُ يَنْتَهِي.
Meaning here: *just about to end.* In German, you would translate it as *bald vorbei* or *fast vorbei.*	

Notice the grammatical difference in the following sentences. They both mean: *The train will move soon.*

With أَنْ: The second verb (after أَنْ) needs the subjunctive mood (مَنْصُوبٌ).	أَوْشَكَ الْقِطَارُ أَنْ يَتَحَرَّكَ.
Without أَنْ: The second verb takes the standard indicative mood (مَرْفُوعٌ).	أَوْشَكَ الْقِطَارُ يَتَحَرَّكُ.

Watch out:

- كَادَ cannot be used in the imperative (أَمْرٌ).
- The present tense (الْمُضَارِعُ) of كَادَ is not يَكُودُ. It is يَكَادُ. كَادَ uses the same conjugation pattern as the verbs *to sleep*

(نامَ - يَنامُ) and *to fear* (خافَ - يَخافُ). The reason for the
letter ا in the middle of the present tense lies in the **stem
vowel** of the present tense of such verbs which is "a".

- If كادَ is negated, it denotes *hardly* or *scarcely*! See q. #125.

102. What are the *verbs of hope* (فِعْلُ رَجاءٍ)?

Arabic verbs which are used to express that something is hope-
fully going to happen.

The word رَجاءٌ means *hope*. Verbs of hope (فِعْلُ رَجاءٍ) are
pretty unique in Arabic because they are almost exclusively
used in the past tense, but the sentence conveys the meaning
of the **present tense** or **future!**

All the following verbs may be translated as *to wish*; *per-*
haps; *it could be that*; *it is possible that.*

This verb is only used in the past. It is a *inert, unipersonal verb* (فِعْلٌ جامِدٌ). Usually, such verbs **can't** be conjugated in the **present tense** (الْمُضارِعُ). Furthermore, they can't be used in the imperative (أَمْرُ) and sometimes, they don't have a مَصْدَر. The past tense verb عَسَى is usually **not conjugated** at all. Instead, it takes a **pronoun suffix** to express the subject. عَسَى needs أنْ to be connected to the predicate.	عَسَى
Only used in literature; it goes along with أنْ to get connected to the predicate.	حَرَى إِخْلَوْلَقَ

- All three verbs are *sisters* of كادَ.

- They need a **predicate** (خَبَرٌ) which has to be a <u>verb</u> in the **present tense** (فِعْلٌ مُضارِعٌ). In order to connect the predicate with a *verb of hope*, you need the particle أَنْ. A following verb takes the *subjunctive mood* (مَنْصُوبٌ) - ending "a".

Some examples:

I wish (that) the exam will be easy.	عَسَى الْإِمْتِحانُ أَنْ يَكُونَ سَهْلًا.
The (fem.) student wishes to see the teacher.	الطَّالِبَةُ اِخْلَوْلَقَتْ أَنْ تَرَى الْمُدَرِّسَ.
Perhaps you are...?	عَساكَ...؟

103. *To begin something* - How do you express that in Arabic?

There are many verbs in Arabic which can do that job.

Verbs, which express that something *starts, begins,* or *is being started* are called فِعْلُ شُرُوعٍ. The word شُرُوع means *attempt; embarking on; engaging in.* Thus, we may translate the grammar term as *verbs of beginning* or *initiative.*

The following verbs basically all denote the same: *to start, to begin, to undertake* – **when they are used in the past tense!**

جَعَلَ	شَرَعَ	أَخَذَ	بَدَأَ • اِبْتَدَأَ
to render	to initiate	to take	to begin

أَقْبَلَ	طَفِقَ	قامَ	راحَ
to approach	to set about	to rise	to go

اِبْرَى	عَلِقَ	أَنْشَأَ	هَبَّ
to oppose	to hang upon	to create	to start moving

There are six things you should know about these verbs:

1. They are *inert verbs* (فِعْلٌ جامِدٌ), we can call them *defective*, because you can only use them in the past tense if you want them to function as a *verb of beginning*. In other words, only when they are used in the past tense, they convey the meaning of *to begin*. Otherwise, they retain their original meaning – for example, *to take* (يَأْخُذُ). All other forms as well as derived nouns are treated as being taken from a complete verb (فِعْلٌ نامٌّ).

2. There is one exception: Only the verb بَدَأَ means *to begin* also in the present tense (يَبْدَأُ).

3. They **must be followed by a verb** in the present tense and **never** by a مَصْدَر.

4. **Never** use أَنْ after these verbs!

5. They are all *sisters of* كَادَ which means that the same rules as for كانَ / كَادَ must be applied.

6. Since they are *sisters of* كَادَ, they have a predicate. The predicate (خَبَر) of these verbs is normally a verb in the present tense (الْمُضارِعُ).

Let's check some examples:

She began to cry.	أَخَذَتْ تَبْكِي.	1
She started to laugh.	شَرَعَتْ تَضْحَكُ.	2
The student **starts** answering the questions.	يَبْدَأُ الطَّالِبُ يُجِيبُ عَنِ الْأَسْئِلَةِ.	3

Notice: Here we use the present tense of بَدَأَ which means the concept of a شُرُوعٍ فِعْلُ. However, since يَبْدَأُ literally means to begin, the sentence still conveys the same meaning.

He starts to walk.	يَبْدَأُ الْمَشْيَ. 4

Wait! Didn't we say that you must use a verb after these verbs and never a مَصْدَرٍ? Yes, this is true. So what happened here? Well, we use بَدَأَ here not as a شُرُوعٍ فِعْلُ but as a regular, complete verb which means we simply use a direct object (مَفْعُولٌ بِهِ), i.e., the مَصْدَر of to walk (مَشَى).

104. When do you need to focus on agreement (الْمُطابَقَةُ)?

In basically four situations.

There are four different situations when a word has to correspond with a preceding word and needs agreement (مُطابَقَةٌ). We call them *followers* (تابِعٌ) in Arabic.

example		grammar term		
the nice student	الطالِبُ الجَمِيلُ	adjective	نَعْتٌ	1
the students, both of them	الطَّالِبانِ كِلاهُما	emphasis	تَأْكِيدٌ	2
these lawyers	هؤُلاء المُحامُونَ	apposition	بَدَلٌ	3
Khālid and Muhammad	خالِدٌ ومُحَمَّدٌ	conjunction	عَطْفٌ	4

What do we have to watch out for if we get one of the above situations?

Agreement in Arabic means to adjust 4 things:

1	Determination	definite (مَعْرِفةٌ) or indefinite (نَكِرةٌ)
2	Gender (جِنْسٌ)	masculine (مُذَكَّرٌ) or feminine (مُؤَنَّثٌ)
3	Number	singular (مُفْرَدٌ), dual (مُثَنَّى) or plural (جَمْعٌ)
4	Case (إِعْرابٌ)	Mirror the case of the word to which the word in question refers.

105. How do you express *me* in Arabic?

You use the word إِيّايَ.

The word looks strange. Grammatically speaking, إِيّايَ is the accusative form (مَنْصُوبٌ) of the personal pronoun *I* (أنا): *me*.

It is very rare to come across accusative (مَنْصُوبٌ) or genitive (مَجْرُورٌ) forms of personal pronouns. Why? Because you only use it if you are not allowed to use a pronoun suffix. This may happen, for example, after the particle *except* (إِلّا) – in the expression *without me*.

pronoun	explanation			مَنْصُوبٌ
I	Notice the فَتْحة above the last letter ي	*me*		إِيّايَ
he	Notice the ضَمّة above the last letter o	*him*		إِيّاهُ

translation	example	meaning	syntax	pronoun
except me	إِلّا إِيّايَ	*me*	إِيّايَ	أَنا
except you	إِلّا إِيّاكَ	*you*	إِيّاكَ	أَنْتَ

106. إِيَّاكَ نَعْبُدُ - What does it mean?

It means: It is You we worship.

The sentence is a part of verse 5 of the first sura (الْفَاتِحةُ) of the Qur'an. Grammatically speaking, إِيَّاكَ is the personal pronoun *you* in the accusative case (مَنْصُوبٌ) - see question #105.

It is You we worship and You we ask for help.	إِيَّاكَ نَعْبُدُ وَإِيَّاكَ نَسْتَعِينُ

Here, it is used to show the importance of the word *you* which is the reason why we use a stand-alone form (ضَمِيرٌ بَارِزٌ مُنْفَصِلٌ). This style is only used in literature or texts of very high quality. Since it is preceding the verb, it is a way to **emphasize** the word *you*. We achieve that by forwarding (تَقْدِيمٌ) the direct object. You could even change the word order and still, the meaning would be practically the same: نَعْبُدُ إِيَّاكَ

Watch out: If إِيَّا starts a sentence, and if a particular person is addressed, it may mean: *Beware of...* or *don't...*

(You!) Don't break the glass!	إِيَّاكَ أَلَّا تَكْسِرَ الْكُوبَ!
Note that the word أَلَّا is a combination of لا + أَنْ.	

Remark: The particle إِيَّا can express **with** if it is connected to و - a so-called *Wāw of concomitance* or *association* (واوُ الْمَعِيّةِ). See *Arabic for Nerds 2*, questions #144, #224, #355.

We go **with** her to the room.	نَذْهَبُ وَإِيَّاها إِلَى الْغُرْفةِ.

107. Do you always need أَنْ to connect two verbs?

No, this is not true.

Normally, you need the particle أَنْ to connect two verbs. In German, most verbs are connected directly (*Ich möchte gehen*). In English, most verbs are connected with *to* (*I want to go*). In English, we would call *to* a conjunction.

In Arabic, if you use أَنْ and add a verb in present tense, subjunctive mood (مَنْصُوبٌ), then we produce the meaning of a مَصْدَر – see *question #81*.

However, there are some Arabic verbs which may go along with other words without أَنْ. These verbs, unlike in English, are directly connected with the second verb. How is that possible? Well, it has to do with the so-called *circumstantial qualifier* (الْحالُ), because the second verb is describing the first verb. There is no problem to use a verbal sentence (جُمْلة فِعْلِيّةٌ) as a حال.

Let us look at this sentence:

She let him go.	تَرَكَتْهُ يَذْهَبُ.

Let us put all ingredients under the microscope.

First verb. The subject is a hidden, implied pronoun with the virtual meaning of: she.	تَرَكَتْ	1
This personal pronoun (*him*) is attached to the first verb. It is referring to the target person.	هُ	2
Remark: If there is no other person involved (if we talk about only one person in the entire sentence), then there is no need for a pronoun.		
The second verb has to be in the present tense (الْمُضارِعُ). In our example, it literally means: *he goes*.	يَذْهَبُ	3
The second verb has to be conjugated with respect to the preceding pronoun, which means in our example: 3rd person singular (*he*).		

Remark: All verbs that may express *to begin* (بَدَأَ), *keep on doing* (ما زالَ), and *to be close to do* (كادَ) don't need أَنْ.

Here are some examples:

1	to leave	تَرَكَ, يَتْرُكُ
	He let him writing.	تَرَكَهُ يَكْتُبُ.
2	to begin – see *question #103.*	بَدَأَ, يَبْدَأُ • اِبْتَدَأَ, يَبْتَدِئُ
	He began to work.	اِبْتَدَأَ يَعْمَلُ.
	He started to laugh.	راحَ يَضْحَكُ.
	He started to work.	قامَ يَعْمَلُ.
3	to continue	اِسْتَمَرَّ, يَسْتَمِرُّ
	He continued to work.	اِسْتَمَرَّ يَعْمَلُ.
4	to hear	سَمِعَ, يَسْمَعُ
	I heard him saying.	سَمِعْتُهُ يَقُولُ.
5	to find	وَجَدَ, يَجِدُ
	I found her sleeping.	وَجَدْتُها تَنامُ.
6	still doing	ما زالَ, لا يَزالُ
	He is still working.	ما زالَ يَعْمَلُ.
7	to do again	عادَ, يَعُودُ
	She is not working again.	ما عادَتْ تَعْمَلُ.

| 8 | to keep doing | بَقِيَ, يَبْقَى |
| | He kept stopping. | بَقِيَ يَقِفُ. |

| 9 | to see | رَأَى, يَرَى |
| | I saw him coming. | رَأَيْتُهُ يَأْتِي. |

| 10 | to watch | شاهَدَ, يُشاهِدُ |
| | She watched him going. | شاهَدَتْهُ يَذْهَبُ. |

108. After أَنْ, is it okay to use a verb in the past tense?

Yes, it is! But it is extremely rare.

You use such a construction occasionally if you want to para-
phrase the **past perfect** (pluperfect; *he had written*).

أَنْ here is a particle (حَرْفٌ مَصْدَرِيِّةٍ) that molds an interpreted
infinitive (مَصْدَر مُؤَوَّل).

- If you use a verb in the **present tense** after أَنْ, it has to be
  in the **subjunctive** mood (مَنْصُوبٌ) – which means it gets
  the final vowel "a".

- If you use a **past tense** verb, you don't need a marker –
  just use the regular past tense. You simply can't do that
  because past tense verbs have a **fixed** shape (مَبْنِيٌّ).

For example:

| I was happy that you (had) succeeded. | سَرَّنِي أَنْ نَجَحْتَ. |
| | = سَرَّنِي نَجاحُكَ. |

| Interpreted infinitive (مَصْدَر مُؤَوَّل), built with the help of a past tense verb. | أَنْ نَجَحْتَ |
| Original infinitive noun (مَصْدُر صَرِيحٌ) | نَجاحُكَ |

Watch out: After the words لَمَّا (*when; after*) and لَوْ (*if*), you might find the particle أَنْ followed by a past tense verb!

| I swear, if you studied, you would be respected. | أُقْسِمُ أَنْ لَوْ دَرَسْتَ لَاحْتُرِمْتَ. = أُقْسِمُ لَوْ دَرَسْتَ... |

109. *He gives it to me - How do you say that in Arabic?*

Sounds easy – but it is not. You need to deal with two objects.

The IV-verb أَعْطَى (*to give, to hand over*) can have two objects. This means that it can also have two pronominal objects.

- The first one is attached to the verb directly. In our example, this is the pronoun *me*.

- The second pronoun is detached from the word and is used with the particle إِيّا. In our example: *it*.

So we end up with the opposite structure compared to English, which is important to keep in mind if you translate.

- The **indirect** object (German: *Dativ*) in an English sentence is attached <u>directly</u> to the verb.

- The **direct** object in an English/German sentence is attached to إِيّا.

Some examples:

He gives it (masculine) to me.	يُعْطِينِي إِيَّاهُ.
He gives it (feminine) to me.	يُعْطِينِي إِيَّاها.
You (fem.) give it (e.g., the books) to him.	أَهْدَيْتِهِ إِيَّاها.
You (fem.) give it (e.g., the book) to her.	أَهْدَيْتِها إِيَّاهُ.

This works for all verbs that take two objects – see *quest. #110*.

110. Which verbs may carry two (direct) objects in Arabic?

Quite many.

In English or German, we regularly have a direct and an indirect object in a sentence. So what's the deal here?

The difference to other languages and other Arabic verbs is that you **don't use a preposition** (*to; with; for* – لِ or مَعَ) to include the second object.

In English, you can't have two direct objects. That is why the translation of verbs with two objects is often tricky, because you will end up with a *direct* and an *indirect object* (connected with a preposition, e.g., *with, to, as, for*).

In Arabic, there are **two groups** of verbs which may carry two objects (فِعْلٌ مُتَعَدٍّ إِلَى مَفْعُولَيْنِ):

GROUP I: The objects were originally the subject and predicate of a nominal sentence (جُمْلَةٌ اِسْمِيَّةٌ).

| 1 | **verbs of preponderance, superiority** | أَفْعالُ الرُّجْحانِ |

to think; to suppose	خَالَ - يَخَالُ حَسِبَ - يَحْسِبُ	ظَنَّ - يَظُنُّ	1
to allege		رَعَمَ - يَزْعُمُ	2

→ See also *question #112*.

2	**verbs of certainty**	أَفْعالُ الْيَقِينِ

to know; to perceive	رَأَى - يَرَى	to know	عَلِمَ - يَعْلَمُ
to regard; to consider	عَدَّ - يَعُدُّ	to find	وَجَدَ - يَجِدُ

3	**transmutative verbs**	أَفْعالُ التَّحْوِيلِ

to take (on)	اِتَّخَذَ - يَتَّخِذُ	to make; to reduce to	جَعَلَ - يَجْعَلُ

Some examples:

The teacher found the students present.	وَجَدَ الْمُدَرِّسُ الطُّلَّابَ حَاضِرِينَ.

1	First object (مَفْعُولٌ بِهِ أَوَّلُ)	الطُّلَّابَ
2	Second object (مَفْعُولٌ بِهِ ثانٍ)	حَاضِرِينَ

The second part was originally a nominal sentence (جُمْلَةٌ اِسْمِيَّةٌ):
The students are present (الطُّلَّابُ حَاضِرُونَ.)

The student thinks (that) his colleagues are present.	ظَنَّ الطَّالِبُ الزُّمَلاءَ مَوْجُودِينَ.
The student alleges that the grammar is difficult.	زَعَمَ الطَّالِبُ النَّحْوَ صَعْبًا.

People perceive knowledge as useful.	رَأَى النَّاسُ الْعِلْمَ نافِعًا.
The man found the door closed.	وَجَدَ الرَّجُلُ الْبابَ مُغْلَقًا.
The professor considered the answer as correct.	عَدَّ الْأُسْتاذُ الإِجابَة صَحيحَةً.
The goldsmith made a ring from gold.	جَعَلَ الصَّائِغُ الذَّهَبَ خاتَمًا.

GROUP II: The two objects did not (and could not) form a nominal sentence (جُمْلَةُ اِسمِيَّةٌ).

to grant; to donate	مَنَحَ - يَمْنَحُ	to dress	أَلْبَسَ - يُلْبِسُ	IV-verb
to ask for	سَأَلَ - يَسْأَلُ	to give	أَعْطَى - يُعْطِي	
to give sustenance	رَزَقَ - يَرْزُقُ	to nourish	أَطْعَمَ - يُطْعِمُ	

Let us try to understand this better by looking at an example:

The student gave his colleague a book.	أَعْطَى الطَّالِبُ زَميلَهُ كِتابًا.

This sentence fragment wouldn't make sense if it stood alone! → That's different to the verbs in group A.	زَميلُهُ كِتابٌ

Here are some more examples of group B:

The director granted the student a prize.	مَنَحَ الْمُديرُ الطَّالِبَ جائِزَةً.
The mother dressed her child with his clothes.	أَلْبَسَتِ الْأُمُّ طِفْلَها مَلابِسَهُ.
The student asked his colleague for help.	سَأَلَ الطَّالِبُ زَميلَهُ الْمُساعَدَةَ.

111. Are there verbs which may carry three objects?

Yes, there are.

In Arabic, there are verbs which may carry three (direct) objects (فِعْلٌ مُتَعَدٍّ إِلَى ثَلاثةِ مَفاعِيلَ). In English or German, you would build a subordinate clause (*Nebensatz*) which carries the information of the second and third object. Let us look at the following sentence:

He showed him that the car is nice.	أَراهُ السَّيارةَ جَمِيلةً.

him	**First object** (مَفْعُولٌ أَوَّلُ). The pronoun has a fixed shape (مَبْنِيٌّ عَلَى الضَّمِّ), but we say that it is located in the position of an accusative (فِي مَحَلِّ نَصْبٍ) since it is a direct object.	هُ
the car	**Second object** (مَفْعُولٌ ثانٍ) - it takes the accusative case (مَنْصُوبٌ).	السَّيارةَ
nice	**Third object** (مَفْعُولٌ ثالِثٌ) - also in the accusative case (مَنْصُوبٌ).	جَمِيلةَ

Here is another example:

She told him that Karim is lazy.	حَدَّثَتْهُ كَرِيمًا كَسُولًا.

Most of the verbs which may carry three objects convey the meaning of *to inform; show; to tell*. They are usually verbs of the II- or IV-stem.

to show	أَرَى - يُرِي		to tell	حَدَّثَ - يُحَدِّثُ
to inform	أَنْبَأَ - يُنْبِئُ		to let to know	أَعْلَمَ - يُعْلِمُ
to inform	أَخْبَرَ - يُخْبِرُ			

112. *I thought that...* - How do you express that in Arabic?

You should not translate it word by word.

There are many verbs in English or German which are usually followed by the word *that*. For example: *I assume that... I think that... I claim that... I believe that... I expect that...*

The verbs above are not followed by *that* (أَنَّ) in Arabic. Instead, you use **one or two direct objects.**

I thought **that** he is lazy.	زَعَمْتُهُ كَسُولًا.
Did you (f.) think **that** Fatima is his sister?	هَلْ خِلْتِ فاطِمَةَ أُخْتَهُ؟
I thought **that** the guy is present.	ظَنَنْتُ الرَّجُلَ مَوْجُودًا.

Here is a list of some verbs that work like that:

to proclaim	زَعَمَ - يَزْعُمُ	to assume	حَسِبَ - يَحْسِبُ
to think	ظَنَّ - يَظُنُّ	to deem	حَجا - يَحْجُو
to suppose	خالَ - يَخالُ	to find	أَلْفَى - يُلْفِي

113. Can an Arabic sentence start with the (actual) object?

Yes, it can. But we need some tuning.

Here is an example:

word order	meaning	example	
verb + subject + object	*The professor wrote the letter.*	كَتَبَ الأُسْتاذُ الرِّسالةَ.	1
object + verb + subject		الرِّسالةُ كَتَبَها الأُسْتاذُ.	2

Let us look at the construction. Note that we use the terms of the original sentence (number 1).

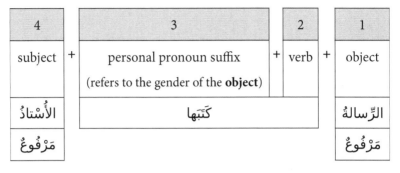

4		3	2		1
subject	+	personal pronoun suffix (refers to the gender of the **object**)	+ verb	+	object
الأُسْتاذُ مَرْفُوعٌ		كَتَبَها			الرِّسالةُ مَرْفُوعٌ

If you want to give the listener a hint that the first word is not the actual subject (but the object!), you may pause after the object – with the effect that the verb, which comes after it, is automatically stressed.

Excursus: You also have to add a pronoun at the end of the verb if you have a sentence with a *relative pronoun* (اِسْمٌ مَوْصُولٌ). Let's quickly go over the major forms of الَّذِي.

	masc.	feminine
singular	الَّذِي	الَّتِي
dual nominative (مُثَنَّى مَرْفُوعٌ)	اللَّذانِ	اللَّتانِ
dual acc. (مَنْصُوبٌ) and genitive (مَجْرُورٌ)	اللَّذَيْنِ	اللَّتَيْنِ
plural (جَمْعٌ)	الَّذِينَ	اللَّوَاتِي / اللَّائِي

Now what about the pronoun? You need it to link the relative clause to the main word to which it refers. See *Arabic for Nerds 2, question #74.*

The book that/which I knew...	...الْكِتابُ الَّذِي عَرَفْتُهُ

114. *A man who went...* - How do you say that in Arabic?

In no case with a relative clause.

Non-native Arabic speakers often translate sentences like our example (*A man who went...*) word by word – and fall into a grammatical trap:

> In Arabic, you **can't** link a relative pronoun (الَّذِي) to an **indefinite** word.

Let's see what it is all about.

NOT possible	Such sentences do not work in Arabic.	1 رَجُلٌ الَّذِي ذَهَبَ...
		...رَجُلٌ مَنْ ذَهَبَ...
CORRECT	This sentence works, however, it means: **The** man who went...	2 الرَّجُلُ الَّذِي ذَهَبَ...

So, how do you express: *A man who went...*?

Answer: رَجُلٌ ذَهَبَ. But there is a problem. In Arabic, without knowing the context, such a sentence could express several things. You need to understand the context. Here are some possible translations:

1	**A** man went...	
	A man, he went...	رَجُلٌ ذَهَبَ.
2	**A** man **who/that** went...	

Another example:

A man, who also went to Austria, called me.	رَجُلٌ ذَهَبَ أَيْضًا إِلَى النَّمْسا اتَّصَلَ بِي .

115. *One student* - How do you say that in Arabic?

You only use the number *one* if you want to stress that you really mean only one. Otherwise, you may use the indefinite article – which is express in Arabic by nunation (تَنْوِينْ). What is the difference between the definite and indefinite article?

The difference between definite and indefinite refers to whether the information in the noun phrase is shared by the speaker and the listener. If you call your friend and tell him: *Bring **the** book tomorrow*, then you indicate that you want a particular book, and that your friend knows which one. If you tell him *Bring **a** book*, your friend could bring any title. If you want to stress that your friend should only bring **one** book or **some book** (German: *irgendein*), you add the number.

In English, the word *one* is a word which always stays the same, no matter what the position or function in the sentence is. In Arabic, we have to words: أَحَدُ (*one unit*) and واحِدْ.

- أَحَدْ (masculine form) and إِحْدَى (feminine). They both serve as the first part of a إِضافة-construction.

- واحِدْ and واحِدةٌ (f.) are used as adjectives (صِفةٌ) and are placed after the main word. Or you use them with مِنْ. Usually they are used if you want to stress the meaning *one* or want to express *a single one*.

the student	A particular student.	الطّالِبُ
a student	It could be any student.	طالِبٌ
one student	أَحَد + definite plural	أَحَدُ الطُّلّابِ
	singular noun + واحِد	طالِبٌ واحِدٌ
one (f.) student	إِحْدَى + def. feminine plural	إِحْدَى الطّالِباتِ

	singular noun + واحِدة	طالِبةٌ واحِدةٌ
one of the students	واحِدٌ + definite plural form	واحِدٌ مِن الطُّلّابِ

But **which gender is our reference** for أَحَدٌ or إِحْدَى when we have a more complex construction? In other words, when they are placed as the predicate (خَبَرٌ). It is up to you: You can use harmonize them with the subject (مُبْتَدَأ) or with the second part of the إِضافة-construction (مُضافٌ إِلَيْهِ).

Money is one of two happi-nesses.	الْمالُ أَحَدُ السَّعادَتَيْنِ.	**Both are**
	الْمالُ إِحْدَى السَّعادَتَيْنِ.	**correct**

Watch out:

- واحِدٌ may be used in a **negative** or **positive** sense.

- أَحَدٌ, however, if it is used as a single word (*anyone, one, someone*) and not in a إِضافة-construction, is only used to convey a **negative** context. In other words, if there is a negation in the sentence, you use أَحَدٌ. In Arabic litera-ture, أَحَدٌ is <u>hardly ever</u> used in a positive sense – except in the Qur'an with reference to Allah.

Say, He is Allah, [who is] One... (*Sura 112:1*)	...قُلْ هُوَ اللهُ أَحَدٌ.

However, if you place أَحَدٌ as the first part of a إِضافة and add another word, it can be used in a **positive** sense as well. It then conveys *one of*...

one of the travelers	أَحَدُ الْمُسافِرِينَ

Some examples.

There is **no one** present.	لَيْسَ أَحَدٌ مَوْجُودًا.	1
I haven't hit **anyone**.	لَمْ أَضْرِبْ أَحَدًا.	
I don't know **anyone**.	لا أَعْرِفُ أَحَدًا.	
There is **someone** present.	مَوْجُودٌ واحِدٌ.	2
In don't want **a single** word from you.	لا أُرِيدُ مِنْكَ كَلِمةً واحِدةً.	

- Never **combine** أَحَدٌ and مِنْ. Why? Because both words indicate a vague number. You can only use one of them.

	correct	مِن الْأَسْبابِ	1
one reason		أَحَدُ الْأَسْبابِ	2
	incorrect	مِنْ أَحَدِ الْأَسْبابِ	3

116. Is there a German *man* (*one*) in Arabic?

Yes, there is.

The German word *man* (which has nothing to do with the English word *man*) is an indefinite pronoun. It is the 58th most common word in German. It refers to one or more people with an unspecified identity. The translation depends on the context: *one, someone, a person, you, they, people.* Also the passive voice in English may fit.

In Arabic, you usually don't need to translate the German *man,* the French *on,* or the English *one.*

It is said that... (**Man sagt, dass...**)	...يُقالُ إنَّ...	1
Here, you use the passive voice of قالَ-يَقُولُ		

As they say... (*Wie **man** sagt...*)	...كَما يَقُولُونَ	2
Here, like in English, you use the third person plural (they)		
One could say... (***Man** kann sagen...*)	...يُمْكِنُ الْقَوْلُ	3
Here you use the IV-verb *to be possible* (أَمْكَنَ-يُمْكِنُ)		
It is generally believed that... (***Man** ist allgemein der Meinung, dass...*)	يُجْمِعُ النّاسُ عَلَى...	4
Here you use the word *people* (النّاسُ) with the verb *to agree unanimously* (أَجْمَعَ-يُجْمِعُ).		
One has to... (***Man** muss...*)	ـمِن الْواجِبِ...	5
This is a common construction. We will examine it in *question #117*.		
Common rumor has it (***Man** munkelt, dass...*)	شاعَتْ الشّائِعةُ أَنَّ/حَوْلَ	6
Lit. meaning: *the rumor is circulating, spread...*		

However, there is also another way. You may encounter it in literature and in the Qur'an.

		fem.	masc.
1	*Men* or *women* (in general). The masculine form equals more or less the English *one* or the German *man*.	مَرْأَةُ الْمَرأةُ	مَرْءٌ الْمَرْءُ
	Plural form:	نِساءُ	not used (مَرْءُونَ)

2	If you talk about a *man* or a *woman* in particular.	اِمْرَأَةٌ	اِمْرُؤٌ

Notice: If اِمْرُؤٌ starts the sentence, you have to pronounce the first letter as a glottal stop – *Hamza of rupture* (هَمْزَةُ وَصْلٍ). So you actually say اِمْرُؤٌ. The same is true for اِمْرَأَةُ.	

Some examples:

One cannot…	...ـ لا يَسْتَطِيعُ الْمَرْءُ
One would think....	...ـ يَظُنُّ الْمَرْءُ
Know that God comes between a man and his heart, and that you will be gathered to Him. *(Sura 8:24)*	وَاعْلَمُوا أَنَّ اللهَ يَحُولُ بَيْنَ الْمَرْءِ وَقَلْبِهِ.
Does every one of them expect to enter a Garden of bliss? *(Sura 70:38)*	أَيَطْمَعُ كُلُّ امْرِئٍ مِّنْهُمْ أَن يُدْخَلَ جَنَّةَ نَعِيمٍ.
I found a woman ruling over them. *(Sura 27:23)*	إِنِّي وَجَدْتُ امْرَأَةً تَمْلِكُهُمْ.

117. *One must...* - How do you say that in Arabic?

There are several ways to express that.

It is a quite tricky in Arabic as you don't use a verb. Let us see how it works:

It is necessary to = one must	مِن الْواجِبِ (عَلَيْهِ) أَنْ	1
You use the active participle (اِسْمُ فاعِلٍ) of the verb *to be necessary* (وَجَبَ - يَجِبُ عَلَى).		

You (one) must write.	مِنَ الْواجِبِ عَلَيْكَ أَنْ تَكْتُبَ.

it is someone's duty = one must	مِن اللّازِمِ (عَلَيْهِ) أَنْ	2

You use the active participle (اِسْمُ فاعِلٍ) of the verb *to be some-one's duty* (لَزِمَ - يَلْزَمُ عَلَى).

You (one) must write.	مِن اللّازِمِ عَلَيْكَ أَنْ تَكْتُبَ.

it is necessary, inescapable, unavoidable that	لا بُدَّ (مِن) أَنْ	3

- The word بُدّ means *escape* or *way out*.

- The لا is a device for the *generic negation* or *complete denial* (لا النَّافِيةُ لِلْجِنْسِ). It intervenes in the nominal sentence and puts the following word into the **accusative** case (مَنْصُوبٌ); so you have to put a فَتْحة on بُدّ (see *question #248*).

- لا بُدَّ thus denotes *definitely, certainly; by all means.*

- لا بُدَّ مِنْ has the meaning of: *it is necessary; inevitable.*

- لا بُدَّ is normally followed by a prepositional or adverbial phrase.

- The preposition مِن may be put between بُدَّ and أَنْ, how-ever, it is usually omitted.

- Notice: أَنْ and أَنَّ are sometimes preceded by the conjunc-tion وَ (last example).

You (one) must write to succeed.	لا بُدَّ (مِن) أَنْ تَكْتُبَ كَيْ تَنْجَحَ.
He simply must do it.	لا بُدَّ لَهُ مِنْهُ.
One must be alert.	لا بُدَّ مِنَ التَّنْبِيهِ.

| She must have told him something. | لاَ بُدَّ أَنْ تَكُونَ قَدْ قَالَتْ لَهُ شَيْئًا. |

| No doubt he is here. | لا بُدَّ وَأَنَّهُ مَوْجُودٌ. |

to be necessary to (وَجَبَ - يَجِبُ)	يَجِبُ أَنْ	4
You (one) must write.	يَجِبُ عَلَيْكَ أَنْ تَكْتُبَ.	

118. خِدْمَةٌ (*service*) - What is the Arabic plural of this word?

The easiest way is a sound feminine plural.

But is it really that easy? Well, we will see. The building of a sound feminine plural (جَمْعُ الْمُؤَنَّثِ السّالِمُ) is done by adding ات. Now comes the more difficult part. What about the correct vowels? Is it: خَدَماتٌ or خِدْماتٌ or خِدَماتٌ or خَدْماتٌ؟

Many native Arab speakers say خَدَماتٌ – but is this form correct? Let us check all options of **sound feminine plurals**.

Pattern: فَعْلَةٌ	1
a) First letter has a فَتْحَة.	
b) Second letter (root letter in the middle) has a سُكُونٌ.	
c) Second root letter is not a weak letter.	
d) → The سُكُون is replaced by a فَتْحَة in the plural. (**Remark:** If there is a weak letter, the سُكُون remained.)	

rings	حَلَقَاتٌ	حَلْقَةٌ		views	نَظَرَاتٌ	نَظْرَةٌ

Pattern: فُعْلَةٌ or فِعْلَةٌ	2

e) First letter has a ضَمّةٌ or كَسْرةٌ.

- Second root letter is not a weak letter

Then, you have three options:

a) you can put a سُكُون on the second letter;

b) you can put a فَتْحة on the second letter;

c) or you use the first vowel, copy it and put it also on the second letter.

meaning	option (c)	option (b)	option (a)	singular
services	خِدِماتٌ	خِدَماتٌ	خِدْماتٌ	خِدْمَةٌ
rooms	حُجُراتٌ	حُجَراتٌ	حُجْراتٌ	حُجْرَةٌ

Eventually, it is a matter of taste. You can choose – but don't say what many people say: خَدَماتٌ! It is wrong.

Don't forget that a sound feminine plural (definite **and** indefinite) takes كَسْرةٌ in the accusative (مَنْصُوبٌ) and never فَتْحة.

I bought chicken.	اِشْتَرَيْتُ دَجاجاتٍ.

119. *He jumped like a tiger. - How do you say that in Arabic?*

The most elegant way is to use a special type of the مَصْدَر.

If you want to describe how somebody did an action, for example, *he jumped like a tiger*, you can use a certain paradigm in Arabic.

It is called اِسْمُ هَيْئَةٍ or مَصْدَرُ هَيْئَةٍ and comes from the word هَيْئَةٌ which means *form, shape, condition*. It describes a **noun of manner** and may be rendered into English as **in the manner of** or in **the way of (to)**. E.g., *in the manner of walking* (مِشْيَةٌ).

- If you want to produce such type of noun, take the root and fill it into the pattern فِعْلَةُ.

- You can only form it from standard **triliteral verbs** (فِعْلٌ ثُلاثِيٌّ مُجَرَّدٌ) which means that their past tense form consists of only three letters. Therefore, this form is **only possible for I-verbs** (stem I فَعَلَ).

- You need a إضافة-construction to express the missing part of *way of* ... Thus, you place the اِسْمُ هَيْئَةٍ as the first part of the إضافة, the so-called مُضافٌ.

- Since it serves as an object of the verb, it has to be in the accusative case (مَنْصُوبٌ).

He jumped like a tiger. Lit.: He jumped *the jump in the way* of the tiger.	قَفَزَ اللّاعِبُ قِفْزَةَ النَّمِرِ.
I ate like someone who is hungry.	أَكَلْتُ إِكْلَةَ الْجائِعِ.
The mother looked at the child with a glance of love.	تَظْهَرَتِ الأُمُّ إِلَى طِفْلِها نِظْرَةَ الْحُبِّ.

Watch out: The اِسْمُ هَيْئَةٍ looks very similar to the *noun of one act* (اِسْمُ مَرّةٍ.) Only the pronunciation is different! It is فِعْلَةُ ("fi3la") and not فَعْلَةُ ("fa3la")!

120. *To eat three times* - How do you say that in Arabic?

You use a special pattern of the noun.

Let's have a look at the following two sentences:

قَفَزَ اللَّاعِبُ قَفْزًا.	1
قَفَزَ اللَّاعِبُ قَفْزَةً.	2

What is the difference? The first two words are the same and mean *the player jumped*. So what about the object? First of all, both sentences are correct, but the meaning is different.

In Arabic, there is a way to **emphasize** if a person has done...

A.   ...something in general.

You use the **standard** مَصْدَر and place it after the verb as the *absolute, inner object* (مَفْعُولٌ مُطْلَقٌ) - *see question #122*. It emphasizes the core meaning of the action (verb). You don't know how often the action was done.

The player jumped (vigorously).	قَفَزَ اللَّاعِبُ قَفْزًا.

B.   ...something only once or a certain amount of times.

You use a **special type** of the مَصْدَر – the so-called *noun of one act* (اِسْمُ مَرَّةٍ). It denotes that the action was done only one time – however, by using a number, you can adjust the amount of times.

How do you build it? You use the pattern فَعْلَةٌ. You can easily recognize this form – it is the مَصْدَر plus ة. The plural is built by the usual pattern for feminine nouns: ات. Since it serves as an object of the verb, it has to be in the accusative (مَنْصُوبٌ).

The player jumped <u>once</u>.	قَفَزَ اللَّاعِبُ قَفْزَةً

Let us look at some examples:

I ate in this restaurant **once**. (only/exactly one time)	أَكَلْتُ فِي هٰذا الْمَطْعَمِ أَكْلَةً.
I ate in this restaurant. (unknown how often)	أَكَلْتُ فِي هٰذا الْمَطْعَمِ أَكْلًا.
I ate in this restaurant 3 times.	أَكَلْتُ فِي هٰذا الْمَطْعَمِ ثَلاثَ أَكَلاتٍ.*

The player jumped.	قَفَزَ اللَّاعِبُ قَفْزًا.
The player jumped once.	قَفَزَ اللَّاعِبُ قَفْزَةً.
The player jumped two times. (dual!)	قَفَزَ اللَّاعِبُ قَفْزَتَيْنِ.
The player jumped three times.	قَفَزَ اللَّاعِبُ ثَلاثَ قَفَزاتٍ.*

The child smiled (one time only).	إِبْتَسَمَ الطِّفْلُ إِبْتِسامَةً.
The child smiled (unknown how often).	إِبْتَسَمَ الطِّفْلُ إِبْتِسامًا.

* You have two options for the plural: قَفَزات or قَفْزات. The same is true for أَكْلات or أَكَلات.

Remark: What happens if the standard مَصْدَر looks like the إِسْمُ الْمَرَّةِ? Let's see.

verb	إِسْمُ مَرَّةٍ	explanation
to call (دَعا)	دَعْوَةٌ واحِدَةٌ *one call*	As the regular مَصْدَر of the verb is دَعْوَةٌ, you need to add a word (number) to make clear that you emphasize the amount of times.
to have mercy (رَحِمَ)	رَحْمَةٌ واحِدَةٌ *having compassion one time*	Same here: The standard مَصْدَر of the verb looks like the إِسْمُ الْمَرَّةِ which is رَحْمَةٌ. You need additional information to indicate that you put the stress on the amount of times.

121. What does لَسْتُ بِفاهِمٍ mean?

It means: I don't understand, really.

In our example, the preposition بـ is **extra/additional** (حَرْف زائِدٌ or حَرْفُ زِيادةٍ) and just there to emphasize the meaning.

However, since there is the preposition بـ involved, the indefinite word فاهِمٍ gets كَسْرة (plus nunation: "*-in*") because after a preposition, a noun has to be genitive (مَجْرُورٌ).

Regarding the grammar, the expression فاهِم is still placed in the location of the **predicate** (خَبَرُ لَيْسَ) which means that it actually needs to be in the accusative case (مَنْصُوبٌ). Since the preposition drags the word into the genitive case, we can only assign a place value (فِي مَحَلِّ نَصْبٍ) for the accusative case.

Let us see the difference:

Without the preposition (without emphasizing) the sentence means *I don't understand*.	لَسْتُ **فاهِمًا**.	1
فاهِمًا is مَنْصُوبٌ because it is the predicate لَيْسَ.		
I don't understand, really.	لَسْتُ بِفاهِمٍ.	2
Here, فاهِمٍ is مَجْرُورٌ because of بِ.		

122. What is an *absolute object* (مَفْعُولٌ مُطْلَقٌ)?

It confirms or strengthens the action.

The infinitive in Arabic (مَصْدَرٌ) speaks of an action without any regard to the subject or the circumstances of time and mood under which it takes place.

Let us check the literal meaning of مُطْلَقٌ.

It is the passive participle (اِسْمُ مَفْعُولٍ) of the IV-verb أَطْلَقَ which denotes *to undo; to set free*. Thus, مُطْلَقٌ means *free; unlimited, unrestricted (without exception), absolute (in any respect, under any circumstances); general; stark or perfect*. That is also probably the main reason why the term مَفْعُولٌ مُطْلَقٌ is usually translated as *absolute object*.

With an *absolute object* you can emphasize an action. Here is how you use it. You need two steps:

1. Take the verb and build the مَصْدَر.

2. Add the مَصْدَر as the object of a sentence.

You will eventually find the verb and its مَصْدَر in the same sentence. For English speakers, this sounds like a redundancy. But in Arabic, it works perfectly fine to emphasize the meaning this way, and it is used a lot.

The مَفْعُولٌ مُطْلَقٌ occurs only in three forms:

translation	example	type of مَصْدَر	
extraction	مُسْتَخْرَجًا	مَصْدَرٌ مِيمِيٌّ	1
thankfulness	شُكْرًا	مَصْدَرٌ أَصْلِيٌّ	2
shot, strike	ضَرْبَةً	اِسْمُ مَرَّةٍ	3

There are two ways to use the مَفْعُولٌ مُطْلَقٌ for **emphasis**:

1. For **confirmation** (تَأْكِيدٌ).

I (definitely) hit Zayd.	ضَرَبْتُ زَيْدًا ضَرْبًا.

2. For further **specification** (تَحْدِيدٌ).

I hit Zayd hard / slightly.	ضَرَبْتُ زَيْدًا ضَرْبًا شَدِيدًا / خَفِيفًا.

Watch out:

In the location of a مَفْعُولٌ مُطْلَقٌ, sometimes the original مَصْدَر is substituted by another expression. This means: You don't write the مَصْدَر of the verb but choose something else. The meaning is implicitly understood – and the idea to give emphasis remains.

Let us check examples of possible representatives of the مَصْدَر. We call them نَائِبٌ عَن الْمَفْعُولِ الْمُطْلَقِ.

	original sentence	example of a substitute
1	فَرِحْتُ بِالنَّجاحِ فَرَحًا.	فَرِحْتُ بِالنَّجاحِ سُرُورًا.

Meaning: *I am **really** glad/delighted about the success.*

A synonym (مُرادِفٌ) for *happiness* (سُرُورًا) is used instead of the original الْمَفْعُولُ الْمُطْلَق – which is فَرَحًا.

2	تَكَلَّمَ الْخَطِيبُ تَكَلُّمًا حَسَنًا.	تَكَلَّمَ الْخَطِيبُ كَلَامًا حَسَنًا.

Meaning: *The speaker talked **very well**.*

Here, we use another form of the مَصْدَر, the *noun of origin* (اِسْمُ الْمَصْدَرِ), which is easier to pronounce – see *question #82*.

3	رَجَعَ الْجَيْشُ رُجُوعَ الْقَهْقَرَى.	رَجَعَ الْجَيْشُ الْقَهْقَرَى.

Meaning: *The army moved **back**.*

The word الْقَهْقَرَى already means *backward movement*, so the result is the same (نَوْعٌ مِن أَنْواعِهِ).

4	وَثَبَ الْقِطُّ وُثُوبَ النَّمِرِ.	وَثَبَ الْقِطُّ وِثْبَةَ النَّمِرِ.

Meaning: *The (male) cat jumped **like** a tiger.*

Here, we use the *noun of manner* (اِسْمُ الْهَيْئةِ) instead of the original مَصْدَر to describe how the cat jumped. Notice the difference between the *noun of one time* (فَ <- first vowel is "a": اِسْمُ الْمَرَّةِ) and the *noun of manner* (فِ <- first vowel is "i": اِسْمُ الْهَيْئةِ).

5	فَهِمْتُ الدَّرْسَ فَهْمًا أَيَّ فَهْمٍ.	فَهِمْتُ الدَّرْسَ أَيَّ فَهْمٍ.

Meaning: *I **totally** understood the lesson.*

Here, we use a إِضافة-construction with أَيّ.

6	فَهِمْتُ الدَّرْسَ الْفَهْمَ كُلَّهُ.	فَهِمْتُ الدَّرْسَ كُلَّ الْفَهْمِ.

Meaning: *I **completely** understood the lesson.*

Here, we use a إِضافة-construction with كُلّ.

7	فَهِمْتُ الدَّرْسَ الْفَهْمَ بَعْضَهُ.	فَهِمْتُ الدَّرْسَ بَعْضَ الْفَهْمِ.

Meaning: *I understood **some parts** of the lesson.*

Here, we use a إِضافة-construction with بَعْض.

8	فَهِمْتُ الدَّرْسَ فَهْمًا أَحْسَنَ الْفَهْمِ.	فَهِمْتُ الدَّرْسَ أَحْسَنَ الْفَهْمِ.

Meaning: *I understood the lesson **as best as** I can.*

Here, we use a special إِضافة-construction with a comparative/superlative (اِسْمُ تَفْضيلٍ).

9	فَهِمْتُ الدَّرْسَ فَهْمًا جَيِّدًا.	فَهِمْتُ الدَّرْسَ جَيِّدًا.

Meaning: *I understood the lesson **well**.* Here, we use a word that was originally attached as an **adjective** (صِفةٌ) to the مَصْدَرُ.

10	قَفَزَ اللَّاعِبُ قَفَزاتٍ ثَلاثًا.	قَفَزَ اللَّاعِبُ ثَلاثَ قَفَزاتٍ.

Meaning: *The player jumped **three times***. Here, we have changed the sentence into a normal sentence with a number (عَدَدٌ).

11	سَقَيْتُ الظَّمْآنَ سَقْيَ كُوبٍ.	سَقَيْتُ الظَّمْآنَ كُوبًا.

Meaning: *I gave the thirsty person **a cup***.

Here, we use the tool or mean (آلة, وَسِيلة) that is connected with the مَصدَرٌ and can substitute it.

12	لَيْتَكَ تُعامِلُني مَعامَلَةً هٰذِهِ الْمُعامَلةِ.	لَيْتَكَ تُعامِلُني هٰذِهِ الْمُعامَلةِ.

Meaning: *I wish you'd treat me **like** that*.

Here, we use a demonstrative noun (اِسْمُ إِشارةٍ) instead of the original مَصْدَر.

→ For an in-depth-analysis, see also *Arabic for Nerds 2, question #324.*

123. *Why not?* - How do you say that in Arabic?

You say: لِمَ لا؟

Let us start with a common mistake:

Doesn't really make sense (in grammar) unless the context is clear and you dropped the verb because it is implicitly understood.	*Why not?*	لِماذا لا؟
Better style. لِمَ is the short version of لِما		لِمَ لا؟

As a rule we could say that you should only use لِماذا

- if there is a **verb** in the sentence, similar to the interrogative particle لِماذا (see *question #25*);

- if you need an **amplifier** – to emphasize (ex. 4 below).

The word لِماذا is a compound (كَلِمَةٌ مُرَكَّبَةٌ) of:

demonstrative noun ذا (*this*)	+	interrogative ما (*what*)	+	preposition لِ (*for*); denotes cause
ذَا الْإِشَارِيَّةِ		مَا الْإِسْتِفْهَامِيَّةِ		لَامُ التَّعْلِيلِ

What's (why) the hurry?	لِمَ الْعَجَلَةُ؟	1
Why all this fear?	لِمَ كُلُّ هٰذا الْخَوْفِ؟	2
Why do you laugh? Note: We have a verb!	لِماذا تَضْحَكُ؟	3
Why (on earth)???	لِماذا؟؟؟	
Note: Here we have actually a nominal sentence: *This* (ذا) *is what for* (لِما). The word ما is the forwarded predicate (خَبَرٌ مُقَدَّمٌ) and ذا is the subject (مُبْتَدَأٌ).		4

Note: For a grammatical analysis of sentences with ماذا, see *Arabic for Nerds 2, question #161.*

The interrogative *why not* can also be introduced by the word هَلَّا. Watch out: It can also denote *isn't...* or *doesn't...?* since it is actually built from the expression: هَلْ لا.

Why wasn't that possible?	هَلَّا كانَ هٰذا مُمْكِنًا؟
Wouldn't you like to sit down? With the second person, هَلَّا may express a polite request.	هَلَّا جَلَسْتَ؟

124. Why do you write دَعا (with I) but مَشَى (with ى)?

It has to do with the root.

The verb مَشَى means *to walk* and دَعا *to call*. The pronunciation of both last letters is the same: *"a"*. So how can you know the correct spelling of the last letter?

As always, you have to think about the root. For this, you have to build the **present tense** (الْمُضارِعُ):

translation	الْمُضارِعُ	root	verb
to call, invite	يَدْعُو	د-ع-و	دَعا
to walk	يَمْشِي	م-ش-ي	مَشَى

Here are the rules:

- If you have و in the root – write ا at the end.
- If you have ي in the root – write ى.

125. *Barely, hardly* - How do you express that in Arabic?

Not by a single word. You need a work-around.

As in most languages, often the simple words are the ones which give you a headache if you want to translate them.

In Arabic this is true for the words *barely* or *hardly*.

There are many ways in Arabic to express the idea that a statement is true to an insignificant degree.

1	Use قَلَّما plus verb (any tense).
The director hardly went to the office.	قَلَّما ذَهَبَ الْمُدِيرُ إِلَى الْمَكْتَبِ.

2	Use قَلَّما plus أَنْ plus verb in the subjunctive mood (مَنْصُوبٌ).
I hardly study.	قَلَّما أَنْ أَدْرُسَ.

3	Use نادِرًا ما plus verb (any tense).
The director hardly went to the office.	نادِرًا ما ذَهَبَ الْمُدِيرُ إِلَى الْمَكْتَبِ.

4	Use نادِرًا plus ما plus أَنْ plus verb/subjunctive mood (مَنْصُوبٌ).
I hardly study.	نادِرًا ما أَنْ أَدْرُسَ.

5	Use لَمْ plus يَكَدْ plus present tense verb (فِعْلُ مُضارِعٌ). Watch out: You need to adjust the verb form (يَكَدْ) according to the person which talks. يَكَدْ is the 3rd person singular (*he*).
I could hardly hear. (*see question #97*)	لَمْ أَكَدْ أَسْمَعُ.

126. How many things can the letter ل express?

Some people say 10, some 12, some claim there are 40!

During the Abbasid Caliphate (ٱلْخِلافَةُ ٱلْعَبّاسِيَّةُ), which lasted from 750 (132 AH) to 1258 (656 AH), entire books were published in which the function of the letter لام were analyzed. Al-Zajjājī (ٱلزَّجّاجِي), a well-known Persian-born grammarian (892-952 CE), distinguishes thirty-one types of the letter لام.

The letter ل is probably the most powerful and sophisticated Arabic letter. It can denote many things: *to*; *because*; *I swear by*; *in view of*; *indeed*; *so that, that*; *then*; *with*, etc.

Around half of the applications of the letter ل are very common. For example: The ل is used as a **short form of إِلَى** when talking about **directions**. It may express **possession**. ل can also be used to express an aim: *in order to* (German: *um zu*):

I went to Egypt to study Arabic.	ذَهَبْتُ إِلَى مِصْرَ لِدِراسَةِ اللُّغةِ الْعَرَبِيّةِ.

It may be used to express **astonishment** (تَعَجُّبٌ) - in the latter application, ل takes فَتْحةٌ. This can happen in other situations too: If a (regular) لِ is followed by a pronoun, the ل may also take a فَتْحةٌ instead, for example, *to/for him* (لَهُ).

Let us look at some sentences. Note that in the examples, the letter ل is not a preposition! It is used to emphasize (لامُ التَّأْكِيدِ) a word. The ل is usually not translated, but you could translate it as *indeed* if you want to put stress on something.

The pollution is *(indeed)* harmful.	إِنَّ التَّلَوُّثَ لَمُضِرٌّ.
The solution of this problem is *(indeed)* very easy.	إِنَّ حَلَّ هذِهِ الْمُشْكِلةِ لَسَهْلٌ جِدًّا.
You are *(indeed)* a clever student.	إِنَّكَ لَطالِبٌ زَكِيٌّ.

- The ل has a فَتْحةٌ on top of it and is pronounced *"la"*. You have to be very careful when you hear a text or speech because you might confuse it with a negation! The negation, of course, is written with a long vowel: لا (*"lā"*).

- **Watch out:** ل <u>doesn't induce any case ending</u> on any word (اللَّامُ غَيْرُ الْعامِلةِ). A following noun (اِسْمٌ) is in the nominative case (مَرْفُوعٌ).

- A hint: If you have to do the إعْراب and put case endings on the words of a sentence, read it as if the letter ل was not there.

It is essential to know the different forms of ل if you want to avoid any mistranslation. Let us look at the most important applications. They offer a playground for enthusiasts:

1	ل having a slight meaning of بَعْدَ (*after*).

Fast when you see it (the new moon), and stop fasting when you see it (the new moon). *(Hadith: Saḥīḥ Muslim 1081)*	صُومُوا لِرُؤْيَتِهِ، وَأَفْطِرُوا لِرُؤْيَتِهِ.

2	The ل to **strengthen** the meaning (تَقْوِيةٌ). This ل is put before the **object**. This ل takes a كَسْرة and the word after it is in the genitive case (مَجْرُورٌ). It is an extra, additional preposition.

Mastering your work is your duty.	إِتْقانُكَ لِلْعَمَلِ واجِبٌ عَلَيْكَ.
Of course I beat Zayd.	لَزَيْدٌ ضَرَبْتُ.

3	The ل that induces the **jussive mood** (اللَّامُ الْجازِمـةُ لِلْفِعْـلِ). This ل is mostly used in the **imperative** (أَمْرٌ). This type of ل has كَسْرة and the verb after it is in the jussive mood (مَجْزُومٌ). Grammarians also call this type *Lām of request* (لامُ الأَمْرِ) or *Lām of the imperative* (لامُ الطَّلَبِ).

Be a responsible man!	لِتَكُنْ مَسْؤُولًا!
Let us (two) be friends!	لِتَكُنْ صَدِيقَيْنِ!
Watch out: If the ل is used after فَ or وَ, then the ل takes a سُكُون. You say: "faltakun".	فَلْتَكُنْ صَدِيقَيْنِ!

---

4 | The ل that induces the **subjunctive mood** (اللَّامُ النَّاصِبَةُ لِلْفِعْلِ الْمُضَارِعِ). This type is also called *Lām of denial* (لام الْجُحُودِ) or *Lām of negation* (لام النَّفْي). It is a *Lām* with "i" (كَسْرةٌ): لِ.

Let us see how it works:

- Step 1 and 2: First of all, you have to use a negated form of كَانَ at the beginning of the sentence.

- Step 3: Then put لِ.

- Step 4 and 5: The verb after ل has to be in the present tense (الْمُضارِعُ), subjunctive mood (مَنْصُوبٌ).

- All this together conveys the meaning of *something that is totally impossible*. It confirms the negative verb *to be*.

Here is the formula:

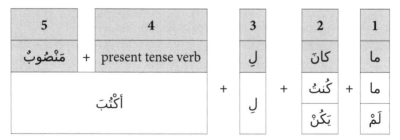

5		4	3	2	1
مَنْصُوبٌ	+	present tense verb	لِ	كَانَ	ما
أَكْتُبَ			+ لِ	+ كُنْتُ / يَكُنْ	ما / لَمْ

Let us check some examples of the *Lām of denial* (لام الْجُحُودِ).

I was not a tyrant to people.	لَمْ أَكُنْ لِأَظْلِمَ النَّاسَ

I didn't know that.	لَمْ أَكُنْ لِأَعْرَفَ ذَلِكَ.
This student didn't neglect his studies.	ما كانَ هذا الطَّالِبُ لِيُهْمِلَ دُرُوسَهُ.
I (indeed, truly) didn't neglect my studies. (pronunciation: "li'uhmila")	ما كُنْتُ لِأُهْمِلَ دُرُوسِي.
Zayd was not late for the lecture.	لَمْ يَكُنْ زَيْدٌ لِيَتَأَخَّرَ عَنْ مَوْعِدِ بَدْءِ الْمُحاضَرَةِ.

| ...Allah will not forgive them, nor will He guide them on any path. *(Sura 4:137).* | ...لَمْ يَكُنِ اللهُ لِيَغْفِرَ لَهُمْ وَلَا لِيَهْدِيَهُمْ سَبِيلًا. |

Note: Here we use the future tense for an appropriate translation as the meaning does not relate to something that is in the past.

| 5 | The ل that **doesn't induce any case in any word.** In other words, a following word simply gets the case which it would also get without the preceding ل. Grammarians say that this type of ل has <u>no</u> ruling or governing power (لامُ غَيْرُ الْعامِلةِ). |

There are several types:

| 5.1 | *Lām of introduction* (لامُ الْإِبْتِداءِ): the ل to emphasize a word. |

Such ل can precede:

a) the subject (مُبْتَدَأٌ);

b) the words نِعْمَ or بِئْسَ - see *question #155 and #183*;

c) the subject or predicate of إِنَّ;

d) the devices to denote the future tense: سَ or سَوْفَ;

a) لَكَرِيمٌ حَاضِرٌ.	Indeed, Karim is present.
b) لَنِعْمَ الْخُلُقُ الصِّدْقُ۔	Verily the best character is honesty.
c) إِنَّ الطُّلَّابَ لَحَاضِرُونَ.	Indeed, the students are present.
c) إِنَّ الصِّدْقَ لَيَنْفَعُ صَاحِبَهُ.	Indeed, honesty is beneficial to the honest person.
c) إِنَّ النَّجَاحَ لَفِي الْعَمَلِ الْجَادِّ.	Indeed, success is found in hard work.
d) لَسَوْفَ يَكُونُ الْحَفْلُ جَمِيلًا.	Certainly the ceremony will be magnificent.
c) إِنَّ فِي الرَّبِيعِ لَجَمَالًا.	Indeed, in spring there is beauty.

5.2 *Lām of the answer* (لَامُ الْجَوَابِ). Used to start the <u>main</u> (second) part of a conditional *if-sentence* or of an **oath**.

5.2.1 The ل which introduces the **main part of an oath** (لَامُ الْقَسَمِ). Note: This type of ل can also be placed after قَدْ plus verb in the past tense.

وَاللهِ لَزَيْدٌ حَاضِرٌ!	By God, Zayd is here!
وَاللهِ لَأَعْمَلَنَّ بِجِدٍّ!	By God, I indeed/truly work hard!
وَاللهِ لَأُكْرِمَنَّكَ!	By God, I will honor you!

5.2.2 The ل which starts the **main part** of an **if-sentence** (فِي جَوَابِ لَوْ). Notice: The ل is not used if the second part of the conditional sentence is negated with مَا or لَمْ.

| If you had listened to the explanation, you would understand. | لَوْ أَنْصَتَّ لِلشَّرْحِ لَفَهِمْتَ. |
| If people cooperated, they would not fail. Notice: Here, since you have a negation, you don't use ل! | لَوْ تَعَاوَنَ النَّاسُ مَا أَخْفَقُوا. |

5.2.3   This ل is used in the second part (فِي جَوَابِ لَوْلا) of a sentence that starts with لَوْلا.

You can only use ل if the answer (second part of the) sentence consists of a verb in the past tense. **Watch out:** Don't use ل if the answer (part after لَوْلا) is negated by مَا.

If it was not for schools, people would have been ignorant.	لَوْلا الْمَدَارِسُ لَكَانَ النَّاسُ جُهَلاءَ.
If it was not for schools, no one would have learned. Here, you don't use ل because of مَا.	لَوْلا الْمَدَارِسُ مَا تَعَلَّمَ أَحَدٌ.
Hadn't it been you, I would have been lost.	لَوْلاكَ لَضَلَلْتُ.

6   In a complex sentence that combines an if-clause and an oath, you use the ل as a helping device – it introduces an oath.

The ل intervenes in conditional sentence (usually with إِنْ) and **paves the way** to another part of the sentence (لامُ مُوَطِّئَةٌ): the part where the oath begins (جَوَابُ الْقَسَمِ). By doing that it tells the reader or listener that the main part (جَوَابٌ) which comes after ل belongs to the oath.

| I swear if you come to visit us, we will be generous to you! | وَاللهِ لَئِنْ زُرْتَنا لَنُكْرِمَنَّكَ! |
| Allah! There is no god but Him! He | اللَّهُ لَا إِلَهَ إِلَّا هُوَ لَيَجْمَعَنَّكُمْ |

will surely assemble you for [account on] the Day of Resurrection, about which there is no doubt. *(Sura 4:87)*	إِلَىٰ يَوْمِ الْقِيَامَةِ لَا رَيْبَ فِيهِ.

In this verse, the ل refers to the first part which includes an oath.

Remark: If you are not sure why we use the ending ـُنَّ in some sentences – see *question #156.*

127. What is the difference between 3,000 and thousands?

The plural form which you need.

So let us check the plural forms of the Arabic word for *thousand* (أَلْفٌ) which is of masculine gender (مُذَكَّرٌ). There are two main plural forms: آلَافٌ and أُلُوفٌ

This brings us to the question: When do we use which form?

a) for **small numbers** (three to ten thousands): آلَافٌ;

b) for **big** (undefined) **numbers:** أُلُوفٌ. It is actually the plural of the plural. أُلُوفٌ is only used for **indefinite** numbers and then donates *thousands*.

c) There is a rare plural form آلُفٌ. It is only used and documented in the expression **3,000** (ثَلَاثَة آلُفٍ).

Here are some examples (the numbers refer to the list above):

translation	example	type
for thousands of years	مُنْذُ آلَافِ السِّنِينَ	a
Since we have a إِضافة-construction, the word آلاف is		

treated as definite (مَعْرِفة); so we cannot use option b).		
hundreds of thousands of...	مِئاتُ الْآلافِ مِنْ	a
The word آلاف is definite (مَعْرِفة); we can't use option b).		
Thousands and thousands (German: zigtausende).	أُلُوفٌ مُؤَلَّفةٌ or آلافٌ مُؤَلَّفةٌ	a or b
Four thousand nine hundred and eighty-five (4985) girls	أَرْبَعَةُ آلافٍ وَتِسْعُ مِئَةٍ وخَمْسٌ وثَمانُونَ بِنْتًا	a

[Prophet], consider those people who abandoned their homeland in fear of death, even though there were thou-sands of them.... *(Sura 2:243)*	أَلَمْ تَرَ إِلَى الَّذِينَ خَرَجُوا مِن دِيارِهِمْ وَهُمْ أُلُوفٌ حَذَرَ الْمَوْتِ ...

Watch out: The word أَلْفٌ is masculine (مُذَكَّرٌ). So, don't mess up the gender-agreement!

4,000	أَرْبَعَةُ آلافٍ
14,000	أَرْبَعَةَ عَشَرَ أَلْفًا
400,000	أَرْبَعُمِائَةِ أَلْفٍ
Watch out for the correct agreement: If you only say the number 400,000, you have to use the singular form! And watch out for the correct endings: The word أَرْبَعمائة, in fact, consists of two words. The first word takes the case ending according to the word's role in the sentence. (Thus it can never be a سُكُون).	
This is one thousand.	هٰذا أَلْفٌ واحِدٌ.

128. What is the plural of *month*? أَشْهُرٌ or شُهُورٌ?

Both are correct.

أَشْهُرٌ or شُهُورٌ are both **broken plural forms** (جَمْعُ التَّكْسِيرِ) of شَهْرٌ which means *month*. The original meaning of the word is *the new moon, when it appears.*

In Arabic, some words have more than one plural forms, and so does شَهْرٌ. So how do we know which form is appropriate? Well, it depends on the number you want to refer to. In our example, on the amount of months.

Few and many – the rules for choosing the correct plural:

1. Normally, the form فُعُولٌ is used for **big numbers** and is called *major plural* (جَمْعُ كَثْرَةٍ). There are four patterns of this kind.

2. The form أَفْعُلٌ is used for **small numbers** (3 to 10) and is called *minor plural* (جَمْعُ قِلَّةٍ). There are sixteen patterns of this kind. See also *question #239.*

meaning	plural **big number**	plural **small number**	singular
face	وُجُوهٌ	أَوْجُهٌ	وَجْهٌ
month	شُهُورٌ	أَشْهُرٌ	شَهْرٌ
line	سُطُورٌ	أسطُرٌ	سَطْرٌ
star	نُجُومٌ	أنْجُمٌ	نَجْمٌ

Let us look at an example.

several months	عِدَّةُ الشُّهُورِ

four months	أَرْبَعةُ أَشْهُرٍ

As we have already said, there are many patterns for the **minor plural** (جَمْعُ قِلَّةٍ), for things between 3 and 10 in number. Let us examine the most common patterns.

meaning	plural	singular pattern: **فَعِيلُ**	plural pattern	1
loafs	أَرْغِفَةٌ	رَغِيفٌ	أَفْعِلةٌ	
pillars	أَعْمِدَةٌ	عَمُودٌ		

meaning	plural	singular pattern: **فَعْلُ**	plural pattern	2
months	أَشْهُرُ	شَهْرُ	أَفْعُلُ	
souls	أَنْفُسُ	نَفْسُ		

The above words are of masculine gender (مُذَكَّرٌ). However, the broken plural pattern أَفْعُلُ is also used for feminine nouns (مُؤَنَّثٌ) consisting of <u>four letters</u> in total (رُباعِيُّ - <u>not</u> 4 root letters). It has a long vowel before the last letter, like in the Arabic words *arm* or *tongue/language* which are being treated as feminine in gender.

meaning	plural	singular
tongue	أَلْسُنٌ	لِسانٌ

meaning	plural	singular
arms	أَذْرُعٌ	ذِراعٌ

Remark: لِسانٌ can be treated as masculine or feminine.

- If the meaning is *language*, it is mostly treated as masculine.
- If the meaning is *tongue*, it is mostly treated as feminine.

meaning	plural	singular pattern: **فَعَل**	plural pattern	3
young men	فِتْيةٌ	فَتًى	فِعْلةٌ	

meaning	plural	singular patterns: فَعِلٌ • فُعْلٌ • فَعَلٌ فَعُولٌ • فَعِيلٌ	plural pattern	4
actions	أَعْمالٌ	عَمَلٌ		
vigilant people	أَيْقاظٌ	يَقِظٌ		
enemies	أَعْداءُ	عَدُوٌّ	أَفْعالٌ	
noble people	أَشْرافٌ	شَرِيفٌ		
sides	أَجْنابٌ	جُنْبٌ		

The word فتية - without vowels - may denote many things:

youthfulness, juvenility	فَتِيَّةٌ
youthful (feminine, singular)	فَتِيَّةٌ
young men, juveniles; plural of فَتًى	فِتْيَةٌ

129. Which (Gregorian) year is 1435 Hijri?

It is the year 2014.

The name هِجْرَةٌ (*hijrah*) denotes the migration of the Islamic prophet Muhammad and his followers from Mecca to Yathrib (later renamed by him to Medina) in 622 CE. This also marks the beginning of the Hijri calendar (التَّقْوِيمُ الْهِجْرِيُّ الْقَمَرِيُّ).

The Muslim calendar is a lunar calendar and doesn't follow the solar system like the Gregorian calendar. In Arabic, a Hijri year is marked by the letter هـ. It is written in this peculiar form, i.e., the form of the letter Hā' when it starts a word (هـ) –

and not the stand-alone form ٥. Maybe so it is not confused with the number 5. The Gregorian (Christian) calendar is marked by the letter م which stands for مِيلادِيٌّ (A.D.).

Now let us return to our question: Which (Gregorian) year is 1435 Hijri? First of all, one lunar year has about 354 days. 33 solar year correspond to 34 lunar years. The easiest way is to use a corrective factor (354 divided by 365) ≈ 0.97. This brings us to a formula:

1. If you want to convert a Hijri to a Gregorian date, you need to multiply the original Hijri year by 0.97 and add 622:

Year Gregorian ≈ Year Hijri × 0.97 + 622
You could also do the following: **G**= H-(H/33)+622

2. If you want to convert a Gregorian to a Hijri date, you have to subtract 622 from the year and multiply it by 1.03:

Year Hijri ≈ (Year Gregorian– 622) × 1.03
You could also do the following: **H**= G-622+(G-622)/32

In our example, the result is: 1435 x 0.97 + 622 = 2013.95. It is the year 2014.

130. ...*has become unacceptable* - What is that in Arabic?

You need to find a good way to express the prefix -un.

If you would like to express that *something has become unacceptable,* you should watch out. Why? Let's see.

131. Can the word ما unite with other words?

Yes, it can.

The word ما is a powerful device in Arabic. The meaning depends entirely on its function and position in the sentence (see *question #134*). In this *question*, we focus on ما as an interrogative noun (اِسْمُ اِسْتِفْهامٍ). It is used to ask questions and means *what*.

In this application, ما can merge and unite with other words. The main result is that the **Aleph vanishes**. Some of the resulting words can be difficult to identify. As a **general rule** we can say that ما doesn't form compounds with words ending in "a" (فَتْحةٌ) such as بَعْدَ or قَبْلَ.

What happens grammatically when we merge ما with other words? Well, ما is dragged into the genitive case (مَجْرُورٌ) due to the preceding preposition. Although we say interrogative *particle* in English, in Arabic we deal with an interrogative *noun* (اِسْمُ اِسْتِفْهامٍ) as ما in this application is a اِسْم, and only a اِسْم can get case endings. However, you don't see all this because the expression has a fixed, indeclinable shape.

Let's put the word عَمَّ under the microscope (إِعْرابٌ).

Preposition which is fixed/cemented on the سُكُون. But since the ن has vanished during the merging process, we say that the fixed سُكُون is found, in fact, on the deleted letter. (حرفُ جَرٍّ مَبْنِيٌّ عَلَى السُّكُونِ عَلَى النُّونِ الْمَحْذُوفةِ)	عَنْ
Question word/interrogative noun. In its original form, the word has a fixed shape and has a سُكُون on the letter Aleph. The fixed shape is the reason why we cannot put visible case markers. But since it is a noun in Arabic, we have to assign a place value, in our situation, since it follows a preposition, it	ما

is placed in the location of a genitive case.

Now comes the tricky part. The Aleph vanishes during the merging process. That's the reason why we say that ما is fixed (cemented) on the سُكُون on the deleted letter Aleph (اِسْمُ (اِسْتِفْهامٍ مَبْنِيٌّ عَلَى السُّكُونِ عَلَى الْأَلِفِ الْمَحْذُوفةِ).

Let's do some merging.

meaning; question word	result	construction
about what?	عَمَّ or عَمَّا	عَنْ + ما
from what? of what?	مِمَّ or مِمَّا	مِنْ + ما
concerning what? what about?	عَلَامَ	عَلَى + ما
to what?	إِلَامَ	إِلَى + ما
concerning what? in what? why?	فِيمَ	فِي + ما
with what?	بِمَ	بِ + ما
why?	لِمَ	لِ + ما

Let's use some of these crafted question words in sentences.

What are you driving with?	بِمَ تُسافِرُ؟
And why not?	وَلِمَ (لِما) لا؟
How does it concern you?	فِيما يَتَعَلَّقُ بِكَ؟
What are you thinking about?	فِيمَ تُفَكِّرُ؟
He asked me about what had happened.	سَأَلَنِي عَمَّا حَصَلَ.
What does the river consist of?	مِمَّ يَتَكَوَّنُ النَّهْرُ؟

Watch out:

- الَّذِي = فِيمَا: Here, ما works as a relative pronoun (اِسْمٌ مَوْصُولٌ) and conveys *this* or *that*; *which*. In this application, you don't get rid of the Aleph!

- Furthermore, if the preposition consists of **three** or more **letters**, then it does <u>not</u> merge with ما (i.e., when ما serves as a relative pronoun): عَلَى ما and إِلَى ما.

Strive for what you desire!	اِسْعَ إِلَى ما تَبْتَغِي!
Note: We use the I-verb سَعَى in the imperative which is the reason why the last letter ى gets cut-off. The VIII-verb اِبْتَغَى means *to desire, to want* and is based on the root بَغَى/يَبْغِي (*to seek*).	
How does it concern you?	فِيمَا يَتَعَلَّقُ بِكَ؟

- Thus, the expression فِيمَ is only used for questions.

132. Is there a difference whether you negate with ما or لَمْ؟

Yes, a tiny one. However, both convey almost the same meaning.

Let us start with ما. In this application, ما is a **negation particle** (حَرْفُ نَفْيٍ) and not a noun which is the situation when ما is used to ask questions (*what*).

1. The ما when used to negate has to stand at the **beginning of a sentence.**

2. ما, if used to <u>negate the past tense</u>, **denies the entire matter** – it strengthens the meaning of the negation.

3. In the <u>present tense</u>, ما **denies** not only the action –but also its **possibility.**

4. Thus, in English, we may translate ما with *not at all*. In German with *gar nicht*.

What about لَمْ? It is a negation particle (حَرْفُ نَفْيٍ) that induces the <u>jussive</u> mood (مَجْزُومٌ) in a following verb.

- The striking thing about this particle is that it **converts** the meaning of the present tense form **into** the **past tense** (يَقْلِبُ الْمُضارِعَ ماضِيًا).

- The negation particle لَمْ, which is used to negate the past tense, does **not express a complete denial**.

Some examples:

I did not hear a thing.	ما سَمِعْتُ شَيْئًا.
I didn't get (wasn't) thirsty at all.	ما عَطِشْتُ.
I wasn't thirsty.	لَمْ أَعْطَشْ.

Watch out: If you see لا together with a verb in the **past tense**, it conveys a different meaning: It may connote a prayer or wish (قَسَمٌ)! Note that the past tense is used for wishes, curses and prayers irrespective of whether it is preceded by لا or not. See also *question #206*. For example:

| May Allah spare you bad things! | لا أَراكَ اللهُ مَكْرُوهًا! |

133. Can you negate a nominal sentence with ما?

Yes, you can.

Normally, you negate a nominal sentence (جُمْلةٌ اِسْمِيّةٌ) by using the verb لَيْسَ. However, it is possible to use ما as well.

- ما precedes the part of the sentence that is to be denied.

- ما can be used together with مِنْ to strengthen the meaning of the negation.

Let us look at some examples.

He is not a teacher.	ما هُوَ مُدَرِّسٌ.
Karim is not traveling.	ما كَرِيمٌ مُسافِرٌ.
Karim doesn't understand.	ما كَرِيمٌ فاهِمٌ.
I have nothing.	ما عِنْدِي شَيْءٌ = لَيْسَ عِنْدِي شَيْءٌ = لا شَيْءَ عِنْدِي.
Is there no alternative?	ما مِنْ بَدِيلٍ؟
Not a single person.	ما مِنْ أَحَدٍ.

In the above examples, we used the nominative case (مَرْفُوعٌ) in the predicate (خَبَرٌ). In some texts, the negative particle ما is used in the sense of لَيْسَ which has a grammatical impact. Don't forget that لَيْسَ heavily interferes in a nominal sentence:

- The subject (مُبْتَدَأٌ), as usual, is nominative (مَرْفُوعٌ);

- the predicate (خَبَرٌ) in a sentence with لَيْسَ, however, is in the **accusative** case (مَنْصُوبٌ).

If we treat ما in the way of لَيْسَ, we get exactly the above implications. This application of ما is called ما الْحِجازِيّةُ. It is only used in Classical Arabic. The name relates to the *Hejaz* which is a region in present-day Saudi Arabia.

The weather is not hot.	ما الجَوُّ حارًّا.
This is not a human being. (*Sura 12:31*). The sentence means *he cannot be mortal.*	ما هٰذا بَشَرًا.
In both examples, the predicate is in the accusative case (مَنْصُوبٌ).	

Watch out: You can only use ما like that if the subject <u>precedes</u> the predicate. You cannot use it if the word-order is reversed.

→ see *Arabic for Nerds 2*, quest. *#142, #272, for a deep analysis.*

134. How many different jobs may ما have in Arabic?

More than ten.

ما is a genuine jack-of-all-trades. By throwing this tiny word into a sentence, you can dramatically change the meaning.

In my opinion, the letter لِ and the ما are the keys to a proper understanding of Arabic.

It is essential to know which functions the word ما may have in a sentence.

| If it had been God's will, they would not have joined other gods with Him. *(Sura 6:107)* | وَلَوْ شَاءَ اللهُ مَا أَشْرَكُوا. |

Without the conditional particle لَوْ, the **negation** particle ما would have turned into a particle to form an **infinitive** (ما الْمَصْدَرِيّة). It would overthrow the entire meaning.

| God willed their joining others with him. | شَاءَ اللهُ مَا أَشْرَكُوا. |

Here are the most common possibilities.

| 1 | **Negation particle** | حَرْفٌ | ما النّافِيةُ |

Normally ما is used to <u>negate a past tense verb</u> (الْماضي). But as shown in *question #133*, ما may also negate a nominal sentence (جُمْلةٌ اِسْمِيّةٌ). Furthermore, you could even negate the present tense (الْمُضارِعُ) with ما. This is very rare; you may find it in the expression *still* (ما يَزالُ).

| The students did not show up yesterday. | ما حَضَرَ الطُّلّابُ أَمْسِ. |

| 2 | **The question *what?*** (interrogative noun) | اِسْمٌ | ما الْاِسْتِفْهامِيّةُ |

| What is your name? | ما اسْمُكَ؟ |
| What are you thinking about? | فِيمَ تُفَكِّرُ؟ |

| 3 | **Relative pronoun** (def. conjunctive noun) | اِسْمٌ | ما الْمَوْصُولةُ |

I found what I love.	وَجَدْتُ ما أُحِبُّ.
I do understand what you say.	إِنَّني أَفْهَمُ ما تَقُولُهُ.
Read what I wrote.	اِقْرَأْ ما كَتَبْتُهُ.

| 4 | **Conditional noun** | اِسْمٌ | ما الشَّرْطِيّةُ |

This ما induces the jussive mood (مَجْزُومٌ) in both verbs of the sentence (in the first and second part). In other words, the verbs will take a سُكُون at the end.

| Whatever good that you do comes back to you. | ما تَفْعَلْ مِنْ خَيْرٍ تَجِدْ جاءَكَ. |
| What(ever) you sow, you will reap. | ما تَزْرَعْ تَحْصُدْ. |

| 5 | **This is used to strengthen the conditional meaning** | حَرْف | ما لِتَأْكِيدِ مَعْنَى الشَّرْطِ |

| If you had worked hard, you would have succeeded.

 Notice that it is not a negation! | إذا ما عَمِلْتَ بِجِدٍّ نَجَحْتَ. |

| 6 | **The ما that produces an (interpreted) infinitive.** | حَرْف | ما الْمَصْدَرِيَّةُ |

It introduces a clause equivalent to a مَصْدَر and **often replaces an adverb of time** (حَرْفٌ مَصْدَرِيٌّ ظَرْفِيٌّ يَنُوبُ عَن ظَرْفٍ، الزَّمانِ الْمَحْذُوفِ الْمُضافِ إلَى الْمَصْدَرِ الْمُؤَوَّلِ).

The ما then is used like the particle أَنْ and has the same meaning and implications – see *question #81*.

The student came after the lesson had started.	حَضَرَ الطّالِبُ بَعْدَما بَدَأَ الدَّرْسُ.
I will fight as long as I live.	سَأُكافِحُ ما دُمْتُ حَيًّا.
I will think of you as long as I live.	سَأَظَلُّ أَتَذَكَّرُكَ ما حَيِيْتُ.
Although the land was wide, they found it narrow.	ضاقَتْ عَلَيْهِم الْأَرْضُ بِما رَحُبَتْ.
In the last example, ما does not step in for an adverb of time (حَرْف مَصْدَرِيَّةٍ غَيْرُ ظَرْفِيٍّ).	

| 7 | **The ما that denotes generality & vagueness**
 some (or *other*); *a certain* | اِسْمٌ | ما الْإِبْهامِيّةُ |

In this application, ما has to be at the end of the sentence and always follows an <u>in</u>definite noun. The ما here functions as an adjective (صِفةٌ) for the preceding word.

I came for a certain reason.	جِئْتُ لِأَمْرٍ ما.
The man who sat next to me in the plane was reading some book.	كانَ الرَّجُلُ الَّذِي جانِبِي فِي الطَّائِرَةِ يَقْرَأُ كِتابًا ما.
There is certainly some mistake.	ثَمَّةَ بِالتَّأْكِيدِ خَطَأٌ ما.

Note: The word ثَمَّةَ (ثَمَّتَ) is a demonstrative noun (اِسْمَ إِشارَةٍ) and has the meaning of هُناكَ; it denotes *there is*. ثَمَّةَ does not change its shape and is negated with لَيْسَ: *there isn't* (لَيْسَ ثَمَّةَ).

I lost something.	أَضَعْتُ شَيْئًا ما.
some day; sometime in the future	يَوْمًا ما
for some reason	لِسَبَبٍ ما

| 8 | **The neutralizing (hindering) ما** | حَرْفٌ | ما الْكافّةُ |

It works as a neutralizer. It actually neutralizes the governing power of a preceding word.

If you place ما after إِنَّ, then the grammatical force of إِنَّ doesn't get through, so you won't have to think about special case endings. Such ما may neutralize particles but also verbs.

Indeed, the bird is free.	إِنَّ الطَّائِرَ طَلِيقٌ.	1
	إِنَّما الطَّائِرُ طَلِيقٌ.	2

In sentence 1, the particle إِنَّ guards the word الطَّائِرَ ("subject" or

إِنَّ اِسْمُ) in the accusative case (مَنْصُوبٌ). In sentence 2, ما is like a wall and neutralizes the power of إِنَّ, so إِنَّ can't get through with its grammatical force. However, both sentences mean the same!

The ما may also neutralize the demand of verbs for having a subject (الْكافَّةُ عَنِ الْفاعِلِ). We can say that the verb then cannot exercise its power and govern a word (the subject) in he *nominative case.*

This happens with verbs such as *to be few* (قَلَّ), *to be extended* (طالَ), *to be often* (كَثُرَ), *to be extensive* (شَدَّ), etc.

| sometimes, perhaps | رُبَّما | frequently; as long as | طالَما | seldom, rarely, hardly | قَلَّما |

| The lazy man rarely succeeds. | قَلَّما يَنْجَحُ الْكَسُولُ. |

If you place such ما after a preposition (حَرْفُ جَرٍّ) or an adverb of time or place (ظَرْفٌ), then you neutralize the governing power of them, in other words, you neutralize the genitive case. This happens ins expressions such as *while* (بَيْنَما) or as, just as (كَما).

| 9 | ما - to denote **surprise** and **astonishment** | اِسْمُ | ما التَّعَجُّبِيَّةُ |

| What a nice spring! | ما أَجْمَلَ الرَّبِيعَ! |
| What fortunate I got here! | ما أَسْعَدَني بِوُجُودي هُنا! |

We will examine this in *question #194.* See also *Arabic for Nerds 2,* questions #5, #294, #434.

135. Is there a word in Arabic which consists of only 1 letter?

Yes, for example the word for and (وَ). But there are also more exciting forms as well.

They are very rare and only possible in the **imperative** (أَمْرٌ). We need to look for verbs with **two weak root letters** (حَرْفُ عِلَّةٍ). Only the strong consonant will survive our operation.

meaning	verb		imperative		meaning
to beware, preserve	وَقَى-يَقِي		! قِ	*qi!*	Protect!
to pay attention to	وَعَى-يَعِي	→	! عِ	*'i!*	Pay attention!
to live up a promise or agreement; to fulfill	وَفَى-يَفِي		! فِ	*fi!*	Fulfill!

It may be difficult to get the correct meaning of such verbs.

...protect us from the torment of the Fire! *(Sura 2:201)*	...قِنَا عَذَابَ النَّارِ!

Note the spelling! In general, it is **impossible** to have a single stand-alone letter in Arabic. For example, the interrogative particle أ is **always written together** with the word that follows after. Other examples are وَ ● لِ ● فَ ● بِ.

Never use a space after them – you must connect them with the following word!

the book and the pen	wrong	الْكِتَابُ وَ الْقَلَمُ
	correct – no space!	الْكِتَابُ وَالْقَلَمُ
Is Zayd at home?	correct! (although it may be difficult to read)	أَفِي الْبَيْتِ زَيْدٌ؟
Didn't Zayd come?		أَلَمْ يَأْتِ زَيْدٌ؟

136. Because, since, as - How do you express that in Arabic?

There are several ways to express this idea.

As, because, and since are conjunctions. They introduce subordinate clauses (the part after since) which is the reason. The conjunctions are used to link the reason to the result.

An example: *I studied Arabic* (= result) *because I was in Egypt* (= reason). Now, how do we express that idea in Arabic?

1	Standard word order: The *because*-part (= reason) comes later in the sentence.

because; since, as; in so far as	حَيْثُ أَنَّ	إِذْ أَنَّ	لِأَنَّ

He did not come (show up) **because** he was lazy.	لَمْ يَحْضُرْ حَيْثُ أَنَّهُ كَانَ كَسُولًا.
I will go to Egypt **since** my heart tells me that I love you.	سَأَذْهَبُ إِلَى مِصْرَ إِذْ أَنَّ قَلْبِي يُحَدِّثُنِي أَنَّنِي أُحِبُّكِ.
He won't come tomorrow because he is ill.	لَنْ يَجِيءَ غَدًا لِأَنَّهُ مَرِيضٌ.

Remark: Watch out for the correct vowels!

in order to	لِأَنْ	≠	because	لِأَنَّ

2	Inversed word order: The sentence starts with the *because*-part (i.e, the causative part).

as, since	بِما أَنَّ + فَ

| Since I don't like the room I'll move (go) to another hotel. | بِما أَنَّ الغُرْفَة لا تُناسِبُني فَسَأَذْهَبُ إِلَى فُنْدُقٍ آخَرِ. |
| Since the weather is nice, I will go to the garden. | بِما أَنَّ الْجَوَّ جَمِيلٌ فَسَأَذْهَبُ إِلَى الْحَدِيقَةِ. |

137. *Because of...* How do you say that in Arabic?

There are several ways to express because of; for the sake of.

It all depends on the context.

- In Egyptian Arabic, there is the word عَلَشان or عَشان.
- In Standard Arabic, you could use جَرّاءُ which is a اِسْمُ.

Here is how you can use جَرّاءُ:

because of; by what; as a result of	جَرّاءُ ما + verb	1
because of what happened there	جَرّاءُ ما لَحِقَ	
because of; due to	مِنْ جَرّاءِ + noun/pronoun	2

I did this for you.	قُمْتُ بِذَلِكَ مِنْ جَرّائِكَ.
	فَعَلْتُ ذَلِكَ مِنْ جَرّائِكَ.
→ The examples on the right mean the same as the sentence above!	بِسَبَبِكَ = وَمِنْ جَرّاكَ =مِنْ أَجْلِكَ

| because of the money | مِنْ جَرّاءِ الْمالِ |
| As a result, countless problems have occurred. | مِنْ جَرّاءِ ذَلِكَ وَقَعَتْ مَشَاكِلُ لا حَصْرَ لَها. |

A woman got into Hell-Fire because of a cat whom she had tied. (*Hadith; Sahih Muslim 2619*)	دَخَلَتِ امْرَأَةُ النَّارَ مِنْ جَرَّاءِ هِرَّةٍ لَهَا - أَوْ هِرٍّ - رَبَطَتْها.

There is another way of writing جَرَّاءُ; the meaning is the same.

because of	مِن جَرَّى
because of you; on your account; for your sake	مِن جَرَّاكَ

However, there are other options too. In the following expres-sions, you have to add a pronoun or a noun as the second part of the إضافة-construction.

Watch out for the case endings.

because of this/as a result	لِذلِكَ + sentence	1
for the benefit of	عَلَى ذِمَّةِ + noun	2
In view of; in regard to; seeing that; because of/for	نَظَرًا لِ + noun	3
for the sake of	مِنْ أَجْلِ or لِأَجْلِ + noun/pronoun	4

Since you have helped him in the past...	...نَظَرًا لِمُساعَدَتِكَ لَهُ فِي الْماضِي	3

138. What do أَخْرَجَ ,عَلَّمَ and ناقَشَ have in common?

The pronunciation of the first letter in the present tense.

Let's see what they have in common.

meaning	present tense	past tense	stem
to discuss	يُناقِشُ	ناقَشَ	III
to oust, to extract	يُخْرِجُ	أَخْرَجَ	IV
to teach	يُعَلِّمُ	عَلَّمَ	II

All three verbs consist of four letters (<u>not</u> root letters). Grammarians call them *triliteral augmented verbs* (فِعْلٌ مَزِيدٌ ثُلاثِيٌّ). They have one thing in common: the **pronunciation**.

In the present tense (الْمُضارِع) the **first vowel** is ضَمّة ("*u*") and not فَتْحة ("a") as in all other verb patterns: **I** and **V to X**.

comparison: verb pattern I		meaning	مُضارِع		وَزْنٌ	stem
he leaves	يَخْرُجُ	he extracts	"y**u**khriju"	يُخْرِجُ	أَفْعَلَ	IV
he paints	يَنْقُشُ	he discusses	"y**u**nāqishu"	يُناقِشُ	فاعَلَ	III
he learns	يَعْلَمُ	he teaches	"y**u**ʿallimu"	يُعَلِّمُ	فَعَّلَ	II

Thus, every time you see a verb consisting of four letters, you can be sure that the first vowel is "u".

139. Does a weak letter cause trouble in the مَصْدَر-form?

Yes, it does.

If you have و or ي in the root, you have to roll up your sleeves:

- Sometimes the weak letter simply disappears.
- However, it may also change into a different letter.

Note that in the following examples the weak letter (حَرْفُ عِلَّةٍ) is not always in the same position.

	problem	meaning	مَصْدَر	verb	stem
1	و at the beginning	*stopping*	إيقافٌ	أَوْقَفَ	IV
2	ا in the middle	*desire; will*	إرادةٌ	أَرادَ	IV
3	ء at the beginning plus ى at the end	*damage; injury*	إيذاءٌ	آذَى	IV
4	و in the middle and ى at the end	*takeover; seizure*	اسْتيلاءُ	اِسْتَوْلَى	X
5	و in the root; instead of تَفْعيلٌ, you use تَفْعِلةُ	*education; pedagogy*	تَرْبِيةٌ	رَبَّى	II

Here are the rules that help you to build a مَصْدَر:

1. و becomes ي

2. ا (Aleph) in the middle stays, but you have to add ة

3. آ (Aleph madda) turns into ي

4. ى at the end becomes ء

   Exception: ى at the end of a II-verb becomes ية

140. What does the ّ do in the word *connection* (اِتِّصالٌ)?

It is the result of an assimilation.

اِتِّصالٌ denotes *connection; communication; relation* and is the مَصْدَر of the VIII-verb اِتَّصَلَ. The root is و-ص-ل.

Now, what about the ّ? Where does it come from?

If و is the first letter of a root, the و will transform into ت with a شَدّة in the VIII-stem اِفْتَعَلَ. Some examples:

meaning	مَصْدَر	verb		root
to be united	اِتِّحادٌ	اِتَّحَدَ		و-ح-د
to agree	اِتِّفاقٌ	اِتَّفَقَ	اِفْتَعَلَ	و-ف-ق
to get in touch with; be connected	اِتِّصالٌ	اِتَّصَلَ		و-ص-ل

141. Why does سَماءُ take nunation ("un") but زَرْقاءُ doesn't?

Because زَرْقاءُ is a so-called diptote (مَمْنُوعٌ مِن الصَّرْفِ).

سَماءُ means *sky*; زَرْقاءُ *blue* (feminine form). First of all, we see that both words end with ء. So why do we have to use different case endings when we put nunation (تَنْوِينْ)?

Let's put both words into a sentence.

In the blue sky	فِي سَماءٍ زَرْقاءَ

We see that سَماءٍ gets nunation (تَنْوِينْ) but زَرقاءَ not. Why is that? Let's check the root.

explanation	root	
ء is part of the root as the و changes into a ء!	س-م-و	سَماءُ
The ء is **extra** (زِيادة) and **not part of the root**. This is the reason why it doesn't take تَنْوِينْ. The additional هَمْزة leads to a certain pattern which is treated as a diptote (مَمْنُوعٌ مِن الصَّرْفِ).	ز-ر-ق	زَرْقاءُ

142. مَساءًا or مَساءً - Which spelling is correct?

It is مَساءً *which means* in the evening.

Our question is about the correct spelling of the ending: With an Aleph at the end, or not? First of all, it is necessary to write the تَنْوِين above the هَمْزة, but do you also need an additional Aleph (ا) after it?

Let's check similar examples to understand the problem:

Aleph?	meaning; explanation		root	word
yes	If the word functions as a direct object and thus takes the accusative case (مَنْصُوبٌ), it is written like this: جُزْءًا *I want a piece* (أُرِيدُ جُزْءًا).	*a piece; portion*	ج-ز-ء	جُزْءًا
no	The root literally means *to spend the winter*. The ء belongs to the root. It was originally و that was transformed to ء.	*in winter*	ش-ت-و	شِتاءً
	in the evening		م-س-و	مَساءً

The rules are simple:

1. If there is an <u>Aleph</u> before the هَمْزة, you <u>don't write</u> an Aleph after the هَمْزة if the word is مَنْصُوبٌ.

2. If there is **no** <u>Aleph</u> before هَمْزة, you have to put an Aleph after it. Why? Because هَمْزة is part of the root!

Bad style!	أَصْبَحَ لَيْسَ مَقْبُولًا.
The verb أَصْبَحَ can't go along with the verb لَيْسَ directly as a predicate (خَبَر أَصْبَحَ) – this wouldn't make sense.	

This is much better!	أَصْبَحَ غَيْرَ مَقْبُولٍ.
Here, the predicate (خَبَر) of أَصْبَحَ is a إضافة-construction. The first part is the word غَيْرِ. Therefore, مَقْبُولٍ is in the genitive case.	

Let's try to find a solution without أَصْبَحَ.

This is not acceptable (unacceptable).	لَمْ يَعُدْ مَقْبُولًا.
I could not stand it any longer.	لَمْ أَعُدْ أَسْتَطِيعُ صَبْرًا.

- These sentences may also express that something is not acceptable (anymore). In its original meaning, the verb عَادَ / يَعُودُ denotes to *return* and is therefore usually connected with a **preposition**, e.g., إِلَى (*to return to*).

- But if you don't use a preposition and instead attach a **direct object** (مَفْعُولٌ بِهِ), the verb will denote *to become xy again*. For example: It became clean again (عَادَ نَقِيًّا).

- If عَادَ (without a preposition) is **negated** and immediately followed by a **verb in the present tense** (الْمُضارِعُ), it will mean *to do something no more* or *no longer*. Note that you connect the second verb directly without أَنْ and conjugate it according to the subject indicated by عَادَ.

143. عَظيمٌ and رَحيمٌ - Same pattern, same form?

No, they are of different kind although they share a pattern.

Let us examine both words:

- In English, both words would be **adjectives**. رَحيمٌ means *merciful;* عَظيمٌ means *great.*

- In Arabic, we could come to the same conclusion and call both words نَعْتٌ or صِفةٌ which is usually translated as attribute or adjective. However, unlike in English which knows the word type adjective, we can only say for the Arabic words that they are adjectives according to their **function** in the sentence. Regarding the word type, they are nouns (اِسْمٌ).

So far, so good. But what about the meaning of the respective noun pattern? First of all, the function in the sentence doesn't concern us here. It is the meaning of the form and how these words are derived from the root.

Let's see why رَحيمٌ and عَظيمٌ have a different morphological personality and character. For our analysis, we first try to build an **active participle** (اِسْمٌ فاعِلٍ) of the root:

1. The root ر-ح-م means *to have mercy; to have compassion.* An active participle, literally meaning *somebody who is merciful,* makes sense.

2. The root ع-ظ-م means *to become grandiose.* An active participle **wouldn't** make sense.

Now, let's see where رَحيمٌ and عَظيمٌ would fit.

الصِّفَةُ الْمُشَبَّهةِ	صيغةُ الْمُبالَغةِ	اِسْمُ الْفاعِلِ	root
---	رَحِيمٌ	راحِم	ر-ح-م
عَظِيمٌ	---	---	ع-ظ-م

What should we make out of that?

- The صيغةُ الْمُبالَغةِ describes something that is done extensively or often. It indicates **exaggeration** or superlativeness. We could say that it is a relative of the *active participle* - see *question #86*.

- An *active participle* (اِسْمُ فاعِلٍ) always points at the occurrence/happening (الْحُدُوث) of an action.

- On the contrary, a صِفةٌ مُشَبَّهةٌ (*quasi participle; similar quality*) is describing a quality (state, action) as natural and permanent! It indicates a meaning of **firmness** and **constancy**.

- *Similar quality* here means that they indicate a quality similar to the active participle. The long version of the term is *adjectives which are made like the participles* (صِفةٌ مُشَبَّهةٌ بِاسْمِ الْفاعِلِ وَالْمَفْعُولِ).

- Since some roots can't form an active participle (اِسْمُ الْفاعِلِ) but only a صِفةٌ مُشَبَّهةٌ, we could say that the صِفةٌ مُشَبَّهةٌ is a substitute for the non-existing active participle. Thus, we could call them *pseudo participles* or *quasi-participles*.

- Regarding the morphology (صَرْفٌ), the صِفةٌ مُشَبَّهةٌ belongs to the *derived nouns* (اِسْمُ مُشْتَقٌّ).

- The صِفةٌ مُشَبَّهةٌ can only be built from triliteral, intransitive verbs (فِعْلٌ ثُلاثِيٌّ لازِمٌ). An intransitive verb cannot carry a direct object.

There is one important rule you should know about:

- You <u>cannot</u> build the <u>active participle</u> (اِسْمُ فاعِلٍ) of a I-verb if it has the vowel <u>**"u"**</u> (ضَمَّةٌ) on the <u>second</u> root letter in the past tense. Such verbs don't build an active participle (اِسْمُ فاعِلٍ). This gap is filled by the صِفَةٌ مُشَبَّهةٌ.

- Notice: This rule also applies for some verbs which have the vowel "i" (كَسْرةٌ) under the second root letter.

Some examples:

root	past tense verb		اِسْم الْفاعِل	صِفَةٌ مُشَبَّهةٌ	
ك-ث-ر	كَثُرَ	to be much	---	كَثِيرٌ	*many*
ك-ب-ر	كَبُرَ	to be big	---	كَبِيرٌ	*big*
ص-غ-ر	صَغُرَ	to be small	---	صَغِيرٌ	*small*
ك-ر-م	كَرُمَ	to be generous	---	كَرِيمٌ	*generous*
ش-ج-ع	شَجُعَ	to be courageous	---	شُجاعٌ	*brave*

How do we know which pattern we should use? We need to check the **vowel of the second root letter** – if it is "u" or "i".

- Some forms are diptotes (مَمْنُوعٌ مِن الصَّرْفِ) and don't take nunation (تَنوينٌ) - they are marked in black.

- If I don't mention the feminine form, you simply add ة.

A	Verbs having "i" (كَسْرةٌ) under the second root letter (فَعِلَ).

	صِفَةٌ مُشَبَّهةٌ	past tense verb		pattern	
happy	فَرِحٌ	to be glad	فَرِحَ	فَعِلٌ	1

lame	أَعْرَجُ - عَرْجاءُ	to be lame	عَرِجَ	أَفْعَلُ - فَعْلاءُ	**2**
green	أَخْضَرُ - خَضْراءُ	to be green	خَضِرَ		

thirsty	عَطْشانُ - عَطْشَى	to be thirsty	عَطِشَ	فَعْلانُ - فَعْلَى	**3**

B	Verbs that have "u" (ضَمَّة) on the second root letter (فَعُلَ).

	صِفَةٌ مُشَبَّهَةٌ	past tense verb		pattern	
noble	شَرِيفٌ	to be noble	شَرُفَ	فَعِيلٌ	**1**
clean	نَظِيفٌ	to be clean	نَظُفَ		
difficult	صَعْبٌ	to be hard	صَعُبَ	فَعْلٌ	**2**
easy	سَهْلٌ	to be easy	سَهُلَ		
brave	شُجاعٌ	to be brave	شَجُعَ	فُعالٌ	**3**
coward(ly)	جَبانٌ	to be a coward	جَبُنَ	فَعالٌ	**4**
brave	بَطَلٌ	to be brave	بَطُلَ	فَعَلٌ	**5**
beautiful	حَسَنٌ	to be fine	حَسُنَ		
hard; solid	صُلْبٌ	to be firm	صَلُبَ	فُعْلٌ	**6**
sweet	حُلْوٌ	to be sweet	حَلُوَ		

144. السَّيَّارَةُ الْجَمِيلَ لَوْنُها - Is there a mistake?

No, there isn't!

If you thought that الْجَمِيلَ should be written with a ة, you might have misunderstood the meaning of the sentence.

I saw the car **whose color is beautiful**. Or: I saw the car with the **beautiful color**.	رَأَيْتُ السَّيَّارَةَ الْجَمِيلَ لَوْنُها.
The sentence doesn't mean: I saw the **beautiful car**.	

The second part of the sentence is a so-called *causative description* or *semantically linked adjective* (نَعْتٌ سَبَبِيٌّ). I prefer the term *connected description*.

In such constructions, the **adjective** is also called the *connected* (مُسَبَّبٌ) and belongs to the **following** noun. To make the construction work, we need a **binder** or **connector** (سَبَبٌ) which is usually a **referring pronoun**. The adjective plus the word after it both together form an adjective/attribute for the word earlier in the sentence.

	second part		head	
ها	لَوْنُ	الْجَمِيلَ	السَّيَّارَةَ	رَأَيْتُ
binder or connector (سَبَبٌ) which links the second part to the first word. It is a referring pronoun.	This is the word to which the adjective relates in meaning.	*the connected* (مُسَبَّبٌ)	The main word which we actually want to describe.	
	Both together work as an attribute or adjective (صِفة) for *car*. Grammarians call it a qualificative clause.		direct object (مَفْعُولٌ بِهِ)	verb + subject

Let's see the difference.

نَعْتٌ حَقِيقِيٌّ	The successful student	الطَّالِبُ النَّاجِحُ
نَعْتٌ سَبَبِيٌّ	The student whose sister is successful	الطَّالِبُ النَّاجِحَةُ أُخْتُهُ

Let us check the different parts of the نَعْتٌ سَبَبِيٌّ.

نَعْتٌ مُؤَنَّثٌ	Although it is a نَعْتٌ, it doesn't describe the word before but after it! The word *sister* (أُخْت) is the logical target of the adjective because it is not the (male) *student*, who is successful.	النَّاجِحَةُ
فَاعِلٌ	Subject; the thing which is described (مَنْعُوتٌ)	أُخْتُهُ

Don't get confused: The sentence does not start with a verb. Thus, the main, primary sentence is a nominal sentence (جُمْلَةٌ اِسْمِيَّةٌ). The word الطَّالِبُ is the subject (مُبْتَدَأ) as the مُبْتَدَأ has to be placed at the beginning of a sentence.

Now, what about أُخْتُهُ? Why do we say that it is the الْفَاعِلُ? Well, grammarians regard it as the الْفَاعِلُ. That might sound strange. But it is a tricky construction (two sentences combined). The word النَّاجِحَةُ is an active participle (اِسْم فَاعِلٍ) which does the job of a verb here (تَعْمَلُ عَمَلَ فِعْلِها).

Still difficult? Let's rewrite the sentence and use a relative clause (اِسْمُ إِشارةٍ).	الطَّالِبُ الَّذِي نَجَحَتْ أُخْتُهُ.

Let's stop for a second and repeat the main points:

- In Arabic, the "adjective" must follow the noun. In this construction it is the opposite: The adjective (الْمُسَبَّبُ) belongs to the <u>following</u> noun. So the adjective isn't for the person/thing which we primarily want to describe – but for someone/something that is related to it.

• The noun after the adjective needs a *connector; binder,* also called *semantic link* (السَّبَبُ). This is almost always a referring pronoun to mark the relation with the word earlier in the sentence.

• The two together (*the connected* and *the word after the adjective*) form the description (نَعْت) for the preceding noun (مَنْعُوت), with which the adjective agrees in case only by attraction.

In practice, you need to follow 5 steps:

1. The نَعْت سَبَبِيٌّ is <u>always</u> **singular**.

2. It is placed **before** the word to which it logically (and in meaning) refers.

3. It agrees with this <u>preceding</u> noun in **determination** (definite/indefinite) and **case** (إِعْرابٌ)

4. It agrees with the <u>following</u> noun in **gender** (masculine/feminine). Furthermore, it is the regent (عامِلٌ) of the following noun which means that the adjective works like a verb. Therefore, the following noun is always the **subject** (فاعِلٌ) of the adjective (which does the job of a verb) – and has to be in the **nominative** case (مَرْفُوعٌ).

5. The noun after the adjective needs a suitable **pronoun** which refers to the head (main word) in the sentence!

Let us look at some examples to understand the rules.

The man whose brother is honorable came.	جاءَ الرَّجُلُ الْفاضِلُ أَخُوهُ.

The man whose two brothers are honorable came.	جاءَ الرَّجُلُ الْفاضِلُ أَخَواهُ.
Two men whose two brothers are honorable came.	جاءَ رَجُلانِ فاضِلٌ أَخَواهُما.
The two men whose sisters are honorable came.	جاءَ الرَّجُلانِ الْفاضِلةُ أَخَواتُهُما.
Ladies whose sisters are honorable came.	جاءَتْ سَيِّداتٌ فاضِلةٌ أَخَواتُهُنَّ.

Let's see the difference and check both types of adjectives.

1	I passed by a handsome man.	مَرَرْتُ بِرَجُلٍ حَسَنٍ.
	Standard adjective (نَعْتٌ حَقِيقِيٌّ). حَسَنٍ agrees in gender, number, case, and determination (definiteness) with its **head** (رَجُلٍ).	
2	I passed by a man with a beautiful mother (lit.: I passed by a man beautiful his mother.)	مَرَرْتُ بِرَجُلٍ حَسَنةٍ أُمُّهُ.
	The adjective حَسَنةٍ agrees only in **case** (مَجْرُورٌ) and **determination** (indefinite) with its **grammatical head** (رَجُلٌ). However, it agrees in **gender** (feminine) with its **logical head** (أُمُّهُ). Here, the adjective (نَعْتٌ) has a dual function: • Syntactically (regarding the grammatical arrangement), it is an attribute of *man* (رَجُلٍ). • Semantically (logically; in meaning), it is a predicate of *mother* (أُمٌّ). • The connection (سَبَبٌ) is expressed by a referring pronoun: ه	

Some more examples.

The students with the following names succeeded. Or: The students whose names follow (are listed below) succeeded.	الطُّلَّابُ الْآتِيةُ أَسْماؤُهُمْ نَجَحُوا.
الْآتِيةُ is the نَعْتٌ and has verbal power. The word أَسْماؤُ is the subject (فاعِلٌ) and therefore in the nominative case (مَرْفُوعٌ).	
If you are not sure about the meaning, re-write the sentence and use a relative clause:	الطُّلَّابُ الَّذينَ أَتَتْ أَسْماؤُهُمْ نَجَحُوا.

The car whose color is nice...	السَّيّارَةُ الْجَميلُ لَوْنُها...
الْجَميلُ is the نَعْتٌ and has verbal power. The word لَوْنُ is the subject (فاعِلٌ) and therefore in the nominative case (مَرْفُوعٌ).	

This is a man whose mother is standing.	هٰذا رَجُلٌ قائِمَةٌ أُمُّهُ.
The word قائِمَةٌ is the نَعْتٌ; the word أُمُّ is the subject (فاعِلٌ).	

To sum it up:

- The نَعْتٌ حَقيقيٌّ comes <u>after the noun</u> which it describes. It follows the noun in gender (m./f.), case, determination (definite, indefinite) and number (singular/dual/plural).

- The نَعْتٌ سَبَبيٌّ <u>comes before the word</u> which it describes. It is always singular!

→ For a detailed analysis, see *Arabic for Nerds 2, qu. #172 and #175.*

145. What is the اِسْمُ الْفَاعِلِ of أَتَى (*to come*)?

It is آتٍ.

The verb أَتَى is tricky because of two things:

1. The **first** root letter – which is هَمْزة.
2. The **last** root letter – which is ى.

In other words, the regular rules don't work. In order to build the active participle (*coming*), we use the pattern فاعِلٌ.

Let us first deal with the هَمْزة. The rule is: ء + ا equals آ

Now, what about the letter ى? If the active participle is indefinite, we have to drop the ى and add nunation (تَنْوينٌ) under the second root letter. The result is تٍ. If the word is definite, the letter ى will turn into ي. Finally, we get:

definite	الْآتِي	the coming		indefinite (*ātin*)	آتٍ	coming

146. أَفْعَلُ - This is the comparative pattern, isn't it?

Yes and no.

The pattern أَفْعَلُ is used for two different derived nouns of the root (مُشْتَقّاتٌ):

1. The *measure of preference* (اِسْمُ التَّفْضيلِ): comparative or superlative

2. The *pseudo participle* (صِفةٌ مُشَبَّهةٌ): the adjective that resembles an active participle. It denotes a firm and durable state or condition and usually indicates color, deficiency, or ornament. See *question #143*.

Now, why does that matter?

1. They both share the same pattern for the <u>masculine form</u>. Note that أَفْعَلُ is a diptote (مَمْنُوعٌ مِن الصَّرْفِ) and does not take nunation (تَنْوِينٌ).

2. The <u>feminine form</u>, however, is <u>different</u>.

Let us check both patterns in depths.

meaning	feminine pattern	feminine form	اِسْمُ التَّفْضِيلِ
bigger/biggest	فُعْلَى	كُبْرَى	أَكْبَرُ
smaller/smallest		صُغْرَى	أَصْغَرُ

meaning	feminine pattern	feminine form	الصِّفَةُ المُشَبَّهَةُ
shining	فَعْلاءُ	زَهْراءُ	أَزْهَرُ
red	Used for colors and handicaps; it is also a diptote.	حَمْراءُ	أَحْمَرُ
blind		عَمْياءُ	أَعْمَى

147. What does the word دُنْيا mean?

The word دُنْيا is usually translated as world.

That's correct. However, what is the literal meaning of the word? It is totally different. Let us check the root: د-ن-و.

The literal meaning of الدُّنْيا is *the lowest* or *the closest* or *the nearest* – and not *the world*. How so? If we look at the DNA of دُنْيا, we identify the pattern فُعْلَى. This is the feminine form of the pattern أَفْعَلُ which is the comparative or superlative (ela-

tive) form (اِسْمُ تَفْضِيلٍ). The pattern فُعْلَى is tricky: if the last
root letter is و, it gets converted into ي; and the ى becomes ا.

meaning	comparative, feminine form	comparative, masculine form	root
closer; closest	دُنْيا	أَدْنَى	د-ن-و
higher; highest	عُلْيا	أَعْلَى	ع-ل-ى
further; furthest	قُصْوَى	أَقْصَى	ق-ص-و
Notice the feminine form in the last example! It's an exception that became the standard form. According to the rule it should be قُصْيا.				

The word دُنْيا is generally used with the definite article: الدُّنْيا.
The plural of دُنْيا is دُنْيَياتٌ or دُنَّى.

In ancient times, people used the term الْحَياةُ الدُّنْيا (*the closest, nearest life*) to describe the present life (الْحَياةُ الْحاضِرَةُ).
Eventually, the word الْحَياة was deleted, and we got الدُّنْيا.

The expression الدُّنْيا is already found in the Qur'an.

...there is a reward in this **present world** for those who do good, but their home in the Hereafter is far better:... (*Sura 16:30*)	... لِلَّذِينَ أَحْسَنُوا فِي هَذِهِ الدُّنْيا حَسَنَةٌ وَلَدَارُ الْآخِرَةِ خَيْرٌ...

- The same can be said about *afterlife/hereafter*. The expression الْحَياةُ الْأُخْرَى denotes *the other life* (which we don't
  know). Eventually, الْحَياةُ was dropped and we got
  الْأُخْرَى. Another expression for *afterlife* is الْآخِرَةُ.

- The most famous mosque in Jerusalem, which is also one
  of the most important in Islam, is called *al-Aqsa-Mosque*.
  It is called الْأَقْصَى as in ancient times it was the mosque

that was the most remote from Mecca (الْمَسْجِدُ الْأَقْصَى). The word الْأَقْصَى literally means *the farthest*.

| I said, "O Allah's Messenger! Which mosque was built first?" He replied, "Al-Masjid-ul-Haram." I asked, "Which (was built) next?" He replied, "Al-Masjid-ul-Aqsa (i.e. Jerusalem)." (*Hadith Sahīh al-Bukhārī 3425*) | قُلْتُ: يَا رَسُولَ اللَّهِ أَيُّ مَسْجِدٍ وُضِعَ أَوَّلُ؟ قَالَ: الْمَسْجِدُ الْحَرَامُ. قُلْتُ ثُمَّ أَيٌّ؟ قَالَ: ثُمَّ الْمَسْجِدُ الْأَقْصَى. |

148. How do you mark the مَجْرُورٌ -case in the word الدُّنْيَا؟

Just do nothing.

The Aleph at the end of الدُّنْيَا (*the world* or *the nearest/closest*) doesn't change in any case. It is always an Aleph.

الدُّنْيَا is a *noun with shortened ending* (اِسْمٌ مَقْصُورٌ), see *question #13*. Such a noun can take the nominative (مَرْفُوعٌ), genitive (مَجْرُورٌ), or accusative (مَنْصُوبٌ) case. However, the case marker is always hidden. Instead, we use a **virtual, presumptive marker** (مُقَدَّرةٌ).

When you see such a word, keep these two things in mind:

1. The case marker it is not pronounced.

2. The word looks the same in any case.

An example.

| king of the world | مَلِكُ الدُّنْيَا |

149. Why is عُلْيَا written with an Aleph but كُبْرَى not?

Because the last root letter is different.

عُلْيَا means *higher* and كُبْرَى *larger/greater*.

Both words are the comparative or superlative form (اِسْمُ التَّفْضِيلِ) in the feminine form (مُؤَنَّثُ). The pattern is فُعْلَى. The masculine is أَفْعَلُ.

They have something else in common. They are both *nouns with shortened endings* (اِسْمُ مَقْصُورٌ). The last letter is pronounced as a long "ā"-vowel (*see question #13*). However, the **spelling** is different. It has to do with the last root letter.

explanation	root	اِسْمُ التَّفْضِيلِ (f.)
The last root letter is **weak.** → You have to write an Aleph at the end. Why do we write ي before the Aleph? This happens in this pattern (فُعْلَى): The final root letter و is converted into ي. So, instead of دُنْوَى we write دُنْيَا.	د-ن-و	دُنْيَا
The last root letter is ر (not weak). → You have to write ى, pronounced as long "ā".	ك-ب-ر	كُبْرَى

150. How do you express *still* in Arabic?

Unfortunately, there is no simple word for still.

The English adverb *still* may convey several ideas. In this *question*, I will show how to express that something is continuing to happen now.

In Arabic, you have to express this idea of *still* by a **negated verb**. This is the most common, elegant and convenient solution. But which verbs are suitable for this job? The verbs which we use here are special because they follow the rules of كانَ. They count as *sisters of* كانَ, so called كانَ وَأَخَواتُها.

Let us quickly check the special rules of كانَ.

The weather was nice.	كانَ الْجَوُّ جَمِيلًا.
Weather is the "subject" (اِسْمُ كانَ); it is nominative (مَرْفُوعٌ). *Nice* is the predicate (خَبَرُ كانَ) and takes the accusative case (مَنْصُوبٌ).	

Let us return to *still*. The striking thing about the verbs which we are going to examine is the **tense**: You can use them in the present or past tense – the **meaning in Arabic is the same**.

But don't forget:

- The <u>present</u> tense (الْمُضارِعُ) is negated with لا.

- If you want to express the <u>future</u>, you negate the present tense with لَنْ and use the subjunctive mood (مَنْصُوبٌ) of the verb: you put the vowel "*a*" (فَتْحةٌ) on the final letter.

- The <u>past</u> tense (الْماضِي) is negated with لَمْ or ما. After ما, you simply use a verb in the past tense. After لَمْ, you need the jussive mood (مَجْزُومٌ) which means that you use the present tense and put سُكُونْ on the final letter.

Notice that you can place a verb (فِعْلٌ) or a noun (اِسْمٌ) directly after the following expressions.

still; yet	ما زالَ • لا يَزالُ
If you don't negate the verb, it means *to come to an end; to vanish; to abandon*.	

He is still sick.	ما زالَ مَريضًا.
She is still sitting.	لا تَزالُ جالِسةً.
He still needs it.	لا يَزالُ في حاجةٍ إِلَيْهِ.
Zayd is still a student.	ما زالَ زَيْدٌ طالِبًا.
He was still in Damascus.	كانَ لا يَزالُ (باقِيًا) في دِمَشْقَ.
Do you want anything else?	أما زِلْتَ تُريدُ شَيْئًا؟

| *not stop doing; keep doing* | ما انْفَكَّ ● لَمْ يَنْفَكَّ ● لا يَنْفَكُّ |

It is a VII-verb following the pattern اِنْفَعَلَ (يَنْفَعِلُ). If it is not negated, it means *to be separated; be disconnected; be undone*. The root verb فَكَّ denotes *to separate; disjoin; disconnect*.

| The man is still writing. | ما انْفَكَّ الرَّجُلُ كاتِبًا. |

| *not to cease to be* | ما فَتِئَ ● لَمْ يَفْتَأْ ● لا يَفْتَأُ |

Without negation, the verb means *to desist, refrain or stop*.

He is still doing...	ما فَتِئَ يَفْعَلُ...
He is still thinking about her.	ما فَتِئَ يَذْكُرُها.
He always will be.	لَنْ يَفْتَأَ.
Khalid is always trying to travel.	مَا فَتِئَ خالِدٌ يُحاوِلُ السَّفَرَ.
He is still a prisoner.	لَمْ يَفْتَأْ أَسيرًا.

| *to continue to be* | ما بَرِحَ ● لَم يَبْرَحْ ● لا يَبْرَحُ |

If the verb is not negated, the meaning is *to leave; to depart*.

He is still rich.	.مَا بَرِحَ غَنِيًّا
They are still in Egypt.	.مَا بَرِحوا فِي مِصْرَ
He is still speaking.	ـمَا بَرِحَ يَقُولُ

151. How do you say *yet* and *not yet* in Arabic?

This is more sophisticated in Arabic than in English.

Even in English, the expressions *yet* and *not yet* are tricky. Negatives with *yet* mean that something has not happened up to now. It is related to *still* – but there is a difference: If you use a negation with *still,* you suggest that the situation should have changed, but it has not. For example.

We usually put *yet* after the main **verb.**	We usually put *still* **after** the subject.
I haven't finished yet.	I **still** *haven't finished*. Meaning: I've been working on it for quite some time and should have finished it by now.

In this *question*, we will have a look at a group of expressions that are related to each other: *still; yet; not yet; not any more.*

1	*yet (still); in spite of it* (German: *dennoch*)	مَعَ أَنَّ • مَعَ ذلِكَ

He is still your brother!	!مَعَ ذلِكَ كُلُّهُ فَهُوَ أَخُوكَ
She forbade it, but he did it anyway.	.فَعَلَ ذلِكَ مَعَ أَنَّها قَدْ مَنَعَتْهُ مِنْهُ

2	*not yet*	حَتَّى الْآنَ

He has not written yet.	لَمْ يَكْتُبْ حَتَّى الْآنَ.

3.1	*not yet; not any more*	negated verb plus بَعْدُ

- In this application, the word بَعْدُ has a fixed shape (مَبْنِيٌّ عَلَى الضَّمِّ) and always stays like that. Why? You have to write بَعْدُ with a final "u" if it is cut off from a إضافة, i.e., if no other word follows it. The idea is that although the second part of the إضافة is missing, the meaning is still understood – we can say that it is cut off from the إضافة by pronunciation and not by meaning. In verbal sentences it sounds most natural to put it at the end of a sentence (and not between the verb and the direct object).

- Watch out: It is possible to use بَعْدُ without a negation.

- Notice the difference: بَعْدَ with "a" (فَتْحة) means *after* and serves as the **first** part of a إضافة-construction. *See question #221.* However, بَعْدُ with "u" (ضَمّة) may be preceded by a preposition, but doesn't change its shape then.

not yet	لَيْسَ بَعْدُ
He has not written the letter yet.	لَمْ يَكْتُبْ بَعْدُ الْجَوابَ.
	ما كَتَبَ الْجَوابَ بَعْدُ.

Notice: It is usually better to put بَعْدُ at the end of the sentence. But to place it immediately after the verb would also be correct.

He had not written the letter yet.	لَمْ يَكُنْ قَدْ كَتَبَ بَعْدُ الْجَوابَ.
	ما كانَ قَدْ كَتَبَ بَعْدُ الْجَوابَ.
He won't have written the lett. yet.	كانَ لَنْ يَكْتُبَ بَعْدُ الْجَوابَ.

	كانَ سَوْفَ لا يَكْتُبُ بَعْدُ الْجَوابَ.
Nobody else came then (after).	لَمْ يَأْتِ أَحَدٌ بَعْدُ.
She doesn't write anymore.	هِيَ لا تَكْتُبُ بَعْدُ.

Watch out: A negation particle may change the meaning.

not yet; not longer; not any more	لَيْسَ بَعْدُ
She is still young. (She is only a small girl.) Notice that we don't use the negation.	هِيَ بَعْدُ صَغِيرةٌ.
He is yet to come.	سَيَأْتِي بَعْدُ.
He has not come yet.	لَمْ يَأْتِ بَعْدُ.

3.2	*never* (German: *noch nie*)	مِنْ قَبْلُ

I have never seen her.	لَمْ أَرَاها مِنْ قَبْلُ
	لَمْ أَرَاها قَطُّ.

4	*not yet*	particle لَمَّا plus verb in the jussive mood (مَجْزُومٌ)

Here, لَمَّا is a particle of negation which induces the jussive mood in a following verb (حَرْفُ نَفْيٍ وَجَزْمُ لِلْمُضارِعِ). Watch out: It is possible to **delete** the verb and the meaning is still understood.

He has not written the letter yet.	لَمَّا يَكْتُبْ الْجَوابَ.
The train hasn't arrived yet.	لَمَّا يَأْتِ الْقِطارُ.
I came close to the city yet. Notice: We have deleted the verb here!	قارَبْتُ الْمَدِينةَ وَلَمَّا.

I came close to the city (but) haven't arrived yet.	قَارَبْتُ الْمَدِينَةَ وَلَمَّا أَصِلْ إِلَيْها.

5	not any more	negation (ما - لَمْ - لا) plus عَادَ / يَعُود plus verb in the present tense.

The director did not go to the office any more.	لَمْ يَعُدْ الْمُدِيرُ يَذْهَبُ إِلَى الْمَكْتَبِ.
	ما عَادَ الْمُدِيرُ يَذْهَبُ إِلَى الْمَكْتَبِ.
The director doesn't go to the office any more.	لا يَعُودُ الْمُدِيرُ يَذْهَبُ إِلَى الْمَكْتَبِ.

The director did not go to the office any more.	لَمْ يَعُدْ الْمُدِيرُ يَذْهَبُ إِلَى الْمَكْتَبِ.
	ما عَادَ الْمُدِيرُ يَذْهَبُ إِلَى الْمَكْتَبِ.
The director doesn't go to the office any more.	لا يَعُودُ الْمُدِيرُ يَذْهَبُ إِلَى الْمَكْتَبِ.

152. Does the Egyptian word لِسَّه mean *still* or *yet*?

It can mean both: still or yet.

When I started learning Egyptian Arabic, there was one word which gave me a headache: *lissa* (لِسَّه), sometimes also written لِسّة or لِسّى. Let's see why.

- *Lissa* means **not yet** in negated sentence. This is also true when *lissa* is used as a stand-alone expression.

- In non-negated sentences (affirmative), *lissa* usually denotes **still** or **just**.

1   *Just* versus *not yet*.

This can be very confusing for beginners.

1.1	*Lissa in the meaning of just or only recently.*

I have just arrived.	لِسَّه واصِل.
They just came.	لِسَّه جايِّين.
He was standing next to me just a second ago.	ده لِسَّه واقِف جَنْبِي مِن ثانْيَة.

Watch out: *lissa* is frequently used in combination with an **active participle** (إِسْمُ فاعِلٍ) to denote a past tense meaning (meaning of *just*): لِسَّه plus إِسْمُ فاعِلٍ.

1.2	The meaning of *not yet.*

I haven't arrived yet.	ما وَصَلْتِش لِسَّه.
They haven't come yet.	لِسَّه ماجُوش.
It is not yet a month since he has left.	سافِر لِسَّه مافِيش شَهْر.

Watch out: If you want to express the meaning of *not yet*, you use the **past tense** (الْماضِي) in Arabic in combination with the negation (ما+ش).

2	The meaning of *still.*

2.1	There is **no verb** (action) involved.

How do we use *lissa* if there is no action (no verb) mentioned in the sentence, but an **adjective** or **adverb of time**?

It is still early.	لِسَّه بَدْرِي.
There is still time.	لِسَّه فيه وَقْت.
There is still one week (to go);	لِسَّه أُسْبُوع.
He's still young.	هُوَّ لِسَّه صُغَيَّر.
It's still to soon for…	لِسَّه بَدْرِي عَلَى…
She is still young.	هِيَ لِسَّه صُغَيَّرة.
Still three dollars (to go; owing).	لِسَّه ثلاثة دولار.

2.2	Which **verb** form do you use if you want to express *still*? You use the present tense (الْمُضارِع) if the action happens right now or the future if the action is yet to happen.

I am still eating.	لِسَّه بآكُل.
I am still studying at the center.	لِسَّه بادْرِس في الْمَرْكَز.
I've still to deliver the menu (food).	لِسَّه حاوَدِّي الْوَجْبة.
I've still to read the magazine.	لِسَّه هأْقْرَأ الْمَجَلّة.

Watch out: In Egyptian Arabic, you have to use the **present tense** (ب+فِعْل مُضارِع) to express *still*. You should not use the active participle (اِسْم فاعِل) because this would express *just* – see number 1.

3	*Just* in the meaning of *just now; only recently.*

Lissa is often used with the Egyptian Arabic expression for *now*, i.e., *dilwa'ti* (دِلْوَقْتِي).

They just now left.	لِسَّه طِلْعوا دِلْوَقْتِي.

| She was standing next to me just a second ago. | دي لِسَّه كانِت واقِفة جنبي مِن ثانية. |
| The lady who had just come from the doctor... | السِتّ اللّي كانِت لِسَّه جايّة مِن عَنْد الدُّكْتُور... |

4 *Lissa* as a stand-alone word.

4.1 *Lissa* conveys the meaning of: *Have... yet?*

Oftentimes, *lissa* is used in **yes-or-no-questions**.

| Question: Have you written it? | كِتِبْته وَلا لِسَّه؟ |
| Answer: Not yet. | لِسَّه. |

Haven't you gone yet?	إنتَ لِسَّه مارُحْتِش؟
Has he come yet or not?	جاء وَلّا لِسَّه؟
Have you seen the student? - Not yet.	شُفْت الطّالِب؟ - لِسَّه.

4.2 *Lissa* is directly connected to a sentence.

| She put up with a lot, and there's more to come. | اِسْتَحْمِلِتْ كْتِير، وَلِسَّه. |

Remark: In some Arabic dialects, *lissa* (لِسّا) goes along with a pronoun (ضَمِيرٌ).

| Haven't you... | لِسَّاكُو... |

153. مُتْحَفٌ or مَتْحَفٌ – What is the word for *museum?*

In Standard Arabic, it is مُتْحَفٌ *("muthaf").*

Many native Arabic speakers call a *museum* مَتْحَف, pronounced with the vowel "a" (فَتْحة) on the first letter. Although there is only a tiny difference, it is strictly speaking wrong although the *Academy of the Arabic Language* in Cairo has approved it in the meantime.

Let's do some analysis. The word مُتْحَفٌ is based on the Arabic root ت-ح-ف which denotes *to present; to show*. However, this root is only used as a IV-verb following the pattern أَفْعَلَ.

If we want to build the *noun of place* (اِسْمُ مَكانٍ) of this action (the place where something is being displayed), we need to be careful.

meaning	اِسْمُ الْمَكانِ	verb		pattern
museum	مُتْحَفٌ	to present	أَتْحَفَ	أَفْعَلَ

The word is pronounced with "u" (ضَمّة) at the beginning. So why to people say مَتْحَف then?

مَتْحَفٌ would be the اِسْمُ الْمَكانِ of a I-verb (ثُلاثِيٌّ مُجَرَّدٌ). But this stem is not used. The I-verb تَحَفَ doesn't exist.

This brings us to a general rule:

- To build the اِسْمُ الْمَكانِ of the stems II to X, you use the **same pattern** as for the **passive participle** (اِسْمُ مَفْعُولٍ).

Let's take the word مُبْتَعَثٌ. Depending on the context, it may mean *source* (اِسْمُ الْمَكانِ) or *sent* (اِسْمُ الْمَفْعُولِ). Some other examples.

stem	verb	meaning	اِسْمُ الْمَكانِ	meaning
II	صَلَّى	to pray	مُصَلَّى	place of prayer
IV	أَتْحَفَ	to present	مُتْحَفٌ	museum
VII	اِنْبَعَثَ	to originate	مُنْبَعَثٌ	place of origin
VIII	اِجْتَمَعَ	to gather together	مُجْتَمَعٌ	gathering place
X	اِسْتَشْفَى	to seek a cure	مُسْتَشْفَى	hospital

154. مُبْتَدَأٌ - Why do we use this grammar term for *subject*?

It is the central figure (keyman) in the sentence. The term describes what a subject, in fact, is: **that with which a beginning is made** (الْمُبْتَدَأُ بِهِ).

In grammar, we call the subject of a nominal sentence (جُمْلَةٌ اِسْمِيَّةٌ) the مُبْتَدَأٌ. That is correct. But have you ever thought about what مُبْتَدَأٌ actually means?

The root of مُبْتَدَأٌ is ب-د-ء. Let's try to form VIII-verb by using the pattern اِفْتَعَلَ. Now, we get the verb اِبْتَدَأَ which denotes *to begin; to start; to bring out something*. Let's return to the word مُبْتَدَأٌ. It can mean two things:

1. It may be the *passive participle* (اِسْمُ الْمَفْعُولِ) of the verb اِبْتَدَأَ. The مُبْتَدَأٌ would then mean *begun*.

2. It may be the *noun of place* (اِسْمُ الْمَكانِ) which would then mean: *the place where it* (the sentence) *begins*.

Why is that? The اِسْمُ الْمَفْعُولِ and اِسْمُ الْمَكانِ of a VIII-verb share the same pattern as shown in *question #172*.

If we use the term *subject of a nominal sentence*, we basically mean the first word. I also use the term *subject*. However, it doesn't harm to think about the literal meaning of grammar terms when studying grammar.

What are the main features of the مُبْتَدَأٌ in Arabic?

- The subject of a nominal sentence <u>cannot</u> be a verb, nor a prepositional or adverbial phrase (شِبْهُ الْجُمْلةِ).

- If a nominal sentence starts with a preposition or an adverb, then this is the **predicate** – more precisely, the *forwarded predicate* (خَبَرٌ مُقَدَّمٌ). You reverse the word-order if you want to emphasize a certain part of the sentence.

What about the predicate (خَبَرٌ) of a nominal sentence? It may consist of:

- a single noun

- a verbal or nominal sentence

- a prepositional or adverbial phrase (شِبْهُ الْجُمْلةِ).

Now, let's see the difference between a nominal and verbal sentence.

| verbal sentence (جُمْلةٌ فِعْلِيّةٌ) | ذَهَبَ مُحَمَّدٌ إِلَى الْمَدِينةِ. | 1 |
| nominal sentence (جُمْلةٌ اِسْمِيّةٌ) | مُحَمَّدٌ ذَهَبَ إِلَى الْمَدِينةِ. | 2 |

Both sentences more or less mean the same: *Muhammad went to the city*. However, if we look at them from a grammatical perspective, there is a big difference. Let's see why.

- In the <u>first sentence</u>, مُحَمَّدٌ is the subject of a **verbal** sentence (فاعِلٌ). If we only used the first word of this sentence, it would be enough to form a meaningful sentence, even without the word *Muhammad*.

Thus, the expression ذَهَبَ is a complete sentence: *he went*. There is a hidden, concealed pronoun in ذَهَبَ which stands for *he*. And this hidden pronoun is, in fact, the subject (فَاعِلٌ) of the verb.

- In the <u>second sentence</u>, مُحَمَّدٌ is the subject of a **nominal** sentence (مُبْتَدَأ). If we only used the first word (i.e., Muhammad), it would not be enough to form a sentence.

The subject of a nominal sentence needs a **predicate**. The predicate completes the meaning. Now, what is the function of the verb in a nominal sentence? It is the predicate!

Thus, we end up with a full sentence within the predicate itself (a compound): *Muhammad, he went to the city.*

	element 2		element 1
1st sentence: element 1 plus 2: *Muhammad went to the city.*	ذَهَبَ إِلَى الْمَدِينةِ. The predicate (خَبَرٌ) is an entire verbal sentence!	+	مُحَمَّدٌ subject (مُبْتَدَأٌ)
2nd sentence: only element 2: *He went to the city.*	If we dropped the word *Muhammad*, we would still have a full sentence.		

→ If you want to know how nominal and verbal sentences differ in meaning, see *Arabic for Nerds 2*, question #208ff.

155. Can you use the letter ل to emphasize a word in Arabic?

Yes, you can.

In Arabic, *emphasis* is called تَأْكِيد or تَوْكِيد. It is a huge play-ground for language lovers. You can use additional words, you can change the word-order – or you use the letter *Lām* (ل). Let's see how we can use the ل as an amplifier. Note that if we use ل to convey emphasis, it has the vowel "*a*" on top (لَ).

1	The *Lām of introduction.*	لامُ الْإِبْتِداءِ

الْإِبْتِداءُ means *the beginning*. This type of ل is <u>never</u> combined with a **verb**! Notice that it does not influence any word regarding cases.

a) This type of ل is placed before the <u>subject</u> of a nominal sentence (مُبْتَدَأ) or

b) before the <u>forwarded predicate</u> (خَبَر مُقَدَّم).

You are (truly, indeed) a faithful friend.	لَأَنْتَ صَدِيقٌ وَفِيٌّ.	a)
(Indeed) Zayd is courageous.	لَزَيْدٌ شُجاعٌ.	
You are great. (Indeed great you are.)	لَعَظِيمٌ أَنْتَ.	b)

2	*What a wonderful... What a bad...!*	نِعْمَ • بِئْسَ

Both expressions can be used with ل in order to boost the empha-sis. See *question #183* for more details.

The best thing a person can do is to seek knowledge.	لَنِعْمَ ما يَفْعَلُهُ الْإِنْسانُ طَلَبُ الْعِلْمِ.
The worst character is lying.	لَبِئْسَ خُلُقًا الْكَذِبُ.

3 ل plus **far future** with سَوْفَ.	لَسَوْفَ

I will (definitely) attend the party.	لَسَوْفَ أَحْضُرُ الْحَفْلَ.

4 The *Lām of the answer* (حَرْفُ جَوابٍ). This type of ل is used in the 2nd part of an **if-clause** with لَوْ or لَوْلا.	لامُ الْواقِعِ

If he studied, he would succeed.	لَوْ دَرَسَ لَنَجَحَ.
If it weren't for the doctor, the situation of the patient would become bad.	لَوْلا الطَّبِيبُ لَساءَتْ حالةُ الْمَرِيضِ.
Were it not for you, I would have been lost.	لَوْلاكَ لَضَلَلْتُ.

5 ل before the **predicate** of إِنَّ.	خَبَرُ إِنَّ

Zayd is indeed generous.	إِنَّ زَيْدًا لَكَرِيمٌ.
The satisfaction of people is difficult indeed.	إِنَّ رِضا النّاسِ لَصَعْبٌ.

6 ل before the **delayed "subject"** of إِنَّ (اِسْم إِنَّ). We call this type of *Lām* also the slipping or wandering *Lām* (لامُ مُزَحْلَقَةٌ). For an in-depth analysis, *see Arabic for Nerds 2, question #260.*	

There is (indeed) benefit in traveling.	إِنَّ فِي السَّفَرِ لَمَنافِعَ.
Indeed, in history there are many lessons.	إِنَّ فِي التّارِيخِ لَعِبَرًا.

| 7 | ل before قَدْ. To express *already* or the past perfect. |

| Zayd is already gone. | لَقَدْ ذَهَبَ زَيْدٌ. |

→ For other ways to convey emphasis, see *questions #155, 157, 159*.

156. Can you use an extra ن to give emphasis?

Yes, you can.

The letter *Nūn* (ن), when added to a conjugated verb, has enough power to function as an amplifier and convey emphasis. We call such *Nūn a Nūn of confirmation* (نُونُ التَّوْكِيدِ) or *energetic Nun*.

The idea of connecting a *Nūn* with the verb is to show the speaker's determination to carry out the action without hesitation. Note that sometimes, the *Nun of confirmation* is left untranslated.

There is a "light" and a "strong" version. You can use this with the **present tense** (الْمُضارِعُ) and the **imperative** (الْأَمْرُ) – but you can't use it with the past (الْماضِي).

Let's see how it works.

1. Delete the ضَمّة on the verb (marker for the indicative mood) or delete the final ن if the verb form belongs to the so-called *five verbs* (أَفْعالٌ خَمْسة) → see *question #83*.

2. Add the vowel "*a*" (فَتْحة) on the last letter. We fix this construction with this sound (مَبْنِيٌّ عَلَى الْفَتْحِ).

3. Finally, add ّن for the heavy *Nūn* or ْن for the light *Nūn*.

4. Note: For the imperative, you do exactly the same.

A	The *light Nūn of confirmation* is formed by adding a نْ with سُكُونْ to the verb.	نُونْ خَفِيفَةٌ

Obey your parents! (imperative of IV-verb أَطاعَ).	أَطِعَنْ والِدَّيْكَ!
Will you go certainly?	هَلْ تَذْهَبَنْ؟

B	The *strong* or *heavy Nūn of confirmation* is more common and its confirmation is bolder.	نُونْ ثَقِيلَةٌ

Do you (certainly) help your friend?	هَلْ تُساعِدَنَّ زَمِيلَكَ؟

Let's see the *heavy Nūn* in action.

1.	نّ – used to express a **demand** or **inquiry**.	مُضارِعٌ جائِزٌ

1.1	Used with the imperative.	أَمْرٌ

In this application, you have to use the *Lām of request* (لامُ الطَّلَبِ), namely لِ, before the imperative. See *question #126*.

Beware of overeating!	لِتَحْذَرَنَّ الإِفْراطَ فِي الطَّعامِ!
Oh our people, be cautious!	يا قَوْمَنا اِحْذَرَنَّ!

1.2	Used to express warnings or prohibitions.	نَهْيٌ

Don't think that success in life is easy!	لاَ تَحْسَبَنَّ النَّجاحَ فِي الْحَياةِ سَهْلاً!

1.3	Used with questions to express a request.	اِسْتِفْهامٌ

Could you help your colleague?	هَلْ تُساعِدَنَّ زَمِيلَكَ؟

1.4	Used to give advice/offer	عَرْضٌ

Shouldn't you certainly help your colleague!	أَلا تُساعِدَنَّ زَمِيلَكَ!

1.5	Used to goad somebody.	تَحْضِيضٌ

Would you stop lying!	هَلَّا تَتْرُكَنَّ الْكَذِبَ!

1.6	Used to express a wish, hope, or desire.	تَمَنٍّ

I wish that you would do good deeds!	لَيْتَكَ تَعْمَلَنَّ طَيِّبًا!

2	After the **negation** with لا. → to put stress on the thing you won't do or accept.

I like honesty and I (certainly) won't tolerate lying.	أُحِبُّ الصِّدْقَ وَلا أَرْضَيَنَّ الْكَذِبَ.

3	After the word إِمَّا in a conditional sentence (شَرْطِيَّةٌ).

Notice the سُكُون in the second part of the sentence as the verb has to be مَجْزُوم.

If you really work hard you will certainly succeed in your life.	إِمَّا تَعْمَلَنَّ بِجِدٍّ تَنْجَحْ فِي حَيَاتِكَ.

| 4 | After an **oath** - if there is a conditional meaning involved. You need to use a combination of ل and the ن in the so-called *answer* (جَوابُ الْقَسَمِ). |

The verb gives the details why you swear and what you prom-ise (جَوابُ قَسَمٍ). It is not negated and although the verb is in the present tense, it has a future meaning. Notice: After an oath you need the particle ل - see *question #205*.

| I swear, I will definitely work hard! | وَاللهِ لَأَعْمَلَنَّ بِجِدٍّ! |

| I swear, I write a letter now! | وَاللهِ لَأَكْتُبُ رِسالَةَ الْآنَ! |

| If there is no conditional meaning involved, you usually don't use the ن of confirmation. |

→ For an in-depth analysis of the *Nūn of confirmation*, see *Arabic for Nerds 2, question #94*.

157. What are the particles of attention?

Words which are used to call someone's attention like "hey!"

In Arabic, grammarians call such words حَرْفُ تَنْبِيهٍ. The word تَنْبِيهٌ means *warning*. These devices help to clarify the matter for the listener.

| أَلا | Mainly a *particle of inauguration* (حَرْفُ اِسْتِفْناحٍ). The word اِسْتِفْناح means *beginning, opening*. A special application is the one as a particle of premonition (= a strong feeling that some-thing is about to happen, often something unpleasant.)

أَلا literally means ***is it not***. It is an **intensifying interjection** |

which introduces sentences. It is often found in the Qur'an.

It may be translated as *nay; verily; truly; indeed; oh yes.*

Nay, it is with knowledge that nations advance.	أَلَا بِالْعِلْمِ تَتَقَدَّمُ الْأُمَمُ.
Unquestionably, it is Allah who is the Forgiving, the Merciful. *(Sura 42:5)*	أَلَا إِنَّ اللّهَ هُوَ الْغَفُورُ الرَّحِيمُ.
O guilty one, won't you amend yourself?	أَلَا أَيُّهَا الْمُذْنِبُ كَفِّرْ عَنْكَ؟

	أَما
Same meaning as أَلَا (i.e., *isn't it*) – but watch out: أَما is usually combined with an **oath** (قَسَمٌ). Furthermore, أَما is placed at the beginning too since it is a *particle of inauguration* (حَرْفُ اِسْتِفْتَاحٍ).	

I swear he is truly honest!	أَما وَاللّهِ إِنَّهُ لَصَادِقٌ!
By God, who made you cry and made you laugh!	أَما وَاللّهِ الَّذِي أَبْكَى وَأَضْحَكَ!

	ها
The particle ها has an emphatic meaning and is used to express attention. It may be connected with other words, especially with pronouns and demonstrative pronouns (*this, that*). It basically just means: *look here, oh!*	

Here I am.	هَأَنَذَا حَاضِرٌ.
Here	هَاهُنَا
and so forth (and so on)	وَهٰكَذَا
Hey you there!	ها أَنْتَ ذَا!!

| Hey you (fem.) there! | ها أَنْتِ ذي! |
| Here, take it! There you are! There you have! | هاكَ / هاكُم (pl.) |

158. Can you use بِ and مِنْ to emphasize?

Yes, this is possible.

The prepositions بِ and مِنْ can be used to give emphasis. For this type of application, they do not exercise their original job which is to direct or give direction.

Instead, they are **extra, additional particles** (حَرْفٌ زائِدٌ). Nevertheless, they do keep their governing power which means that the word which comes after بِ or مِنْ has to be in the genitive case (مَجْرُورٌ).

The letter بِ	
Traveling is not difficult at all.	لَيْسَ السَّفَرُ بِصَعْبٍ.
Knowledge is sufficient to advance.	كَفَى بِالْعِلْمِ وَسِيلَةً لِلتَّقَدُّمِ.
Allah is the best protector!	كَفَى بِاللهِ وَكِيلًا!

Note: The verb كَفَى basically means *to be enough*. However, it can also denote *to protect*; *to spare*. It is used <u>without</u> a preposition. The preposition بِ here is only there to give emphasis.

The preposition مِنْ

You need to put a singular noun (اِسْمٌ نَكِرَةٌ) after it.

An extra preposition مِنْ doesn't dramatically change the meaning like a real preposition. As a حَرْفٌ زائِدٌ it is just there for emphasis!

Nobody came to me.	ما جاءَنِي مِنْ أَحَدٍ.

→ See also *Arabic for Nerds 2, question #178.*

159. What does a (separate) personal pronoun express?

It can express emphasis and may help to identify the predicate.

You can easily emphasize a noun (اِسْمٌ) by just adding the corresponding personal pronoun in its stand-alone form.

This form is called *pronoun of separation* (ضَمِيرُ فَصْلٍ) because it separates the subject (مُبْتَدَأ) from the predicate (خَبَرٌ) and provides some space in-between.

Why can that be useful? Usually, the predicate in a nominal sentence is <u>indefinite</u>.

If both the subject and the predicate are <u>definite</u>, it may be difficult to grasp the correct meaning.

This is because you may mistake the predicate for an adjective (صِفة) since an adjective has to agree also regarding the *determination* (i.e., the definite article) with the word to which it refers. Thus, this pronoun is called *pronoun of support* (ضَمِيرُ الْفَصْلِ) because it is used to distinguish the predicate and clarify the subject.

Some examples.

It is **Khalid** who sits there.	خالِدٌ هُوَ الْجالِسُ هُناكَ.

The **engineers** were the ones responsible for the success of the project.	كانَ الْمُهَنْدِسُونَ هُمْ الْمَسْؤُولِينَ عَنْ نَجاحِ الْمَشْرُوعِ.
I have done my duty.	قُمْتُ أَنَا بِالْواجِبِ.
He wrote the lesson himself.	كَتَبَ هُوَ الدَّرْسَ.
Zayd, **he** is the generous.	زَيْدٌ هُوَ الْكَرِيمُ.
The mothers, **they** are the most virtuous.	الْأُمَّهاتُ هُنَّ الْفاضِلاتُ.

In sentences with إِنَّ (*verily, indeed*), you will encounter the *pronoun of separation* (ضَمِيرُ فَصْلٍ) as well. It is actually the same situations as above. Before the particle إِنَّ entered the sentence, we had a standard nominal sentence (جُمْلةٌ اِسْمِيّةٌ) with subject (مُبْتَدَأٌ) and predicate (خَبَرٌ).

If both are **definite** (مَعْرِفة), the sentence may be difficult to understand. The *pronoun of separation* helps to identify both parts clearly, i.e., subject and predicate. Once the particle إِنَّ enters the sentence, the subject is called اِسْمُ إِنَّ and the predicate خَبَرُ إِنَّ.

Indeed, the boy (he) is diligent.	إِنَّ الْوَلَدَ هُوَ الْمُجْتَهِدُ.
Let's delete إِنَّ and see what we get: .الْوَلَدُ الْمُجْتَهِدُ	
This is a nominal sentence with both subject and predicate having the definite article. Therefore, we should use a personal pronoun.	

Watch out: We also use a *pronoun of separation* if the predicate is **close to a definite noun**. This happens if we have a comparative noun (اِسْمُ تَفْضِيلٍ).

Nobody (he) is more knowledgeable than	لَيْسَ أَحَدٌ هُوَ أَعْلَمَ مِنْ

your brother.	أَخِيكَ.

Usually, such a pronoun does not have a job in the sentence. It is merely there for **separation**. We say that it has no place in the analysis (لَا مَحَلَّ لَهُ مِنَ الْإِعْرَابِ). In other words, it cannot function as the subject, predicate, object, etc.

However, there is one tricky situation when we have to treat it differently and assign a grammatical function (which means we need to think about a hypothetical case ending). This happens when we have a nominal sentence (جُمْلَةٌ اِسْمِيّةٌ) in which the **second noun** is <u>connected</u> to the **first noun** by the *pronoun of separation*. The personal pronoun then functions as the subject (مُبْتَدَأٌ) of the second nominal sentence. Sounds complicated? Let's check an example:

The student was (he is/himself) Zayd.	كَانَ الطَّالِبُ هُوَ زَيْدٌ.

Let's first check the sub-sentence: The pronoun هُوَ is the subject (مُبْتَدَأٌ) and زَيْدٌ is its predicate (خَبَرٌ). What about the main, primary sentence? The word الطَّالِبُ is the "subject" of كَانَ (اِسْمُ كَانَ) and the **entire sentence** هُوَ زَيْدٌ is the predicate of كَانَ (خَبَرُ كَانَ).

160. Which expressions can be used for emphasis?

There are many!

If you want to add weight to your statement, there are some powerful expressions in Arabic that will do the job. You usually use a *generic, absolute negation* (لَا النَّافِيةُ لِلْجِنْسِ) which translates as *there is no…*

If you use this type of negation, the "subject" (لا اِسْمُ) will take the accusative case (مَنْصُوبٌ). Although the "subject" has to be indefinite (نَكِرَةٌ - no definite article!), it does not take nunation (تَنْوِينٌ). It only gets one فَتْحَةٌ, the vowel "a". → See also *question #248.*

Such expressions are usually followed by a prepositional or adverbial phrase. However, although the expression may need to go along with a preposition (مِنْ or فِي), the preposition is often dropped. You also find that in the expression *it is unavoidable* which is لَا بُدَّ مِنْ أَنَّ. Instead, you often see the conjunction وَ resulting in: لَا بُدَّ وَأَنَّ...

doubtless; not doubt that...	لا رَيْبَ فِي...
There is no doubt about it.	لا رَيْبَ فِيهِ.
She will come, no doubt about it.	سَتَحْضُرُ وَلا رَيْبَ.

| doubtless; without doubt | لا شَكَّ أَنَّ... |
| You know him, without doubt. | تَعْرِفُهُ وَلا شَكَّ. |

Note: Such expressions are often introduced with the conjunction وَ and are placed at the end of the sentence.

| There is absolutely no doubt that many of you did not go. | لا شَكَّ أَبَدًا أَنَّ الْكَثِيرَ مِنْكُمْ لَمْ يَذْهَبْ. |

| You have certainly crossed the line. | لا بُدَّ وَأَنَّكَ تَجاوَزْتَ الْخَطَّ. |
| I must know it. | لا بُدَّ أَنْ أَعْرِفَهُ. |

Note: Since the expression is followed by a verb here and not a noun, we use أَنْ plus verb instead of أَنَّ plus noun.

| indisputably | لا جِدالَ أَنَّ... |

unquestionable	لا مِراءَ أَنَّ...

I say firmly...	أَقُولُ جازِمًا إِنَّ...
I say for sure...	أَقُولُ عَنْ يَقينٍ إِنَّ...

In these two examples, we use إِنَّ ("inna") since we use the verb قالَ - see *question #229* and *Arabic for Nerds 2, question #256*.

161. When do you use a pronoun in a relative clause?

When you would decline the relative pronoun in English.

In German, you have to decline the relative pronoun (*welch - welcher - welche – welches*) according to its position in the sentence. In English, you sometimes do it.

In Arabic, however, you almost never decline relative pronouns (اِسْمُ مَوْصُولٍ). For example, the word الَّذِي (*which, that*) stays the same in all cases, no matter if it denotes *which, who,* or *whom.* The only exception is the dual - see *quest. #113*.

So, what happens in Arabic? We may need a **connector**, a *returning pronoun* (ضَمِيرٌ عائِدٌ) which relates back to the main word. Let's see how it works.

Without a referring pronoun: the nominative case (مَرْفُوع)	
The lazy man	الرَّجُلُ الْكَسُولُ
= The man who is lazy	= الرَّجُلُ الَّذِي هُوَ كَسُولٌ
Here, the relative pronoun would be in the <u>nominative case</u> in Eng-	

lish. The information in the relative clause has the same case as the subject. Since we do not have any other person or object involved, there is **no need for a connector/link**.

The man who came...	...الرَّجُلُ الَّذِي جَاءَ.ـ

You wouldn't decline the relative pronoun in English. Imagine the sentence without a relative pronoun: الرَّجُلُ جَاءَ. (*The man came.*) This would make sense – thus, you don't need a referring pronoun.

With a referring pronoun:
the genitive (مَجْرُورٌ) or accusative case (مَنْصُوبٌ)

The man whom I knew.... (attached to a verb)	...الرَّجُلُ الَّذِي عَرَفْتُهُ
Have you found the keys that you lost? (attached to a verb)	هَلْ وَجَدْتَ الْمَفَاتِيحَ الَّتِي فَقَدْتَهَا؟
This is the pen that you asked for. (attached to a preposition)	هٰذا هُوَ الْقَلَمُ الَّذِي سَأَلْتَ عَنْهُ.
This is the professor whose book I read. (attached to a noun)	هٰذا هُوَ الْأُسْتَاذُ الَّذِي قَرَأْتُ كِتَابَهُ.

Try to imagine the sentences in the above table without the relative pronoun – they wouldn't make sense. In all these examples, the relative pronoun **would be declined in English** (*whom*) or in German (*Der Mann, den...*).

In other words, when the main word (*antecedent*) is <u>not the subject</u> of the verb in the **clause**, then you need a **link (returning pronoun)**.

The last sentence literally means: This is the professor whose book **I read it**. The subject of the verb in the clause is "*I*". Since we talk about the book of the professor, we need an object pronoun that refers to the professor. The object pronoun agrees with the main word (*professor*) in the usual ways.

Excursus I: The nature of the relative pronoun/noun الَّذِي.

In Arabic, the word الَّذِي is considered **definite** (مَعْرِفَةٌ) and **indeclinable** (مَبْنِيٌّ). Therefore, we cannot put case endings and can only assign a place value. Although it can't change its form, we say that it is فِي مَحَلِّ رَفْع (*in the position of a nominative*) or نَصْبٍ (*accusative*) or جَرٍّ (*genitive*).

Lit.: *He came, he who...*	ـ...جَاءَ الَّذِي
الَّذِي here is the **subject** (فَاعِلٌ) of the verbal sentence! It would thus take the nominative case (مَرْفُوعٌ). However, since it has a fixed shape, we can only **assign a place value** – that of a nominative case (فِي مَحَلِّ رَفْعٍ).	

Wait! Why do we say that the relative "pronoun" takes on a grammatical function in the sentence? This has to do with its origin and nature. Contrary to English, the relative noun in Arabic has a **demonstrative nature**. It is a compound of لَ plus ذِي which got enhanced by the definite article (الـ) resulting in الَّذِي. Let's see what this means.

I hit the man who came.	ضَرَبْتُ الرَّجُلَ الَّذِي جَاءَ.
If I apply the nature of الَّذِي, the inner and literal meaning of the sentence is as follows: *I hit the man, **this one** (t)here, he came.* (German: Ich schlug den Mann, **den da**, er kam.)	

Excursus II: What can be used in a relative clause (صِلَةُ الْمَوْصُولِ)? You have four options.

The man who lives there.	الرَّجُلُ الَّذِي يَسْكُنُ هُناكَ.	verbal sentence (جُمْلَةٌ فِعْلِيَّةٌ)	1
He came, he who was absent.	حَضَرَ الَّذِي كانَ غائِبًا.		

Those who are my friends attended.	حَضَرَ الَّذِينَ هُمْ أَصْدِقائِي.	nominal sentence (جُمْلَةُ اِسْمِيَّةٌ)	2

Notice: When the relative clause is made of a nominal sentence, then the subject (مُبْتَدَأٌ) serves as the *returning pronoun*! In our example: هُمْ.

Look at the panel that is in front of you.	أُنْظُرْ إِلَى اللَّوْحَةِ الَّتِي أمامَكَ.	adverbial phrase (ظَرْفٌ)	3
The flowers which were in the garden, were picked up.	قُطِفَتْ الْأَزهارُ الَّتِي فِي الْحَدِيقةِ.	prepositional phrase (جارٌّ وَمَجْرُورٌ)	4

In 3 and 4, we assume that there is a virtual, estimated verb or active participle to which the adverbial or prepositional phrase relate – for example: كائِنٌ or اِسْتَمَرَّ. For an in-depth discussion about that (التَّعَلُّقُ), see *Arabic for Nerds 2, question #140*.

Watch out: A single word after الَّذِي is not possible. If you have such a situation, just add a personal pronoun, and the sentence works.

162. الَّذِي and مَنْ - When do you use which word for *who*?

It depends on whether you talk about a specific person or not.

First of all, both words express the meaning of a **relative pronoun** (اِسْمُ مَوْصُولٍ): *this; that; the one; which; whom; who.*

regarding a specific person	اَلَّذِي	1
for a general statement	مَنْ	2

I like the professor who cares about his students.	أُحْبُّ الأُسْتاذَ الَّذِي يَهْتَمُّ بِطُلَّابِهِ.	1
I like (one) who cares about students.	أُحِبُّ مَنْ يَهْتَمُّ بِطُلَّابٍ.	2

This is similar to ما which is also used for general statements.

I like the (two) dresses that my (two) friends have bought.	أُحِبُّ الْفُسْتانَيْنِ اللَّذَيْنِ اِشْتَرَتْهُما صَديقَتَي.	1
I like what I bought.	أُحِبُّ ما اِشْتَرَيْتُهُ.	2
Watch out: You don't use ها in the second sentence. It is ه – because in <u>general statements</u>, the <u>masculine pronoun</u> is used!		

163. *Exactly twenty or more than twenty. How do you know?*

If there's مِنْ involved, you know that the number is a bit vague.

In Arabic, there is a nice way of expressing that you talk about an exact amount of people/things or only about an approximate amount. Look at these two examples:

I met *(exactly)* twenty students.	قابَلْتُ عِشْرينَ طالِبًا.	1
I met *(about/more than)* twenty	قابَلْتُ عِشْرينَ مِنَ الطُّلَّابِ.	2

students.		

Thus, if we use the construction مِنْ plus the **plural form** of a noun, we can indicate that we are not talking about an exact number. However, you often don't translate this nuance. You would just say: *I met twenty students.*

164. If a verb is transitive, what does that mean?

A transitive verb is one that is used with an object.

Let's see how a **transitive** verb (فِعْلٌ مُتَعَدٍّ) works in English.

He	sends	her	a letter
subject	(**transitive**) verb	**indirect** object	**direct** object

An **intransitive** verb (فِعْلٌ لازِمٌ) does not have a direct object.

We	walked	for hours
subject	(**intransitive**) verb	adverb

Some examples now in Arabic.

The player ran. (There is no object.)	جَرَى اللّاعِبُ.	intransitive
The child sat down.	جَلَسَ الْوَلَدُ.	intransitive
It is impossible to use a direct object with *to sit*, as the action can only be done by the doer – but the doer can't do it to a thing or an object.		

The child broke the cup.	كَسَرَ الطِّفْلُ الْكُوبَ.	transitive
The verb needs an object (*cup*); otherwise the sentence would not work. The object is the answer to the question: **what?**		

In Arabic, there are **verbs** which can have **two** or **three objects**. If a verb can carry only one object, we call it مُتَعَدٍّ إِلَى مَفْعُولٍ واحِدٍ. If a verb can carry two objects, we say مُتَعَدٍّ إِلَى مَفْعُولَيْنِ. See *question #109* for more details.

165. What is the root of the word تَارِيخٌ (*history*)?

The root is ء-ر-خ.

It is worthwhile to take a closer look at this root.

- The corresponding **verb** for *history* is أَرَّخَ which is a II-verb following the paradigm فَعَّلَ.

- The person *who writes down the history* (اِسْمُ الْفاعِلِ), is the مُؤَرِّخٌ.

- The مَصْدَر of II-verbs is built after the pattern تَفْعِيلٌ. Thus, the مَصْدَر of أَرَّخَ is تَأْرِيخٌ – notice the هَمْزة on top of the Aleph.

- The word تَأْرِيخٌ describes the **process** of *writing down history* or *dates*.

- The **result** of تَأْرِيخٌ is تارِيخٌ = *history*. Notice here that the Aleph doesn't take a هَمْزة!

Hence, the word تارِيخٌ is a noun (اِسْمٌ) which denotes the **result,** whereas the مَصْدَر of the verb is describing the **process** of reaching the goal (هَدَفٌ) of the action.

Remark: ع-ر-خ is probably not an Arabic root. It is an ancient Semitic root that is already found in Accadian, Aramaic, and Hebrew. The Hebrew word יָרֵחַ ("yareah") means *moon* and יֶרַח (first vowel is close to German "ä" and English "a" as in "land") means *month* – from which perhaps the idea of a *calendar* and *date* arose. Some scholars, however, say that it is a pure Arabic root. There is even the idea that تَارِيخ is formed by transposition from تَأْخِير (*delay*).

166. How do you convert transitive into intransitive verbs?

You play with the stems: you add or delete letters.

Every verb has a subject, but not every verb has an object. A verb which can carry an object is a transitive verb (فِعْلٌ مُتَعَدٍّ).

A verb which **can't** carry an object and thus only has a subject is called *intransitive* verb (فِعْلٌ لَازِمٌ). A single letter – added or deleted – can **convert a transitive verb into an intransitive verb** or vice versa.

Let's see how it works and start with the conversion operation transitive → **intransitive.**

	translation	**transitive**		translation	**intransitive**
1		أَفْعَلَ	→		فَعَلَ
	The policeman threw the thief out of the house.	أَخْرَجَ الشُّرْطِيُّ اللِّصَّ مِن الْبَيْتِ.		The thief got out of the house.	خَرَجَ اللِّصُّ مِن الْبَيْتِ.

2	فاعَلَ	→	فَعَلَ
Muhammad sat with the guest.	جالَسَ مُحَمَّدُ الضَّيْفَ.	The guest sat.	جَلَسَ الضَّيْفُ.

3	اِسْتَفْعَلَ	→	فَعِلَ
The company brought tourists to Egypt.	اِسْتَقْدَمَتِ الشَّرِكةُ السُّيّاحَ إلَى مِصْرَ.	The tourists came to Egypt.	قَدِمَ السُّياحُ إلَى مِصْرَ.

4	فَعَّلَ	→	فَعُلَ
The student improved his handwriting.	حَسَّنَ الطّالِبُ خَطَّهُ.	The handwriting of the student is nice.	حَسُنَ خَطُّ الطّالِبِ.

Now, what about the other direction? Let's see some options for the conversion operation intransitive → **transitive.**

	translation	**intransitive**		translation	**transitive**

1		اِنْفَعَلَ, تَفَعَّلَ	→		فَعَلَ
	The cup got broken.	اِنْكَسَرَ الْكُوبُ.		The child broke the cup.	كَسَرَ الطِّفْلُ الْكُوبَ.

2		اِفْتَعَلَ	→		فَعَلَ
	The cup is filled with water.	اِمْتَلَأَ الْكُوبُ بِالْماءِ.		The child filled the cup with water.	مَلَأَ الطِّفْلُ الْكُوبَ بِالْماءِ.

167. What is so special about *a kilogram of sugar*?

In Arabic, it is the grammar.

When you say *I buy a kilo, a liter,* or *a hectare,* it is a vague information because you don't say what kind of good you are buying. The sentence becomes clearer as soon as you add a **specification** (تَمْيِيزٌ). It answers the question: *what?* (مَاذَا؟)

However, there are several grammar issues we have to solve.

Let us first check the grammar terms.

I have one pound (a *ratl* ~ half a kilo) of honey.	عِنْدِي رَطْلُ عَسَلًا.
He gives me a liter (of) milk.	يُعْطِينِي لِتْرًا لَبَنًا.

رَطْلُ in example 1 is the *subject* (مُبْتَدَأٌ); in example 2, لِتْرًا is the *direct object* (مَفْعُولٌ بِهِ); We also call them the *distinguished (specified)*: الْمُمَيَّزُ.	*liter* *ratl*	لِتْرًا رَطْلُ
This is the *specification* or *distinctive* (التَّمْيِيزُ). It clears the ambiguity of *liter* and *ratl* (one pound).	*milk* *honey*	لَبَنًا عَسَلًا

> **Rule:** The classical *specification* (تَمْيِيزٌ) has to be a **singular** (مُفْرَدٌ) word in the **accusative** case (مَنْصُوبٌ).

But that is not the end of the story. If you want to express *one pound (of) oil,* you have **four different options** which all mean the same. However, the case markers may be different:

You add the word *oil* directly as a تَمْيِيزٌ	عِنْدِي رَطْلُ زَيْتًا.	1
Oil has to be in the accusative case (مَنْصُوبٌ) because it is a classical **specification** (تَمْيِيزٌ).		

You use a إضافة-construction.	عِنْدِي رَطْلُ زَيْتٍ.	2
Oil is the second part of the إضافة and has to be مَجْرُورٌ.		

You use a construction with مِن.	عِنْدِي رَطْلٌ مِن زَيْتٍ.	3
Oil follows a preposition and therefore has to be مَجْرُورٌ.		

You use an apposition (بَدَلٌ).	عِنْدِي رَطْلُ زَيْتٌ.	4
Oil stands in apposition to one pound (ratl). It therefore takes the same case – here it is the nominative case (مَرْفُوعٌ) since the word رَطْلُ is the subject (مُبْتَدَأ) of the nominal sentence.		

The specification doesn't have to be a classical unit like *kg*, *liter*, etc. It can also be of other type (no measurement).

I bought (a bouquet) of flowers.	اِشْتَرَيْتُ باقَةً زَهْرًا.
I bought a bag (sack) of tea.	اِشْتَرَيْتُ كِيسًا شايًا.

Watch out: Almost all numbers in Arabic follow the logic of the specification. Some use a إضافة-construction (option 2), other numbers carry the *distinctive* as a تَمْيِيزٌ (option 1) which is the reason for the accusative case (مَنْصُوبٌ). The word كَمْ (*how much, how many*) is also followed by a *specification*. The numbers marked gray use a **specification** (تَمْيِيزٌ).

	distinctive	translation	example
3-10	plural in the genitive (جَمْعٌ مَجْرُورٌ) (إضافة-construction)	*In the room are 7 students.*	فِي الْغُرْفةِ سَبْعةُ طُلّابٍ.
11 - 99	singular in the accu-	*In the room are 11 stu-*	فِي الْغُرْفةِ أَحَدَ

		dents.	عَشَرَ طالِبًا.
20, 30, 40, ...	sative (مُفْرَدٌ مَنْصُوبٌ) specification (تَمْييزٌ)	There are 20 men in the house.	فِي الدَّارِ عِشْرُونَ رَجُلًا.
100	singular in the geni-tive (مُفْرَدٌ مَجْرُورٌ) (إضافة-construction)	The faculty has 100 professors.	فِي الْكُلِّيَّةِ مِئَةُ أُسْتاذٍ.
1000		The faculty has 4000 students.	فِي الْكُلِّيَّةِ أَرْبَعةُ آلافِ طالِبٍ.
how many	singular in the accu-sative (مُفْرَدٌ مَنْصُوبٌ) specification (تَمْييزٌ)	How many books do you have?	كَمْ كِتابًا عِنْدَكَ؟

There are two <u>exceptions</u>: The **numbers 1** and **2**. They use a different idea: the adjective.

In the office, there is one (male) em-ployee and two (female) employees.	فِي الْمَكْتَبِ مُوَظَّفٌ واحِدٌ، وَمُوَظَّفَتانِ اِثْنَتانِ.

The number comes **after** the noun! It is an adjective (صِفةٌ) and needs agreement. It corresponds in number, case, gender and de-termination (definite, indefinite) with the preceding noun.

Remark: Also a **comparison** may be a specification (تَمْييزٌ).

Cairo is more crowded than Alexandria.	الْقاهِرةُ أَكْثَرُ اِزِدِحامًا مِن الإِسْكَنْدَرِيَّةِ.

اِزِدِحامًا is a **specification** (تَمْييزٌ). It tells the reader or listener what you are talking about; the sentence wouldn't make sense without it.

168. اِمْتَلَأَتْ الْبُحَيْرَةُ سَمَكًا. - How do you translate that?

The lake is full of fish.

The construction of the sentence اِمْتَلَأَتْ الْبُحَيْرَةُ سَمَكًا is pretty sophisticated. In fact, we deal with a sentence that has changed its word order.

In Arabic grammar, such constructions are called *distinctive/specification of the sentence* (تَمْيِيزُ الْجُمْلةِ) or *distinctive/specification of the relation* (تَمْيِيزُ الْنِسْبةِ).

Now, what about the sentence? If we dropped the last word سَمَكًا, the sentence would still work.

The lake was filled.	اِمْتَلَأَتْ الْبُحَيْرَةُ.

It would be a general saying as you have removed the additional information, the specification (التَّمْيِيزُ), which made it specific. We only know that the lake is filled now, but full of what? Water, garbage, or fish?

That is the reason why we need to give additional information and tell the reader and listener what it actually was that filled the lake.

Another example:

People differ culture-wise (يَخْتَلِفُ النَّاسُ ثَقافةً).

The culture of people differs.	يَخْتَلِفُ ثَقافةُ النَّاسِ.	1
This was the original sentence. We used a إضافة-construction.		
People differ culture-wise	يَخْتَلِفُ النَّاسُ ثَقافةً.	2
This is how we can rewrite the first sentence – without changing the meaning. Notice three things:		

1. The different form of the verb: Now, we use the masculine form; above, we used the feminine form تَخْتَلِفُ .

2. The word *culture* takes the accusative case (مَنْصُوبٌ) because it is a تَمْيِيزٌ.

3. The subject in both sentences is different: In example 1, it is ثَقافةُ; in example 2, it is النَّاسُ.

What we have seen above can be applied to different parts of a sentence. In the following examples, the original sentence and the sentence that uses a specification (تَمْيِيزٌ) mean the same.

what has changed	with **specification** (تَمْيِيزٌ)	original sentence
subject	اِشْتَعَلَتِ النَّارُ فِي الْبَيْتِ.	اِشْتَعَلَ الْبَيْتُ نارًا.
	The house caught fire.	
object	نَظَّمَ الْقائِدُ الْجُنُودَ صُفُوفًا.	نَظَّمَ الْقائِدُ صُفُوفَ الْجُنُودِ.
	The leader organized the soldiers to stand in a line.	
	Notice: You have to change the order of the إِضافة and delete the definite article.	
comparative, superlative	هذا الطَّالِبُ أَشَدُّ ذَكاءً.	---
	This student is the most intelligent.	

169. What is the passive participle (اِسْمُ الْمَفْعُولِ) of دَعَا؟

It is مَدْعُوٌّ.

The I-verb دَعَا means *to call, to invite*. The passive participle is مَدْعُوٌّ which means *called*. How do we end up with such a weird form?

The passive participle (اِسْمُ مَفْعُولٍ) of a I-verb is formed by using the pattern مَفْعُولٌ. Some examples:

meaning	اِسْمُ مَفْعُولٍ	I-verb
to understand - *understood*	مَفْهُومٌ	فَهِمَ - يَفْهَمُ
to read - *was read*	مَقْرُوءٌ	قَرَأَ - يَقْرَأُ
to break - *broken*	مَكْسُورٌ	كَسَرَ - يَكْسِرُ

Remember that the glottal stop – the Hamza (هَمْزة) – is not a weak letter! The verb قَرَأَ (*to read*) follows the standard rules, except that you have to pay attention how to write the هَمْزة correctly. In our example, we get مَقْرُوءٌ.

Now, what happens if we have a root that contains و or ي, a **weak letter** (حَرْفُ عِلَّةٍ)? It gets tricky.

- Verbs with a weak letter in the **middle** (مُعْتَلُّ الْوَسَطِ) are called *hollow* (فِعْلٌ أَجْوَفُ). For example: قَالَ.

- Verbs with a weak letter **at the end** (مُعْتَلُّ الْآخِرِ) are called *defective* (فِعْلٌ ناقِصٌ - مُعْتَلٌّ). See *question #98.*

Some examples.

meaning	اِسْمُ مَفْعُولٍ	verb
to invite or call - *invited* or *called*	مَدْعُوٌّ	دَعا - يَدْعُو
to say - *said*	مَقُولٌ	قَالَ - يَقُولُ

meaning	اِسْمُ مَفْعُولٍ	verb
to sell - *sold*	مَبِيعٌ	باعَ - يَبِيعُ
to forget - *forgotten*	مَنسِيٌّ	نَسَى - يَنْسَى
to throw - *thrown*	مَرمِيٌّ	رَمَى - يَرْمِي

Now we have the answer to our question: مَدْعُوٌّ.

How can you know the correct (middle or last) letter for the passive participle? Just check the present tense (الْمُضارِعُ). The الْمُضارِعُ shows you how the weak letter changes.

> If the present tense verb ends in و or ى, the passive participle will have a شَدّة on the last letter.

The passive participle of II to X-verbs is easily formed.

- You only have to add مُ to the past tense verb.
- If it starts with ا, then delete the ا.

Watch out: The active participle (اِسْمُ فاعِلٍ) looks exactly the same if the vowels are not written. The only difference is just **one** vowel. For example, the VIII-verb *to respect* (اِحْتَرَمَ):

passive participle (اِسْمُ الْمَفْعُولِ)	*respected*	مُحْتَرَمٌ	1
	The vowel on the second root letter is فَتْحةٌ.		
active participle (اِسْمُ الْفاعِلِ)	*one who respects*	مُحْتَرِمٌ	2
	The vowel of the second root letter is كَسْرةٌ.		

How does the plural of the passive participle مَدْعُوٌّ look like? You add the usual suffix -ونَ. Thus, you have to write two و!

the invited students	الطُّلّابُ الْمَدْعُوُّونَ

170. How do you build the *noun of place* (إِسْمُ مَكانٍ)؟

You use the pattern مَفْعَلٌ *or* مَفْعِلٌ.

In Arabic, it is easy to build a word for the place where the action happens. It is called *noun of place* (إِسْمُ مَكان) and belongs to the derived nouns of the root (إِسْمُ مُشْتَقٌّ).

For a **I-verb** (ثُلاثِيٌّ) there are two patterns:

A. The pattern مَفْعَلٌ.

It is used either...

1. if the verb has a **weak** letter <u>at the end</u> (defective ending);

2. if the second root letter takes the vowel "a" (فَتْحةٌ) or the vowel "u" (ضَمّةٌ) in the **present tense**.

translation	إِسْمُ مَكانٍ		translation		verb
principle; basis	مَبْدَأٌ		to begin	*a*	بَدَأَ يَبْدَأُ
playground	مَلْعَبٌ		to play	*a*	لَعِبَ يَلْعَبُ
amusement center	مَلْهًى		to be amused	*u*	لَها يَلْهُو

Here are some roots that do not use this pattern (exceptions). There are no rules – it is just based on how people use them.

translation	إِسْمُ مَكانٍ		translation		verb
school	مَدْرَسةٌ		to learn	*u*	دَرَسَ يَدْرُسُ
farm	مَزْرَعةٌ		to plant	*a*	زَرَعَ يَزْرَعُ
place of sunset*	مَغْرِب		to depart	*u*	غَرَبَ يَغْرُبُ
mosque*	مَسْجِدٌ		to bow down	*u*	سَجَدَ يَسْجُدُ

| graveyard | مَقْبَرَةٌ | to bury | *u* | يَقْبُرُ | قَبَرَ |

* Notice: According to the rules it should be مَسْجَدُ and مَغْرَبٌ.

B. The pattern مَفْعِلٌ.

It is used either...

1. if the verb <u>starts</u> with a <u>weak letter</u>;
2. if the second root letter takes the vowel "i" (كَسْرَةُ) in the **present tense**.

translation	إِسْمُ مَكانٍ	translation		verb	
position, station	مَوْقِفٌ	to stop		يَقِفُ	وَقَفَ
appointment	مَوْعِدٌ	to promise		يَعِدُ	وَعَدَ
birthplace	مَوْلِدٌ	to give birth to		يَلِدُ	وَلَدَ
native country	مَوْطِنٌ	to settle down	*i*	يَطِنُ	وَطَنَ
runway	مَهْبِطٌ	to descend		يَهْبِطُ	هَبَطَ
place of retreat	مَرْجِعٌ	to return		يَرْجِعُ	رَجَعَ
residence	مَنْزِلٌ	to stay		يَنْزِلُ	نَزَلَ

There are well-known exceptions:

| airport* | مَطارٌ | to fly | يَطِيرُ | طارَ |

* Notice: According to the rules it should be مَطِيرٌ

If you want to know how to build the إِسْمُ مَكانٍ for other verb forms (II to X), have a look at *question #172*.

171. Does مَوْلِدٌ mean *birthday* or *birthplace*?

It can mean both.

Depending on the context, the اِسْمُ مَكانٍ can function as the *noun of time* (اِسْمُ زَمانٍ).

The *noun of time* indicates the time (moment) when the action happens. Sometimes this can be tricky because the اِسْمُ مَكانٍ and the اِسْمُ زَمانٍ look exactly the same as they share the same pattern. Moreover, they may even denote approximately the same. An example:

اِسْمُ زَمانٍ	My birthday is in October.	مَوْلِدِي فِي شَهْرِ أُكْتُوبِر.
اِسْمُ مَكانٍ	My birthplace is in London.	مَوْلِدِي فِي مَدِينَةِ لُنْدُن.

172. What do verbs of stem II to X have in common?

Four types of derived nouns look exactly the same: noun of place, noun of time, passive participle, and مَصْدَرٌ مِيمِيٌّ.

Augmented verbs (فِعْلٌ مَزِيدٌ) are easier to handle than just the plain I-verb. There are only few patterns and almost no exceptions. *Augmented* means that you add extra letters to the root. The result is what we call the different verb stems.

Let us examine the VIII-verb اِلْتَقَى بِ which means *to meet (someone); to encounter*. It uses the past tense pattern اِفْتَعَلَ. We formed it by adding the letters ا and ت to the basic I-verb لَقِيَ (*to find, to meet*).

What happens if we want to form nouns of this verb?

For example, we want the passive participle, the noun of place or time? Answer: We will end up with the same word.

This does not only happen to VIII-verbs – but to all augmented verbs (stem II to X). In other words, some derived nouns (اِسْمٌ مُشْتَقٌّ) use the same pattern.

1	اِسْمُ مَكانٍ	The center is the meeting point of the students.	الْمَرْكَزُ مُلْتَقَى الطُّلَّابِ.
2	اِسْمُ زَمانٍ	The students meet at nine o'clock.	السَّاعَةُ التَّاسِعَة مُلْتَقَى الطُّلَّابِ.
3	اِسْمُ مَفْعُولٍ	The students have met.	الطُّلَّابُ مُلْتَقَى بِهِمْ.
4	مَصْدَرٌ مِيمِيٌّ	The meeting of the students was nice.	كانَ مُلْتَقَى الطُّلَّابِ جَمِيلًا.
		The original مَصْدَرٌ (مَصْدَرٌ أَصْلِيٌّ) is الاِلْتِقاءُ.	

Let's summarize the most important points:

- The اِسْمُ مَفْعُولٍ and اِسْمُ مَكانٍ and اِسْمُ زَمانٍ as well as the share the same pattern. This is true for all stems except for the plain I-verb.

- Only a I-verb has special patterns for the اِسْمُ زَمانٍ and اِسْمُ مَكانٍ. They are مَفْعَلٌ and مَفْعِلٌ.

Let us now check some stems.

pas. p. (اِسْمُ مَفْعُولٍ)	pattern	passive	meaning	verb	
decided	مُقَرَّرٌ	مُفَعَّلٌ	قُرِّرَ	*to decide*	قَرَّرَ	II
controlled	مُراعًى	مُفاعَلٌ	رُوعِيَ	*to control*	راعَى	III
closed	مُغْلَقٌ	مُفْعَلٌ	أُغْلِقَ	*to close*	أَغْلَقَ	IV

instructed	مُتَعَلَّم	مُتَفَعِّل	نُعُلِّم	to study	تَعَلَّم	V
prevented	مُتَدارَك	مُتَفَاعَل	نُدُورِكَ	to prevent	تَدارَكَ	VI
depressed	مُنْحَدَر	مُنْفَعَل	---	to descend	إنْحَدَر	VII
concise	مُخْتَصَر	مُفْتَعَل	أُخْتَصِر	to shorten	إخْتَصَر	VIII
The passive participle is not used with IX-verbs. However, the active participle (اِسْمُ فاعِلٍ) of this stem is often mistaken as the passive participle. It follows the pattern: مُفْعَلّ. For ex., the active participle of *to be black* (اِسْوَدَّ) is مُسْوَدٌّ.						IX
extracted	مُسْتَخْرَج	مُسْتَفْعَل	أُسْتَخْرِج	to extract	إسْتَخْرَج	X

173. What is the root مُسْتَشْفَى (hospital)?

It is ش-ف-ي.

The word مُسْتَشْفَى means *hospital* and is the اِسْمُ مَكانٍ of the X-verb اِسْتَشْفَى. It literally denotes *the place to seek cure.*

Watch out: The *noun of place* (اِسْمُ مَكانٍ) and the *passive participle* (اِسْمُ مَفْعُولٍ) of a X-verb share the same pattern! *See question #172.*

translation	اِسْمُ مَكانٍ		translation	X-verb
meeting place	مُلْتَقَى		to meet	إلْتَقَى
hospital	مُسْتَشْفَى		to seek a cure	إسْتَشْفَى
society	مُجْتَمَع		to meet	إجْتَمَع

If you are not sure whether the word مُسْتَشْفَى is masculine or feminine, have a look at *question #174.*

174. Is مُسْتَشْفَى (*hospital*) masculine or feminine?

It is masculine (مُذَكَّرٌ).

Stop! But isn't it true that a final ى is usually an indicator for a feminine word? Yes, this is true. But there are exceptions.

> Rule: Most *nouns of place* (اِسْمُ مَكانٍ) are **masculine**.

Now, what happens if we add an adjective? What about the agreement? The adjective has to take the masculine form!

| a nightclub | مَلْهًى لَيْلِيٌّ (not لَيْلِيَّةٌ) |
| a big hospital | مُسْتَشْفًى كَبِيرٌ |

175. How do you build words for tools (اِسْمُ آلةٍ)?

There are many patterns.

Scissors, spoon, or car – it is easy to form a word for a **tool** or an **instrument** with which the action (of the verb) is being done. We call such words *noun of instrument* (اِسْمُ آلةٍ). The word آلةٌ means *instrument* or *machine*.

We deal with derived nouns (اِسْمُ مُشْتَقٌّ) of the root. There are several patterns to build it:

> pattern: مِفْعَلٌ

meaning	plural	اِسْمُ آلةٍ		I-verb
microscope	مَجَاهِرُ	مِجْهَرٌ	to be brought to light	جَهَرَ - يَجْهَرُ

meaning	plural	اِسْمُ آلةٍ		I-verb
scissors	مَقَاصُّ or مِقَصَّاتٌ	مِقَصٌّ	to cut	قَصَّ - يَقُصُّ

pattern: مِفْعَلةٌ

meaning	plural	اِسْمُ آلةٍ		I-verb
sweeper	مَكَانِسُ	مِكْنَسةٌ	to sweep	كَنَسَ - يَكْنِسُ
spoon	مَلاعِقُ	مِلْعَقةٌ	to lick	لَعِقَ - يَلْعَقُ

pattern: مِفْعالٌ

meaning	plural	اِسْمُ آلةٍ		I-verb
key	مَفَاتِيحُ	مِفْتاحٌ	to open	فَتَحَ - يَفْتَحُ
weight scales	مَوازِينُ	مِيزانٌ	to weigh	وَزَنَ - يَزِنُ

pattern: فَعّالةٌ

meaning	plural	اِسْمُ آلةٍ		I-verb
eyeglasses	نَظّاراتٌ	نَظّارةٌ	to see	نَظَرَ - يَنْظُرُ
car; vehicle	سَيّاراتٌ	سَيّارةٌ	to ride	سارَ - يَسِيرُ

Sometimes the active participle is used for describing tools:

You use the active participle (اِسْمُ فاعِلٍ).

meaning	plural	إِسْمُ آلَةٍ		verb	
air plane	طَائِرَاتٌ	طَائِرَةٌ	to fly	طَارَ - يَطِيرُ	I
air conditioner	مُكَيِّفَاتٌ	مُكَيِّفَةٌ	to adjust	كَيَّفَ - يُكَيِّفُ	II

Watch out: Not all words for tools are derived from roots. Some are **inert, static nouns** (إِسْمٌ جَامِدٌ). Some examples:

Not related to roots – inert, static noun (إِسْمٌ جَامِدٌ)					

plural	tool		plural	instrument	
أَقْلَامٌ	قَلَمٌ	*pen*	أَسْيَافٌ or سُيُوفٌ	سَيْفٌ	*sword*
سَكَاكِينُ	سِكِّينٌ	*knife*	رِماخٌ or أَرْماحٌ	رُمْحٌ	*spear*

176. مِئْذَنَةٌ or مَأْذَنَةٌ - What is the word for *minaret*?

Both are used – however, there is a difference in meaning.

This question deals with the correct first vowel. Today, most people use مَأْذَنَةٌ with the vowel "a" (فَتْحَة) on the first letter. In the early times of Islam, however, the spelling and pronunciation for *minaret* was مِئْذَنَةٌ – with the vowel "i" (كَسْرَة). In old dictionaries like *Lane's Lexicon* مَأْذَنة is called a *vulgar word*.

Let's examine both. The root is ع-ذ-ن and means *to hear*.

- The II-verb أَذَّنَ means *to call to prayer*.

- The IV-verb آذَنَ means *to make public; to announce*.

Why do مِئْذَنة and مَأْذَنة have different prefixes?

First of all, both are derived nouns (اِسْمٌ مُشْتَقٌّ).

1. The word مِئْذَنة is a *noun of instrument* (اِسْمُ آلةٍ). →
   مِئْذَنة is an instrument to do the call to prayer.

2. The word مَأْذَنة is a *noun of place* (اِسْمُ مَكانٍ). It is the
   place where the call to prayer happens.

If we take that seriously, it could probably mean that the مِئْذَنة
was originally a structure small enough justifiably to be called
an instrument.

Remark: In the film *The Message* (1976), which was approved
by several Muslim historians and scholars, the first muezzin,
Bilāl, went up to the roof to make the very first call to prayer
in Islam. The earliest mosques most probably lacked minarets.

According to Islamic tradition, Bilāl and his early successors
gave the call to prayer from a high or public place, such as the
doorway or roof of a mosque, an elevated neighboring structure or even the city wall, but never from a tall tower. The idea
of a minaret first arose under the Umayyad Caliphate (الْخِلافةُ
الأُمَوِيَّةُ) in Syria where Muslims came in contact with Syrian
church towers. They converted the churches into mosques and
adapted the towers.

177. How do you say *write!* in Arabic?

You can simply use the imperative mood: أُكْتُبْ!

The imperative (أَمْر) is the most common way. But there are
other ways too. The following examples basically all denote
write! Notice that the verbs – in both constructions – end with
سُكُون as we need the jussive mood (مَجْزُومٌ).

imperative		prefix
'uktub	أُكْتُبْ!	---
litaktub. We use the *Lām of the imperative* (لامُ الأَمْرِ). This type of لِ takes the vowel "i" (كَسْرةٌ).	لِتَكْتُبْ!	لِ

You can use the *Lām of the imperative* also with فَ or وَ. In such situations, the لْ has no vowel. This is necessary because otherwise it would be difficult to combine و with لْ. Try to speak both letters very quickly – eventually, you will end up producing *"wal"* and *"fal"*.

| *falyastajībū* | Let them comply, and let then believe! (We mark the jussive here by dropping the final ن) | فَلْيَسْتَجِيبُوا | فَلْ... |
| *walyu'minū* | | وَلْيُؤْمِنُوا! | وَلْ... |

178. Is there a mistake? - ذٰلِكُم الْكِتابُ مُفِيدٌ يا أَصْدِقائي

No, there isn't. But let us check why.

The sentence means: *That book is useful, my friends!*

The first expression ذٰلِكُمْ looks strange. Since the meaning is *that book,* why is it not just ذٰلِكَ الْكِتابُ ?

For English speakers, it is not logical that the *demonstrative pronoun* (اِسْمُ إِشارةٍ) **agrees** in **gender** and **number** (singular/plural) with the person that gets called – in our example: *my friends!* In Arabic, this is only true if you use the so-called *Kāf of allocution* (كافُ الْخِطابِ). You find it with the demonstrative nouns *that* and in special expressions.

| Hey Karim, that notebook is useful! | ذٰلِكَ الدَّفْتَرُ مُفِيدٌ يا كَرِيمُ! |

Hey my (two) friends, that note-book is useful!	‏ذٰلِكُما الدَّفْتَرُ مُفيدٌ يا صَديقَيَّ!‏
Hey my friends, that notebook is useful!	‏ذٰلِكُم الدَّفْتَرُ مُفيدٌ يا أَصْدِقائِي!‏
Hey (my)ladies, that notebook is useful!	‏ذٰلِكُنَّ الدَّفْتَرُ مُفيدٌ يا سَيِّداتِي!‏

tell me	‏أَرَأَيْتَكَ‏	slowly!	‏رُوَيْدَكَ‏

→ See also *Arabic for Nerds 2*, question #95.

179. What does ‏إِمَّا‏ mean?

The word ‏إِمَّا‏ could be translated as: either.... (or).

The word *either* is used when there are two possibilities only. So how do we use it in Arabic?

If there is doubt (‏شَكٌّ‏) – particle of separation	‏حَرْفُ تَفْصيلٍ‏
This man is either stupid or insane.	‏هٰذا الرَّجُلُ إِمَّا أَحْمَقُ وَإِمَّا مَجْنُونٌ.‏
Either Samir or Zayd will pay me a visit.	‏يَزُورُنِي إِمَّا زَيْدٌ وَإِمَّا سَميرٌ.‏

Letting choose – particle of selection	‏حَرْفُ تَخْيِيرٍ‏
You have to meet either the director or the secretary.	‏يَجِبُ عَلَيْكَ أَنْ تُقابِلَ إِمَّا الْمُديرَ وَإِمَّا السِّكْرِتيرَ.‏

| إِخْتَرْ إِمَّا الْجِدَّ وَإِمَّا الْكَسَلَ! | You have to choose, either diligence or laziness! |

Some important points:

- You have to put إِمَّا <u>twice</u> – and in the second part, you have to connect it with وَ.
- The letter إِمَّا always stays the same. It <u>does not get cases</u>, nor does it take on a function in the sentence (لا مَحَلَّ لَهُ مِن الْإِعْرابِ).
- It <u>does not influence</u> other words regarding cases.

180. What kind of word is لَيْسَ (*not to be*)?

It is a defective verb (فِعْلٌ مَاضٍ نَاقِصٌ) which means that it does not form all tenses and moods.

The word لَيْسَ literally means *not to be; not to exist*. In fact, the existence itself is absolutely denied. It is a verb and used to negate a nominal sentence (جُمْلَةٌ اِسْمِيَّةٌ), a sentence that has no other verb. It changes the meaning from affirmative to negative (مِن الْإِثْباتِ إِلَى النَّفْيِ). We say that لَيْسَ **excludes the predicate from the subject**.

It is a special verb. It **only** exists in the **past tense** (الْماضِي). لَيْسَ **cannot** form the **imperative** (الْأَمْرُ) nor can it be used in the present tense (الْمُضارِعُ).

- In Arabic, verbs like لَيْسَ which are only used in the past tense are called *inert, aplastic verbs* (فِعْلٌ جامِدٌ). Another example is the verb عَسَى which means *to wish*.

- The reason for this name (*inertia*) is the similarity to particles (حَرْفٌ) which do not change their forms. For example, the particles of negation.

- All other verbs are called *variable verbs* (فِعْلٌ مُتَصَرِّفٌ).

لَيْسَ is also a *sister of* كَانَ. This implies that...

- the **"subject"** (اِسْمُ لَيْسَ) is in the **nominative** (مَرْفُوعٌ);

- the **predicate** (خَبَرُ لَيْسَ) is in the **accusative** (مَنْصُوبٌ).

> **Watch out:** Although لَيْسَ is only used in the past tense, it has the **meaning of the present tense**!

Only in very few situations, when the context is clear, you could translate لَيْسَ with a past tense meaning. Since لَيْسَ is a verb, you don't need to add a personal pronoun (أَنا, هُوَ, ...) as it is included in the verb. We call that an implied, hidden pronoun (ضَمِيرٌ مُسْتَتِرٌ).

There are several ways to negate a nominal sentence. Let's analyze an example: *She is not generous.*

كَرِيمَةً has to be مَنْصُوب because it is the predicate of لَيْسَ – similar to the خَبَرُ كَانَ.	لَيْسَتْ كَرِيمَةً	1
We use a construction with بِ to emphasize the negation, sometimes in addition with the definite article.	لَيْسَتْ بِكَرِيمَةٍ	2

Watch out: Also here, كَرِيمَة is the خَبَرُ لَيْسَ. However, the additional, extra preposition for emphasis drags the word into the genitive case (مَجْرُورٌ). This is the reason for "-in" (two كَسْرَة). For a deep analysis, see *Arabic for Nerds 2, question #128.*

Here, we use a construction with غَيْرُ instead of لَيْسَ – note that this is a إِضافة-construction. Therefore, كَرِيمَةٍ takes the genitive case.	هِيَ غَيْرُ كَرِيمَةٍ 3

Similar to بِ, also the preposition مِنْ can be used to accentuate the negation:

No one knows everything.	لَيْسَ مِنْ إِنْسانٍ يَعْرِفُ كُلَّ شَيْءٍ.

181. لَيْسَ لَدَيْهِ سَيَّارَةٌ. - Is there a mistake?

No, there isn't. The sentence means: He doesn't have a car.

If you translate it into English, you won't find a mistake anyway as the subject is *he* and the predicate is *car*. But it is not that obvious in Arabic because we have a tricky construction.

The verb لَيْسَ has to agree with the subject (اِسْمُ لَيْسَ). You can easily identify the subject in a sentence with لَيْسَ by the marker for the nominative case (مَرْفُوع) because the predicate has to be in the accusative case (مَنْصُوبٌ). So, the subject is *car*.

The director is **not in the office**.	لَيْسَ الْمُدِيرُ فِي الْمَكْتَبِ.	subject of لَيْسَ	1
He is **not the director** in the office.	لَيْسَ الْمُدِيرَ فِي الْمَكْتَبِ.	predicate of لَيْسَ	2
The subject is the hidden pronoun *he* (هُوَ) found in لَيْسَ.			

However, *car* (سَيَّارَةٌ) is **feminine** in Arabic and لَيْسَ has the third person singular **masculine** form. Is there a mistake? The feminine subject *car* is separated from the other parts of the sentence.

That is why لَيْسَ can have the masculine form. This is pretty common in Arabic.

Watch out: The predicate (خَبَر لَيْسَ) in our sentence is لَدَيْهِ. It is an adverbial phrase (ظَرْفُ مَكَانٍ). Okay, some say that this is not entirely correct, which I totally agree, but I don't want to go into the details here (see *Arabic for Nerds 2, question #220*).

In sentences like our example, the predicate of لَيْسَ is often mistaken as the subject, especially in sentences that express possession which is due to the **inverted word-order.** Let us remember what inverted <u>word</u> order means.

He has a book. (Lit.: At/with him is a book.)	عِنْدَهُ كِتابٌ.

This adverbial phrase (ظَرْفُ مَكَانٍ) is the forwarded predicate (خَبَر مُقَدَّمٌ). The predicate appears at the first position where you would expect the subject = inverted word order. عِنْدَهُ is the predicate of the sentence and should be in the accusative (مَنْصُوبٌ) – but you don't see that because you cannot put case markers on عِنْدَهُ. We can only assign virtual case markers, i.e., the place value of an accusative case.	عِنْدَهُ
Subject (مُبْتَدَأٌ) of the nominal sentence (جُمْلَةٌ اِسْمِيَّةٌ).	كِتابٌ

He does not have a book. (Lit: At him a book does not exist.)	لَيْسَ عِنْدَهُ كِتابٌ.

What is actually negated? The subject or the predicate? We say that لَيْسَ **excludes the predicate from the subject.**

Let's play with this sentence.

wrong	If you rearrange the sentence like this, it looks wrong – and it is wrong!	لَيْسَ سَيَّارَةٌ لَدَيْهِ.
correct	This is a correct sentence because the "subject" is **not** separated from لَيْسَ.	لَيْسَتْ سَيَّارَةٌ لَدَيْهِ.
correct	This looks correct and most scholars say it is, although the verb here doesn't agree with the "subject".	لَيْسَ لَدَيْهِ سَيَّارَةٌ.
	There is another part of the sentence (لَدَيْهِ) between the اِسْمُ لَيْسَ ("subject") and the verb لَيْسَ, so you can do it.	

Remark: If you use لَيْسَ similar to a particle (you don't conjugate it), it **negates single elements** of the sentence:

It was not I who killed him.	لَيْسَ أَنا قَتَلْتُهُ

182. لَسْتُ أَدْرِي - Is there a mistake?

No, there isn't.

The expression لَسْتُ أَدْرِي means *I don't know*.

Usually, we use the verb لَيْسَ only to negate a nominal sentence (جُمْلَةٌ اِسْمِيّةٌ). But here we have a verb after لَيْسَ. It is the I-verb يَدْرِي/دَرَى which means *to know; to be aware*.

The negation with لَيْسَ conveys a very strong idea of non-existence and is mainly used in literature. You may negate any verbal sentence with لَيْسَ. The verbal sentence then is placed as the predicate (خَبَرٌ) of لَيْسَ. However, it is very rare and mostly used with the first person singular (*I*).

Don't forget: Although لَيْسَ is a past tense verb, you **negate the present tense.**

We do not come to you.	لَسْنا نَصِلُ إِلَيْكَ.
I don't remember.	لَسْتُ أَذْكُرُ.

183. Can you praise or condemn something with one word?

Yes, you can. You use نِعْمَ for the good and بِئْسَ for the bad.

These two words are verbs and convey an emphatic meaning. Let us look at the main two verbs:

what a good / superb / perfect / wonderful / truly excellent ...	نِعْمَ
what bad / miserable ...	بِئْسَ

We call such constructions *praise* and *criticism* (أُسْلُوبُ الْمَدْح وَالذَّم). Both verbs are *inert, static verbs* (فِعْلٌ جامِدٌ) like the verb لَيْسَ. Such verbs do not form all tenses. In fact, نِعْمَ and بِئْسَ are only used in the past tense (الْماضِي). You cannot form the present tense (الْمُضارِعُ), nor the imperative (الأَمْرُ).

- Moreover, these two verbs never change their form. They have a fixed shape.

- The word after نِعْمَ or بِئْسَ (the word being qualified) must be a **definite noun** in the nominative case (مَرْفُوعٌ).

- The feminine forms نِعْمَت / بِئْسَت are rarely used.

Let us look at some examples.

| What an excellent man Karim is! | لَنِعْمَ الرَّجُلُ كَرِيمٌ! |

Notice: The لَ at the beginning is used to intensify the meaning.	
He is a wonderful friend indeed. Notice: The particle إِنَّ is used to emphasize.	إِنَّهُ نِعْمَ الْخَلِيلُ.
What bad men you both are!	لَبِئْسَ الرَّجُلانِ أَنْتُما!

Both نِعْمَ and بِئْسَ may be used with a relative pronoun (اِسْمٌ مَوْصُولٌ), i.e., with ما or مَن. Merged with the particle ما, the meaning is slightly different and often translated as *indeed*.

Indeed, bad things you did! (German: *Gar Schlechtes hast du getan!*)	بِئْسَما صَنَعْتَ!

There are other words in Arabic that follow the same rules: They are unchangeable and connected to a noun in the nominative case. Furthermore, they are also used emphatically.

what/how a great..., monumental...	جَلَّ	عَزَّ
	شَدَّ	هَدَّ

what a big...	كَبُرَ
what a bad..., wicked...	ساءَ
what a nice..., beautiful...	حَسُنَ - حُسْنَ - حَسْنَ
what a great..., powerful...	عَظُمَ - عُظْمَ - عَظْمَ
how lovely..., what lovely...	حَبَّ + ذا
how terrible, bad...	لا حَبَّ + ذا

Some examples.

How lovely you are!	حَبَّذا أَنْتَ!
How dear/strong you loved her!	لَشَدَّ ما أَحْبَبْتَها!
What big/bad word comes out of your mouth!	كَبُرَتْ كَلِمَةً تَخْرُجُ مِن أَفْواهِكُمْ.

In the last example we used the feminine form. But this is optional! You can also use just كَبُرَ. Watch out: The word فَمٌ is tricky!. If you want to say *your mouth* (singular), it is فَمِكَ or فِيكَ (if مَجْرُورٌ).

| What an annoying hypocrisy! | لا حَبَّذا النِّفاقُ! |

Some remarks:

- The verb حَبَّ is used as a فِعْلٌ جامِدٌ which is merged with a demonstrative pronoun (اِسْمُ إِشارةٍ).

- The demonstrative pronoun ذا is the subject (فاعِلٌ) and thus should get the nominative case. Since it has a fixed shape, we can only use a virtual case marker and assign the place value of the nominative case (فِي مَحَلِّ رَفْعٍ).

- If you want to express criticism, use the negation: لا حَبَّذا

For an in-depth analysis of such sentences, see *Arabic for Nerds 2, question #446.*

184. When does a verb need the مَنْصُوبٌ-mood?

This mood indicates that an action is intended or expected.

There are certain devices after which a verb must be used in the *subjunctive* mood (مَنْصُوبٌ). In Arabic grammar, the term

مَنْصُوب denotes *with open ending*. The word *open* here means that it ends in the vowel "*a*" (فَتْحَةٌ).

What does such a vowel at the end of a verb tell us? There are several possibilities: The verb may relate to a state or act that you want to do, that you won't do, that you would like to have, that you could do.

Thus, the subjunctive mood cannot be used on its own. **It is connected to a possibility, to a wish or a duty** (which usually stands at the beginning of the sentence). Certain devices induce the subjunctive mood in the verb.

that; in order to	Device to mold an interpreted infinitive (حَرْفٌ مَصْدَرِيّةٍ). See *question #81*.	أَنْ	1

not to; don't	The لا is a *particle of interdiction* (حَرْفُ نَهْيٍ). Used to request leaving a matter, to refuse it, and to forbid it.	أَنْ لا = أَلَّا	2

I wrote to him not to slow down = that he should not slow down.	كَتَبْتُ إِلَيْهِ أَلَّا تُبْطِئَ.

in order to; so that; so	The *Lām of causality* and *justification* (لامُ تَعْلِيلٍ). The لِ may also be used to mold an interpreted infinitive (حَرْفُ مَصْدَرِيّةٍ).	لِ	3

We assume that the particle أَنْ is implicitly there. Thus, in fact, we have لِأَنْ, but usually, you only write لِ. However, if you want to negate the verb, you need to write أَنْ. The result is: لِئَلَّا.

Be audacious in order to reach glory!	غَامِرْ لِتَبْلُغَ الْمَجْدَ!
Study so that you don't fail!	أُدْرُسْ لِئَلَّا تَرْسُبَ!

He said: "So that there would not be any hardship on his Ummah." (Hadith; Sunan al-Nasā'ī 609).	قَالَ لِئَلَّا يَكُونَ عَلَى أُمَّتِهِ حَرَجٌ.

(emphasis)	The *Lām of denial* (لامُ الْجُحُودِ). It occurs after the negated form of *to be* (كانَ) in order to confirm the negation.	لِ	4

I was not a tyrant to people.	لَمْ أَكُنْ لِأَظْلِمَ النّاسَ.

so that	The *Fā' of occasion* or *causality* (فاءُ سَبَبِيَّةٌ). Used if there is a preceding word indicating a wish, a command, a question or a prohibition – usually expressed by an imperative.	فَ	5

Be generous, so that you will prevail.	جُودُوا فَتَسُودُوا.
Stand up, then I will stand up!	قُمْ فَأَقُومَ!

in order to; so that	The *Kāf of causality* and *justification* (كافُ تَعْلِيلٍ). It may be used instead of أَنْ to produce interpreted infinitive (حَرْفُ مَصْدَرِيَّةٍ).	كَيْ / لِكَيْ	6

Be active, so that you can succeed!	اِعْمَلْ كَيْ تَنْجَحَ!

in order not to	This works similar to أَلّا – see number 2.	كَيْ لا = كَيْلا لِكَيْ لا = لِكَيْلا	7

until; so that; in order to	The word حَتَّى may convey many meanings and may take on several jobs in a sentence. Here, we only look at two functions:	حَتَّى	8

a) حَتَّى as a particle of causality (حَرْفُ تَعْلِيلٍ). It can be used as a synonym to the *Lām of causality* and *justification* (لامُ تَعْلِيلٍ). The reason why we use the subjunctive is that we assume that there is a virtual, hypothetical particle أَنْ involved.

b) حَتَّى as a *particle of finality* (حَرْفُ غايةٍ). It is used to indicate an intention or the result plus its consequences.

Be active, so that you can succeed !	اِعْمَلْ كَيْ تَنْجَحَ! a)
I ate the fish in order to leave only its head. (See *Arabic for Nerds 2*, #189)	أَكَلْتُ السَّمَكَةَ حَتَّى رَأْسِها. b)

will not	Particle to negate the occurrence of the verb in the future (حَرْفُ مَعْنًى مَبْنِيٌّ يَنْفِي وُقُوعَـهُ فِي الْمُسْتَقْبَل).	لَنْ	9

I will not help the corrupt people.	لَنْ أَكُونَ مُناصِرٍ لِلْفاسِدِينَ.

in that case; therefore; so; then	This particle (حَرْفٌ) has a fixed shape (مَبْنِيٌّ). It is placed at the start of an answer (صَدْرُ الْجَوابِ). Note: The verb after إِذَنْ in the subjunctive mood expresses the future!	إِذَنْ	10

In that case you will succeed.	إِذَنْ تَنْجَحَ.
In that case I will leave after your visit.	إِذَنْ أَذْهَبَ بَعْدَ زِيارَتِكَ ـ

Watch out if the <u>last root letter</u> is و or ي – a weak letter (حَرْفُ عِلّةٍ) – and you need the subjunctive (مَنْصُوبٌ).

What matters is the **vowel** of the **second root-letter** in the **present tense**!

	example	What is the مَنْصُوب-ending?	last letter	verb	
he won't be pleased	لَنْ يَرْضَى	hidden "a"	ى	يَرْضَى	1
he won't complain	لَنْ يَشْكُوَ	قَتْحَةٌ on top of و	و	يَشْكُو	2
he won't throw	لَنْ يَرْمِيَ	قَتْحَةٌ on top of ي	ي	يَرْمِي	3

185. *Nice flowers.* Should you say زَهْرُ جَميلٌ or زَهْرٌ جَميلةٌ?

You should say زَهْرٌ جَميلٌ.

The word زَهْرٌ is the *collective plural* (اِسْمُ جِنْسٍ جَمْعِيٌّ) for *flowers*. The singular form is زَهْرَةٌ which means *a flower* or *blossom*. This is typical for collective plurals: if you want to form the singular, you use ة or a Nisba (ياءُ النِّسْبَةِ).

عَرَبِيٌّ	an Arab		عَرَبٌ	Arabs
عَسْكَرِيٌّ	a soldier		عَسْكَرٌ	army (camp)
تُفّاحَةٌ	an apple	◄	تُفّاحٌ	apples
زَهْرَةٌ	a flower		زَهْرٌ	flowers
دَمْعَةٌ	a tear		دَمْعٌ	tears
حَديدَةٌ	a piece of iron		حَديدٌ	iron

The crucial point here is that we do not form the regular plural of the singular unit. Otherwise, we would end up with زَهَراتٌ or تُفّاحاتٌ.

Since we do not have real plural forms, we call words like زَهْرٌ *quasi-plurals* (شِبْهُ الْجَمْعِ).

Collective nouns don't describe a specific group, but species. For example: شَجَرٌ (*trees*) or عِلْمُ الشَّجَرِ (*dendrology; the science of trees;*). Another example: لَحْمُ الْبَقَرِ (*beef; meat*). Collective nouns, in comparison to English, tend to have a distinction between being collective and being countable, often related to elements in nature.

This explains why we have different plural forms in Arabic for such words. The difference between شَجَرٌ and أَشْجَارٌ is like the difference between *Gebirge* (species) and *Berge* in German. Both mean *mountains*. Regarding *Gebirge*, you are thinking of the mountains as **one entity**; regarding *Berge*, you are thinking of them as **individual entities**.

Now, what about the **gender of collective nouns?**

Generic collectives (collective plurals) are **masculine** (مُذَكَّرٌ).

Since adjectives need to agree with the word they want to describe, collective plurals go along with a **masculine** singular adjective. That is striking because in Arabic, we normally use the feminine form of the adjective when they relate to a plural.

An example.

tall trees	شَجَرٌ طَوِيلٌ

But this is only true for this pseudo-plural.

There is another plural of زَهْرَةٌ - the word أَزْهارٌ. It is used to describe a small amount of flowers, like a bouquet or a bunch of. In this situation, the adjective follows the regular rules of plurals. So, we need the feminine form: أَزْهارٌ جَمِيلَةٌ.

Watch out: Only **collective names of tribes and people** are treated as <u>feminine</u>!

يَهُودِيٌّ	a Jew	◄	يَهُودٌ	Jews
هِنْدِيٌّ	an Indian		هِنْدٌ	Indians
قُرَيْشِيٌّ	a Qurayshite		قُرَيْشٌ	Quraysh

Some collective plurals do not form a singular unit. For example, the word طَيْرٌ means *bird* <u>or</u> *birds*! The collective plural is understood to be the individual noun as well. If you want to express flocks of birds, you may use the plural form طُيُورٌ.

186. How do you say *not at all* in Arabic?

You have several options.

If you want to stress on the fact that you have not done anything or that you have never done a certain thing, you add the expression *not at all* (German: *überhaupt; überhaupt nicht*).

In Arabic, you could use the following expressions:

with negation: *not at all; never; by no means.* Since it is used as an adverb of time, the noun غَيْر has the vowel "a" (فَتْحَة).	غَيْرَ مَرَّةٍ لا...بِالْمَرَّةِ	1
never; not at any point; in any respect; by no means	مُطْلَقًا لا...عَلَى الْإِطْلاقِ	2
<u>never</u>; <u>not at all</u> (with the future tense only! See *Arabic for Nerds 2*, question #350).	أَبَدًا	3
not at all; in the first place	أَصْلًا	4

totally not; not at all	بِأَكْمَلِها	5
not at all; (بِصِفَةٍ عامَّةٍ *means in general*)	لا...بِصِفَةٍ عامَّةٍ	6
absolutely not, definitely not. It comes from the root ب-ت-ت which means to *complete*.	الْبَتَّةَ or بَتَّةً	7

Some examples:

I've seen him more than once.	رَأَيْتُهُ غَيْرَ مَرَّةٍ.	1
I haven't seen him at all.	لا رَأَيْتُهُ غَيْرَ مَرَّةٍ.	1
It will not be accepted at all.	لَنْ يُقبَلَ مُطْلَقًا.	2
not a thing.	لا شَيْءَ مُطْلَقًا	2
I won't scream at all!	لَنْ أَصْرُخَ أَبَدًا!	3
There were no people there at all.	لَمْ يَكُنْ هُناكَ ناسٌ أَصْلًا.	4
She won't be in Cairo at all.	لَنْ تَكُونَ فِي الْقاهِرةِ بِأَكْمَلِها.	5
A: Are you ill? B: Not at all!	أَأَنتَ مَريضٌ؟ لا لَسْتُ مَريضًا أَلْبَتَّةَ.	7

A: Thank you very much! B: You are welcome/Not at all.	شُكْرًا جَزيلًا! الْعَفْوُ = لا شُكْرَ عَلَى واجِبٍ!

187. The girl is bigger than... - Why is that tricky in Arabic?

You need to decide whether you should use أَكْبَر or كُبْرَى.

For the translation of this sentence, we need to form a **comparative**. In linguistics, a comparative is the form of an adjective (or adverb) that expresses a difference in amount, number, degree, or quality.

An adjective (in English) can exist in three forms: positive, comparative, and superlative. You will encounter several grammar terms:

positive	comparative	superlative	elative
big	*bigger*	*biggest*	*very big; especially big*

For example:

This boy is bigger than his brothers.	هٰذا الْوَلَدُ أَكْبَرُ مِن إِخْوَتِهِ.

	term	explanation
الْوَلَدُ	الْمُفَضَّلُ	Lit. meaning: *the preferred*. The thing which has more of it. It is placed <u>before</u> the comparative.
أَكْبَرُ	اِسْمُ تَفْضِيلٍ	The *noun of preference* (اِسْمُ تَفْضِيلٍ) is a derived noun (اِسْمٌ مُشْتَقٌّ). It uses the pattern أَفْعَلُ. In its pure form, it is an **elative**. By using certain constructions, you can give it the meaning of a **comparative** or **superlative**.
إِخْوَتِهِ	الْمُفَضَّلُ عَلَيْهِ	The thing which is inferior. Placed <u>after</u> مِن of the comparative. Note that there is no الْمُفَضَّلُ عَلَيْهِ in the superlative.

For example, the comparative of *big* (كَبِيرٌ) is *bigger* (أَكْبَرُ). This is the **masculine** (مُذَكَّرٌ) form. However, in the sentence *The girl is bigger than...* we talk about a female person. So, does that mean that we have to use the feminine form of *bigger*, which would be كُبْرَى? Well, we will see.

We have several options to translate our example. Let's have a look at them. Pay attention to the vowels at the end!

1	Comparative meaning: ***bigger than***	أَنْ يَكُونَ مُجَرَّدًا مِن أل وَالْإضافة

It is always أَكْبَرُ مِن. You always use the **masculine** form!

There are some important things you should know:

- Don't use the definite article. It is only أَكْبَر and not الْأَكْبَر.
- This isn't a إِضافة-construction. Note the preposition مِن after the word أَكْبَر.

English translation	example	
This boy is bigger than his brothers.	أَكْبَرُ مِن إِخْوَتِهِ.	هٰذا الْوَلَدُ
This girl is bigger than her sisters.	أَكْبَرُ مِن أَخَواتِها.	هٰذِهِ الْبِنْتُ
These two boys are bigger than their brothers.	أَكْبَرُ مِن إِخْوَتِهِما.	هٰذانِ الْوَلَدانِ
These two girls are bigger than their sisters.	أَكْبَرُ مِن أَخَواتِهِما.	هاتانِ الْبِنْتانِ
These boys are bigger than their brothers.	أَكْبَرُ مِن إِخْوَتِهِمْ.	هٰؤُلاءِ الْأَوْلادُ
These girls are bigger than their sisters.	أَكْبَرُ مِن أَخَواتِهِنَّ.	هٰؤُلاءِ الْبَناتُ

Therefore, the answer to our question is: الْبِنْتُ أَكْبَرُ مِن.... No-tice that أَكْبَرُ مِن stays the same in every sentence! In the comparative, we don't use the feminine form nor dual/plural, and there is no agreement!

- It **always** has the same form: **masculine** and **singular**.

- أَكْبَرُ doesn't take nunation (تَنْوِينٌ) because this pattern (morpheme) is a diptote (مَمْنُوعٌ مَن الصَّرْفِ).

2	Superlative meaning: *the biggest*	أَنْ يَكُونَ مَعْرِفًا بِأَل

- أَكْبَرُ changes its gender and number. It needs the **definite article**.

- The *preferred thing* (الْمُفَضَّلُ) needs the **definite article** as well.

- We need to apply the rules of <u>adjectives</u> (صِفَةٌ).

English translation	اِسْمُ التَّفْضِيلِ	الْمُفَضَّلُ		
This is the biggest boy.	الْأَكْبَرُ.	الْوَلَدُ	هوَ	هٰذا
This is the biggest girl.	الْكُبْرى.	الْبِنْتُ	هِيَ	هٰذِهِ
These two are the biggest (two) boys.	الأَكْبَرانِ.	الْوَلَدانِ	هُما	هٰذانِ
These two are the biggest (two) girls.	الْكُبْرَيانِ.	الْبِنْتانِ	هُما	هاتانِ
These boys are the biggest.	الْأَكْبَرُونَ or الْأَكْبَرُ.	الْأَوْلادُ	هُمْ	هٰؤُلاءِ
These girls are the biggest.	الْكُبْرَياتُ or الْكُبَرُ.	الْبَناتُ	هُنَّ	هٰؤُلاءِ

Some remarks:

- The اِسْمُ التَّفْضِيلِ has to follow the الْمُفَضَّلُ for the correct agreement.

- If you have a feminine dual, you have to write ي and not ت because there is ى at the end of the feminine form! For example, الْكُبْرَيانِ.

- When the اِسْمُ التَّفْضيلِ is the object of a sentence, then it has to be in the accusative case (مَنْصُوبٌ)! For example:

| I saw the two big (biggest) girls. | شاهَدْتُ الْبِنْتَينِ الْكُبْرَيَيْنِ. |

| 3 Superlative meaning: *the biggest* | أَنْ يَكُونَ مُضافًا إِلَى نَكِرَةٍ |

- We again only use أَكْبَرُ.
- The اِسْمُ التَّفْضيلِ is <u>always</u> masculine and singular.
- We use a إِضافة-construction.
- The *preferred thing* (الْمُفَضَّلُ) is **indefinite** and serves as the second part of the إِضافة - it is in the genitive case.
- This type conveys the strongest superlative meaning!

English translation	الْمُفَضَّلُ	اِسْمُ التَّفْضيلِ		
This is the biggest boy.	وَلَدٍ.	أَكْبَرُ	هُوَ	هٰذا
This is the biggest girl.	بِنْتٍ.	أَكْبَرُ	هِيَ	هٰذِهِ
These two are the biggest boys.	وَلَدَيْنِ.	أَكْبَرُ	هُما	هٰذانِ
These two are the biggest girls.	بِنْتَيْنِ.	أَكْبَرُ	هُما	هاتانِ
These are the biggest boys.	أَوْلادٍ.	أَكْبَرُ	هُمَ	هٰؤُلاء
These are the biggest girls.	بَناتٍ.	أَكْبَرُ	هُنَّ	هٰؤُلاء

| 4 Superlative meaning: *the biggest* | أَنْ يَكُونَ مُضافًا إِلَى مَعْرِفَةٍ |

- You have the choice: You can use أَكْبَرُ or the appropriate form that corresponds in gender and number with the *preferred thing* (الْمُفَضَّلُ).

- The الْمُفَضَّلُ has the **definite** article.

- The comparative (اِسْمُ التَّفْضِيلِ) is **indefinite** (نَكِرَةٌ).

English translation	الْمُفَضَّلُ	اِسْم التَّفْضِيل		
This is the biggest boy.	الأَوْلادِ	أَكْبَر	هوَ	هٰذا
This is the biggest girl.	الْبَناتِ	أَكْبَر - كُبْرى	هِيَ	هٰذه
These two are the biggest boys.	الأَوْلادِ	أَكْبَر - أَكْبَرا	هُما	هٰذانِ
These two are the biggest girls.	الْبَناتِ	أَكْبَر - أَكْبَريا	هُما	هاتانِ
These are the biggest boys.	الأَوْلادِ	أَكْبَر - أَكْبَروا	هُمْ	هٰؤُلاء
These are the biggest girls.	الْبَناتِ	أَكْبَر - كُبْرَيات	هُنَّ	هٰؤُلاء

Now, does it matter which construction you use? No, it doesn't. Most sentences are translated in the same way. But you have to watch out to spot the nuances.

1	هٰذا هُوَ أَكْبَرُ الأَوْلادِ.	We cannot tell from the construction how many children we compare. It may be only two.
2	هٰذا هُوَ أَكْبَرُ وَلَدٍ.	The superlative here has an **absolute sense**: the biggest **(known)** child.

1	أَعْلَى الْجِبالِ	the highest of the mountains
2	أَعْلَى جَبَلٍ	the highest (known) mountain

188. What is the stem of the verb *to be reassured* (اِطْمَأَنَّ)?

It is a IV-verb – but that's not all.

The root of the verb contains **four** letters: ط-م-ء-ن. Thus, the basic I-verb of this root with four letters is طَمْأَنَ which means *to pacify, to reassure*. Which pattern should we use for a IV-verb with 4 root letters?

→ It is اِفْعَلَّ. You add a connecting هَمْزة to the beginning and double the **last** radical (فِعْلٌ مَزِيدٌ رُباعِيٌّ).

The conjugation of a IV-verb of four root letters is similar to the conjugation of a IX-verb based on three root letters. For example, the IX-verb *to turn red; to blush* (اِحْمَرَّ).

- Many IV-verbs (four root letters) express a **reflexive** or **superlative meaning**. Reflexive verbs show that the person who does the action is also the person who is affected by it. What is meant by superlative? Two examples:

The hair trembled. This means that the hair rose up and stood upright because of fear, weather, or any other reason.	اِقْشَعَرَّ الشَّعْرُ.
The night was dark. Here, the verb tells you that darkness grew up and blackened.	اِكْفَهَرَّ اللَّيْلُ.

- Many of these verbs don't form the passive voice.
- Thus, also the passive participle (اِسْمُ مَفْعُولٍ) is rarely used. Theoretically, you would use the pattern مُفْعَلَلٌّ. In our example, we would get مُطْمَأَنٌّ.

Let's check the most important **derived nouns** of this pattern.

meaning	pattern	kind	word
he was reassured	اِفْعَلَلَّ	الْماضِي	اِطْمَأَنَّ
he is reassured	يَفْعَلِلُّ	الْمُضارِعُ	يَطْمَئِنُّ
tranquillity; serenity	اِفْعِلّالٌ	الْمَصْدَرُ	اِطْمِئْنانٌ
be reassured!	masculine	الْأَمْرُ (imperative)	اِطْمَأْنِنْ
	feminine		اِطْمَئِنِّي
	plural		اِطْمَئِنُّوا
calm	مُفْعَلِلٌّ	اِسْمُ الْفاعِلِ	مُطْمَئِنٌّ

189. How do you say *more crowded* in Arabic?

Not by a single word. You can't express "more crowded" by building the comparative of "crowded" – it is simply impossible.

So, what should we do instead? We need to change the form of the word. I will explain this step by step. Adjectives in Arabic are not a certain type of word like the English word *beautiful*.

In Arabic, we use nouns that can qualify to work as adjectives. These nouns are derived from the root (اِسْمٌ مُشْتَقٌّ) and have different shapes, patterns, and grammatical origins.

How do we translate expressions like *more respected; more crowded; more intense red; feeling more not like going to*?

There are 7 conditions that need to be fulfilled if we want to build the *noun of preference* (اِسْمُ تَفْضِيلٍ).

1	Our source must be the most standard form of the verb: **stem I** of a **triliteral** root.	فِعْلٌ ثُلاثِيٌّ

2	The word of which we want to build the comparative **isn't a quasi participle**, an active participle-like adjective. In other words, it is not an adjective that indicates firmness. It should not be derived from a stative verb.	أَلَّا تَكُونَ صِفَةً مُشَبَّهَةً
3	Our starting point is the **active voice** - not the passive.	أَنْ يَكُونَ الْفِعْلُ مَبْنِيًّا لِلْمَعْلُومِ
4	The verb is **not negated** (i.e., affirmative).	أَنْ يَكُونَ الْفِعْلُ مُثْبَتًا، لَيْسَ مَنْفِيًّا
5	The verb is **not defective** and has a **subject**.	أَنْ يَكُونَ الْفِعْلُ تامًّا, لَهُ فاعِلٌ
6	The verb can be **conjugated in all tenses and moods**.	أَنْ يَكُونَ الفِعْلُ مُتَصَرِّفًا
7	A **comparison** is **meaningful** and does make sense.	أَنْ يَكُونَ الْفِعْلُ قابِلًا لِلتَّفاوُتِ

But what happens if one of the above conditions is violated? Let's see.

> **CONDITION 1:** It is not a I-verb and its pattern has more than three letters. possible

We can fix this by using a construction called أُسْلُوبُ التَّفْضِيلِ. Let us take the VIII-verb *to be crowded* (اِزْدَحَمَ). Now, we want to say the following: *Cairo is more crowded than Beirut*. How do you translate that into Arabic?

Here is a step by step guide:

1. Build the مَصْدَر. The root of اِزْدَحَمَ is زَحَمَ. Note that the letter د is not part of the root. Since we have a VIII-verb of the pattern اِفْتَعَلَ, it should actually be ت, but it was replaced by a د to make the pronunciation easier. The مَصْدَر is اِزْدِحامُ.

2. Choose an auxiliary word (اِسْمُ تَفْضيلٍ). Usually you use one of the following words (مُساعِدٌ) for the construction.

more; bigger	أَكْثَرُ	more; more intense	أَشَدُّ	less	أَقَلُّ

3. Combine both words. We use a trick here. We do not use a إِضافة-construction. We use a **specification** (تَمْييزٌ). This is the reason for the accusative case (مَنْصوبٌ) - see *question #167* and *Arabic for Nerds 2, question #381*.

Cairo is more crowded than Beirut.	الْقاهِرةُ أَكْثَرُ اِزْدِحامًا مِن بَيْروتَ.

CONDITION 2: The comparative of an active partici-ple-like adjective (الصِّفةُ الْمُشَبَّهةُ).	possible

These two patterns form pseudo participles (صِفةٌ مُشَبَّهةٌ):

masculine	أَفْعَلُ	feminine	فَعْلاءُ

In the pattern فَعْلاءُ, notice the فَتْحة above the first letter! If it was ضَمّةٌ, it would be a regular comparative form and not a صِفةٌ مُشَبَّهةٌ! For example, the feminine form of *bigger*: كُبْرى. Some examples of the صِفةٌ مُشَبَّهةٌ.

meaning	feminine form	masculine form	root/verb
red	حَمْراءُ	أَحْمَرُ	حَمِرَ
blind	عَمْياءُ	أَعْمى	عَمِيَ

A صِفَةٌ مُشَبَّهَةٌ cannot form a comparative in Arabic. If we insist on expressing the idea, we need a helping construction. Here is a step by step guide:

1. Build the مَصْدَر. Let us take a look at these examples:

meaning	مَصْدَر	pattern	root
redness; red color	حُمْرةٌ	فُعْلَةٌ	ح-م-ر
blueness; blue color	زُرْقةٌ		ز-ر-ق

Watch out – there are two famous exceptions:

meaning	مَصْدَر	root
whiteness; white color	بَيَاضٌ	ب-ي-ض
blackness; black color	سَوادٌ	س-و-د

2. Choose an auxiliary word (اِسْمُ تَفْضِيلٍ).

more; bigger	أَكْثَرُ		more; more intense	أَشَدُّ		less	أَقَلُّ

This is the result – also here, we use a **specification** (تَمْيِيزٌ).

The flower has more redness than the other flower.	الْوَرْدةُ أَشَدُّ حُمْرةً مِن الْوَرْدةِ الأُخْرى.

CONDITION 3: The comparative of a passive voice.	possible

In Arabic, you can't build a comparative form by using the passive voice itself. For example: *more respected*. Before we dig into this matter, let us quickly check what we are talking about.

The passive voice of a I-verb is built by the pattern فُعِلَ for the past tense and يُفْعَلُ for the present tense.

active voice (مَعْلُومٌ) of the verb *to listen*	يَسْمَعُ	سَمِعَ
passive voice (مَجْهُولٌ) of the verb *to listen*	يُسْمَعُ	سُمِعَ

Let's check now the VIII-verb *to respect* (اِحْتَرَمَ).

passive, present tense		past tense		pattern	root
he is respected	يُحْتَرَمُ	he respected	اِحْتَرَمَ	اِفْتَعَلَ	حَرِمَ

If we want to express *more crowded*, we need another solution and can apply a new trick. Here is a step by step guide.

1. Build the interpreted infinitive (مَصْدَرٌ مُؤَوَّلٌ). → see question #81. This is easy.

interpreted infinitive (مَصْدَرٌ مُؤَوَّلٌ)	original infinitive (مَصْدَرٌ أَصْلِيٌّ)
أَنْ يُحْتَرَمَ	اِحْتِرامٌ

2. Choose an auxiliary word (اِسْمُ تَفْضِيلٍ).

The following words mean basically the same, you can choose any of them. Don't forget that all of them are diptotes and don't take nunation (مَمْنُوعٌ مِن الصَّرْفِ).

meaning	اِسْمُ تَفْضِيلٍ	root
worthier; more deserving	أَحَقُّ	حَقَّ
more appropriate, suitable, deserving	أَوْلَى	وَلَى

worthier; more suitable	أَجْدَر	جَدُرَ

3. Combine both. Here is the result:

The father is more respected.	الأَبُّ أَحَقُّ أَنْ يُحْتَرَمَ.

CONDITION 4: The verb is negated.	possible

Let's see how we can fix a sentence if we have لا يَعْرِفُ. We will follow and apply the same procedure as shown in CONDITION 3. The only thing we must not forget is the negation!

1. Build the interpreted infinitive (مَصْدَرٌ مُؤَوَّلٌ).

This is tricky since we have a negation (see *question #208*).

أَلَّا يَعْرِفَ	=	يَعْرِفُ	+	لا	+	أَنْ

Notice that أَنْ plus لا becomes أَلَّا

2. Choose an auxiliary word (اِسْمُ تَفْضِيلٍ).

As explained above, the following words mean basically the same, you can choose any of them: أَحَقُّ • أَوْلَى • أَجْدَر

3. Combine both. Here is the result:

It is better for humans not to lie.	الإِنْسانُ أَجْدَرُ أَلَّا يَعْرِفَ الْكِذْبَ.
My colleague deserves not to go.	زَمِيلِي أَحَقُّ أَلَّا يَذْهَبَ.

CONDITION 5: We have a verb that does not have a subject/doer of the action (فَاعِلٌ). Furthermore, it is *defective*.	**impossible**

There are verbs in Arabic which are not satisfied with only a subject. Unless you add a **predicate**, they would not provide a meaningful sentence. That is the reason why such verbs are called *deficient* (فِعْلٌ ناقِصٌ) opposite to *complete* verbs (فِعْلٌ تامٌّ). A deficient verb does not give you information by itself. A well-known example is the verb *to be* (كانَ).

The weather was nice.	كانَ الْجَوُّ جَمِيلًا.

Regarding كانَ, there is no way to express a comparison. This is logical because what should be the comparative of *to be*?

CONDITION 6: The verb can't be conjugated in all tenses and moods.	**impossible**

There are verbs in Arabic which can't be conjugated in all tenses and moods (فِعْلٌ ناقِصُ التَّصْرِيفِ). For example, لَيْسَ which is used to negate nominal sentences (جُمْلةٌ اِسْمِيّةٌ) is only known in the past tense (الْماضِي). It cannot form the present tense (الْمُضارِعُ) nor the imperative (الْأَمْرُ).

Such verbs are also called inert, static verbs (فِعْلٌ جامِدٌ). They do not accept changes in their forms which also makes them close to particles (حَرْفٌ).

Regarding لَيْسَ, there is no way to express a comparison.

Therefore, we need a complete/full verb (فِعْلٌ مُتَصَرِّفٌ).

CONDITION 7: You can't make a real comparison.	**possible**

If someone is dead, he is dead. You can't be *more dead.* But what if it is meant in the sense of time? For example: *he has died before...* Or: *he has been sitting on the chair longer than...* That makes sense.

We could form the comparative of such words if we have the idea of time in mind (the amount of time; length). Let us use the verb *to sit* (جَلَسَ).

1. Build the original infinitive (مَصْدَرٌ أَصْلِيٌّ).

This is easy: جُلُوسٌ.

2. Choose an auxiliary word (اِسْمُ تَفْضِيلٍ).

Here we need words connected to time.

meaning	اِسْمُ تَفْضِيلٍ	root
previous; former; earlier	أَسْبَقُ	سَبَقَ

3. Combine both. We use a **specification** (تَمْيِيزٌ). Here is the result:

Meaning: The child sat down before the teacher.	الطِّفْلُ أَسْبَقُ جُلُوسًا مِن الْمُدَرِّس.
Meaning: ʿAbd al-Naser died earlier than al-Sadāt.	عَبْدُ النَّاصِرِ أَسْبَقُ مَوْتًا مِن السَّدَاتِ.

190. Why shouldn't you say "I buy a Qur'an" in Arabic?

Since we assume that you want to buy a physical book, the word الْقُرْآنُ *doesn't really fit.*

The root of الْقُرْآنُ is ق-ر-ء. Many dictionaries say that it is the infinitive noun (مَصْدَرٌ) of the verb *to read* (قَرَأَ / يَفْرَأُ). Thus, قُرْآن denotes the action of *to read* or *to recite*.

The origin of the word is not entirely clear. Mainly Western scholars say that the word is borrowed from Aramaic.

Others say that the word الْقُرْآنُ uses the pattern فُعْلانٌ. This pattern is used for the مَصْدَر of a triliteral verb. However, it is not the standard pattern but the **common usage** of such verbs (وَزْنٌ سَماعِيٌّ). Other examples of this pattern are *thankfulness* (شُكْرانٌ) or *pardon* (غُفْرانٌ).

According to *Lane's Lexicon*, some scholars suggested that الْقُرْآنُ was originally the *noun of origin* (اِسْمُ الْمَصْدَرِ) of the expression: قَرَأْتُ الشَّيْءَ which means *I **collected** together the thing* or of قَرَأْتُ الْكِتابَ which means *I read (or recited) the book or scripture*. It was later conventionally applied *to signify the Book of God that was revealed to Muhammad*.

Precisely speaking, قُرْآن describes all the words that are in the book. So it doesn't make sense to use this term if you want to say that you want a physical copy of the book.

Instead, it is better to use the expression الْمُصْحَفُ with the definite article (= الْمُصْحَفُ الشَّرِيفُ). The word مُصْحَفٌ (plural: مَصاحِفُ) means *volume* or *binder*.

Let us now try to translate the sentence: *I bought a Qur'an.*

This is understandable – but poor style.	اِشْتَرَيْتُ قُرآنًا.
This is much better.	اِشْتَرَيْتُ مُصْحَفًا.

191. Why is the verb *to wish* (عَسَى) of special kind?

It is allergic to morphological changes.

The original meaning of عَسَى is *to be possible; it could be*. It belongs to a special group of verbs. They are called *inert verbs* (فِعْلٌ جامِدٌ) because they lack the flexibility to form tenses and moods. عَسَى is only used in the past tense (الْماضِي); present tense, future tense, the imperative simply don't exist. Furthermore, عَسَى is only used in the third person singular (masculine)! Basically it is never conjugated and always stays عَسَى.

The verb is usually followed by أَنْ plus verb in the subjunctive mood (مَنْصُوبٌ). It can be followed by the subject of a sentence which then has to be in the accusative case (مَنْصُوبٌ) because عَسَى follows the same rules as كَادَ (see *questions #97* and *#98*). Remember that the predicate of كَادَ has to be in the nominative case (مَرْفُوعٌ).

The verb عَسَى may have a personal pronoun suffix which makes the expression personal: *perhaps you; perhaps we, …*

It could be; it was possible; wishfully; maybe. عَسَى expresses a wish or rhetorical question.	
What should I do?	ماذا عَسَى أَنْ أَفْعَلَ؟
What could he say?	ماذا عَساهُ يَقُولَ؟
The weather should be nice.	عَسَى الْجَوُّ يَكونَ جَميلًا.
Perhaps you are lazy?	عَساكَ كَسُولٌ؟
Perhaps I... (ن is needed to connect ي)	عَساني...ـ
Maybe Allah (مَنْصُوبٌ!) will...	عَسَى اللهُ أَنْ...

For an extensive analysis of عَسَى, see *Arabic for Nerds 2*, *questions #241 and #242*.

192. How do you say *dark/deep red*?

This construction is actually pretty similar to English.

You can use the word دَاكِنٌ which means *dark* or *blackish*. It is the active participle (اِسْمُ فَاعِلٍ) of the root دَكِنَ which means *to darken*. Since it functions as an adjective (صِفَةٌ), it is put **after** the color. Therefore, a possible translation of *dark red* is أَحْمَرُ دَاكِنٌ.

However, like any other صِفَةٌ, it may be put into a *figurative (impure) possessive construction* (إِضَافَةٌ غَيْرُ مَحْضـةٍ) which practically means that the صِفَةٌ **precedes** the noun. Let's see the difference.

Zayd's book (the book of Zayd)	كِتَابُ زَيْدٍ

This is a pure possessive construction (إِضَافَةٌ حَقِيقِيَّةٌ). Why? Because it would be impossible to use a different case marker in the second part (Zayd). It has to be the genitive case (مَجْرُورٌ).

In a pure إِضَافة-construction, you will find its original idea: determination (تَعْرِيفٌ) and specification (تَخْصِيصٌ).

The thief of the house	سَارِقُ الْمَنْزِلِ

What's the issue? We have an impure إِضَافة-construction (إِضَافَةٌ غَيْرُ حَقِيقِيَّةٍ). Why is that? The first part of the إِضَافة here is an active participle (اِسْمُ فَاعِلٍ). It has verbal power and could theoretically have a direct object (مَفْعُولٌ بِهِ). It includes a hidden, implied pronoun (in the nominative case).

This hidden pronoun brings a separation between the first and second part of the إِضَافة. Any type of **separation** weakens the bond and link between the two words.

Theoretically, we could interpret the sentence differently. When we use the hidden pronoun *he,* we could transform the phrase into a meaningful sentence. We just need to use the verbal power of the active participle (it can work as a regent for the direct object). Thus, we use the accusative case (مَنْصُوبٌ) in the second word. What would be the result? *He steals the house* (هُوَ سَارِقُ الْمَنْزِلَ.)

Let's return to our question. The active participle (اِسْمُ فَاعِلٍ) the passive participle (اِسْمُ مَفْعُولٍ,) the quasi-participle (صِفَةٌ مُشَبَّهَةٌ) may be put as the first part of a إِضافة. The very same words could also work as adjectives (but then put behind).

An adjective has to agree with the word which it wants to describe. When the modified noun is definite, the adjective has to be definite as well. This is not possible in a إِضافة!

So let's use a figurative إِضافة.

dark green	دَاكِنُ الْخُضْرِةِ	dark red	دَاكِنُ الْحُمْرِةِ
dark blue	دَاكِنُ الزُّرْقِةِ	dark black	دَاكِنُ السَّوادِ

This brings us to a common mistake.

The second part of the إِضافة must be the infinitive noun (*redness*, *blueness*) and not an adjective (*red*, *blue*).

dark black	دَاكِنُ السُّوداءِ	incorrect
dark red, deeply red	داكِنُ الْأَحْمَرِ	

Remark: What we showed above has nothing to do with an <u>inverted word-order</u> which means that the predicate (خَبَر) precedes the subject (مُبْتَدَأ) in a nominal sentence. For example:

Smoking is forbidden.	مَمْنُوعٌ التَّدْخِينُ.

Forwarded predicate (خَبَرٌ مُقَدَّمٌ); it takes the nominative	مَمْنُوعٌ

case (مَرْفُوعٌ بِالضَّمَّةِ): "*un*".	
Delayed subject (مُبْتَدَأٌ مُؤَخَّرٌ); it also takes the nominative case (مَرْفُوعٌ بِالضَّمَّةِ).	النَّذْخِينُ

193. بَيْنًا or بَيْنَاً - Where do you add the two lines at the end?

*The very correct view is that you should put it **before** the Aleph.*

The two lines are the case ending. Thus, we need to find out how we should express the *nunation* (تَنْوِينٌ) if we have an **indefinite noun** (اِسْمٌ) that needs to be marked with the accusative case (مَنْصُوبٌ). What is correct? On top of the Aleph (بَيْنَاً) or before the Aleph (بَيْنًا)?

You will encounter both spellings in books, movie subtitles, newspapers, even in calligraphies.

Most grammarians, especially Egyptian linguists, argue that the تَنْوِينٌ should be written on the last letter <u>before the Aleph</u>.

The reason is rather simple: The Aleph is a silent letter (حَرْفٌ ساكِنٌ) and can't take any vowel. It always carries a سُكُونٌ and looks like اْ.

If we explicitly wrote the ن of nunation, we would get بَيْنَنْ. Thus, it becomes clear that the vowel "*a*" of the nunation "*an*" should be put on the last letter of the word (in our example, on the ت). The same is true for the other two cases. You can find an extensive analysis in *Arabic for Nerds 2, question #59*.

Some people break this rule in a certain situation: If a word ends in ل, we will add the Aleph and get لا in the accusative case (مَنْصُوبٌ). In this situation, many people don't put the

تَنْوِين before the last letter because the تَنْوِين would separate the Aleph from the ل. Instead, they write the تَنْوِين on top of the Aleph. The result is لَا.

Let's check two examples: كَسُولٌ (*lazy*), رَسُولٌ (*prophet*).

spelling many prefer	correct
رَسُولاً	رَسُولًا
كَسُولاً	كَسُولًا

But watch out if you have ى at the end which is also pro-nounced as Aleph. For example, the word for *meaning*.

wrong	مَعْنىً
correct	مَعْنًى

Remember that there are four situations in which you don't add an Aleph after the last letter in the مَنْصُوب-case. Then the تَنْوِين will be on the last letter – except when the last letter is already a "long Aleph" like in no. 2 in the following examples:

last letter:

water (مَاء), *finishing* (اِنْتِهَاءً)	separate Hamza (هَمْزَةٌ)	1
stick (عَصًا), *Mustafa* (مُصْطَفًى)	shortened Aleph (أَلِفٌ مَقْصُورَةٌ)	2
library (مَكْتَبَةً)	feminine ending ة (تَاءُ تَأْنِيثٍ)	3
refuge (مَلْجَأً)	Hamza written as أ	4

194. When would you use the word أَجْمَلَ in Arabic?

If you want to express astonishment or admiration.

If we just look at the word أَجْمَلُ, it could be a *noun of prefer-ence* (اِسْمُ تَفْضِيلٍ) expressing a comparative: *more beautiful*.

But there is another possibility. أَجْمَلَ can be used to express **astonishment, surprise, or admiration** (أُسْلُوبُ التَّعَجُّبِ).

In this situation, the word أَجْمَلَ is not a noun (اِسْمٌ) as it would be in the *comparative* – but a <u>verb</u> (فِعْلُ التَّعَجُّبِ). It is an *inert verb* (فِعْلٌ جَامِدٌ) which never changes its form and is always in the singular. Some examples.

| What a beautiful view of the sea! | مَا أَجْمَلَ مَنْظَرَ الْبَحْرِ! |
| How beautiful is the rose! | مَا أَجْمَلَ الْوَرْدَةَ! |

The following I-verbs are often used in such constructions:

كَبُرَ	كَثُرَ	صَدَقَ	عَظُمَ	عَذُبَ	جَمُلَ
to be big	to be many	to be sin-cere	to be great	to be sweet	to be beautiful

There are two patterns in Arabic which convey such a mean-ing. You use the same source (and apply the same conditions) that you also use to form a *noun of preference* (اِسْمُ تَفْضِيلٍ) - see *question #189*. Let's see how it works.

You use the particle مَا **plus** the verb pattern for astonishment (فِعْلٌ مَاضٍ عَلَى وَزْنِ أَفْعَلَ) **plus** a noun in the accusative case (اِسْمٌ مَنْصُوبٌ)	مَا + أَفْعَلَ	1

What a beautiful sky!	مَا أَجْمَلَ السَّماءَ!

Subject (مُبْتَدَأٌ) of the nominal sentence (جُمْلةٌ اِسْـمِـيّةٌ). Since we cannot mark this word visibly with case markers, we can only apply a place value (اِسْمٌ نَكِرةٌ فِي مَحَلِّ رَفْعٍ). مَا here has the implicit meaning of *something great*.	مَا
The **predicate** (خَبَرٌ). This is an inert past tense verb; the (verbal) subject (فاعِلٌ) is a hidden/implied pronoun.	أَجْمَلَ
Direct object (مَفْعُولٌ بِهِ) of the verb. Therefore, it takes the accusative case (مَنْصُوبٌ).	السَّماءَ

Use another verb measure for astonishment (فِعْلٌ) (ماضٍ عَلَى وَزْنِ أَفْعِلْ) **plus** the additional preposition بِ **plus** the subject (فاعِلٌ) **plus** a noun in the accusative (تَمْيِيزٌ مَنْصُوبٌ).	2 أَفْعِلْ + بِ

What a beautiful sky!	أَجْمِلْ بِالسَّماءِ!
What a noble woman is she!	أَكْرِمْ بِها فَتاةً!
	= أَكْرِمْ بِها مِن فَتاةٍ!

Inert past tense verb in the imperative (فِعْلُ أَمْرٍ جامِدٌ).	أَكْرِمْ
Redundant/extra preposition (حَرْفُ جَرٍّ زائِدٌ).	بِ
This is the **subject** (فاعِلٌ). The preceding preposition forces the genitive case (مَجْرُورٌ) - which you cannot see the pronoun suffix has an indeclinable, fixed shape. From a grammatical perspective, ها is located in the position of a nominative case (فِي مَحَلِّ رَفْعٍ).	ها
This is a **specification** (تَمْيِيزٌ) which is the reason why it	فَتاةً

takes the accusative case (مَنْصُوبٌ).	

See *Arabic for Nerds 2, question #382*, for a detailed analysis.

If you are dealing with verb stems II to X, a negation, or the passive voice, the أُسْلُوبُ التَّعَجُّبِ is still possible but tricky. You can fix these constructions with some tricks – it works similar to the *comparative* (see *questions #189*).

An example if there is *to be* (كان) involved.		1
The rain was heavy.	كانَ الْمَطَرُ شَدِيدًا.	
What a heavy rain! Construction: auxiliary word + مَصْدَر.	ما أَضْعَبَ كَوْنَ الْمَطَرِ شَدِيدًا!!	
What a heavy rain! Construction: instead of the regular مَصْدَر, use an interpreted infinitive (مَصْدَرٌ مُؤَوَّلٌ) molded by أَنْ.	ما أَضْعَبَ أَنْ يَكُونَ الْمَطَرُ شَدِيدًا!!	

An example of a verb other than stem I (الْفِعْلُ غَيْرُ ثُلائِيٍّ).		2
What an effort of the professor! Construction: auxiliary word + مَصْدَر	ما أَحْسَنَ إِجْتِهادَ الأُسْتاذِ!	
What an effort of the professor! Instead of the مَصْدَر, use an interpreted infinitive (مَصْدَرٌ مُؤَوَّلٌ)	ما أَحْسَنَ أَنْ يَجْتَهِدَ الأُسْتاذُ!	

195. الْمَدِينَةُ قَرطاجُ or مَدِينةُ قَرطاجَ - **What is correct?**

Both are correct.

However, the grammatical construction is different, and so are the case endings! Let us check the differences:

Carthage is an **apposition** (بَدَلٌ) and must take the same case as *city*: the nominative case (مَرْفُوعٌ). It literally means: *The city, Carthage, ...*	الْمَدِينةُ قَرطاجُ
Carthage is the **second part** of the إضافة-construction – and needs the genitive case (مَجْرُورٌ). Foreign names of cities are diptotes (مَمْنُوعٌ مِن الصَّرْفِ) which is the reason for the vowel "a". It literally means: *The city of Carthage...*	مَدِينةُ قَرطاجَ

196. Why do we read numbers from left to right?

Actually, you could also read them from right to left.

Arabic is written from right to left. But numbers are usually written (and spoken) from left to right. Some say that this is linked to contemporary Arabic and Western influence.

However, Ibn ʿAbbās (ابْن عَبَّاس), the cousin of prophet Muhammad and one of the early Qurʾan scholars, is said to have already used the numbers from left to right.

It is a matter of taste as both reading directions are regarded as correct. For example, the year 1997.

7+90+ 900+1000	فِي عام سَبْعةٍ وَتِسْعِينَ وَتِسْع مِئةٍ وَأَلْفِ
1000+900+7+90	فِي عام أَلْفِ وَتِسْع مِئةٍ وَسَبْعةٍ وَتِسْعِينَ

Note that the word *hundred* in Arabic is written as a compound and with long Aleph before the Hamza: (تِسْعِمِائةٍ).

197. Why are there "an"-endings in أَهْلًا وَسَهْلًا؟

Because we assume that there is an underlying, virtual verb.

In Arabic, several words are used with the ending *"an"*, i.e., nunation (تَنْوِينٌ) in the accusative case (مَنْصُوبٌ).

These words were originally part of a sentence, but the verbs which were responsible for the case endings were deleted. The only thing that remained was a مَصْدَر in the مَنْصُوب-case.

In most situations, the words in the accusative case served as an **absolute** or **inner object** (مَفْعُولٌ مُطْلَقٌ) which is mainly used to confirm or emphasize the verb or to show its nature – see *question #122*. This is true for, words like شُكْرًا (*thanks*). Sometimes, it may also be a **direct object** (مَفْعُولٌ بِهِ) of a deleted verb as in the word أَهْلًا (*welcome*).

Many of these expressions have developed into independent expressions.

	original sentence	expression (عِبَارَةٌ)
صَادَفْتَ أَهْلًا لَا غُرَبَاءَ وَوَطِئْتَ سَهْلًا لَا وَعْرًا.	welcome!	أَهْلًا وَسَهْلًا
Literal meaning: You have found (met with) kinsfolk, not strangers, and set foot on a place that is even and not rugged. (May you arrive as part of the family, and tread an easy path as you enter.)		
أَشْكُرُكَ شُكْرًا.	thanks!	شُكْرًا
I really want to thank you.		
آضَ or يَئِيضُ إِلَى شَيْءٍ أَيْضًا.	as well	أَيْضًا
He returned to the thing, i.e., to the doing of the thing; he did the thing again.		

Only some adjectives (صِفة) may lose their case ending as they are not a مَصْدَر and do not function as a مَفْعُولٌ مُطْلَقٌ. Since we stop after the one and only word, we put سُكُوت at the end.

wonderful!	عَظيمْ!	congratulations!	مَبْرُوكْ!
Quasi participle (صِفة مُشَبَّهة) of the verb عَظُمَ.		Passive participle (اِسْـمُ مَفْعُولٍ) of the verb بَرَكَ.	

198. النَّوْمَ, النَّوْمَ! - Why do these words get a فَتْحة؟

Because they function as a warning.

There is a special form in Arabic if you want to warn or instigate someone. It is called أُسْلُوبُ التَّحْذِيرِ وَالْإِغْراءِ which literally means: *warning and instigation.* For example: النَّوْمَ, النَّوْمَ!

So what does it mean? When a student is sitting in class and almost falls asleep, the teacher can warn the person by saying النَّوْمَ, النَّوْمَ which means *beware of sleep!*

The tricky thing about this construction is the case. We need the accusative case (مَنْصُوبٌ). Let us see some examples.

Fire!	النَّارَ!
Fire and drowning!	النَّارَ وَالْغَرَقَ!

You can also enhance the construction by adding the receiver of the warning.

All three sentences mean the same: *(you) beware of fire!*	إِيّاكَ النَّارَ!	1
	إِيّاكَ وَالنَّارَ!	2
	إِيّاكَ مِن النَّارِ!	3

- The pronoun إِيَّاكَ is the accusative (مَنْصُوبٌ) of *you*.
- If the fire is confirmed, repeat the vocative: إِيَّاكَ إِيَّاكَ النَّارَ!

See also *Arabic for Nerds 2, question #421ff.*

199. How do you express *although; despite* in Arabic?

Not so easy. It depends on where you put them in a sentence.

We need to form a so-called concessive clause which expresses an idea that suggests the opposite of the main part of the sentence. For example: *Although it was raining, he came to the party.* In Arabic, such sentences are often difficult to grasp because you don't use plain, clear words like in English.

Let's see how it works.

subordinate clause; final clause	main clause
Although he was tired,	*he couldn't sleep.*

1	Words that may stand at the **start** of the **main** or **subordinate** clause. They always go along with a nominal sentence (جُمْلة اسْمِيَّة) which means that you can never have a verb after them.

although; even though	رَغْمَ أَنَّ · عَلَى الرَّغْمِ مِنْ أَنَّ · بِالرَّغْمِ مِنْ أَنَّ

Note: The expressions بِالرَّغْمِ مِنْ أَنَّ with ب is widespread now, but it is not found in the classical works of Arabic. You cannot find بِالرَّغْمِ but only عَلَى الرَّغْمِ. Why? Probably because the preposition عَلَى simply fits better as it denotes **compulsion** (الْإِجْبارُ). The ب, on the other hand, conveys accompanying (الْمُصاحَبةُ).

مَعَ أَنَّ بَيْدَ أَنَّ غَيْرَ أَنَّ	*although; whereas; nevertheless; however*

حَضَرَ مَعَ أَنَّهُ كَانَ كَسُولًا.	He showed up **although** he was lazy.
عَلَى الرَّغْمِ مِن أَنَّهُ كَانَ مَرِيضًا فَقَدْ قَرَّرَ أَنْ يَحْضَرَ الْمُحَاضَرَةَ.	**Although** he was sick, he decided to attend the lecture.
هُوَ كَثِيرُ الْمَالِ بَيْدَ أَنَّهُ بَخِيلٌ.	He has a lot of money, **however**, he is stingy.
خَرَجْتُ مِن الْبَيْتِ عَلَى الرَّغْمِ مِنْ أَنَّ الطَّقْسَ كَانَ بَارِدًا.	I left the house **although** the weather was cold (despite the cold weather).

> 2 | The expression إِلَّا أَنَّ is put at the **start** of the **main clause**. It is common to use it with رَغْم and other expressions shown above.

إِلَّا أَنَّ	yet; however; but; nevertheless

مَعَ أَنَّ الْفُنْدُقَ كَانَ جَمِيلًا إِلَّا أَنَّهُ يَخْلُو مِنْ دَوْرَةِ مِياهٍ.	**Although** the hotel was nice, it **nevertheless** had no toilet.
مَعَ أَنَّ هَذِهِ الشَّرِكَةَ مَشْهُورَةٌ إِلَّا أَنَّ إِنْتَاجَها صَارَ قَلِيلًا وَضَعِيفًا.	**Although** this company is famous, **yet** its output has become little and weak.
عَلَى الرَّغْمِ أَنَّ الِامْتِحَانَ كَانَ صَعْبًا إِلَّا أَنِّي أَجَبْتُ عَلَى كُلِّ الْأَسْئِلَةِ.	**Even though** the test was difficult, **yet** I answered all the questions.

> 3 | Devices that are placed **in-between** a sentence or at the beginning of the **subordinate** clause. See also *question #265*.

even if; though	وَإِنْ
even if (you use a past tense verb but the meaning is the present tense)	وَلَوْ

Call me, even if you are on the train!	كَلِّمْنِي بِالْمَحْمُولِ وَلَوْ كُنْتَ فِي الْقِطارِ!
You will visit Cairo again even if you have visited Cairo before.	أَنْتَ - وَإِنْ زُرْتَ الْقاهِرَةَ مِنْ قَبْلُ - سَوْفَ تَزورُها مَرَّةً أُخْرَى.

200. How do you spell after...? بَعَدَما or بَعَدَ ما (with space)?

It depends on if you want to use ما as a relative pronoun (which, that) or if ما should produce an interpreted infinitive.

Both applications of ما are often misunderstood. We could derive the following two rules which are almost always correct:

- You leave space before ما when it is used as a relative pronoun (ما الْمَوْصُولُ). A good indicator for this type of ما is when the verb after ما contains a pronoun suffix.

- You connect ما with the preceding word immediately (without space) if ما is the device to produce an expression that can be interpreted as a مَصْدَر (ما الْمَصْدَرِيّةُ).

The whole issue has been subject of a long debate. Take for example the following sentence:

1	أُحِبُّ ما كَتَبْتَ.

Theoretically, the ما could be **both**: a relative pronoun and a device to form an infinitive.

type of ما	How we could rewrite the sentence
ما الْمَصْدَرِيّة	أُحِبُّ كِتابَتَكَ.
Meaning: *I like the way you write* (طَرِيقَتُكَ فِي الْكِتابَةِ).	
ما الْمَوْصُولةُ	أُحِبُّ الَّذِي كَتَبْتَ.
Meaning: *I like what is written on the paper* (الْمَكْتُوبُ فِي الْوَرَقِ)	

However, if we have the following sentence, then ما can **only** be a **relative pronoun**. Why? Because of the *binder, connector* – the *returning pronoun* (ضَمِيرُ الْعائِدِ). The ه is referring to the word ما. Sometimes, however, the referrer may be omitted.

2	أُحِبُّ ما كَتَبْتَهُ.

All that matters if other words get involved, like عِنْدَ before ما.

ما الْمَصْدَرِيّة	I stop talking when I want.	أَتَوَقَّفُ فِي الْحَدِيثِ عِنْدَما أَرْغَبُ.	correct
Meaning: *at/when my wish is to stop* (عِنْدَ رَغْبَتِي التَّوَقُّفَ).			

ما الْمَوْصُولةُ	I stop talking (at the position) that I want.	أَتَوَقَّفُ فِي الْحَدِيثِ عِنْدَما أَرْغَبُهُ.	**incorrect.** You need space.

Notice the pronoun! This is a hint that we have a relative pronoun. The ه here is a returning pronoun. The meaning is عِنْدَ الَّذِي أَرْغَبُهُ. It denotes *when my wish is to stop* (عِنْدَ رَغْبَتِي التَّوَقُّفَ).

ما الْمَوْصُولةُ	I stop talking (at the position) that I want.	أَتَوَقَّفُ فِي الْحَدِيثِ عِنْدَ ما أَرْغَبُهُ.	correct

> Remark: We would also use give some space if the pronominal suffix, the ه in our example, would be concealed/hidden which occasionally happens in such sentences with ما in Classical Arabic. The ه here is the direct object (مَفْعُولٌ بِهِ) of the verb أَرْغَبُ.

Let us use the expression *after* (بَعْدَ) and analyze the difference.

ما الْمَصْدَرِيّةُ	I came after we had finished.	جِئْتُ بَعْدَما اِنْتَهَيْنا.	correct
ما الْمَوْصُولةُ		جِئْتُ بَعْدَ ما اِنْتَهَيْنا.	incorrect

ما الْمَوْصُولةُ	I came after what happened.	جِئْتُ بَعْدَ ما حَدَثَ.	correct
ما الْمَصْدَرِيّةُ		جِئْتُ بَعْدَما حَدَثَ.	incorrect

If ما is preceded by a preposition, mistakes occur. Only if the preposition before ما is very short (1 or 2 letters), you write them together – otherwise, you should leave space in-between.

Correct what follows.	صَحِّحْ فِيما يَلِي!	understandable
	صَحِّحْ فِي ما يَلِي!	better (الصَّوابُ)
	The meaning of ما here is: صَحِّحْ فِي الَّذِي يَلِي	

Excursus: How do you build and use adverbs of time?

Adverbs have many meanings and functions. They are especially important for indicating the time, manner, place, degree and frequency of something.

Adverbs work very different in Arabic.

You have to identify the appropriate spot in a sentence where an adverb of time, place, or manner would fit.

Then you have a choice of different types of words and forms which could fit at that location. For example, you may use *particles* (حَرْفٌ), *indeclinable nouns* (اِسْمٌ مَبْنِيٌّ) but also *absolute objects* (مَفْعُولٌ مُطْلَقٌ) or *specifications* (تَمْيِيزٌ).

Let's see some expressions that function as *adverbs of time*.

Note that in the following expressions, the مَا is either a particle to produce an **infinitive** (مَا الْمَصْدَرِيّة) or a **relative pronoun** (مَا الْمَوْصُولةُ).

I	Let's start with constructions in which مَا is a **relative pronoun** (مَا الْمَوْصُولةُ).

1	after; later; in the future.	فِيما بَعْدُ

Note: The expression فِيما alone would denote *while, as* (and may be followed by a nominal or verbal sentence). The مَا here is a **relative pronoun** (مَا الْمَوْصُولةُ). The expression literally denotes *in what is after* (فِي الَّذِي بَعْدَهُ).

Why do we write it together? This is optional because only if the word before مَا has more than 3 letters, you have to write them together.

He came **later**.	جاءَ فِيما بَعْدُ.
She remembered the word later.	تَذَكَّرَت الْكَلِمةَ فِيما بَعْدُ.

2	before; earlier; in the past	فِيما مَضَى

The Prophet said: "Amongst the people **preceding you** there used to be *Muhaddithun*	قَالَ: إِنَّهُ قَدْ كَانَ فِيما مَضَى قَبْلَكُمْ مِنْ

(i.e. persons who can guess things that come true later on, as if those persons have been inspired by a divine power), and if there are any such persons amongst my followers, it is Umar bin al-Khattāb. *(Sahīh al-Bukhārī 3469)*	الأُمَمِ مُحَدَّثُونَ، وَإِنَّهُ إِنْ كَانَ فِي أُمَّتِي هَذِهِ مِنْهُمْ، فَإِنَّهُ عُمَرُ بْنُ الْخَطَّابِ.

3	as much as; to the same extent as	بِقَدْرِ مَا
	You are as free as I am.	أَنْتَ حُرٌّ بِقَدْرِ مَا أَنَا حُرٌّ.

4	as soon as; the moment when	أَوَّلَ مَا
	As soon as the negotiations started…	أَوَّلَ مَا بَدَأَت الْمُحَادَثَاتُ…

II Now let's check constructions in which مَا produces an **interpreted infinitive** (مَا الْمَصْدَرِيَّةُ) that has the same meaning as the مَصْدَر itself.

5	after…	past tense verb + مَا + بَعْدَ/قَبْلَ
	before…	(مَنْصُوبٌ) present tense subjunctive + أَنْ + بَعْدَ/قَبْلَ

Both of the above constructions produce an **interpreted infinitive** (مَصْدَر مُؤَوَّل). This is also the reason why we need مَا or أَنْ because after بَعْدَ only a noun can follow.

The interpreted infinitive, as an entity, replaces the مَصْدَر and means exactly the same.

| After he had left... | بَعْدَما اِنْصَرَفَ = بَعْدَ اِنْصِرافِهِ |

Don't forget that the word بَعْدُ expresses yet or later.

| He is yet to come. (Or: He will come later.) | سَيَأْتِي بَعْدُ. |

| 6 | when; whenever; as soon as | past or present tense + عِنْدَما |

عِنْدَما is used to indicate the time in which the action expressed in the main clause takes place (فِي الْوَقْتِ الَّذِي). It may precede or follow the main clause. Note that the عِنْدَما was not used in the prime of Classical Arabic!

When he came...	عِنْدَما جاءَ...
When he goes...	عِنْدَما يَذْهَبُ...
Whenever he began to walk...	عِنْدَما يَبْدَأُ الْمَشْيَ...

| 7 | until; while; as long as | رَيْثَما or رَيْثَ أَنْ |

| Sit down while I am out – until I am back. | اِجْلِسْ رَيْثَما أَعُودُ. |

| 8 | often; frequently | past tense verb + طالَما |
| | Literally: *as long as*. It comes from the verb طال - *to be long*. |

| that occurred often | طالَما حَدَثَ ذٰلِكَ |

Watch out: You may hear that people use طالَما as a synonym of ما دَامَ. However, this doesn't really make sense.

As long as you fear, Allah will be with you.	‏ما دُمْتَ تَتَّقِي اللهَ فَسَيَكُونُ مَعَكَ.‏	correct
	‏طالَما تَتَّقِي اللهَ فَسَيَكُونُ مَعَكَ.‏	incorrect

Why is that? The **verb** طال denotes that its subject (فاعِلٌ) is present during the entire period of the action.

If we say, for example, طالَما سِرْنا مَعًا (*as long as we walked together*), the meaning would be that the duration of the act of walking (=subject) was long. The interpretation of the sentence would be: طالَ سَيْرُنا مَعًا because the ما in this expression produces an interpreted infinitive! However, the actual subject نا (*we*) is suddenly the second part of the إِضافة and the main subject is *walking*.

The expression ما دَامَ, on the other hand, needs a subject and a predicate – because it is a sister of كانَ. If we say

As long as the truth is among the people, ignorance won't spread.	‏ما دَامَ الْحَقُّ بَيْنَ النّاسِ فَلَنْ يَنْتَشِرَ الْجَهْلَ.‏

The "subject" is الْحَقُّ. The predicate is بَيْنَ النّاسِ. The answer is فَلَنْ يَنْتَشِرَ الْجَهْلَ. This is exactly what we want to express.

Remark: Some scholars say that ما in type II is a **hindering (neutralizing) particle** (حَرْفٌ كافٌّ). See *Arabic for Nerds 2*, question #296.

III A special type of the مَا: It produces an **adverbial inter-preted infinitive** (مَا الْمَصْدَرِيَّةُ الزَّمَانِيَّةُ).

9	every time when; whenever

كُلَّمَا

- Although you use past tense verbs, they convey a present tense meaning!

- It conveys a conditional meaning if both verbs are in the past tense.

- The مَا is special (مَا الْمَصْدَرِيَّةُ الزَّمَانِيَّةُ). It is a particle that produces a *circumstantial, adverbial infinitive* (حَرْفٌ مَصْدَرِيٌّ ظَرْفِيٌّ). We say that it replaces the *adverb of time* (ظَرْفُ الزَّمانِ) which was deleted and had been holding the place of the first part of the إِضافة. Therefore, if we look at its position, it gets the place value of an ad-verb in the accusative case (فِي مَحَلِّ نَصْبٍ). We can pic-ture مَا as conveying a notion of time which expresses **si-multaneousness**.

Whenever he studies, he is happy.	كُلَّمَا دَرَسَ فَرِحَ.
Whenever they are given sustenance from the fruits of these Gardens, they will say, "We have been given this before" *(Sura 2:25)*	كُلَّمَا رُزِقُوا مِنْها مِن ثَمَرَةٍ رِّزْقًا قَالُوا هَٰذَا الَّذِي رُزِقْنَا مِن قَبْلُ

IV Expressions with مَا plus verbs such as *to be many* (كَثُرَ), *to be few* (قَلَّ), *to be often* (شَدَّ), etc.

- Such مَا is a *hindering, neutralizing Mā* (مَا الْكَافَّةُ). It neu-tralizes the regimen of the verb (مَا الْكَافَّةُ عَنِ الْفَاعِلِ). In other words, we get rid of the subject (فَاعِلٌ) of the verb.

By neutralizing, we mean that these verbs do not request a subject (an agent, the doer of the action) anymore.

- If we add a **verb** in the past tense, it denotes a conditional or future meaning.

10	maybe; possibly; perhaps; sometimes	رُبَّما

| Perhaps Zayd is in the house. | رُبَّما زَيْدٌ فِي الْبَيْتِ. |
| Maybe I would leave Egypt; perhaps I shall leave Egypt. | رُبَّما غادَرْتُ مِصْرَ. |

رُبَّما may be introduced by the emphatic particle لَ. Note that رُبَّما is a tricky expression – for an analysis, see *Arabic for Nerds 2, qu. #137*.

| Perhaps he has escaped. | لَرُبَّما نَجا. |

201. How do you say *so that* in Arabic?

There are many options.

Sentences starting with *so that...* are subordinate clauses and give a cause or result. In Arabic, there are several possibilities to express this idea. Let us look at three main constructions.

so that; to the point where; in such a manner that	بِحَيْثُ	1

Usually a جُمْلة فِعْلِيّة (present or past tense) follows. Sometimes, it can be followed by أَنَّ and a جُمْلة اِسْمِيّة.

| You had a lot of money, **so that** you could travel to Germany. | كانَ لَدَيْكَ مالٌ كَثِيرٌ بِحَيْثُ اِسْتَطَعْتَ أَنْ تُسافِرَ إِلَى أَلْمانِيا. |

فَ can also denote *so that* and expresses a wish, a command, or a question. Note that you need the subjunctive mood (مَنْصُوبٌ) of the verb.	فَ	2

He hoped/wished to see me so that we could discuss the topic.	تَمَنّى لَوْ رَآني فَنُناقِشَ الْمَوْضُوعَ.

حَتّى is usually translated as *until*. It may also denote *so that*. If the situation which you describe is still ongoing, then use the present tense in the subjunctive (مَنْصُوبٌ) because there is a virtual, estimated أَنْ which is understood, but not written. If the action is already over, you should use the past tense after حَتّى.	حَتّى	3

Do good, so that you (can) enter the Garden.	اِعْمَلْ الْخَيْرَ حَتّى تَدْخُلَ الْجَنَّةَ.

202. How do you recognize a reported (indirect) speech?

After قالَ you will see the particle إِنَّ.

In Arabic, the reported speech (كَلامٌ مَنْقُولٌ, غَيْرُ مُباشِرٍ) is not different from the direct speech regarding tense or word-order. You don't have to change words like in English where *yesterday* becomes *the day before*. In German, the reported speech is easy to recognize as you have to use the *Konjunktiv I*.

What happens in Arabic?

1	Direct speech
He said: "I wrote you a letter."	قالَ: "(إِنّيِ) كَتَبْتُ لَكَ رِسالةً."

2	Reported speech
He said that he had written me a letter. (Both mean the same.)	قالَ إِنَّهُ كَتَبَ لِي رِسالةً.
	قالَ بِأَنَّهُ كَتَبَ لِي رِسالةً.

A hint: If you want to make clear that a sentence is a reported speech you could use بِأَنَّ = *that*. Notice the vowel "a" (فَتْحة) on top of the Aleph in بِأَنَّ. After the preposition بـ, we don't have to use إِنَّ – for more information about إِنَّ *see question #231*.

203. How do you build reported questions?

This is more difficult than the reported speech.

Let us try to translate the following sentence: *He asked me whether/if...*

whether / if...	إنْ + كانَ ...	1
	إذا + كانَ (ما) ...	2
→ If you have a verb with a preposition, e.g., سَأَلَ عَنْ (*to ask about*).	عَمّا إذا ◄ ما إذا + عَنْ	3
	فيما إذا ما إذا + في	

Now let us check the tenses.

	direct question		reported question
present tense	الْمُضارِعُ		الْماضِي or كانَ + الْمُضارِعُ
past tense	الْماضِي		كانَ + قَدْ + الْماضِي
future tense	الْمُسْتَقْبَلُ		كانَ + الْمُسْتَقْبَلُ
nominal sentence	جُمْلة اِسْمِيّة		كانَ + خَبَرٌ

Some examples.

direct question	reported question
لا أَعْرِفُ: "هَلْ ذَهَبَ أَمْ لا؟"	لا أَعْرِفُ ما إِذا (=إِنْ) كانَ قَدْ ذَهَبَ أَمْ لا.
I don't know: "Did he go or not?"	I don't know if he had gone or not.
سَأَلْتُهُ: "هَلْ تُحِبُّ الْقَهْوَةَ أَمْ الشَّايَ؟"	سَأَلْتُهُ إِنْ (= عَمَّا إِذا) كانَ يُحِبُّ الْقَهْوَةَ أَمْ الشَّايَ.
I asked him: "Do you like coffee or tea?"	I asked him if he liked coffee or tea.

204. لَبَّيْكَ (*at your service*) - What form is that?

It is pretty sophisticated and has to do with the dual.

Muslims use this expression all the time. It means *Praise Allah*! Or *Allah be praised*!

لَبَّيْكَ اللَّهُمَّ لَبَّيْكَ is said during the pilgrimage before the Muslim pilgrims enter Mecca. It means *Here I am! At your service!* The expression is tricky.

Let us check the construction.

1. The root: It is ل-ب-ي. This root is only used as a II-verb and means *to follow, to obey* (*a call, an invitation*).

2. The مَصْدَر: The مَصْدَر of لَبَّى – a II-verb (فَعَّلَ) – would be تَلْبِيَةٌ. But we don't use this word for our expression. Instead, we use لَبٌّ which is the *noun of origin* (اِسْمُ الْمَصْدَرِ) of the verb لَبَّى. (*See question #82 and Arabic for Nerds 2, #110*).

3. Form the dual: لَبٌّ is put into the dual form for the sake of corroboration (emphasis) meaning *answer after answer, saying after saying* (إِلبابًا بَعْدَ إِلبابٍ ، وإِجابةً بَعْدَ إِجابةٍ). The dual is لَبَّانِ if nominative (مَرْفُوعٌ) or لَبَّيْنِ if genitive (مَجْرُورٌ) or accusative (مَنْصُوبٌ).

4. Put the word into in مَنْصُوب: This expression is used as an exclamation of admiration – a special form of the expression of admiration (أَسْلُوبُ التَّعَجُّبِ). Thus, we get لَبَّيْنِ.

5. Add the personal pronoun: Since we want to add the personal pronoun *you* (*you* refers to Allah) and since we use the word as an absolute, inner object (مَفْعُولٌ مُطْلَقٌ), the ن is dropped because it is linked to a personal pronoun – in other words, we have a إِضافة-construction.

6. Result: Finally, we get: لَبَّيْكَ.

There is a bunch of expressions that are similarly constructed using an absolute object (مَفْعُولٌ مُطْلَقٌ); sometimes in dual form, e.g., سَعْدَيْكَ).

meaning	original meaning	expression
Praise God!	أُسَبِّحُ اللهَ تَسْبِيحًا.	سُبْحانَ اللهِ !
God forbid! God save (protect) me (us) from that!	أَعُوذُ بِاللهِ مَعاذًا.	مَعاذَ اللهِ !
Here I am! At your service!	أُلَبِّيكَ تَلْبِية بَعْدَ تَلْبِية أي أُلَبِّيكَ كَثِيرًا.	لَبَّيْكَ !
And all good is in your hands.	أُسْعَدْثُكَ إِسعادًا بَعْدَ إِسعادٍ.	سَعْدَيْكَ !

Other expressions using an exclamation of admiration or surprise (أُسْلُوبُ النَّعَجُّبِ):

Meaning: *how capable, how excellent he is!* Literally: *His achievement is due to God.*	لِله دَرُّهُ !
What a hero!	ياألَهُ مِنْ بَطَلٍ!

Excursus: Why do we use اللَّهُمَّ ("*allahumma*") for God?

The word اللَّهُمَّ is used in the Qur'an five times. The origin of
the expression is not entirely clear.

- Muslim scholars say that it just means يا اللّٰه (O God!). The م,
  they say, was added to compensate the omission/suppression
  of the vocative particle يا.

- Other scholars say that it is a short form of: يا اللّٰهُ أُمَّنا بِخَيْرٍ
  which means *O God! Bring us good!* Or: *O God! Instruct us in
  righteousness!*

- There is even another idea: Bible scholars said that it comes
  from Biblical Hebrew because a word for *God* is אֱלֹהִים which
  is pronounced *ĕlohīm*. However, Muslim scholars say that
  God's name in Hebrew is the plural form which is true.

  אֱלֹהִים is the plural of אֱלוֹהַּ or אֱלָהַּ (*Eloah*). Jewish scholars
  hold that אֱלֹהִים is singular (it governs a singular verb or adjective) when referring to the Hebrew God, but grammatically
  plural (taking a plural verb or adjective) when used to denote
  pagan divinities.

  The Hebrew plural may also be explained by a *plural of respect*
  (*pluralis excellentiae*). And what do secular scholars say? They
  attribute the plural אֱלֹהִים to a polytheistic origin of the Is-
  raelite religion.

205. Why do you have to be careful when you say وَاللهِ؟

At least because the grammar is tricky.

In Arabic, the word قَسَمٌ means *oath*.

The principle meaning of the root is *to share, to part*; but also *to destine*. From this root, the IV-verb أَقْسَمَ بِ عَلَى is used to express the English verb *to swear*. The preposition بِ here means *by*. The most famous oath is وَاللهِ which literally means *by God!* It is usually translated as *I swear*.

Now comes the fun stuff: Do you know why the word God takes the genitive case (مَجْرُورٌ)? Well, in fact, the particle و stands for a verb (أَقْسَمَ بِ) and the بِ in this suppressed and unpronounced verb is also the reason for the genitive case. This type of و is called وَاوُ الْقَسَمِ.

Watch out: Never use the verb أَقْسَمَ with و. So don't say: أُقْسِمُ وَاللهِ

In Arabic, the person or thing you swear by (الْاِسْمُ الْمُقْسَمُ بِهِ) has to take that case. We will see why. There are three help-ing devices which introduce an oath (أَدَوات الْقَسَمِ):

- وَ: the most common particle. Never use it with a verb.

- بِ: is the only particle that may be used with the verb it-self: *I swear by* (أُقْسِمُ بِ)

- تَ: the تَ is exclusively used with *God* (اللهُ or رَبُّ).

By the sky with its towering constellations (Sura 85:1)	وَالسَّمَاءِ ذَاتِ الْبُرُوجِ

Let us check the grammar grammatical implications:

1. If the sentence after the oath is a <u>nominal sentence</u> (جُمْلَة اسْمِيّةٌ), you'll have to use either إِنَّ or إِنَّ combined with لِ.

I swear that certainly life is a struggle!	وَاللهِ إِنَّ الْحَيَاةَ كِفَاحٌ!
I swear that certainly life is a struggle! In this sentence we use the preposition لِ. The meaning is the same.	وَاللهِ إِنَّ الْحَيَاةَ لِكِفَاحٍ!

2. If the sentence after the oath is a <u>verbal sentence</u> (جُمْلَة فِعْلِيّةٌ) in the <u>past tense</u>, you'll have to use قَدْ or لَقَدْ.

By Allah, I have obeyed your command!	تَاللهِ لَقَدْ أَطَعْتُ أَمْرَكَ!
By Allah, I obeyed your command!	تَاللهِ قَدْ أَطَعْتُ أَمْرَكَ!

3. If the sentence after the oath is a <u>verbal sentence</u> (جُمْلَة فِعْلِيّةٌ) in the <u>present tense</u>, you'll have to add the letter لَ after the oath and use the letter ن for emphasis – the so-called نُونُ التَّوْكِيدِ (see *question #156*). In short: you put a فَتْحة at the end of a verb and add نَّ.

I swear, I will certainly do it!	وَاللهِ لَأَفْعَلَنَّ!

4. If the sentence after the oath is <u>negated</u>, there is no need to add any kind of emphasis (تَأْكِيدٌ).

By God, there is no success with laziness!	وَاللهِ لَا نَجَاحَ مَعَ الْكَسَلِ!
After the oath there is a negated nominal sentence (جُمْلةٌ اسْمِيّةٌ).	

By God, I do not agree!	وَاللهِ لَمْ أُوَافِقْ!
After the oath there is a negated verbal sentence (جُمْلةٌ فِعْلِيّةٌ).	

206. If we curse in the name of God, why do we use the past?

Because we want to express a wish.

When we curse in the name of God, we use a past tense verb to express the present tense. The same goes for wishes that refer to God. Let us see some examples (notice the past tense).

God kill them!	قَتَلَهُمْ اللهُ !
God assist you!	نَصَرَكَ اللهُ !
May God protect you from diseases!	حَماكَ اللهُ مِن الْأَمْراضِ!

May God not make you prosper!	لا أَصْلَحَكَ اللهُ !
If you want to negate a verb (and want to express a curse or wish), you use لا plus past tense (الْماضِي). This is a rare exception as normally, you only negate the present tense (الْمُضارِعُ) with لا.	

207. Can you use مَنْ to start a conditional sentence?

Yes, you can.

In literature or formal Arabic, you can choose from a variety of words to start a conditional sentence (*if; when*).

The word مَنْ generally denotes *who* but it can also be used to introduce an (indefinite) conditional sentence. It then conveys the meaning of *whoever; whatever; wherever; however.* مَنْ is used for general assumptions. For example: *Whatever you do, you will be my friend.*

If you use مَنْ, you have to watch out for the correct mood of the verbs. We need the jussive mood (مَجْزُومٌ).

| Whoever strives, succeeds in life. | مَنْ يَجْتَهِدْ يَنْجَحْ فِي حَيَاتِهِ. |

- The verb يَنْجَحْ ends in سُكُون which is the standard way of marking the jussive mood (مَجْزُومٌ) of regular verbs.

| Whoever visits Egypt meets a friend. | مَنْ يَزُرْ مِصْرَ يَلْقَ صَدِيقًا. |

- The verb يَزُورُ becomes يَزُرْ (with سُكُون) in the jussive mood (مَجْزُومٌ), so we got rid of the weak letter و.

- The verb يَلْقَ ends with "a" (فَتْحَةٌ). Why? Because the present tense (indicative mood) of this I-verb is يَلْقَى. We got rid of the last letter because it is weak (حَرْفُ عِلَّةٍ). The vowel on top of the second (and now last letter) is a فَتْحَةٌ. This is true for all verbs which have و or ي as the final root letter and follow the past tense pattern فَعِلَ such as to meet (لَقِيَ). Don't mix it up with the IV-verb يُلْقِي/أَلْقَى which means to throw.

Note: The same would have happened to the I-verbs to remain (بَقِيَ), to be pleased (رَضِيَ), or to forget (نَسِيَ) in the مَجْزُومٌ-mood.

208. What is the difference between أَلَّا and إِلَّا?

إِلَّا means except. أَلَّا denotes not to.

These two words almost look the same. The only difference is the Hamza (هَمْزَةٌ).

It is written either on top (أَلَّا) or at the bottom (إِلَّا). The position is decisive.

- إِلَّا is a *particle of exception* (حَرْفُ اسْتِثْناءٍ). It means *except* (see *question #215*).

- أَلَّا is a combination of two words (تَكُونُ مُرَكَّبَةً مِنْ أَنَّ النَّاصِبَةِ لِلْمُضارِعِ وَلَا النَّافِيَةِ) and means *not to*.

أَلَّا has a فَتْحة upon the هَمْزة. It means *that not*; *unless*; *if not* and is the result of a grammatical construction:

3		2		1
أَلَّا	=	لَا	+	أَنْ

The verb after أَلَّا has to be in the subjunctive mood (مَنْصُوبٌ) due to the particle أَنْ. Here are some examples:

...that you don't travel...	أَلَّا تُسافِرَ = أَنْ لا تُسافِرَ
that you don't (didn't) do it...	...أَلَّا تَفْعَلَهُ
I think that he didn't drink.	أَظُنُّ أَلَّا يَشْرَبَ.
I want you not to pull back.	أُرِيدُ أَلَّا تَتَراجَعَ.

Let us look at a sentence in which you find both words:

He decided not to take anything with him except the book.	قَرَّرَ أَلَّا يَأْخُذَ مَعَهُ إِلَّا الْكِتابَ.

After أَنْ the verb is in the subjunctive (مَنْصُوبٌ), so the verb has to take فَتْحَة at the end (يَأْخُذَ). | أَنْ + لا = أَلَّا

But why has the word الْكِتابَ a فَتْحَة at the end? Here, the word إِلَّا means *except*. The grammatical construction is called أُسْلُوبُ الْقَصْرِ and follows certain rules. If you don't know them, have a look at *question #217*. | إِلَّا

Hint: If you want to put the correct vowels on the words, just delete the negation in your mind and you'll get يَأْخُذ الْكِتابَ. The word الْكِتاب is the direct object (مَفْعُولٌ بِهِ) and has to be in the accusative case (مَنْصُوبٌ).

Watch out: The expression إِلَّا may denote a <u>conditional meaning</u>. It is a compound of the *conditional* إِنَّ (إِنَّ الشَّرْطِيَّةُ) and the *negation device* لا (لا النَّافِيَةُ).

| If you don't study, you will fail. | إِلَّا تَدْرُسْ تَرْسُب. |
| Even if you do not help the Prophet, God helped him. (*Sura 9:40*) | إِلَّا تَنْصُرُوهُ فَقَدْ نَصَرَهُ اللَّهُ. |

209. What is the function of a بَدَل (*apposition*)?

An apposition refers to the same person or thing which is already mentioned in a sentence.

Literally, بَدَل means *substitute*. An apposition takes the same case as the word it is accompanying.

| Karim, the driver, was in the house. | كانَ كَرِيمٌ السَّائِقُ فِي الْبَيْتِ. |

| → This is the origin of the above sentence! | كانَ كَرِيمٌ, كانَ السَّائِقُ, فِي الْبَيْتِ. |

Let us check the grammar terms:

- The first part (*Karim*) is called مُبْدَل مِنْهُ (*substituted for*).
- The second part (*the driver*) is the بَدَل (*apposition*).

What about the position of the بَدَل in a sentence?

1. The بَدَلٌ follows the subject of a sentence.

This student came.	جاءَ هذا الطَّالِبُ.

This is the subject of the sentence.	فاعِلٌ / مُبْدَلٌ مِنْهُ	هذا
The student is not the subject of the sentence. It is an apposition.	بَدَلٌ	الطَّالِبُ

2. The بَدَلٌ follows the object of a sentence.

I met this student.	قابَلْتُ هذا الطَّالِبَ.

Direct object of the sentence. The word هذا never changes its shape.	مَفْعُولٌ بِهِ مُبْدَلٌ مِنْهُ	هذا
The student is not the object of the sentence! It is an apposition and needs agreement. Therefore, you have to use the accusative case (مَنْصُوبٌ) as well.	بَدَلٌ	الطَّالِبَ

Now a tricky example: The بَدَلٌ has an attributive meaning. See also *Arabic for Nerds 2*, question #185.

The doctor treated the leg of the patient. (Lit. meaning: The doctor treated the patient, his leg.)	عالَجَ الطَّبِيبُ الْمَرِيضَ رِجْلَهُ.

Direct object (مَفْعُولٌ بِهِ).	الْمَرِيضَ
Apposition (بَدَلُ الْبَعْضِ مِن الْكُلِّ). This type of apposition needs a **connector** (رابِط) which is a possessive pronoun. Such pronoun may be shown or is implicitly understood (unwritten).	رِجْلَهُ

This pronoun always ends in ضَمَّةٌ as it is مَبْنِيّ (fixed). Grammatically speaking, the pronoun is the second part of a إِضافةٌ-construction (مُضافٌ إِلَيْهِ).	٥

210. What is the root of the verb *to examine* (اِطَّلَعَ)؟

The root is ط-ل-ع.

The VIII-verb اِطَّلَعَ means *to examine; to study; to check.* It follows the pattern اِفْتَعَلَ.

Thus, watch out: According to the verb pattern, the verb should be اِطْتَلَعَ. As this would be difficult to pronounce, the ت and the ط merge to a double ط – written as طّ.

- The مَصْدَر is اِطِّلاعٌ and means *inspection; examination.*
- The IV-verb almost looks the same: *to teach* (أَطْلَعَ). So, what's the difference? The IV-verb doesn't have شَدَّةٌ and it starts with a *Hamza of rupture* (هَمْزَةُ قَطْعِ), i.e., ء (on top of the Aleph), which you have to pronounce.

211. How do you use وَ, فَ, and ثُمَّ؟

They describe a sequence and do not influence case endings.

All three particles are found between two words which have the same case. وَ, فَ and ثُمَّ are so-called "couplers" or conjunctions (حَرْفُ عَطْفِ).

In other words: The word which comes after it and the preceding word need to agree.

That's for the grammar part. Let's focus on the meaning. These three words are used to describe a chronological sequence.

- وَ means *and*;

- فَ could be translated as *and*; *and so*; *then*. It implies a closer relationship, some development, or a logical order between the words or sentences.

- ثُمَّ could be translated as *then*; *after that*; *thereupon*. It shows that one event is over, and that a new thing starts.

Ahmed **and** Khalid came. We don't know who came first or if they came at the same time. The chronological sequence doesn't matter.	جاءَ أَحْمَدُ وَخالِدُ.	1
Ahmad came, **and right after him** (immediately after) Khalid.	جاءَ أَحْمَدُ فَخالِدُ.	2
Ahmad came, and **thereupon** Khalid.	جاءَ أَحْمَدُ ثُمَّ خالِدُ.	3

Note that words consisting of only one letter are combined with the subsequent word. Thus, you have to attach و and ف to the word which comes after them.

212. What does the verb عاد mean?

It depends on what you add.

The verb عاد (past tense) – يَعُودُ (present tense) – is a sly verb.

It can denote many things and go along with many constructions, for example, you add verbs without أَنْ directly.

Let's see the most common constructions.

No longer to be; to become. Present or past tense meaning.	When عادَ (only past tense) is **negated** plus **two nouns.** Then, we treat عادَ as a *sister of* كانَ. The subject (اِسْمُ عادَ) is in the nominative case (مَرْفُوعٌ) and the **predicate** (خَبَرُ عادَ) is in the accusative case (مَنْصُوبٌ).	1

I am no longer a child.	أَنا لَمْ أَعُدْ صَغِيرًا.
She never became angry with him.	لَمْ تَعُدْ مَرَّةً واحِدَةً غاضِبَةً مِنْهُ.

to return	Especially if عادَ or يَعُودُ (present or past) is used with إلَى. There is no other verb involved. We call عادَ a full or **complete verb** (فِعْلٌ تامٌّ) then.	2

The student returned to Egypt.	عادَ الطّالِبُ إلَى مِصْرَ.

no longer to be	When عادَ (only past tense) is **negated**: لَمْ يَعُدْ plus verb in the present tense, indicative (without أَنْ).	3

I no longer remember....	لَمْ أَعُدْ أَذْكُرُ...
I no longer think...	لَمْ أَعُدْ أُفَكِّرُ...
He didn't (or doesn't) feel anymore.	لَمْ يَعُدْ يَشْعُرُ.
He no longer walked.	ما عادَ يَذْهَبُ.

| *to do again;* | When عاد (only past tense) is **not negated**: | 4 |
| *to repeat* | عاد plus verb in the present tense, indicative (without أَنْ). | |

| He hit me again. | عادَ قَصَرَيَنِي. |
| He walked again. | عادَ يَذْهَبُ. |

| *to do again* | عاد or يَعُود (present or past tense), **not negated**, plus فَ plus verb in the present tense, indicative mood (الْمُضارِعُ الْمَرْفُوعُ) or past tense (الْماضِي). | 5 |

He kissed her again.	عادَ فَقَبَّلَها.
I convinced myself again.	عُدْتُ فَأَقْنَعْتُ نَفْسِي.
I forget again.	أَعُودُ فَأَنْسَى.

213. Do إذا and إذًا and إِذَنْ and إِذْ mean the same?

No way! Only in rare situations, they may denote the same idea.

Three Arabic words almost look the same but mean very different things.

Let's see the main points.

| 1 | when, if; as suddenly | إذا |

- إذا is normally introducing a conditional sentence. The verbal sentence after it is usually in the past tense – but it has the meaning of the present tense or even future tense!

- إذا can only be used if the situation in the conditional sentence can theoretically be achieved (if it is possible, or if it has happened.)

- This is different to إِنْ because إِنْ may be used to introduce a <u>possible or impossible</u> condition – see below.

- إِذا ما is only used to emphasize a sentence (تَأْكِيدٌ).

| If you work hard, you will be successful in your life. (This leaves open if you are successful or not; you could be both.) | إِنْ تَجْتَهِدْ فِي عَمَلِكَ تَنْجَحْ فِي حَيَاتِكَ. |
| When the sun rises (and the sun does rise every day without an exception), people will go to their work. | إِذَا طَلَعَتِ الشَّمْسُ ذَهَبَ النَّاسُ إِلَى عَمَلِهِمْ. |

| If angels come, devils will go. This is an Arabic proverb which means that good and bad do not meet. | إِذَا حَضَرَتِ الْمَلَائِكَةُ، ذَهَبَتِ الشَّيَاطِينُ. |

| 2 | since; as, because; at that time, when | إِذْ |

- It may explain or **indicate the reason** for the preceding event (*as, since* - causal) – note that such إِذْ may be followed by a verb or noun.

- إِذْ may be used to express that two actions happen at the **same time** (*when* - temporal). *See Arabic for Nerds 2, question #342.* Normally, a verbal sentence in the past tense follows, very rarely you see a nominal sentence. It has usually the meaning of عِنْدَ ما.

| She cried because she was sick. | بَكَيْتُ إِذْ كَانَتْ مَرِيضَةً۔ |
| Do they hear you when you call? | هَلْ يَسْمَعُونَكُمْ إِذْ تَدْعُونَ؟ |

| I was late. I made a mistake since I didn't use the train. | وَصَلْتُ مُتَأَخِّرًا. أَخْطَأْتُ إِذْ لَمْ أُسَافِرْ بِالْقِطَارِ. |

| 3 | therefore; so; then; | إِذًا |

- It denotes a **response**. Often used in a dialogue in response to what was said before. Most grammarians say that it does not change any case or mood and thus has **no governing power**.

| A: We will meet at the center. | سَنَلْتَقِي فِي الْمَرْكَزِ. |
| B: Let's have a coffee together then. | إِذًا تَشْرَبُ قَهْوَةً مَعًا. |

| So, what's the problem? | إِذًا مَا الْمُشْكِلَةُ؟ |

| 4 | in that case; if the case be so; well then | إِذَنْ |

- It occurs at the start of an answer (صَدْرُ الْجَواب). It is immediately followed by a verb which has to be in the **subjunctive mood** (مَنْصُوبٌ). The verb expresses the **future**! We call the job of this particle حَرْفُ جَوابٍ وَجَزاءٍ وَنَصْبِ وَاسْتِقْبَال.

In that case you will succeed.	إِذَنْ تَنْجَحَ.
In that case I will leave after your visit.	إِذَنْ أَذْهَبَ بَعْدَ زِيارَتِكَ۔
Note the subjunctive mood – the vowel "a"!	

214. Can إذا and إذْ express something unexpected?

Yes, they can.

إذا and إذْ may have a **special job** in the sentence:

- Both إذا and إذْ may work as a *particle of surprise* (حَرْفُ مُفاجَأَةٍ). They can be used to express that something is unexpected or surprising: *behold! see! wow! suddenly! and all of a sudden there was…*

- إذا (إِذا الْفُجائِيَّةُ) is more common. After such إذا, you have to use a **nominal sentence** (جُمْلةٌ اسْمِيّةٌ). The particle إذا is usually preceded by فَ; but you may also use وَ.

- إذْ, when used to express *when suddenly*, is used after *while* (بَيْنَما). See *Arabic for Nerds 2*, question #349.

I entered the room and (surprisingly) all the students were absent.	دَخَلْتُ الْحُجْرَةَ فَإِذا جَمِيعُ الطُّلّابِ غائِبُونَ.
I opened my bag, and (strangely/surprisingly) it was empty.	فَتَحْتُ حَقِيبَتِي فَإِذا هِيَ خالِيَةٌ.
While I was studying, suddenly my friend came.	بَيْنَما أَنا أَدْرُسُ إِذْ دَخَلَ صَدِيقِي.
While we were sitting, suddenly, a man came up to us.	بَيْنَما نَحْنُ جُلُوسٌ إِذْ طَلَعَ عَلَيْنا رَجُلٌ.
I went out, and all of a sudden, Zayd was at the door.	خَرَجْتُ فَإِذًا زَيْدُ بِالْبابِ.

215. How many words may be used to express *except*?

Around ten.

Arabic knows many words and expressions to denote *except*. Grammarians call these constructions أُسْلُوبُ الْإِسْتِثْناءِ. The word اِسْتِثْناءُ means *exclusion, exception*.

All of the following words and expressions mean basically the same: *except*; *but*; *excluding*; *save*:

إِلَّا • غَيْر • سِوَى • عَدَا • ما عَدَا • خَلا • ما خَلا • حاشا

Note: The expression ما حاشا doesn't exist. حاشا literally means *far be it*. خَلا means *outside of*. عَدَا means *save*. All three may be treated as inert past tense verbs or prepositions.

Let us now examine how we could use them.

- The **excluded** thing is called الْمُسْتَثْنَى. This word is placed <u>after</u> the particle of exception (e.g., إِلَّا). The grammarians regard the الْمُسْتَثْنَى as a **variety of the direct object** (مَفْعُولٌ بِهِ). Therefore, it takes the accusative case (مَنْصُوبٌ). For more details, see *Arabic for Nerds 2*, #401.

- The all-included thing (the majority from which the exception is taken) is called الْمُسْتَثْنَى مِنْهُ. It is placed <u>before</u> the particle denoting *except*.

1. The construction with إِلَّا (except).

The word إِلَّا is a particle of exception (حَرْفُ اسْتِثْناءٍ).

| 1 | All students came except one. | جاءَ الطُّلّابُ إِلَّا طالِبًا. |

الطُّلّابُ is the الْمُسْتَثْنَى مِنْهُ. The word طالِبًا is the الْمُسْتَثْنَى. It has to be in the accusative case (مَنْصُوبٌ) because we assume that طالِبًا is the direct object (مَفْعُولٌ بِهِ) of a suppressed, underlying verb. The hidden, virtual verb may express: I exclude students).

| 2 | Only one student came. | .مَا جَاءَ الطُّلَّابُ إِلَّا طَالِبًا |
| | | .مَا جَاءَ الطُّلَّابُ إِلَّا طَالِبٌ |

Both are correct. You can choose: nominative case (مَرْفُوعٌ) or accusative case (مَنْصُوبٌ).

- Watch out: طَالِبًا in the accusative case (مَنْصُوبٌ) is the **excluded** (الْمُسْتَثْنَى).

- In the second sentence, however, we use the nominative case (مَرْفُوعٌ)! Thus, the grammatical function is different: The word طَالِبٌ is an **apposition** (بَدَلٌ). Hence, regarding agreement, it has to follow the word to which it refers (i.e., the مِنْهُ الْمُسْتَثْنَى); in our example, the word الطُّلَّابُ.

| 3 | Only one student is here. | .مَا جَاءَ إِلَّا طَالِبٌ |

This form is called أُسْلُوبُ الْقَصْرِ and describes **exclusivity** (see *question #217*). The word طَالِبٌ is the subject (فَاعِلٌ).

Hint: Delete the negation in your mind if you want to find the correct function and case. Hence, read it like: جَاءَ الطُّلَّابُ – and then put the case markers.

What about this sentence?

There is only one student in the room.	.لَيْسَ فِي الْغُرْفةِ إِلَّا طَالِبٌ
لَيْسَ is a verb – so it usually stands in the singular form at the beginning! (Note: This is only different if the subject is inherent in the verb, e.g., *they*: لَيْسُوا فِي الْبَيْتِ – *they are not at home*.)	
• فِي الْغُرْفةِ is the predicate (خَبَرُ لَيْسَ).	
• طَالِبٌ is the "subject" (اِسْمُ لَيْسَ).	

2. The construction <u>with</u> ما.

ما is not a negation particle, but a device to imitate a مَصْدَر.
We consider it then as a verb which causes a following verb
to be guarded in the accusative case.

All students came except one.	جاءَ الطُّلَّابُ ما عَدَا طالِبًا.
	جاءَ الطُّلَّابُ ما خَلا طالِبًا.

- In both examples, the word for *except* is expressed by a
  so-called interpreted **infinitive** (ما الْمَصْدَرِيَّةُ), an interpreted مَصْدَر, which we consider as having verbal power
  here. We can simply treat them as verbs.

- Since it is a verb, it guards a direct object (مَفْعُولٌ بِهِ) –
  which is the reason for the accusative case (مَنْصُوبٌ).

- The entire expression ما عَدَا طالِبًا is located in the position of a *circumstantial description; status* (حال) - for an
  analysis, see *Arabic for Nerds 2, question #408*.

3. The construction <u>without</u> ما.

We treat them as inert past tense verbs – we need the accusative case (مَنْصُوبٌ) for the *excluded*.

1	All students came except one.	جاءَ الطُّلَّابُ عَدَا طالِبًا.
	Same meaning as above with ما. The word طالِبًا is a regular ob-ject (مَفْعُول بِه) of the verb عَدَا.	

We treat them as prepositions – we need the genitive (مَجْرُورٌ)
for the *excluded*.

| 2 | All students came except one. | جاءَ الطُّلَّابُ خَلا طالِبٍ.
جاءَ الطُّلَّابُ حاشا طالِبٍ. |

Here, we treat خَلا and حاشا as prepositions (حَرْفُ جَرٍّ). Thus, the word after it has to be مَجْرُورٌ.

4. The construction using غَيْر • سِوَى.

Both words are **nouns** (اِسْمُ اِسْتِثْناءٍ). The word غَيْر means *other*. The word سِوَى denotes *other than*. Both words are considered to be *indefinite* – see *question #216*.

First option: Indefinite noun before غَيْر.

The most elegant way of treating غَيْر is to see it as an **adjective** (صِفةٌ) for an **indefinite** (نَكِرةٌ) noun. But there's an issue: غَيْر needs to be the first part of a إضافة. The second part makes the entire expression definite (مَعْرِفةٌ). Looks like a mismatch (indefinite noun – definite adjective), but it isn't! In Arabic, both غَيْر and سِوَى are always seen as indefinite nouns.

| A man came to me other than you. | جاءَنِي رَجُلٌ غَيْرُكَ. |

Theoretically, the expression غَيْرُكَ is **definite** due to the pronoun suffix كَ. The expression غَيْرُكَ is an adjective for the **indefinite** word *a man*. Wait, but how can it be an adjective for an indefinite word when the expression itself is definite? Good question.

The grammarians say that the pronoun كَ which is attached to غَيْر does not strip the word غَيْر from its indefiniteness. That is also the reason why it takes the nominative (مَرْفُوعٌ) – the case of the word to which it refers since adjectives need agreement (الْمُطابَقةُ).

Second option: <u>Definite</u> noun before غَيْر.

We treat غَيْر itself as *the excluded* (الْمُسْتَثْنَى). This means that we need to mark it with the accusative case (مَنْصُوب). Thus, we actually treat غَيْر like a word that is placed after إلّا! Why? Well, originally, إلّا was involved and was placed before غَيْر.

غَيْر also serves as the first part of the إضافة-construction and drags a following word into the genitive case (مَجْرُور).

All students came except one.	جاءَ الطُّلَّابُ غَيْرَ طالِبٍ.
	جاءَ الطُّلَّابُ سِوَى طالِبٍ.

The word طالِبٍ is the second part of a إضافة-construction, so it has to be in the genitive case (مَجْرُور). Since the sentence is **not** negated, the word غَيْرَ has to be in the accusative case.

Third option: Negated sentence before غَيْر.

Only one student came. (The students didn't come, except for Zayd.)	ما جاءَ الطُّلَّابُ غَيْرَ طالِبٍ.
	ما جاءَ الطُّلَّابُ غَيْرُ طالِبٍ.

You have a choice: You can either write غَيْرَ or غَيْرُ. Both are correct. After a negated sentence (جُمْلَة مَنْفِيَّة), we have two options. We can either treat it as *the excluded* (مَنْصُوب عَلَى الْإِسْتِثْناءِ) → the <u>accusative</u> case; or we say that it stands in *apposition* (بَدَل) to the preceding word → in our example, the nominative case (in apposition to *students*)

Fourth option: negated sentence before غَيْر, but the الْمُسْتَثْنَى مِنْهُ is missing. Only *the excluded* is mentioned.

| Only one student came. | ما جاءَ غَيْرُ طالِبٍ. |
| | ما جاءَ سِوَى طالِبٍ. |

This type of construction is called أُسْلُوبُ الْقَصْرِ. The word طالِبٍ is the second part of a إضافة-construction; hence, it has to be in the genitive case (مَجْرُورٌ). We mark the word غَيْر according to its function in the sentence. In our examples, it is the **subject** (فاعِل) because the الْمُسْتَثْنَى مِنْهُ is not mentioned. It has to take a ضَمّة.

Hint: If you want to find the correct case markers, just delete the negation in your mind. Note: In the sentence with سِوَى, the case marker is hidden/presumptive (مُقَدَّرة).

Fifth option: It is cut off from the إضافة – which can only happen if لَيْسَ is involved.

| I have one penny, nothing more. | قبضتُ دِرْهَمًا لَيْسَ غَيْرُ. |
| → This is the meaning: | لَيْسَ غَيْرُها مَقْبُوضًا |

We deleted the second part of the إضافة as well as the predicate of لَيْسَ - marked in gray above. In this situation, we fix the word غَيْرُ on the vowel "u" (مَبْنِيٌّ عَلَى الضَّمِّ). This happens also with words such as قَبْل in the expression مِنْ قَبْلُ - see *question #221.*

Now, which job may غَيْر have in a sentence? It depends on the position in the sentence.

| *Someone else visited me.* | زارَني غَيْرُكَ. |
| Subject (فاعِلٌ) of the verb → nominative case. | |

I asked someone else.	سَأَلْتُ غَيْرَكَ.

Direct object (مَفْعُولٌ بِهِ) → accusative case.

I looked at someone else (other than you).	تَطَلَّعْتُ إِلَى غَيْرِكَ.

In the genitive case since it is placed after a preposition (مَجْرُورٌ بِحَرْفِ جَرٍّ).

I didn't look at the students, except for Zayd.	مَا تَطَلَّعْتُ إِلَى الطُّلَّابِ غَيْرَ زَيْدٍ.
	مَا تَطَلَّعْتُ إِلَى الطُّلَّابِ غَيْرِ زَيْدٍ.

Negated sentence (جُمْلَةٌ مَنْفِيَّةٌ); so we have a choice. The accusative case or the case of the preceding word (apposition) – see option 3.

Buy another book than this!	اِشْتَرِ كِتَابًا غَيْرَ هٰذا!

Adjective (نَعْتٌ) → accusative here (like كِتَابًا).

The students succeeded, except for Zayd.	نَجَحَ الطُّلَّابُ غَيْرَ زَيْدٍ.

In the accusative case since we treat it as the excluded (مَنْصُوبٌ عَلَى الْإِسْتِثْنَاءِ)

Zayd traveled unsatisfactorily.	سَافَرَ زَيْدٌ غَيْرَ راضٍ.

Circumstantial description; status (حَالٌ) → accusative case.

216. Is the word بَعْضٌ (*some*) definite or indefinite?

It has to be treated as indefinite in any situation.

بَعْضٌ is a special noun.

We call it a noun that *applies the indefiniteness intensively, that is impregnated with incertitude, obscurity* (مُتَوَغِّلٌ فِي الْإِبْهام). In other words, it is always considered indefinite.

The same is true for *one* (أَحَدٌ), *some* or *one part* (بَعْضٌ), *like* (مِثْلٌ), *similar to* (شِبْهُ), *except/other than* (غَيْر and سِوَى). They are considered **indefinite** even if we should treat it as definite by the rules of the Arabic grammar, which would happen in إضافة-constructions, when the part after those words is definite.

- With such words, it is theoretically impossible to form a possessive construction (إضافة) that is treated as definite – because the **first part is immune to definiteness!**

- Furthermore, this also means that such words **never get the definite article** الـ.

one of them	Although the pronoun suffix would make the entire إضافة-construction definite, we treat the whole expression as **indefinite**. This has huge implications. For example, in the last two examples, we use the إضافة-construction, which looks definite on the paper, as an adjective for an indefinite word!	أَحَدُهُمْ
a youth like me		فَتًى مِثْلِي
men other than you		رِجالٌ غَيْرُكُمْ

...except some who got to the Prophet.	...إِلَّا بَعْضَهُمْ لَحِقُوا بِالنَّبِيِّ.

What happened here? The relative clause does <u>not</u> use الَّذِي although the construction before would suggest that (we have a **definite** word, a إضافة-construction which is automatically made definite by the pronoun suffix). However, in Arabic, the expression بَعْضَهُمْ is treated as **indefinite**! See *question #87*.

Some of us watched the others (or: we watched each other)	رَاقَبَ بَعْضُنَا بَعْضًا.	1
بَعْضُنَا is the subject (فَاعِلٌ). بَعْضًا is the direct object (مَفْعُولٌ بِهِ)		

We raised some of them above the others.	رَفَعْنَا بَعْضَهُمْ فَوْقَ بَعْضٍ.	2
بَعْضٍ is part of an adverbial phrase (second part of the إضافة).		

...the people could hardly recognize one another. (Sahīh Muslim 614)	...النَّاسُ لاَ يَكَادُ يَعْرِفُ بَعْضُهُمْ بَعْضًا.	3
بَعْضُهُمْ is the subject (فَاعِلٌ). بَعْضًا is is the direct object (مَفْعُولٌ بِهِ). The entire sentence after النَّاسُ is the predicate (خَبَرٌ)		

If you need to translate such sentence, you have several options for outsmarting the Arabic grammar (the indefiniteness). See also question #87. Let's check a Hadith *(Sahīh Muslim 617)*:

يَا رَبِّ أَكَلَ بَعْضِي بَعْضًا.

- O Lord, part of me has eaten another part.
- O Lord, parts of me have consumed other parts.
- O Lord, parts of me have consumed the others.
- O Lord My different parts eat up each other.
- O Lord! Some parts of me consume other parts.

217. How do you express exclusiveness in Arabic?

There are many options.

If you want to emphasize a fact or person, you can use the words *except* or *only* in English. In Arabic, there are plenty of ways to express this idea (أُسْلُوبُ الْقَصْرِ).

1 Negation plus exception	النَّفْيُ وَالْإِسْتِثْناءُ
Only the serious workers are successful.	لا يَنْجَحُ إِلّا الْعامِلُونَ بِجِدٍّ.

For the correct case endings, just imagine the sentence without the negation!

2 Use a combination of ما + إِنَّ	إِنَّما

Watch out: After إِنَّما, you may use a nominal (جُمْلَةٌ اِسْمِيّةٌ) or verbal sentence (جُمْلَةٌ فِعْلِيّةٌ). What type of ما do we have? A neutralizing particle (ما الْكافّةُ)! Such ما is like a wall through which the grammatical force of إِنَّ doesn't penetrate. In other words, you don't need to think about special case endings.

Success is for serious workers only.	إِنَّما النَّجاحُ لِلْعامِلِينَ بِجِدٍّ or إِنَّما يَنْجَحُ الْعامِلُونَ بِجِدٍّ.

3 Use the words: *but ; rather; on the contrary*	بَلْ لَكِنْ

Generally speaking, the particle بَلْ corrects a statement and confirms and verifies what follows (حَرْفُ إِضْرابٍ). If you see بَلْ in a sentence, you know at least that the information after بَلْ is more important or correct than the statement earlier.

You have to use a **single word** after بَلْ and not a sentence. Only then we treat the particle بَلْ as a **conjunction**/"coupler" (حَرْفُ عَطْفٍ). What is the effect of this? The word before and after بَلْ take the **same case**.

If we want to **overturn** what is said before, we need to start with a **negation**. In this application, بَلْ is a *particle of correction* (حَرْفُ اِسْتِدْراكٍ), also called *adversative particle* which corrects the previous statement.

Note: What we said so far about بَلْ is also true for لٰكِنْ.

Khalid wasn't present but absent.	ما كانَ خالِدٌ حاضِرًا بَلْ غائِبًا.
Fairouz is not a writer, she is a singer.	ما فَيْرُوز كاتِبةٌ لٰكِنْ مُغَنِّيةٌ.
	ما فَيْرُوز كاتِبةٌ بَلْ مُغَنِّيةٌ.

Now, let's focus on بَلْ. There is one tricky situation: If you use لَيْسَ (or ما in the way of لَيْسَ), then you need to use the **nominative case** (مَرْفُوعٌ) after بَلْ and not the accusative case which is normally used for the predicate of لَيْسَ.

| Zayd is not standing, but (he is) sitting. | ما زَيْدٌ قائِمًا بَلْ قاعِدٌ. |
| Zayd is not standing; no, is not sitting. (This is not what you want to express!) | ما زَيْدٌ قائِمًا بَلْ قاعِدًا. |

Some grammarians say that you can only use بَلْ after a negation. However, if you encounter بَلْ in an affirmative (not negated) sentence, then watch out. If you **don't have a negation** before or if you use an **imperative**, then بَلْ may...

a) indicate that the earlier information was incorrect or not important. What follows بَلْ is the correction.

b) indicate the opposite of what was given earlier in the sentence.

→ The command or statement only relates to what follows بَلْ.

| a | Drink water, rather, milk! (Drink | اِشْرَبْ ماءً، بَلْ حَلِيبًا! |

water; no, milk!)	
Zayd came; no, Khalid.	جاءَ زَيْدٌ، بَلْ خالِدُ.
We don't visit the enemy, but the friend.	لا نَزُورُ الْعَدُوَّ، بَلْ الصَّدِيقَ. b

5 Emphasis by word-order	التَّقْدِيمُ وَالتَّأْخِيرُ

I address my words to you.	إِلَيْكَ أُوَجِّهُ كَلامِي or أُوَجِّهُ كَلامِي إِلَيْكَ.

Watch out for the correct cases and use of grammar!

The friendship with an idiot is a burden.	صَداقَةُ الْأَحْمَقِ تَعَبٌ.

Only a burden is the friendship with an idiot.	لَيْسَتْ صَداقَةُ الْأَحْمَقِ إِلّا تَعَبًا.
Here, you have to negate the noun with لَيْسَ The predicate (خَبَرٌ مَنْصُوب has to be (لَيْسَ	

I am a **student** (feminine).	أَنا طالِبَةٌ.
I am (only) a **student**.	لَسْتُ إِلّا طالِبَةً.
(It is that; because; only) I am a **student**.	إِنَّما أَنا طالِبَةٌ.
I am **student**, not a teacher.	أَنا طالِبَةٌ لا مُدَرِّسةٌ.

218. How do you express *I can* in Arabic?

You have many verbs to choose from.

In colloquial Arabic, you will hear مُمْكِن most of the time. In Standard Arabic, you mainly use certain verbs, but it totally depends on the situation.

I. *Can* in the meaning of ***to master***.

to master, to do well (a skill)	أَحْسَنَ / يُحْسِنُ	IV-verb
to master (a language)	أَجادَ / يُجِيدُ	
to bring to perfection; to be proficient	أَتْقَنَ / يُتْقِنُ	

He speaks Arabic very well.	يُجِيدُ الْعَرَبِيَّة.
	يُتْقِنُ الْعَرَبِيَّة.

II. *Can* in the meaning of ***to be able to***.

a person's capability to	Use بِاسْتِطاعَةِ + person + a) noun in the nominative (= what the person can do) **or** b) particle أَنْ plus verb **or** c) فِي plus noun.	ط-و-ع
my capability	بِاسْتِطاعَتِي	
to be able to	إِسْتَطاعَ, يَسْتَطِيعُ + أَنْ	

He can travel.	يَسْتَطِيعُ السَّفَرَ.
	يَسْتَطِيعُ أَنْ يُسافِرَ.

lit. *to know* (used for things that you need to learn in order to exercise them).	عَرَفَ / يَعْرِفُ	ع-ر-ف

He can swim.	يَعْرِفُ الْعَوْمَ.

with my capacity, possibility	بِمَقْدُورِي أَنْ	ق-د-ر
to be able to (often associated with physical capability)	قَدَرَ, يَقْدُرُ أَنْ / عَلَى	

He can walk.	يَقْدُرُ عَلَى الْمَشْيِ.
	يَقْدُرُ أَنْ يَمْشِيَ.

to enable someone to do something	أَمْكَنَ, يُمْكِنُ أَنْ / مِنْ	م-ك-ن
it is possible that…	مِن الْمُمْكِنِ أَنْ	

Can I go with you? (Is it possible for me that...)	هَلْ يُمْكِنُنِي أَنْ أَذْهَبَ مَعَكَ؟
he can do...	يُمْكِنُهُ أَنْ
it is possible that; it may be that...	يُمْكِنُ أَنْ
as much as possible	...أَكْثَرَ مَا يُمْكِنُ

III. If you want to express: *not to be able, to be incapable.*

to be unable to do	عَجَزَ / يَعْجَزُ عَنْ	ع-ج-ز

He couldn't do it.	عَجَزَ عَنْ فِعْلِ الْأَمْرِ
	عَجَزَ أَنْ يَفْعَلَ الْأَمْرَ.

IV. *Can* in the meaning of *__not to be possible__*.

negated: not to be possible for someone	وَسِعَ / يَسَعُ	و-س-ع

I couldn't stop her.	ما وَسِعَنِي مَنْعُها.
She defended him as good as possible.	داقَعَتْ عَنْهُ ما وَسِعَها الدِّفاعُ (ما سَمَحَ الْجَهْدُ)
I cannot say.	لا يَسَعُنِي أَنْ أَقُولَ ـ
I can't do that.	ما أَسَعُ ذَلِكَ.

V. *Can* in the meaning of *__to be allowed to__*.

to allow; to permit	سَمَحَ, يَسْمَحُ لِ + بْ + أَنْ	س-م-ح

Can (may) I enter? (Do you allow me to enter?)	هَلْ تَسْمَحُ لِي بِأَنْ أَدْخُلَ؟ or يُسْمَحُ لَكَ بِأَنْ تَدْخُلَ.
Smoking is permitted.	التَّدْخِينُ مَسْمُوحٌ.

219. Does a simple sentence also mean simple grammar?

Not really.

Sometimes a single word can change the grammar and the meaning of a sentence dramatically. This happens oftentimes when you emphasize words.

Let us look at three examples.

	meaning	explanation	example
1	The student is in the house.		الطَّالِبُ فِي الْبَيْتِ.
		subject (مُبْتَدَأٌ)	الطَّالِبُ
		predicate (خَبَرٌ)	فِي الْبَيْتِ
	The second part of the sentence is a prepositional phrase (شِبْهُ جُمْلةٍ). Grammatically speaking, it is located in the position of a nominative case (مَرْفُوعٌ) – but you cannot see that. We can only assign a place value (فِي مَحَلِّ رَفْعٍ). For a discussion whether the prepositional phrase can be called the predicate or not see *Arabic for Nerds 2*, question #219.		

2	Indeed, safety lies in slowness.		إِنَّ السَّلَامَة فِي التَّأَنِّي.
	Watch out: The "subject" (اِسْمُ إِنَّ) is in the accusative case (مَنْصُـوبٌ). The predicate is in the nominative case (مَرْفُوعٌ).	اِسْمُ إِنَّ	السَّلَامة
		خَبَرُ إِنَّ	فِي التَّأَنِّي

3	Indeed, safety lies in slowness.		إِنَّما السَّلَامةُ فِي التَّأَنِّي.
	We use a neutralizer (ما الْكَافّةُ) with the effect that إِنَّ cannot use its grammatical power. We have a standard nominal sentence after the particle of emphasis (إِنَّما).	مُبْتَدَأ مَرْفُوعٌ	السَّلَامةُ
		خَبَرٌ مَرْفُوعٌ	فِي التَّأَنِّي

220. What are the so-called *five nouns* in Arabic?

They are: father, brother, mother-in-law, owner of, mouth

They are called *the five nouns* (الْأَسْماءُ الْخَمْسةُ) because they are five in number.

These nouns are special because they change their form dramatically when they are connected to a pronoun or are part of a إِضافة-construction. It all depends on the case they need. Let's have a look at them:

meaning	مَنْصُوبٌ	مَجْرُورٌ	مَرْفُوعٌ	word	
his father	أَباهُ	أَبِيهِ	أَبُوهُ	أَبٌ	1
his brother	أَخاهُ	أَخِيهِ	أَخُوهُ	أَخٌ	2
his mother in law	حَماهُ	حَمِيهِ	حَمُوهُ	حَمٌ	3
owner of; with	ذا	ذِي	ذُو	ذُو	4
his mouth	فاهُ	فِيهِ	فُوهُ	فُو (فَمٌ)	5

221. What is the correct spelling of *before*? قَبْلَ or قَبْلُ?

Both are correct – but you have to know in which situation.

The words *before* (قَبْلَ) and after (بَعْدَ) end in "a" (فَتْحةَ) – unless they are preceded by مِنْ. Then, they take "u" (ضَمّةُ).

Why is that? Well, the ضَمّةُ replaces a deleted sequence which would follow otherwise: ...مِنْ قَبْلِ ذٰلِكَ الْوَقْتِ.

That's why you write one ضَمّةُ on the last letter of بَعْدَ orقَبْلُ when it is preceded by مِنْ. Let us look at some examples.

previously; before	مِنْ قَبْلُ
I have not visited Luxor before (this day).	لَمْ أَزُرِ الْأُقْصُرَ قَبْلَ الْيَوْمِ.
I have not visited Luxor before.	لَمْ أَزُرِ الْأُقْصُرَ مِنْ قَبْلُ.

Note the difference:

| *before*; *previously*. It doesn't require further specification. Here, قَبْلُ is built on one ضَمّةُ as we don't have a إِضافة | مِنْ قَبْلُ |

| before xy | قَبْلَ + إِضافةُ |
| before the lesson | قَبْلَ الدَّرسِ |

| After مِنْ, the word قَبْلِ takes كَسْرةُ since it is placed after a preposition. | مِنْ قَبْلِ + إِضافةُ |
| before that | مِنْ قَبْلِ ذٰلِكَ |

222. How do you express *never* in Arabic?

It depends on whether you talk about the past or future.

In Arabic, there is no universal word for *never*. Many people think that أَبَداً would do the job, but in fact, it is often misused. You need to know which word you can use with which tense.

| (1) **negation of the past tense** + (2) قَطُّ | never; ever; at all |
| The word قَطُّ itself comes from the root: *to carve; to cut; to trim.* | |

| The director has never gone to the office. | لَمْ يَذْهَبْ الْمُدِيرُ قَطُّ |

| (Note: You'd need a helping vowel in يَذْهَبْ). | إلى الْمكْتَبِ. |

| (1) **negation** of the **future** + (2) أَبَدًا | never |
| I will never study. | لَنْ أَدْرسَ أَبَدًا. |

| (1) **negation** of the **present tense** + (2) مُطْلَقًا | never |
| I never study. | لا أَدْرُسُ مُطْلَقًا. |

For a deep analysis, see *Arabic for Nerds 2, question #350.*

223. كانَ and إِنَّ are somehow the opposite, aren't they?

Yes, they are – regarding case endings.

If you see the verb كانَ (*to be*) or the particle إِنَّ (*indeed; that*) in a sentence, you have to be very careful.

The standard rules for case endings are overthrown. Both كانَ and إِنَّ have "sisters", i.e., other words that share the same grammar rules.

Let us analyze both groups since they are crucial for under-standing Arabic grammar.

| All sisters of كانَ are **verbs** (فِعْلٌ). | كانَ وَأَخَواتُها |
| All sisters of إِنَّ are particles (حَرْفٌ) | إِنَّ وَأَخَواتُها |

كانَ	إِنَّ
Past tense of the verb *to be*.	To emphasize a nominal sentence (جُمْلةٌ اِسْمِيّةٌ)
← • كانَ • أَصْبَحَ • أَضْحَى • أَمْسَى • باتَ • ظَلَّ - *to be* or *to become*	← إِنَّ • أَنَّ • كَأَنَّ • لَكِنَّ • لَيْتَ • (*if only*) • لَعَلَّ (*perhaps*)
← صارَ - to describe a transformation	Since these particles emphasize a nominal sentence, the word after إِنَّ has to be a noun or a pronoun (ها, ه, ...) which turns it, in fact, into a nominal sentence.
← لَيْسَ - for negation	
← ما دامَ - for proof of duration	
← ما بَرِحَ • ما اِنْفَكَّ • ما فَتِئَ • ما زالَ - to express continuation; *still, as long as* (all have a present tense meaning)	The "sisters" are conjunctions expressing doubt or objection.
"subject": nominative (مَرْفُوعٌ)	"subject": accusative (مَنْصُوبٌ)
predicate: accusative (مَنْصُوبٌ)	predicate: nominative (مَرْفُوعٌ)

an example	
أَصْبَحَ الرَّجُلُ مُدِيرًا.	كَأَنَّ الْحَياةَ حُلْمٌ.
The man became director.	It seems that life is a dream.

224. What is the plural of the word *year* (سَنةٌ)?

There are two correct plural forms: سَنَواتٌ *and* سِنُونَ.

سَنةٌ is a feminine word (مُؤَنَّثٌ).

Nevertheless, we may use **sound masculine plural** (جَمْعُ الْمُذَكَّرِ السَّالِمُ). Let's see what it is all about.

type	explanation	plural
A	regular feminine plural	سَنَواتٌ
B	sound masculine plural pattern for the nominative case (مَرْفُوع).	سِنُونَ
	sound masculine plural pattern for the genitive case (مَجْرُورٌ) and the accusative case (مَنْصُوبٌ).	سِنِينَ

Form B is subsumed under the sound masculine plural (جَمْعُ الْمُذَكَّرِ السَّالِمُ). Thus, the same rules as for sound masculine plural forms have to be applied, i.e., you have to omit the ن in masculine sound plural endings if the word serves as the first part of a إِضافة.

There are several other words which have a sound masculine plural form besides a usually more common plural form. For example the Arabic word for *son* (اِبْن) – see *question #225*.

If you want to know why we are allowed to do that, see *Arabic for Nerds 2, question #100*.

225. What does the word أُولُو mean?

أُولُو *is the plural of the demonstrative pronoun* ذُو *which basically means: master of; in possession of.*

أُولُو *is a very strange plural form. Such patterns are not very common, but, in fact, there are many atypical plural forms in Arabic. Let's take, for example, the word* اِبْن *(son). In the following expression, note that the* ن *was dropped.*

sons of Israel	بَنُو إِسْرائيلَ

Send with us the Children of Israel. (Sura 26:17)	أَنْ أَرْسِلْ مَعَنَا بَنِي إِسْرَائِيلَ.

Let us check the details:

- A: broken plural (جَمْعُ التَّكْسِيرِ).
- B: sound masculine plural pattern (جَمْعُ الْمُذَكَّرِ السَّالِمُ)

	meaning; explanation	plural	type	
	Meaning: *sons*. This is the broken plural.	أَبْنَاءٌ	A	
	Sound masculine plural, nominative (مَرْفُوعٌ).	بَنُونَ	B	اِبْن
	Sound masculine plural, مَنْصُوبٌ and مَجْرُورٌ.	بَنِينَ	B	
	Type B is more common in religious texts. Note that the ن disappears in إِضافة-constructions because it is a sound masculine plural!		بَنُو إِسْرَائِيلَ	
	owner; *people*. It is the masculine plural of ذُو for the nominative case (مَرْفُوعٌ) You can't use it alone; it must be used as the first part of a إِضافة like ذُو – which is why there's no ن.	أُولُو	B	ذُو
	Sound masculine plural, مَنْصُوبٌ and مَجْرُورٌ.	أُولِي	B	
	Meaning: *men of understanding*. It comes from the root ل-ب-ب which means *to be sensible*.		أُولُو الْأَلْبَابِ	

وَلَكُمْ فِي الْقِصَاصِ حَيَاةٌ يَا أُولِي الْأَلْبَابِ لَعَلَّكُمْ تَتَّقُونَ.

Fair retribution saves life for you, people of understanding, so that you may guard yourselves against what is wrong. When death approaches one of you who leaves wealth (Sura 2:179)

Watch out: The word ذُو is sometimes mistaken with اذ and therefore mistranslated as *that*.

226. قَصَيْتُ أَوْقاتًا or قَضَيْتُ أَوْقاتٍ - What is correct?

Correct is قَضَيْتُ أَوْقاتًا. *The sentence means: I spent time.*

Do not let the ending mislead you. It is true that Arabic sound feminine plural (جَمْعُ الْمُؤَنَّثِ السّالِمُ) never take the case ending "-an" (اً) in the accusative case (مَنْصُوبٌ). For example:

I saw (female) teachers.	رَأَيْتُ مُعَلِّماتٍ.

In our sentence, قَضَيْتُ أَوْقاتًا, the word *time* is the direct object (مَفْعُولٌ بِهِ). Let us put أَوْقاتُ under the microscope. At first glance, it looks the feminine ت-ending.

But this is wrong, because أَوْقاتُ is not a feminine plural. The ت is part of the root! Therefore, it has to be قَضَيْتُ أَوْقاتًا.

meaning	plural	word	root
time	أَوْقاتُ	وَقْتُ	و-ق-ت
I had a great time.		قَضَيْتُ أَوْقاتًا سَعِيدةً.	
sound	أَصْواتُ	صَوْتُ	ص-و-ت
I heard sounds.		سَمِعْتُ أَصْواتًا.	

227. What is the active participle of *to point out* (دَلَّ)?

It is دَالٌّ *and means: indicating; pointing.*

Verbs consisting of two root letters having one doubled can be a nasty. The active participle (إِسْمُ فَاعِلٍ) of such roots is often misread because the typical vowel "i" (كَسْرةٌ) is missing.

	active participle (إِسْمُ الْفَاعِلِ)	present tense (الْمُضارِعُ)	past tense (الْماضِي)	root
to point out	دَالٌّ	يَدُلُّ	دَلَّ عَلَى	د-ل-ل
to split	شاقٌّ	يَشُقُّ	شَقَّ	ش-ق-ق

→ The only thing you should keep in mind is that the doubled root letter is not written twice, but gets a شَدّةٌ.

228. How do you express *on the same day* in Arabic?

You use a word expressing time and add إِذْ *resulting in* يَوْمَئِذٍ

There are many ways to express that something happened on the same day, in the same year, etc. There is a **universal formula** to express that smoothly. Our main ingredient is إِذْ, a word denoting past time: *at the time of; then.*

Here is how it works:

Step 1:	Take a word indicating time (or place).	ساعة

Step 2:	Add the vowel "a" (فَتْحةٌ) at the end of the word, because this word will be used as an adverb.	ساعَتَ

Watch out: This is not the marker of the accusative case! What happens is that we first fix it on the vowel "a" (مَبْنِيٌّ عَلَى الْفَتْحِ). Since we made the word indeclinable by that, we say that it is placed in the position of an accusative case (فِي مَحَلِّ نَصْبٍ).

Note that ة will become ت in the next step because this word serves as the first part of a إِضافة.

Step 3	Add إِذْ as the second part of the إِضافة. Thus, it has to take the genitive case, so we get ئِذٍ. The expression means *at the same time; in this/that hour.*	ساعَتَئِذٍ

If you want to know why إِذْ in this situation is capable of taking case endings, see *Arabic for Nerds 2, question #343.*

Some more examples.

They all mean more or less the same: *then* or *at that time*:	وَقْتَئِذٍ	عِنْدَئِذٍ	آنَئِذٍ
	ساعَتَئِذٍ	حِينَئِذٍ	فِي ذَاكَ الْوَقْتِ

You can use إِذْ with other words as well like *day* or *year.*

at the same moment/second	لَحْظَتَئِذٍ
on the same day	يَوْمَئِذٍ
in the same year	سَنَتَئِذٍ

229. What is the difference between إِنَّ and أَنَّ?

The spelling of the Hamza (هَمْزَة). But there is more, of course.

You may have noticed that after *to say* (قَالَ), *the particle* إِنَّ is used and not أَنَّ. Why is that?

Let us first look at the **DNA of** إِنَّ and أَنَّ. Both are particles with a verbal nature (حَرْفٌ مُشَبَّهٌ بِالْفِعْلِ). What do we mean by that? Well, in fact, they both express the meaning of a verb which could be, for example, *to confirm* (أَكَّدَ). So when you say إِنَّ, you actually express *I confirm* (أُؤَكِّدُ). Therefore, the grammarians say that these particles somehow resemble verbs which also is one explanation for the accusative case (مَنْصُوبٌ) which may be interpreted as the object of the virtual verb.

Nevertheless, we say that both particles intervene in a nominal sentence (جُمْلَةٌ اِسْمِيَّةٌ) and give it a special nature. This means that both particles need **two ingredients**:

- a "subject" or noun (اِسْمُ إِنَّ/أَنَّ) which takes the <u>accusative</u> case (مَنْصُوبٌ) and

- a predicate (خَبَرُ إِنَّ/أَنَّ) which has to be in the <u>nominative</u> case (مَرْفُوعٌ).

Let's do some analysis and start with a rule:

> أَنَّ can never stand at the beginning of a sentence.

On the other hand, إِنَّ can only be used:

- To **start a full sentence** – a nominal sentence (جُمْلَةٌ اِسْمِيَّةٌ). إِنَّ then functions as an emphatic particle (*indeed, truly, verily*).

- **After** verbs that don't necessarily take an object (*to say*).

- In the **reported speech** when you have *to say* (قَالَ) and sometimes also with the verb عَلِمَ (*to get to know*).

إِنَّ **can never be placed before a verb.**

In other words, إِنَّ is never followed by a verb.

For this reason you often see a dummy pronoun after إِنَّ, grammatically speaking, a *pronoun of the matter* (ضَمِيرُ شَأْنٍ) in form of a pronoun suffix; for example ه which results in إِنَّهُ.

Instead of starting the sentence directly with a noun (اِسْمُ), the verb is placed after إِنَّهُ, and all is fine. Watch out for the case endings as with the dummy pronoun, the sentence follows the regular rules of a verbal sentence (جُمْلَةٌ فِعْلِيِّةٌ). Thus, you don't need to think about weird case endings.

Let us look at an example. Both sentences mean the same: *He said that the teacher came.*

Here we use a dummy pronoun.	قَالَ إِنَّهُ جَاءَ المُدَرِّسُ.

Teacher takes a ضَمّة as it is the subject (فَاعِلُ) of the verb جَاءَ (!) and therefore in the **nominative** case (مَرْفُوعٌ). The entire sentence after إِنَّهُ is located in the spot of the predicate of إِنَّ (خَبَرُ إِنَّ). And what about the اِسْمُ إِنَّ? It is the dummy pronoun.

The standard construction.	قَالَ إِنَّ المُدَرِّسَ جَاءَ.

Teacher is the "subject" - the noun of the particle إِنَّ (اِسْمُ إِنَّ); so it takes the vowel "a" (فَتْحَةٌ) as it is in the **accusative** case (مَنْصُوبٌ).

Let us dig deeper into the sentence structure.

I said that the lesson is easy.	قُلْتُ إِنَّ الدَّرْسَ سَهْلٌ.

There has to be a full (nominal) sentence after إِنَّ. This is grounded in the nature of the verb *to say* as *to say* doesn't need an object!

The best way to understand why there is إِنَّ after قَالَ is the following rule:

> قالَ is **always followed by a sentence** or clause
> – and <u>never by a single word</u> (e.g., a مَصْدَرٌ).

Why wouldn't this work with اَنَّ (with فَتْحة on the ن)? Try to imagine the following examples with a مَصْدَرٌ (instead of اَنَّ plus verb). Notice also the case endings.

I am pleased that you arrived.	أَسْعَدَنِي اَنَّكَ وَصَلْتَ . = أَسْعَدَنِي وُصُولُكَ.
I mentioned to Karim that you arrived.	ذَكَرْتُ لِكَرِيمٍ اَنَّكَ وَصَلْتَ. = ذَكَرْتُ لِكَرِيمٍ وُصُولَكَ.
I was happy that you arrived. (or: with the fact that you arrived.)	فَرِحْتُ بِاَنَّكَ وَصَلْتَ. = فَرِحْتُ بِوُصُولِكَ.

What do we learn from this? The expression اَنَّكَ وَصَلْتَ (*that you arrived*) could be replaced by وُصُولُكَ (*your arriving/your arrival*) which is the مَصْدَر.

اِنَّ, however, **can't be paraphrased** like that!

The sentence قالَ اِنَّكَ وَصَلْتَ (*He said: truly, indeed, you arrived.*) could not be replaced by قالَ وُصُولُكَ (*He said: your arriving/arrival*) because the latter doesn't make sense.

Thus, اِنَّكَ وَصَلْتَ has the status of a full clause and not that of a مَصْدَر (infinitive). In English, we occasionally leave the word *that* out.

Some important remarks:

- You have to use اِنَّ after قالَ if you **trust** the information that comes after it. If you <u>doubt</u> it, you can use a construction with ب and اَنَّ – to indicate that it may not be the absolute truth. Notice: This construction is also used for the reported speech! (see *question #202*).

Let us check an example (taken from a Syrian textbook):

Some scientists say that the universe is expanding.	يَقُولُ بَعْضُ الْعُلَماءِ بِأَنَّ الْكَوْنَ يَتَمَدَّدُ.

- أَنَّ may start a sentence – but it is not a particle then!

The child moaned.	أَنَّ الطِّفْلُ.
The child moans.	يَئِنُّ الطِّفْلُ.

In this sentence أَنَّ is not a particle (حَرْفٌ) – it is a verb (فِعْلٌ)! The particle أَنَّ can never stand at the beginning of a sentence – unless it is a verb (*to groan; moan*) which looks like this:

past tense (الْماضِي)	أَنَّ	present tense (الْمُضارِعُ)	يَئِنُّ

- Sometimes, you find the letter لـ after a sentence with إِنَّ.

It is you whom I know.	إِنِّي بِكَ لَعارِفٌ.

إِنَّ here is combined with the first person أَنا expressed by the pronoun suffix ي. The information, which comes after it (i.e., the predicate), is often introduced by لـ – which is **not** a negation nor a preposition. It is a *wandering* or *slipping Lām* (اللّامُ الْمُزَحْلَقَةُ).

It was initially put before the "subject"/noun of إِنَّ (اِسْمُ إِنَّ), but since Arabic does not like to have two devices of emphasis next to each other targeting the same word, it slipped towards the end and is now placed before the predicate. **Watch out:** This type of لـ has <u>no</u> influence on the case!

Remark: When you use the verb عَلِمَ in the meaning of *to hear about*; *to be told*; *to get to know*, you can choose between إِنَّ or أَنَّ. See also *Arabic for Nerds 2, question #306*.

Both sentences mean the same: *I was told/got to know that the lesson is easy.*	عَلِمْتُ أَنَّ الدَّرْسَ سَهْلٌ.
	عَلِمْتُ إِنَّ الدَّرْسَ سَهْلٌ.

Note: For an analysis of إِنَّ and أَنَّ, see *Arabic for Nerds 2, q. #253 to #267*.

230. What do you have to put right after the particle أَنَّ?

Certainly <u>not</u> a verb (فِعْلٌ).

أَنَّ is often translated as *that*. For example: *I think that...* After the particle أَنَّ, you usually find a pronoun suffix or a مَصْدَر.

Where's the catch? If you have an English sentence in mind that starts with *I think that..*, oftentimes you should not translate it bit by bit. You may need some tuning. An example.

I think that it isn't clear if...	...أَظُنُّ أَنَّ لَيْسَ مِن الْواضِحِ إذا	1

There is a mistake! After أَنَّ you can never put a verb – and لَيْسَ is a verb! In this sentence, the اِسْمُ أَنَّ would be missing!		

The solution: You can fix the sentence with a pronoun which serves as the اِسْمُ أَنَّ. The word right after أَنَّ is not a verb anymore. Note the pronunciation: *'annahu*.	أَظُنُّ أَنَّهُ لَيْسَ مِن الْواضِحِ إذا...	2

The pronoun converts the sentence to a nominal sentence (جُمْلَةٌ اِسْمِيَّةٌ).	

231. When do you have to use the particle إِنَّ?

There are at least nine important situations.

إِنَّ may be translated as *verily, indeed, certainly* or *that*. Sometimes, you can even ignore it. It depends on the context.

1	At the beginning of a nominal sentence (جُمْلَةٌ اِسْمِيَّةٌ).

Certainly (indeed), work is important for people.	إِنَّ الْعَمَلَ ضَرُورِيٌّ لِلإِنْسانِ.

2	After a quotation.

My professor said: "Indeed, the prices in this shop are high."	قالَ أُسْتاذِي:"إِنَّ الأَسْعارَ فِي هٰذا الْمَحَلِّ مُرْتَفِعَةٌ."

3	After أَلَا which is a so-called *intensifying interjection* or *particle of inauguration* (حَرْفُ اِسْتِفْتاحٍ). It may be rendered as *oh yes, indeed, truly, verily*. It literally means: *is it not*.

Oh yes, everything is ephemeral (lasting for a short time; not permanent)!	أَلا إِنَّ كُلَّ شَيْءٍ زائِلٌ!
By all means they are themselves the conquerors!	أَلا إِنَّهُمْ هُمْ الطّافِرُونَ!
Unquestionably, [for] the allies of Allah there will be no fear concerning them, nor will they grieve. *(Sura 10:62)*	أَلَا إِنَّ أَوْلِياءَ اللَّهِ لَا خَوْفٌ عَلَيْهِمْ وَلَا هُمْ يَحْزَنُونَ.

4	After the word كَلَّا which may denote: *not at all; on the contrary; by no means! Certainly not! Never! No!*

| On the contrary! Health is more important than money! | كَلَّا إِنَّ الصِّحَّةَ أَهَمُّ مِنَ الْمالِ! |
| No! He has been stubbornly hostile to Our revelation. *(Sura 74:16)* | كَلَّا إِنَّهُ كَانَ لِآيَاتِنَا عَنِيدًا. |

---

5   After the particle إِذْ. In such constructions, it often means *when* (not the question!).

| I arrived when the students were leaving. | حَضَرْتُ إِذْ إِنَّ الطُّلَّابَ مُنْصَرِفُونَ. |

---

6   After حَيْثُ and حَتَّى.

- حَيْثُ means *where* (not the question!). The word is used as an *adverb of place* (ظَرْفُ مَكانٍ). In some situations, it may also denote *since, as, due to the fact that; in that...*
- حَتَّى in such constructions often denotes *so that* (and not: *until*).

I sat where the colleagues were sitting.	جَلَسْتُ حَيْثُ إِنَّ الزُّمَلَاءَ جالِسُونَ.
Fire, since (as, because) it is hot, heats water.	النَّارُ مِنْ حَيْثُ إِنَّها حَارَّةٌ تُسَخِّنُ الْمَآءَ.
Zayd became ill, so that verily they have no hope for him.	مَرِضَ زَيْدٌ حَتَّى إِنَّهُمْ لَا يَرْجُونَهُ۔

---

7   To start a sentence used as a *circumstantial description* (حال).

| I said goodbye to my colleague while he was leaving. | وَدَّعْتُ زَمِيلِي وَإِنَّهُ مُنْصَرِفٌ. |

| 8 | At the beginning of a relative clause (جُمْلَةُ الصِّلةِ). |

| I met those who master five languages. | قَابَلْتُ مَنْ إِنَّهُمْ يُجِيدُونَ خَمْسَ لُغاتٍ. |

| 9 | To start the sentence after an oath (جَوابُ الْقَسَمِ). |

| I swear that the temperature has reached fifty below zero. | وَاللهِ إِنَّ دَرَجةَ الْحَرارةِ وَصَلَتْ إِلَى خَمْسِينَ تَحْتَ الصِّفْرِ. |

232. Can you use قال (*to say*) together with أَنَّ?

Yes, you can – but only later in the sentence.

Usually, the indirect (reported) speech after قَالَ is connected by إِنَّ. But what should you do if you have more than just one information? For example: *It is said that.... and that...*

If you have two noun clauses in an indirect speech with قَالَ, there is a common way to deal with it:

- The **first part** is introduced with إِنَّ and
- the **second part** with أَنَّ.

Let us look at an example:

| It is said **that** they are still alive and **that** they need water. | يُقالُ إِنَّهُمْ ما زالُوا أَحْياءً, وَأَنَّهُمْ يَحْتاجُونَ إِلَى مِياهٍ. |
| We have two occurrences of *that*. Notice the spelling! The first *that* is إِنَّهُمْ (*'inna*) and the second *that* is أَنَّهُمْ (*'anna*). |

233. When does a noun (اِسْمٌ) in Arabic need the nominative case (مَرْفُوعٌ)؟

There are six situations.

Subject of a nominal sentence (جُمْلةٌ اِسْمِيّةٌ). The word مُبْتَدَأ literally denotes *where it begins*. It is usually the <u>first word</u> of a sentence.	مُبْتَدَأ	1
Predicate of a nominal sentence (جُمْلةٌ اِسْمِيّةٌ). It completes the meaning of the مُبْتَدَأ. Without the خَبَر, a nominal sentence wouldn't make sense.	خَبَر	2
This is the "subject" (usually the first noun) in a sentence with كانَ. All its *sisters* work pretty similar: *verbs of approximation* (فِعْلُ مُقارَبةٍ), *verbs of hope* (فِعْلُ رَجاءٍ), *verbs of beginning* (فِعْلُ شُروعٍ). See *questions #101, #102, and #103.*	اِسْمُ كانَ and its sisters	3
Predicate of a sentence starting with إِنَّ. Its *sisters* work in the same way and are: أَنَّ • كَأَنَّ • لكِنَّ • لَعَلَّ • لَيْتَ plus the absolute, generic negation (لا النَّافِيةُ لِلْجِنْسِ). For instance: *There is no lasting pleasure* (لا سُرُورَ دائِمٌ).	خَبَرُ إِنَّ and its sisters	4
Subject of a verbal sentence.	فاعِلٌ	5
Subject of a verbal sentence in the passive voice.	نائبُ فاعِلٍ	6

234. What is the difference between قُتِلَ and تَمَّ الْقَتْلُ؟

The meaning is the same: was killed. But there is a finesse.

There is only a minor difference as both constructions express the passive voice.

- قُتِلَ is the regular passive voice of the verb *to kill* (قَتَلَ).

- تَمَّ الْقَتْلُ is another possibility to express roughly the same. We use the construction تَمَّ plus مَصْدَر. The I-verb تَمَّ/يَتِمُّ denotes *to be* or *become complete/finished.*

Let's check the difference.

قُتِلَ الرَّجُلُ.	The man was killed.

We use the verb *to kill* in the passive voice. We don't know who the killer was. *Man* is now the subject of the passive voice (نائِبُ فاعِلٍ) and used to be the direct object (مَفْعُولٌ بِهِ).

تَمَّ قَتْلُ الرَّجُلِ.	The man was killed.

The meaning here is slightly different. The direction is more like: *the killing was completed.* تَمَّ is an intransitive verb; it does not carry a direct object.

If you use this sentence without further information, it will express that there was an *order/assignment that has been fully completed.* It has the meaning of: *Okay, I did it; it is done.*

Killing (قَتْلُ) is an infinitive (مَصْدَرٌ) and functions as the regular subject (فاعِلٌ) of the verbal sentence (جُمْلَةٌ فِعْلِيّةٌ) – and not, like in the previous sentence, as the نائِبُ فاعِلٍ.

Note that the مَصْدَر after تَمَّ must be **definite** (مَعْرِفة): by the article الـ, by serving as the first part of a إِضافة-construction (our example), or by a pronoun suffix.

| The lesson was completed. | تَمَّ الدَّرْسُ. | 3 |

If you use this sentence *without* further information, it will mean: *I have finished the lesson*; *I did it.* (Rather than just: *The lesson is over*).

| The work will be finished. | سَيَتِمُّ الْعَمَلُ. | 4 |

In this sentence, we express a *future* action by conjugating the verb تَمَّ. Note: الْعَمَلُ here is the subject of the sentence (فاعِلٌ).

235. What may the word أَيّ express?

Various things. For example: which, each, what a…!, or that is.

If you want to use أَيّ correctly, it can quickly turn into a nasty word. There are different ways of using أَيّ • أَيَّة (feminine form) – and each way may change the meaning of the sentence.

Grammatically speaking, أَيّ is the first part of a إِضافة-construction and drags the word which follows into the genitive case (مَجْرُورٌ). The word أَيّ may take any of the three case endings according to its position in the sentence.

Let us examine now how we can use أَيّ in a sentence.

1	**Meaning:** *which?*	الْاِسْتِفْهَامُ

Which book is this?	أَيُّ كِتَابٍ هٰذا؟	1

أَيُّ is the **predicate** (خَبَرٌ) of a nominal sentence (جُمْلَةٌ اِسْمِيَّةٌ) and is in the **nominative** case (مَرْفُوعٌ); هٰذا is the subject (مُبْتَدَأٌ).

Which book did you read?	أَيَّ كِتَابٍ قَرَأْتَ؟	2

أَيَّ كِتَابٍ is the **direct object** (مَفْعُولٌ بِهِ) and thus takes the **accusative** case (مَنْصُوبٌ) which might be surprising as it starts the sentence (inverted word-order). أَيّ can also function as other types of objects. For example:

- أَيّ is placed as a **circumstantial qualifier** (حَالٌ): *I passed by Zayd, what a well-mannered man!* (مَرَرْتُ بِزَيْدٍ أَيَّ مُهَذَّبٍ.)
- أَيّ is placed as an **absolute object** (مَفْعُولٌ مُطْلَقٌ) - it usually denotes the exclamatory meaning of "what a..!": *She was very happy with this book.* (سُرَّتْ بِهٰذا الْكِتَابِ أَيَّ سُرُورٍ.)

Which book did you read? (same meaning as 2)	أَيُّ كِتَابٍ قَرَأْتَهُ؟	3

But there is a grammatical difference: أَيّ in example 3 is the **subject** (مُبْتَدَأٌ) of a nominal sentence (جُمْلَةٌ اِسْمِيَّةٌ) and thus takes the nominative case (مَرْفُوعٌ). This is why you have to refer to the word *book* again by using a returning pronoun: هُ.

Rule: If you use a **transitive** verb (a verb that can carry an object), it must be connected with a pronoun. If you have an **intransitive** verb, you don't need a pronoun.

Which student came?	أَيُّ تِلْمِيذٍ حَضَرَ؟	4

أَيّ is the **subject** (مُبْتَدَأٌ) of the nominal sentence (جُمْلَةٌ اِسْمِيَّةٌ). *To come* is an intransitive verb → no pronoun suffix!

| Which nationality? | مِنْ أَيِّ جِنْسِيةٍ؟ | 5 |

أَيّ is placed after a preposition → genitive case (مَجْرُورٌ).

| Which (female) student? | أَيَّةُ طالِبَةٍ؟ | 6 |

We use the feminine form أَيَّةُ because طالِبَةٍ is feminine. However, sometimes you may see the masculine form although the word after أَيّ is feminine.

---

2   Meaning: anyhow; anyone; anyway

It may rain; but anyhow, I shall go out.	قَدْ تُمْطِرُ وَلَكِنِّي سَأَخْرُجُ عَلَى أَيَّةِ حالٍ.
I did not hear anything of…	لَمْ أَسْمَعْ أَيَّ شَيْءٍ مَنْ...
I like anything you like.	أَيُّ شَيْءٍ تُحِبُّهُ فَأَنا أُحِبُّهُ.

In this construction, we have two sentences which are combined. Watch out: The verb تُحِبُّ does not take the jussive mood (مَجْزُومٌ) as this is not a conditional sentence (see number 3).

---

3   *Conditional meaning*   اِسْمُ شَرْطٍ

| A (each/every) student who works hard will succeed. | أَيُّ طالِبٍ يَجْتَهِدْ يَنْجَحْ. |

Both verbs are in the jussive mood (مَجْزُومٌ) since the sentence has a conditional meaning!

| Whomever you honor shall praise you. | أَيًّا تُكرِمْ يَحْمَدْكَ. |

If you skip the second part of the إِضافة-construction after أَيِّ, you have to put *nunation* (تَنْوِينٌ) as a **compensation**. In the accusative case (مَنْصُوبٌ), we get أَيًّا (with "an"). Notice: Both verbs are in the jussive mood (مَجْزُومٌ).

4	**Relative pronoun meaning:** *which, that.* See *Arabic for Nerds 2*, question #120.	اِسْمٌ مَوْصُولٌ

I like the one who carries out his work.	يُعْجِبُنِي أَيِّ أَدَّى عَمَلَهُ.
For a better understanding, we could rewrite the sentence as follows:	أَيِّ يُعْجِبُنِي مَنْ أَدَّى عَمَلَهُ.

5	**Adjective describing an indefinite noun** (نَعْتٌ بَعْدَ نَكِرَةٍ) نَعْتٌ

Zayd is a man, what a man!	زَيْدٌ رَجُلٌ أَيُّ رَجُلٍ.
It is of greatest importance (lit.: it is of importance, and of what importance!)	إِنَّ لَهُ شَأْنًا أَيَّ شَأْنٍ.

Watch out: أَيْ without شَدّةٌ means *that is (to say); namely.*

أَيْ is used to explain a preceding word or information. It may be translated as *this means; that is to say; namely.* It is also used to address somebody (حَرْفُ نِداءٍ).	أَيْ = يَعْنِي

You are accusing me of a crime, namely, that I am a thief.	تَتَّهِمُنِي بِالجُرْمِ، أَيْ أَنا مُجْرِمٌ.

O Lord! (Note: It is read with inclination of voice.)	أَيْ رَبِّ!

236. How do you express *when I was eleven...* in Arabic?

There are several possibilities.

Let us examine a more complicated option.

When I was eleven...	كُنْتُ فِي الْحادِيةَ عَشْرَةَ مِنْ عُمْرِي...

1. Is the word الْحادِيةَ in the accusative case (مَنْصُوبٌ)?

No, it is not! الْحادِيةَ is located in the position of a genitive case (مَجْرُورٌ) since it is placed after a preposition. What you see is not the case marker of an accusative case (مَنْصُوبٌ)!

All numbers between 11 and 19 (cardinal and ordinal) always end in "a" (فَتْحةٌ) whatever the case may be. They are fixed on that shape and thus indeclinable (مَبْنِيٌّ). Other ordinal numbers follow the usual rules.

2. Why do you use the feminine form of the numbers?

Originally, the sentence included the word سَنة (*year*) after the preposition فِي. Even it is not written, the numbers are still declined according to the feminine word سَنةٌ.

When I was twelve...	كُنْتُ فِي الثّانِيةَ عَشْرَةَ مِنْ عُمْرِي...
I am 22 (variation one).	عُمْرِي اثْنانِ وَعِشْرُونَ عامًا.
I am 22 (variation two).	أَنا فِي الثّانِيةِ وَالْعِشْرِينَ مِنْ عُمْرِي.

Watch out: In the last sentence, the number after فِي takes كَسْرة ("*i*")! It is in the genitive case (مَجْرُورٌ) and follows the standard rules (unlike numbers between 11 and 19 – see first example!).

237. What is a causative object (مَفْعُولٌ لِأَجْلِهِ)?

A causative object (مَفْعُولٌ لَهُ or مَفْعُولٌ لِأَجْلِهِ) describes the purpose of an action; the reason why an action is done.

It clarifies the reason for the occurrence of an action which originates from the doer (subject). In order to identify it, you ask: _Why did the subject/agent do it?_ Or: _What for (reason)?_

- The مَفْعُولٌ لِأَجْلِهِ takes the accusative case (مَنْصُوبٌ).

- The مَفْعُولٌ لِأَجْلِهِ is not always just a single word; it may also be an adverbial phrase (شِبْهُ جُمْلَةٍ).

- It has to be indefinite (نَكِرَةٌ); otherwise, we have to use لِ. This particle is called _Lām of causality_ and _justification_ (لامُ تَعْلِيلٍ).

- It has to be a مَصْدَرٌ; otherwise, use the preposition لِ.

- The مَصْدَرٌ, which expresses the purpose, is usually connected to emotions, feelings, etc.

- What is the difference to the _circumstantial description/ status_ (حالٌ)! If you want to identify a حالٌ, you ask: _how?_

causative object (مَفْعُولٌ لِأَجْلِهِ)	
I went to Egypt to study Arabic. (Question: **Why** did I go to Egypt?)	جِئْتُ إِلَى مِصْرَ رَغْبَةً فِي تَعَلُّمِ الْعَرَبِيَّةِ.
The word رَغْبَة describes the cause, the reason why I went to Egypt.	رَغْبَةً فِي = السَّبَب
He cried of fear. (Question: **Why** did he cry?)	بَكَى خَوْفًا.

In the following examples, we are not able to use a causative object (مَفْعُولٌ لِأَجْلِهِ). Let's see why.

| I came for water. (Question: **Why** did I come?) | جِئْتُ لِلْماءِ. |

The word ماءٌ is **not** a مَصْدَرٌ; thus, we use لِ.

| I came to you for my benefit/interest (to take advantage). (Question: **Why** did I come?) | جِئْتُكَ لِلْاِسْتِفادَةِ. |

The word *profit, gain* (الْاِسْتِفادَةُ) is **definite** (مَعْرِفةٌ)! Thus, we need to insert the preposition لِ.

| I went to school for learning. (Question: **Why** did I go to school?) | قَصَدْتُ الْمَدْرَسةَ لِلدَّرْسِ. |

The word دَرْسٌ is not connected to emotions, feelings, or affectivity; thus, we use لِ.

circumstantial description/status (حالٌ)

| He came laughing. (Question: **How** did he come? It describes the subject while it was doing the action.) | جاءَ ضاحِكًا. |

238. How do you express: *at the beginning of the century?*

You could almost use a direct translation – but there's one issue.

In Arabic, we use the plural form of the word that determines the time. Let's have a look.

At the beginning of the 20th century	الْقَرنِ الْعِشرِينَ	أَوائِلِ	خِلالَ
In the middle of the month	الشَّهرِ	+ أَواسِطِ	+ **or** فِي
At the end of the year	السَّنةِ	أَواخِرِ	

at the very outset; at the beginning of; in the early stages of	فِي أَوَائِلِ
at the beginning of the fifties	فِي أَوَائِلِ الْخَمْسِيناتِ
since its beginnings; from the very beginning	مِن أَوَائِلِهِ

The word after خِلالَ (*during; through*) or فِي has to be in the genitive case (مَجْرُورٌ). In our examples, they are broken plurals (جَمْعُ تَكْسِيرٍ) and diptotes (مَمْنُوعٌ مِن الصَّرْفِ) – but since they are definite (first part of a إِضافة), they take the regular ending, i.e., a كَسْرةٌ.

Watch out: Don't mix خِلالَ with the expression مِنْ خِلالِ which means *across; on the basis of; by means of*.

239. What is special about diptotes (؟(مَمْنُوعٌ مِن الصَّرْفِ)

They do not take nunation (تَنْوِينٌ).

What we are going to analyze in this *question* is only important if we deal with **indefinite** (نَكِرةٌ) words. For example, *friends* (أَصْدِقاءُ) or *desert* (صَحْراءُ).

Words which are definite by الـ or are functioning as the first part of a إِضافة follow the standard rules.

Indefinite words get *nunation* (تَنْوِينٌ). In Arabic, we use the term Tanwīn (تَنْوِينٌ) which is the مَصْدَر of the II-verb نَوَّنَ (*adding an n*). At the very beginning of Arabic, it indicated the nasalization of the final vowel of the word, especially in the case ending of the noun. The main function of nunation is to mark the absence of the definite article الـ.

The term مَمْنُوعٌ مِن الصَّرْفِ literally means *prohibited from variation/declension*. In English, we use the term *diptote* (having two cases) and for the standard noun, we use *triptote* (having three cases).

If a noun is a *diptote*, you don't write nunation, you don't write nor pronounce the endings *"un"*, *"in"* or *"an"*. Instead, you only use a simple vowel without the n-sound. If you want to know the idea behind diptotes in Arabic, see *Arabic for Nerds 2, question #46*.

Several types of words are مَمْنُوعٌ مِن الصَّرْفِ. We will check them now in detail.

I. Proper names (عَلَمٌ).

- All names of men and women are diptotes.

- All names of cities are **feminine** and are also diptotes.

Feminine proper nouns (عَلَمٌ مُؤَنَّثٌ)		A
Zaynab (زَيْنَبُ), Suʿād (سُعادُ), Damascus (دِمَشْقُ)	They look masculine – but have a feminine meaning.	1
Osama (أُسامةُ), Hamza (حَمْزةُ)	They look feminine – but have a masculine meaning.	2
Mecca (مَكَّةُ), Fatima (فاطِمةُ), Khadīja (خَدِيجةُ)	They look feminine – and have a feminine gender.	3
Sun (شَمْسُ), Egypt (مِصْرُ), India (هِنْدُ)	They consist of three letters; the second letter has a سُكُون.	4
You can choose if you want to add تَنْوِينٌ or not: مِصْرُ or مِصْرٌ; هِنْدُ or هِنْدٌ - both are correct! But the diptote is more common.		

Non-Arabic names (عَلَمٌ أَعْجَمِيٌّ)		B
Ibrahim (إِبْراهِيمُ), Ramses (رَمْسِيسُ), Iran (إِيرانُ).	Words are borrowed from foreign languages (more than three letters).	1
Noah (نُوحُ), Hud (هُودُ), Lot (لُوطُ)	Foreign names consisting of **three** letters: the 2nd letter has a سُكُون.	2
You can choose if you want to add nunation or not: نُوحُ or نُوحٌ.		

Proper names with three consonants plus Aleph ا and ن = ان	C
Ramadan (رَمَضانُ), Adnan (عَدْنانُ), Marwan (مَرْوانُ)	These words are mostly names.

Proper names having the pattern of a verb (عَلَى وَزْنِ الْفِعْلِ)	D
'Ahmad (أَحْمَدُ), Yazīd (يَزِيدُ), Yathrib (يَثْرِبُ) - the old name of Medina	These words look like verbs (present or past tense).

Proper names that follow the pattern فُعَلُ (fu'al)	E
Omar (عُمَرُ), Zahal (زُحَلُ) - name of the planet Saturn	Words formed of three letters having the vowel pattern "u-a".

Proper names that consist of two names (composite noun).	F
Hadramaut (حَضَرَ مَوْتُ), Bethlehem (بَيْتَ لَحْمُ), Baalbek (بَعْلَبَكُّ)	Two nouns - the 2nd part is declined (receives case endings).

- You cannot apply this rule to numbers like *fifteen* (خَمْسَةَ عَشَرَ) which have an entirely indeclinable shape (مَبْنِيٌّ).

- Names ending in وَيْهِ like *Sībawayhi* (سِيبَوَيْهِ) are indeclinable (مَبْنِيٌّ). They are often Persian names or words.

II. Adjectives (صِفَةٌ)

In Arabic, there are only three types of words: nouns (اِسْمٌ), verbs (فِعْلٌ), and particles (حَرْفٌ). Nouns (اِسْمٌ) may qualify as adjectives in Arabic if they are located in an appropriate position (after a noun; agreement). Note that only nouns get case endings!

	A
Adjectives following the pattern فَعْلانُ (fa'lān) Watch out: words of the measure فُعْلانٌ (fu'lān) get تَنْوِينٌ!	

thirsty (عَطْشانُ), hungry (جَوْعانُ), drunk (سَكْرانُ)	These adjectives have the feminine form فَعْلَى and the plural form فَعالَى.

	B
Adjectives of the pattern أَفْعَلُ ('af'al): comparative and colors	

bigger (أَكْبَرُ), nicer (أَجْمَلُ), more important (أَهَمُّ), smaller (أَصْغَرُ)	These adjectives have the feminine form فُعْلَى.	1
Notice the difference between the feminine form of the *noun of preference* (اِسْمُ تَفْضِيلٍ) and the patterns of colors. Comparative: أَفْعَلُ – فُعْلَى versus colors: أَفْعَلُ – فَعْلاء.		
blind (أَعْمَى * عَمْياءُ), dumb (أَبْكَمُ * بَكْماءُ); deaf (أَصَمُّ * صَمَّاءُ)	Adjectives denoting disabilities (عُيُوبٌ بِالإِنْسانِ).	2

Adjectives that are used as numbers: the patterns فُعَال (fu'āl) and مَفْعَل (maf'al).	C

one by one; in one row (أُحَادُ or مَوْحَدُ)	Both patterns describe how things are arranged. You can choose which form you prefer, they both mean the same. They are **only used with numbers from 1 to 10.** Used mainly in literature.
in pairs (ثُناءُ or مَثْنَى)	
in pairs of ten (مَعْشَرُ or عُشارُ)	

III. Broken plurals (جَمْعُ التَّكْسِيرِ)

Broken plural can give you a headache in Arabic. There are dozens of patterns. The most important one is called *secondary* or *ultimate plural* (مُنْتَهَى الْجُمُوعِ). Why is it called *ultimate plural*? Well, the answer is linked to the *plural of a plural*.

Excursus: The plural of the plural and the ultimate plural

In Arabic, you can form the plural of a plural (جَمْعُ الْجَمْعِ). Sounds strange, but this has to do with the several types of plurals. In Arabic, we have plurals for small and big numbers, and we have collectives. Furthermore, we can interpret the *minor plural* (جَمْعُ قِلَّةٍ) – for small amounts up to ten – as a collective.

Now, can we form the plural of a minor plural? **Yes**, this is possible. The idea is to multiply the units it includes.

The plural of the plural denotes numbers from nine and up – because it indicates plurals of three and more, from plurals including themselves three units.

Some examples:

singular	(minor) plural	plural of the plural
يَدٌ	أَيْدٍ	أَيَادٍ
hand	several hands; assistance	acts of assistance
قَوْلٌ	أَقْوالٌ	أَقاوِيلُ
saying; doctrine	doctrines; sayings	groups of (common) sayings and doctrines
مَكانٌ	أَمْكِنَةٌ	أَماكِنُ
place	several places	groups of places

So, what's the big deal? Some plural patterns can be changed to get what is called the *plural of the plural* (جَمْعُ الْجَمْعِ).

- أَمْكِنَةٌ is the **plural** of the singular word مَكانٌ.

- The **plural** أَمْكِنَةٌ itself, however, can be put into a plural form as well: أَماكِنُ. Now comes the crucial thing: This last form **cannot** form any further plural form (الصِّيغَةُ نِهايَةُ الْجَمْعِ الَّذِي يُمْكِنُ أَنْ تَصِلَ إِلَيْهِ الْكَلِمَةُ).

- That is why a word like أَماكِنُ is called an **ultimate plural**. Why did we mention all this in this chapter? Many ultimate plural forms are **diptotes!**

The *plural of a plural* and the *ultimate plural* are related to each other – but are strictly speaking different concepts.

The *plural of a plural* is used to multiply **units**. Its base is already a plural. The *ultimate plural*, on the other hand, is mainly a morphological concept. Its base can only be a singular form.

Watch out: You may see that the *plural of a plural* is formed by the sound plural patterns (but only empirical/سَماعِيٌّ) - by the sound masculine plural (if the singular is masculine human) or in the other situations by the sound feminine plural pattern (جَمْعُ الْمُؤَنَّثِ السّالِمُ).

groups of houses	بُيُوناتٌ	←	houses	بُيُوتٌ

Now let's get back to our main topic. **Ultimate plurals have the following pattern:**

1		2		3
two letters	+	Aleph	+	two or three letters

After the first two letters, there is an **additional Aleph in the middle,** and after the Aleph, you will find **two or three letters**.

There are 19 patterns. <u>Four patterns</u> are diptotes.

pattern	plural	singular	meaning	
أَقَاعِلُ	أَصَايِعُ	إِصْبَعُ	finger	1
	أَكْارِمُ	كَرِيمٌ	generous	
مَفَاعِلُ	مَساجِدُ	مَسْجِدٌ	mosque	2
	مَكَايِسُ	مِكْنَسةٌ	broom, sweeper	
	مَنازِلُ	مَنْزِلٌ	house	
	مَدارِسُ	مَدْرَسةٌ	school	
	مَصانِعُ	مَصْنَعٌ	factory	
أَقَاعِيلُ	أَضَابِيرُ	إِضبارَةٌ	file, dossier	3

	أَساليبُ	أُسْلُوبٌ	style; method	
مَقَاعِيلُ	عَصافِيرُ	عُصْفُورٌ	bird	4
	مَواثِيقُ	مِيثَاقٌ	contract	
	مَصابِيحُ	مِصْباحٌ	lamp	
	مَفاتِيحُ	مِفْتاحٌ	key	

You can remember the patterns with the following English sentence: You need a **lamp** (مَصابِيحُ) and your **fingers** (أَصابِعُ) to read the **dossier** (أَضابِيرُ) in the **house** (مَنازِلُ).

- This explains why the plural of *men* (رِجالٌ) gets nunation (تَنْوِينٌ) because after the Aleph, there is only **one letter**.

- However, a doubled letter (شَدَّةٌ) counts. Thus, the plural of the following words don't get تَنْوِينٌ and are diptotes.

toil	مَشاقٌّ	مَشَقَّةٌ	harm	مَضارُّ	مَضَرَّةٌ	material	مَوادُّ	مادَّةٌ

IV. Special situations

A noun (إِسْمٌ) ending in Aleph ‍ا indicating a feminine form!

The Aleph ى is additional (إِسْمٌ مَقْصُورَةٌ)	A

We get this special situation when the letter ى (أَلِفٌ مَقْصُورَةٌ or *shortened Aleph*) is preceded by **more than two radicals** (root letters). In other words, the letter ى is additional and not part of the root.

| good news | بُشْرَى | | pregnant | حُبْلَى |
| larger, major | كُبْرَى | | Salma, fem. name | سَلْمَى |

However, if the letter ى is preceded by only two radicals (root letters), it does get nunation! See *question #13*.

| hospital | مُسْتَشْفَى | | meaning | مَعْنًى |

The Aleph ا and the ء are additional (إِسْمٌ مَمْدُودَةٌ)		**B**

We have this situation if the so-called *extended Aleph* (أَلِفٌ مَمْدُودَةٌ) is preceded by **more than two radicals** (root letters) and followed by a Hamza (هَمْزَةٌ) - resulting in اءُ

desert	صَحْرَاءُ		beauty	حَسْنَاءُ
red	حَمْرَاءُ		scientists	عُلَمَاءُ
friends	أَصْدِقَاءُ		arrogance	كِبْرِيَاءُ

Watch out! In the following examples, the ء is either part of the root or was originally و or ي that turned into ء. In other words, Aleph and Hamza are not preceded by more than two radicals. Such words get nunation (تَنْوِينٌ). See *question #12*.

news	تَبَأٌ - أَنْبَاءٌ	ن-ب-ء		building	بِنَاءٌ - أَبْنِيَةٌ	ب-ن-ي
sky	سَمَاءٌ	س-م-و		enemy	عَدُوٌّ - أَعْدَاءٌ	ع-د-و
name	اسْمٌ - أَسْمَاءٌ	س-م-و		member	عُضْوٌ - أَعْضَاءٌ	ع-ض-و

Excursus: What about feminine regular plurals?

They have only **two case endings** ("*un*" and "**in**") – but they can take nunation (تَنْوِينٌ). They are <u>not</u> diptotes (مَمْنُوعٌ مِن الصَّرْفِ)! In the accusative (مَنْصُوبٌ) and genitive (مَجْرُورٌ) case, they share the same ending: ـِ

240. How do you mark cases in diptotes (مَمْنُوعٌ مِن الصَّرْفِ)؟

Instead of "-un", "-in", and "-an", you use two vowels: "u" or "a".

A *diptote* is a word that does not get nunation (تَنْوِينٌ). In order to receive nunation, a word has to be **indefinite** (نَكِرَةٌ). As soon as there is diptote in a sentence, you'd better check it twice before you put case endings. Let's see the whole story.

1. Indefinite diptote - **nominative** case (مَرْفُوعٌ).

| These are clean streets. | هٰذِهِ شَوارِعُ نَظِيفَةٌ. |
| These are new buildings. | هٰذِهِ مَنازِلُ جَدِيدَةٌ. |

We have two diptotes (شَوارِعُ and مَنازِلُ). We can only mark them with one ضَمّةٌ. Now, what about the adjectives which are placed after them? Adjectives need agreement (مُطابَقةٌ). Since they refer to an indefinite noun in the nominative case, we have to mark them as such – in other words, they get nunation: "*-un*".

2. Indefinite diptote - **accusative** case (مَنْصُوبٌ).

| I saw clean streets. | شاهَدْتُ شَوارِعَ نَظِيفَةً. |
| The engineers build new houses. | يَبْنِي الْمُهَنْدِسُونَ مَنازِلَ جَدِيدَةً. |

Same story here. The two diptotes do not get nunation. Instead, we mark them with a simple vowel: "*a*". And what about the adjectives? They need to agree with the word they describe – in both examples, with an indefinite noun in the accusative case. Hence, they get nunation. We mark them with "-*an*".

3. Indefinite diptote - **genitive** case (مَجْرُورٌ).

This may be confusing. If an indefinite diptote needs the genitive case, we mark it with "*a*" (فَتْحةٌ).

In the following examples, only sentences marked in grey contain a diptote (مَمْنُوعٌ مِن الصَّرْفِ).

I walked in clean streets.	1 مَشَيْتُ فِي شَوارِعَ نَظِيفةٍ.
I walked in <u>the</u> streets of the city.	2 مَشَيْتُ فِي شَوارِعِ الْمَدِينةِ.
I walked in <u>the</u> clean streets.	3 مَشَيْتُ فِي الشَّوارِعِ النَّظِيفةِ.

- In the first example, we have an indefinite diptote which is followed by an adjective.

- In the second example, we have a definite diptote since the word serves as the first part of a إِضافة.

- In the third example, we also have a definite diptote (definite article ال).

→ The **indefinite** diptote gets the vowel **"a"** in the genitive.

→ The **definite** diptote is marked as usual with the vowel **"i"**.

241. Is حَسْناءُ the feminine form of أَحْسَنُ (better)?

No, it isn't.

The word أَحْسَنُ is masculine. It is a noun of preference (اِسْمُ تَفْضِيلٍ) and may express a comparative (*better*) or superlative (*best*). If we want to form the feminine form of this word, we apply the pattern فُعْلَى and get حُسْنَى.

Now, what does حسناء mean then? First of all, we have to set the correct vowel on the first letter: it is حَسْناءُ.

The pattern فَعْلاءُ is used to derive the feminine version of words that denote colors or deficiencies.

What is the nature of both words أَحْسَنُ and حَسْناءُ? They are quasi participles (صِفةٌ مُشَبَّهةٌ). The masculine version of such nouns which usually serve as adjectives uses the same pattern as the اِسْمُ تَفْضِيل – which is: أَفْعَلُ.

meaning	feminine	masculine
red	حَمْراءُ	أَحْمَرُ
bigger/biggest	كُبْرَى	أَكْبَرُ

But that is not the end of the story. Is it true that the masculine counterpart of حَسْناءُ is the word أَحْسَنُ? Yes it is, but the meaning then is not *best* – it is *beautiful*.

There are some adjectives of beauty that use the same pattern as colors and deficiencies:

- أَفْعَلُ for masculine and فَعْلاءُ for feminine forms.

The word أَحْسَنُ is rarely applied to a man whereas it is pretty common to use حَسْناءُ to describe a woman as *beautiful*. In-

stead, you should better use حَسَنٌ for men which practically
means the same as أَحْسَنُ. Let us summarize:

meaning	grammatical form	feminine	masculine	
better; best	اِسْمُ التَّفْضِيلِ	حُسْنَى	أَحْسَنُ	1
beautiful; nice	الصِّفةُ الْمُشَبَّهةُ	حَسْناءُ	أَحْسَنُ (not used)	2

Let's check other words which follow the same logic.

meaning	feminine form	masculine form
smooth	مَلْساءُ	أَمْلَسُ
nice; bright	بَلْحاءُ	أَبْلَحُ
brave; courageous	شَجْعاءُ	أَشْجَعُ

Notice that both forms (masculine and feminine) are diptotes!

242. مَشَيْتُ وَالْبَحْرَ - How would you translate that?

The meaning is: I walked along the sea.

The expression وَالْبَحْرَ is an *object of accompaniment* (مَفْعُولٌ
مَعَهُ). You may also hear *concomitant object* (which means: *to
accompany; to be somehow connected*) or *object in connection*.

If you don't know the function of a مَفْعُولٌ مَعَهُ, you will
mistranslate a sentence totally. We could say that such object is
a noun in the accusative case (اِسْمٌ مَنْصُوبٌ) which is directly
placed after the device وَ which conveys the meaning of *with*
(and not: *and*). Thus, you could replace وَ with مَـعَ and
wouldn't change the meaning – however, you would end up

with a different case ending as the noun after مَعَ would take the genitive case (مَجْرُورٌ).

Notice that the verb induces the accusative case in the object – it is not the particle وَ. The وَ is only there to transport the meaning of the verb.

| I walked along the sea. | مَشَيْتُ وَالْبَحْرَ. |
| I walked along the sea. | مَشَيْتُ مَعَ الْبَحْرِ. |

| I work during the night. | أَعْمَلُ وَاللَّيْلَ. |
| I woke up by the chirping of the birds. | اِسْتَيْقَظْتُ وَتَغْرِيدَ الطُّيُورِ. |

Not only the verb may take an *object of accompaniment*.

The father is sitting with his family.	verb (فِعْلٌ)	جَلَسَ الْأَبُ وَالْأُسْرَةَ.
I like your walking on the pavement.	infinitive (مَصْدَرٌ)	يُعْجِبُنِي سَيْرُكَ وَالرَّصِيفَ.
The man is walking in the gardens.	active participle (اِسْمُ الْفَاعِلِ)	الرَّجُلُ سَائِرٌ وَالْحَدائِقَ.
The car is left to the driver.	passive participle (اِسْمُ الْمَفْعُولِ)	السَّيَّارَةُ مَتْرُوكَةٌ وَالسَّائِقَ.
Be patient with the angry man!	verbal noun (اِسْمُ الْفِعْلِ)	رُوَيْتَكَ وَالْغاضِبَ.

243. What is the root of مِينَاءٌ (*port*)?

The root is و-ن-ي.

The Arabic word for *port* was originally مِوْناي following the pattern مِفْعالُ. This pattern is used to form a noun of instrument (اِسْمُ آلةٍ). Like the Arabic word for *minaret* (*question #176*), it was originally meant to be a tool and not a place.

However, مِوْناي would be difficult to pronounce. Therefore, the more convenient مِينَاءُ is used instead. The plural of مِينَاءُ is مَوَانٍ or مَوَانِئُ.

Scholars have suggested that the origin of this word may go back to ancient Egyptian (where port is *mni*), from where it entered Greek (*limen*), Hebrew (*namel* – נָמֵל), and Arabic.

244. How do you express *whereas* or *while* in Arabic?

Basically, you have two options.

- In English, *whereas* is used to express: *in contrast or comparison with the fact that...* → to indicate a contrast between two facts or ideas.

- *While* can be used in two ways. It may denote *during the time that something else happens*. Or: *in contrast with something else*. We only focus on the latter here.

The construction with أَمّا plus فَ.	1

I liked the mountains **whereas** my friends hated them.	أَلْجِبالُ أَعْجَبَتْنِي أَمّا أَصْدِقائِي فَقَدْ كَرِهُوها.

The construction with بَيْنَما.	2

بَيْنَما is an *adverb of time* (ظَرْفُ زَمانٍ or مَفْعُولٌ فِيهِ).

Thus, it is located in the position of an accusative case.

I asked her to come to the party, **whereas** she wants to stay at home.	طَلَبْتُها بِحُضُورِ الْحَفْلة, بَيْنَما هِيَ تُرِيدُ الْبَقاءَ فِي الْبَيْتِ.

Watch out:

بَيْنَما is more often used to join two actions or situations which simultaneously happen. It then has the same meaning as عِنْدَما or حِينَما. In this application, بَيْنَما is followed by either a nominal (جُمْلَةٌ اِسْمِيّةٌ) or verbal sentence (جُمْلَةٌ فِعْلِيّةٌ).

The verb may be used in the past or present tense – but don't forget that the tense (for the translation) is marked by the main clause.

I read a book while you watched a soap opera.	قَرَأْتُ كِتابًا, بَيْنَما أَنْتَ كُنْتَ تُشاهِدُ مُسَلْسَلًا.
She fell asleep while reading.	بَيْنَما كانَتْ تَقْرَأُ غَلَبَها النُّعاسُ.

The expression: فِي/عَلَى حِينِ أَنَّ	3

He is generous whereas she is not.	هُوَ كَرِيمٌ فِي حِينِ أَنَّها لَيْسَتْ كَذَلِكَ.

245. How do you express *his brother came laughing?*

You need a so-called circumstantial description (حالٌ).

If you have a complete sentence and want to modify its meaning, you may use *while, when, although, that is* in English.

You may also use participles (*smiling, crying, ...*) which work as modifiers.

In Arabic, we use a *circumstantial description/status* (حَالٌ). It is added to an already complete sentence as a kind of supplement. The حَال expresses the **state or condition of the subject** (or object) **while the action takes place.** The صَاحِبُ الْحَالِ (*concerned by the status*) is the entity (subject and/or object) whose circumstances are described by the حَال.

If you ask *how are you?* in Arabic, you can say: كَيْفَ الْحَالُ؟

Some people may jokingly answer: .الْحَالُ مَنْصُوبٌ

This is a reference to the حَال which has to take the accusative case (مَنْصُوبٌ). In order to identify the حَال, you ask the question: كَيْفَ؟ In our example: *How did his brother come? Answer: smiling* (ضَاحِكًا).

The حَال can consist of a word (e.g., an active participle) or a full sentence. There are several possibilities to use a حَال.

A. You use a single word.

The man drank the coffee smiling.	.شَرِبَ الرَّجُلُ الْقَهْوةَ **مُبْتَسِمًا**

Question: How did he drink the coffee?

Subject (فَاعِل) of the verbal sentence (جُمْلَةٌ فِعْلِيَّةٌ). It is the صَاحِبُ الْحَالِ.	الرَّجُلُ
Direct object (مَفْعُولٌ بِهِ), accusative case (مَنْصُوبٌ).	الْقَهْوةَ
Circumstantial description (حَالٌ)	مُبْتَسِمًا

If the حَال is not expressed by a single word (مُفْرَدٌ), it will need a connector (رَابِطٌ).

Notice that you don't translate the connector. Thus, never say, for example, *and* or *and he*, etc. There are three possibilities to connect the حالٌ with the preceding sentence:

The device وَ - so-called واوُ الْحالِ.	وَ	1
A pronoun at the end of a verb, for example the ضَمّة (meaning *he*) in the verb: يَتَّحَّدَثُ	pronoun only	2
و plus pronoun (ضَمِيرٌ).	وَهُوَ	3

A. You use a full sentence.

The حالٌ can also be a full sentence:

- If you use a nominal sentence (جُمْلةٌ اِسْمِيّةٌ), you need a connector (رابِطٌ) to link it with the preceding sentence.

- The verbal sentence (جُمْلةٌ فِعْلِيّةٌ) doesn't need a رابِطٌ. The hidden, concealed pronoun (ضَمِيرٌ مُسْتَتِرٌ) which is included in the verb is enough to link both parts.

I repeated my lessons while the people were sleeping.	راجَعْتُ دُرُوسِي وَالنّاسُ نائِمونَ.	• 1

The subject (فاعِلٌ) is a hidden, concealed pronoun expressing *you* (أَنْتَ) which is also the صاحِبُ الْحالِ.	راجَعْتُ

The entire nominal sentence (جُمْلةٌ اِسْمِيّةٌ) is located in the position of a حالٌ.	وَالنّاسُ نائِمونَ

The whole second sentence is placed in the spot of an accusative case (فِي مَحَلِ نَصْبٍ) since it occupies the location of a حال - but you don't see that.

I left the house with open doors/ and left the door open, etc.	تَرَكْتُ الْبَيْتَ وَالْبَابُ مَفْتُوحٌ.	2

The object (مَفْعُولٌ بِهِ) is the صاحِبُ الْحالِ.	الْبَيْتَ

The entire nominal sentence (جُمْلَةٌ اِسْمِيّةٌ) is located in the position of a حال.	وَالْبَابُ مَفْتُوحٌ

The director sat down talking.	جَلَسَ الْمُدِيرُ يَتَحَدَّثُ.	3

Here we use a verbal sentence (جُمْلَةٌ فِعْلِية) as a حال for الْمُدِيرُ which is the صاحِبُ الْحالِ. Notice that we don't need a connector because we use a verbal sentence. The same is true in the following sentence:

The director came driving his car.	أَتَى الْمُدِيرُ يَقُودُ سَيارتَهُ.	4

I started sleeping when the sun rose.	بَدَأْتُ النَّوْمَ وَقَدْ طَلَعَتِ الشَّمْسُ.	5

C. You use a prepositional or adverbial clause (شِبْهُ الْجُمْلةِ).

Such شِبْهُ الْجُمْلةِ may be an adverb of time or place or a prepositional phrase.

I received the prize with joy (joyfully).	اِسْتَلَمْتُ الْجائِزةَ فِي فَرَحٍ.

The prepositional phrase (جارٌ وَمَجْرُورٌ) works as a حال for the subject (the concealed, hidden pronoun أنا) which is also the صاحِبُ الْحالِ.

I left the car in the parking lot.	.تَرَكْتُ السَّيَّارةَ عِنْدَ الْمَوْقِفِ

The adverbial phrase (ظَرْفُ مَكانٍ) is the حال. What about the السَّيَّارةَ? It is the word صاحِبُ الْحالِ.

Watch out: All three possibilities (A, B, and C) mean the same. For example: *He greeted me saying...*

participle	verbal sentence	nominal sentence
سَلَّمَ عَلَيَّ قائِلًا...	سَلَّمَ عَلَيَّ يَقُولُ...	سَلَّمَ عَلَيَّ وَهُوَ قائِلٌ...

Let us summarize the main conditions for a حال:

- The حال has to be <u>indefinite</u> (نَكِرةٌ) and in the <u>accusative</u> case (مَنْصُوبٌ).
- The صاحِبُ الْحالِ has to be <u>definite</u> (مَعْرِفةٌ). It can be either the subject (فاعِلٌ) or the object (مَفْعُولٌ بِهِ).

246. Why are نَعْت and حال often confused?

Because the they may be of the same form – but serve in a different function.

The term نَعْت or صِفةٌ means *description* in Arabic and is translated into English as *attribute* or *adjective*.

The نَعْت is a derived noun (اِسْمٌ مُشْتَقٌّ) which is based on the root.

There are several types – the most common are:

صِيغَةُ الْمُبالَغةِ	الصِّفَةُ الْمُشَبَّهَةُ	اِسْمُ الْمَفْعُولِ	اِسْمُ الْفاعِلِ
form of exaggeration	adjectives similar to active (and passive) participles	passive participle	active participle

Let us check all this in detail:

I bought a new car.	اِشْتَرَيْتُ سَيّارَةً جَدِيدَةً.

The thing that is **described** (مَنْعُوتٌ).	سَيّارَةٌ
The **description** (نَعْتٌ). It needs agreement (مُطابَقةٌ) and takes the same grammatical features as the thing which it describes.	جَدِيدَةٌ

The نَعْت has to agree with the مَنْعُوتٌ in four things:

1	Determination (def. or indefinite)	نَكِرَةٌ ● مَعْرِفةٌ
2	Case marker	مَرْفُوعٌ ● مَجْرُورٌ ● مَنْصُوبٌ
3	Gender (نَوْعٌ - جِنْسٌ)	مُذَكَّرٌ ● مُؤَنَّثٌ
4	Number (عَدَدٌ)	مُفْرَدٌ ● مُثَنّى ● جَمْعٌ

The نَعْت is different from the حَال.

- A sentence following a <u>definite</u> word is a حَال. It describes the subject or object while the action takes place.
- A word (or sentence) following an <u>indefinite</u> word is a نَعْت – a description that is not connected to the action which the subject/object is doing.

| I don't want to see **a crying child**. | لا أُحِبُّ أَنْ أُشاهِدَ طِفْلًا باكِيًا. |

The word باكِيًا is an **adjective** (نَعْت), and not a حَالٌ! Why? Because the حَالٌ can only refer to a definite word. The نَعْت here is a general statement here.

| I don't want to see **the child crying**. | لا أُحِبُّ أَنْ أُشاهِدَ الطِّفْلَ باكِيًا. |

Now باكِيًا don't have an adjective anymore. It is a **circumstantial description** (حَالٌ) for the word الطِّفْلَ which is the صاحِبُ الْحالِ. It describes the condition of a certain child while I am watching the child.

Another example:

| I live in a house close to the beach. | أَسْكُنُ فِي بَيْتٍ بِحَيِّ الشَّاطِئِ. |

| بَيْتٍ | Indefinite (نَكِرَةٌ) → it can't be a حَالٌ. It is the مَنْعُوت. |
| بِحَيِّ الشَّاطِئ | It is possible to use a full sentence or quasi-sentence to function as an adjective (النَّعْتُ وَالْجُمْلَةُ). In our example, it is a prepositional phrase. |

The following two sentences can't work as a حَالٌ as the word which is being described is <u>indefinite</u> → they are adjectives.

| I live in a house with big rooms. | أَسْكُنُ فِي بَيْتٍ غُرَفُهُ واسِعَةٌ. |
| I live in a house opposite the beach. | أَسْكُنُ فِي بَيْتٍ أَمامَ الْبَحْرِ. |

247. Why should you pay attention when you see مَهْما؟

مَهْما *induces the jussive mood (مَجْزُومٌ) in verbs. If you trans-*
late such sentences, you should use the present tense.

مَهْما is a tricky word. It is a conditional noun (اِسْمُ شَرْطٍ)
which conveys the meaning of *despite; although; whatever;*
whatever the case... no matter what/how. مَهْما induces the jussive mood (مَجْزُومٌ) in verbs. How do we use it?

- If مَهْما starts the sentence, you normally use a verb in the
  jussive mood (مَجْزُومٌ). The verb thus ends in سُكُون or
  you need to delete a weak letter (حَرْفُ عِلَّةٍ).

- If مَهْما is placed in the second part of a sentence, you
  normally use a verb in the past tense – which conveys the
  meaning of the present or future tense!

Whatever effort you do, you will find a result.	مَهْما تَجْتَهِدْ تَلْقَ.
I will be the same person whatever people say.	سَأَظَلُّ بِهذا الشَّكْلِ مَهْما قالَ النَّاسُ.
Notice in the last example that we use the past tense of *to say* to express a present tense meaning.	

Let's see some more examples.

Whatever the case…	مَهْما يَكُنْ مِنْ الأَمْرِ...
No matter how I try, I can't.	مَهْما حاوَلْتُ لا أَسْتَطِيعُ.
As long as you do good, we shall not dismiss you.	مَهْما تَصْلُحْ فَلَنْ تَعْزِلَكَ.
They said, "We will not believe in you, no	وَقَالُوا مَهْمَا تَأْتِنَا بِهِ مِنْ

| matter what signs you produce to cast a spell on us." *(Sura 7:132)* | آيَةٍ لِّتَسْحَرَنَا بِها فَمَا نَحْنُ لَكَ بِمُؤْمِنِينَ. |

If you don't want to use مَهْما, you have some options:

$$\text{مَهْما} = \text{حَتَّى لَوْ} = \text{إِذا حَدَثَ}$$

All three expressions introduce an <u>indefinite conditional clause</u>. This is different to the particles لَوْ or إِذا which are limiting the number of possible conditions in the if-part whereas words like *whatever, whoever, wherever* leave it open to almost any situation.

- Indefinite conditional clause: *Whatever the weather will be, we will go.* In indefinite conditional sentences, the verbs are almost always in the jussive mood (مَجْزُومٌ).

- *If the weather is nice, we will go.* In conditional constructions with لَوْ or إِذا, you don't use the jussive mood.

248. . لَا إِلَهَ إِلَّا اللهُ - Why does God have a فَتْحَةٌ ("a")?

The sentence means: There is no God but God.

The long vowel "*ā*" in God (إِلَه) and Allah (اللّٰه) are written with a vertical dash – a *dagger Aleph* (أَلِفٌ خَنْجَرِيَّةٌ); see *quest. #22.*

But this is not our main concern here. If we want to understand the vowel on the last letter of إِلَه ("*la 'ilāha...*"), the single form of God, we have to enter the field of the *generic* or *absolute negation* (لا النَّافِيةُ لِلْجِنْسِ).

Let us first check the different forms of the device لا.

	type	translation	example
1	Negation of a verb (حَرْفُ نَفْي)	The boy doesn't play football in the street.	الْوَلَدُ لا يَلْعَبُ الْكُرَة فِي الشَّارِع.
	The verb *to play* has a ضَمّة at the end which is the marker for the standard, indicative mood (مَرْفُوعٌ). This type of لا does not induce any mood or case.		

	type	translation	example
2	Interdiction, prohibition (لا النّاهِيَة)	Don't play soccer in the street!	لا تَلْعَبْ بِالْكُرةِ فِي الشَّارِع.
	This type of لا conveys the meaning of *don't* (negated imperative). It does influence other words in the sentence. The verb after لا needs the jussive mood (مَجْزُومٌ). Notice the سُكُون at the end of the negated imperative تَلْعَبْ.		

	type	translation	example
3	conjunction (عَطْفٌ)	Nagīb Mahfūz is a writer, not a poet.	نَجيب مَحْفُوظ كاتِبٌ لا شاعِرٌ.
	The word after a conjunction takes the same case as the preceding word. Thus, both words (*writer*; *poet*) take the same case.		

	type	translation	example
4	generic, absolute negation (لا النّافِيةُ لِلْجِنْس)	There is no student in the room.	لا طالِبَ فِي الْغُرْفةِ.

This negation is called *generic* or *absolute negation* because it denies the existence of the entire genus. Therefore, it conveys the meaning of *there is no... (at all)*. Or: *there is not a...* Or: *none at all*.

Some remarks:

- لا intervenes in a nominal sentence (جُمْلَةٌ اِسْمِيّةٌ). There is no verb involved!

- The noun after لا must be **indefinite** (نَكِرَةٌ) and never gets nunation (تَنْوِينٌ).

- The noun has to follow the لا immediately.

- The predicate is in the nominative case (مَرْفُوعٌ) and gets nunation.

- This لا works like the particle إِنَّ. It is a حَرْفٌ نَاسِخٌ, so it abrogates rules. The "subject" (اِسْمُ لا النّافِيةِ لِلْجِنْسِ) is in the accusative (نَصْبُ الْمُبْتَدَإِ) and the predicate (خَبَر لا) takes the nominative case (رَفْعُ الْخَبَرِ).

- But it is not that simple: The noun after لا gets fixed on the vowel "a" (مَبْنِيٌّ عَلَى الْفَتْحِ) which is the reason why we only see one فَتْحَةٌ. This, however, is not the case marker. It is only the vowel on which a noun in this position is built. In fact, we can only assign a place value and say that the اِسْمُ لا النّافِيةِ لِلْجِنْسِ is located in the spot of an accusative case (فِي مَحَلِّ نَصْبٍ)

- **Watch out:** If you are referring to a specific person or thing, you negate the nominal sentence with لَيْسَ.

Let's put the noun after لا under the microscope.

A	It is a **single noun** (مُفْرَدٌ).

The underlying grammar is pretty theoretical. You don't have to worry to much about it because even if you just remember to use the accusative case (without nutation), the result will be fine.

So, what's going on? Although you don't see it, we fix the word after لا on a vowel or letter and thus make it indeclinable (مَبْنِيٌّ). It may look like the regular markers of the accusative, but it is not.

We can only apply place values. See also *Arabic for Nerds 2, q. #278*

There is no popular liar. (Lit. meaning: No liar is popular.) Notice the فَتْحة on *liar*.	لا كاذِبَ مَحْبُوبٌ.	1
There are no popular liars. Notice that و turns into ي here!	لا كاذِبِيْنَ مَحْبُوبُونَ ـ	2
There are no (female) popular liars.	لا كاذِباتِ مَحْبُوباتٌ.	3

Watch out: Feminine sound plurals and duals have two case markers only: for the nominative (مَرْفُوعٌ) and for the so-called *oblique* (مَجْرُورٌ and مَنْصُوبٌ). However, they do not belong to diptotes (مَمْنُوعٌ مِن الصَّرْفِ). Sound feminine plurals get nunation (تَنْوِين) whenever they are indefinite.

B   We use a إِضافة-construction and use **regular case markers.**

- The 1st part of the إِضافة is in the <u>accusative</u> case (مَنْصُوبٌ).
- The 2nd part is indefinite (نَكِرةٌ) and in the <u>genitive</u> (مَجْرُورٌ).

There is no professional who loses his wage. (Lit. meaning: No professional loses his wage.)	لا مُتْقِنَ عَمَلٍ يَضيعُ أَجْرُهُ.	1
There are no professionals who lose their wages.	لا مُتْقِني عَمَلٍ يَضيعُ أَجْرُهُم.	2
Notice that ون turns into ي as the ن disappears in a إِضافة and the و turns into ي in the accusative case (مَنْصُوبٌ).		
There are no (female) professionals who lose their wages.	لا مُتْقِناتِ عَمَلٍ تَضيعُ أَجْرُهُنَّ.	3
Why do we use the كَسْرة ("*i*") here although it is مَنْصُوبٌ؟ Because we have a feminine sound plural! See *question #34*.		

C	A construction that resembles a إِضافةٌ-construction (شَبِيهة بِالْمُضافِ), but grammatically, it isn't.

- The 1ˢᵗ part takes **nunation** (تَنْوينٌ) → the accusative (مَنْصُوبٌ). Either use add "-an" if you have a singular word, or you change و into ي if you have a sound masculine plural.
- The 2ⁿᵈ part is a **direct object** (مَفْعُولٌ بِه) – and therefore takes the accusative case (مَنْصُوبٌ).

There is no professional who loses his wage.	لا مُتْقِنًا عَمَلًا يَضِيعُ أَجْرُهُ.
Note that عَمَلًا is a مَفْعُولٌ بِه. The part after the object is the predicate (خَبَر) – in the form of a جُمْلة فِعْلِيّة.	
There are no professionals who lose their wages.	لا مُتْقِنِينَ عَمَلًا يَضِيعُ أَجْرُهُم.
There are no (female) professionals who lose their wages.	لا مُتْقِناتٍ عَمَلًا تَضِيعُ أَجْرُهُنَّ.

Watch out:

Neither the students nor the professor are present.	لا الطُّلَّابُ حاضِرُونَ وَلا الأُسْتاذُ.

The subject (مُبْتَدَأٌ) is in the nominative case (مَرْفُوعٌ) and is pronounced: at-tullāb**u** because the first word is <u>definite</u>! This sentence is **not a general statement**.

It is addressing a specific situation/certain people. Grammatically speaking, we negate a normal nominal sentence (جُمْلةٌ اِسْمِيّةٌ) with لا, which is possible (see *question #133*). So we have a normal negation (لا النّافِيةُ). After the particle لا, there must be a مُبْتَدَأٌ in the nominative case.

| There is no peace nor justice in the world. | لا فِي الْعالَمِ سَلَامٌ وَلا عَدْلٌ. |

We have our main ingredient for a generic negation (لا النَّافِيةُ لِلْجِنْسِ): the **indefinite** word (نَكِرةٌ). But there is an issue. You are not allowed to separate لا and the denied thing (here: سَلَام). Thus, we have a normal negation (لا النّافِيَةُ).

| You are clever without doubt. | أَنْتَ ذَكِيٌّ بِلا شَكٍّ. |

The preposition بـ turns the sentence into a regular negation (لا النَّافِيَةُ), and a standard لا does not change the case (except in a special application, see *question #133*). For the correct case endings, just treat the sentence as it would be written without لا.

| No doubt. | بِلا رَيْبٍ = لا رَيْبَ فِي ذلِكَ. |

| No doubt in that. | لا شَكَّ فِي ذلِكَ. |

This sentence meets the conditions for an absolute negation (لا النَّافِيةُ لِلْجِنْسِ): indefinite, nothing in between, no preposition!

249. Why are if-clauses often difficult to translate?

The translation depends on the context – not on tenses or moods.

In most languages, if-clauses are pretty abstract constructions. I was teaching German in Egypt. In one lesson, I talked about New York and said a sentence which in English means: *If I had money, I would fly to New York.*

After the lesson a student came to me and said: *Congratulations! When are you going to New York? We will miss you!* The sentence I used is pretty complex.

I asked my listeners to do two things: (1) **imagine** that I am rich and (2) **imagine** what I would to do as a rich person.

In English, we love to speak in *would-*, *could-* and *should-* sentences. But in Arabic, there is no easy way to express this idea. The Arabic verb lacks tenses and moods and specific rules for if-clauses. Instead, it all depends on the context!

Some hints:

- Verbs in conditional sentences have no real temporal significance. The actual tense is determined by the context.

- The verb in the **first part** of the if-sentence is typically in the **past tense** – regardless of whether a reference to a past, present, or future situation is intended.

- The verb in the **second or main clause** is usually in the past tense too – but other tenses are possible as well.

- The actual meaning of the verbs corresponds to a number of English tenses depending on the meaning of the condition and the context.

250. What does the jussive mood (مَجْزُومٌ) express?

Usually, one of the following things: a condition, a prohibition, or an imperative.

The word *jussive* is based on the Latin word *jubeō*: to order, to command. In Arabic, مَجْزُومٌ literally means *cut short; clipped*. In grammar, it denotes *with deleted ending*. So, what's the idea?

Elision (جَزْمٌ) is a grammatical situation that requires to **cut the end of the present tense verb** (الْمُضارِعُ). We achieve that by using a سُكُونٌ. If there is a weak letter involved (حَرْفُ عِلَّةٍ), we drop that to mark this mood.

When should we use it? When you see the مَجْزُومٌ-ending,

a) probably there is a connection to the meaning of *should;*

b) maybe there is a command involved (*imperative*);

c) maybe the sentence has a conditional meaning;

The jussive mood (مَجْزُومٌ) does not occur by itself. It has to be induced by certain devices, so-called *particles of elision* (حَرْفُ جَزْمٍ). They may even have enough power to cut two verbs (often conditional sentences).

cutting **two** verbs		cutting **one** verb	
if; even if	إِنْ	negation (past tense)	لَمْ
whenever	إِذْما	negation	
who	مَنْ	prohibition (لا النَّاهِيَةُ)	لا
that which	ما	(even) if	إِنْ
whatever	مَهْما	since	لَمَّا
what a	أَيُّ	*Lām* of the imperative (لامُ الْأَمْرِ). *To; let's*	لِ
in whatever way	كَيْفَما		
when	مَتَى		
wherever	أَيْنَما		
in what time	أَيَّانَ		
whence	أَنَّى		
wherever	حَيْثُما		

Don't play with fire!	لا تَلْعَبْ بِالنَّارِ!	cutting one verb
Be a responsible man!	لِتَكُنْ مَسْؤُولًا!	
He did not go.	لَمْ يَذْهَبْ.	

| If you are lazy, you will be a loser. | إِنْ تَكْسَلْ تَخْسَرْ. | cutting two verbs |
| Wherever you sit, I sit. | أَيْنَما تَجْلِسْ أَجْلِسْ. | |

251. When do you need the jussive (مَجْزُوم) in if-clauses?

When the condition is expressed by a particle of elision (حَرْف جَزْمٍ).

Several words can start a conditional sentence, but not every device initiates the jussive mood (مَجْزُوم). Most of them, however, do. Let's check them.

| إِنْ | *if*; used for time or place |

| If you put an effort in your work, you will succeed in your life. | إِنْ تَجْتَهِدْ فِي عَمَلِكَ تَنْجَحْ فِي حَيَاتِكَ. |

| مَتَى | *when* |

| If/when you come to Egypt, you will find beautiful weather. | مَتَى تَأْتِ إِلَى مِصْرَ تَجِدْ جَوَّها جَمِيلًا. |
| The weak letter of يَأْتِي (present tense of *to come*; أَتَى) is elided. | |

مَنْ	*who*; for persons

ما	*who*; *whoever*; *which* – for animals, trees; non-human things

Whoever travels a lot will see different people.	مَنْ يُسافِرْ كَثِيرًا يَرَ شُعُوبًا مُخْتَلِفَةً.

The weak letter in يَرَى (present tense of *to see*; رَأَى) is deleted.

Remark: رَأَى is one of the very few extremely irregular verbs. You cannot conjugate it by using the common rules. The Hamza disappears in the present tense and the imperative looks totally weird since it is only one letter: رَ (masculine) and رَيْ (feminine) for the singular and رَوْا (masculine) and رَيْنَ (feminine) for the plural.

مَهْما	*what*; *which*; *whatever*

What you do for the good of the people will make you happy.	مَهْما تُقَدِّمُوا مِن خَيْرٍ لِلنَّاسِ تُصْبِحُوا سُعْداءَ.

أَيْنَما	*where*; for places

Wherever you travel, you will find friends.	أَيْنَما تُسافِرْ تَجِدْ أَصْدِقاءَ۔

كَيْفَما	*how*

The way you treat friends, the way they will treat you.	كَيْفَما تُعامِلْ زُمَلاءَكَ يُعامِلُوكَ.

	every; whoever. For people, places, time. Notice that you need to put a noun (اِسْم) after أَيُّ and never a verb – because أَيُّ is used in a إِضافة-construction.
أَيُّ	

Every worker who works diligently will find the fruits of his work.	أَيُّ عامِلٍ يَعْمَلْ بِجِدٍّ يَلْقَ ثَمَرَةَ عَمَلِهِ.

The weak letter of يَلْقَى (present tense of *to find*; لَقِيَ) is elided.

252. Do you always need the مَجْزُوم- mood in if-clauses?

No, you don't.

Several words may start a conditional sentence without changing anything in the following verbs. In fact, two of the most prominent words for conditional sentences are of that nature: إِذا and لَوْ.

Let's see how they work.

إِذا	*if; when*

The condition expressed by إِذا is a **situation which is likely or expected** – thus, it is usually translated as *when*. The only uncertainty is often just the time of the event.

The verb after إِذا has to be in the **past tense** although it has a **future** meaning.

If morning comes, people will go to their work.	إِذا طَلَعَ الصَّباحُ ذَهَبَ النَّاسُ إِلى أَعْمالِهِم.

لَوْ | if; whether

- لو is used for **hypothetical** situations, for things that are **improbable** or **contrary to fact**. We are either talking about something that has already occurred or we know that the scenario we are introducing doesn't match reality.

- Similar to إِذا, the temporal meaning of the verb is not determined by its form, but by the meaning of the condition.

- Regarding the use of ف in the main clause - see *qu. #253*.

How do we use لَوْ?

- If the first part of the if-clause **cannot be achieved** anymore, the second part (or answer), of course, is also not going to happen. In English, we call such sentences *imagined conditions* or *third conditional*. In Arabic, we say اِمْتِناعُ الشَّرْطِ. The word اِمْتِناع means impossibility; *refraining*.

- That's why you need the **(emphatic) particle** لَ ("*la*") to **connect** the second sentence and underline the hypothetical meaning. It is called *Lām of the complement* (لامُ الْجَوابِ). Such device is used in the second part of a conditional sentence with لَوْ or لَوْلا and in oaths.

Had you put effort into your work, you would have won the prize.	لَوْ اِجْتَهَدْتَ في عَمَلِكَ لَحَصَلْتَ عَلَى الْجائِزةِ.

Watch out: The normal interpretation of this sentence would be as a **counterfactual**. So don't get confused: The sentence does not mean: *If you put an effort in your work, you will earn the prize.*

If I had known (it), I would have walked.	لَوْ عَرَفْتُ لَمَشَيْتُ.

لَوْلا	if not; if it were not for; if it had not been for; if there was no

لَوْلا precedes a single noun or noun phrase and **hypothetically denies** it.

- Immediately after لَوْلا you have to place a **noun** in the nominative case (اِسْمٌ مَرْفُوعٌ).
- In the second part of the sentence, you use the particle لَ. It conveys emphasis and serves as a binder. See *quest. #126.*

If there was no Nile, Egypt would be a desert.	لَوْلا النّيلُ لَأَصْبَحَتْ مِصْرُ صَحَراءَ.

The word مَوْجُودٌ (*found; existing*) is implicitly understood after the word *Nile* – but never written. See *Arabic for Nerds 2, quest. #224.*

كُلَّما	every time; whenever.

Every time I walked in the streets of Cairo, I found a crowd.	كُلَّما سِرْتُ فِي شَوارِع الْقاهِرة وَجَدْتُ اِزْدِحامًا.

Notice: In the second part of the sentence, you have to use the past tense! Such sentences are also often translated with the past tense!

253. When do you use فَ in conditional sentences?

It depends on how you start the second part.

In most conditional sentences which start with لَوْ or مَنْ or إِذا, you will find the particle فَ in the second part. It is used to connect the first sentence (*protasis*) with the main clause (*apo-dosis*). Thus, we call it *Fā' of sanction* (فاءُ الْجَزاءِ). The letter فَـ is used as a conjunction meaning: *then; thus; hence; therefore.*

1. When do you have to use it?

If the second sentence (main clause) doesn't start with the verb directly, you should add فَـ.

Generally speaking, فَـ usually is found before:

هُوَ	إِنَّ	قَدْ	سَـ سَوْفَ	لِ	لَمْ	لَنْ	ما	لا
or any other pro-noun to empha-size and start a nominal sentence (جُمْلةٌ اِسْمِيّةٌ)	to stress the main clause	to empha-size the meaning of the past tense	future indi-cator			negation		

Whoever enters the room is safe.	مَنْ دَخَلَ الْغُرْفةَ فَهُوَ آمِنٌ.
If you get married, you won't marry me.	إِذا تَزَوَّجْتَ فَلَنْ تَتَزَوَّجيني.

If you start the second part (main clause) directly with a verb, you don't need the فَـ – but instead, maybe the particle لَ, which is an amplifier and underlines one thing: The situation, which is described in the second part, will only be true if the first part happens.

Or in other words: If the first part doesn't happen, the sec-ond part won't either. The لَ is normally used for if-clauses type II (*if I was...*) and III (*if I had been...*). Notice the difference to the particle لِ with a كَسْرة – which means *in order to*. Let us look at an example of لِ.

If I had known (it), I would have walked.	لَوْ عَرَفْتُ لَمَشَيْتُ.

2. What is the grammatical impact of such فَ?

> If the second part of a conditional sentence starts with فَ, the **jussive mood** (مَجْزُومٌ) is **prohibited**. The verb takes the standard, indicative mood (مَرْفُوعٌ) and ends in "u".

The following examples more or less mean the same – despite the different tenses: *Whoever works hard, will succeed.*

1	We use only the verb – we don't need فَ.	مَنْ يَعْمَلْ بِجِدٍّ يَنْجَحْ.
2	The second and main clause is a nominal sentence (جُمْلَةٌ اِسْمِيّةٌ). Here, we need فَ! Subject (فَنَجاحُهُ) and predicate (مُؤَكَّدٌ) are in the nominative case (مَرْفُوعٌ).	مَنْ يَعْمَلْ بِجِدٍّ فَنَجاحُهُ مُؤَكَّدٌ.
3	The future tense needs فَ. Note that the second verb ends in ضَمّةٌ (yanjah**u**). Don't get confused. Grammatically speaking, the verb is nevertheless located in the position of a jussive mood (فِي مَحَلِّ جَزْمٍ).	مَنْ يَعْمَلْ بِجِدٍّ فَسَيَنْجَحُ.
		مَنْ يَعْمَلْ بِجِدٍّ فَسَوْفَ يَنْجَحُ.

How can we justify that we don't use the jussive mood? The فَ has the function of a breakwater. After فَ, we now have a nominal sentence (جُمْلَةٌ اِسْمِيّةٌ).

- The **verb** itself functions as the predicate (خَبَر).
- And where is the subject (مُبْتَدَأ)? It was deleted.

Now, it becomes theoretical: The nominal sentence, consisting of the predicate and the deleted subject, is located in the position of a jussive mood (الْجُمْلَةُ مِن الْمُبْتَدَإِ الْمَحْذُوفِ وَالْخَبَرِ تَكُونُ فِي مَحَلِّ جَزْمٍ). We say that predicate (خَبَرٌ = سَتَنْدَمُ) is in place of the deleted second (main) clause of the sentence. Let's use an example to illustrate all this:

If you are lazy, you will be sorry.	إِنْ تَكْسَلْ فَسَتَنْدَمُ.
This is the virtual meaning of the second (main) clause: *you (yourself) will be sorry.*	فَأَنْتَ تَنْدَمُ.

If you want to dig deeper into the nature of this فَ, see *Arabic for Nerds 2*, question #389.

254. What is the difference between إِذَا and إِنْ?

It is a bit like the question: if or when.

Let's start with English: *if* is used to introduce a possible or unreal situation or condition. *When* is used to refer to the time of a future situation or condition that we are certain of.

In Arabic, the difference between *if* and *when* is often fluid. Theoretically, you can use both words to express *if* or *when* – but there is a difference.

This word implies a positive or negative meaning; something may happen – or not! Closer to *if.*	إِنْ
This particle indicates that <u>something is going to happen.</u> Closer to *when.*	إِذَا

Here is an example:

When morning comes (and it will definitely come)...	إذا طَلَعَ الصَّباحُ

Important: It doesn't matter which tense you use! All three sentences in the table have more or less the same meaning: *If you strive in your work, you will be successful in your life.*

1	إِنْ اِجْتَهَدْتَ فِي عَمَلِكَ نَجَحْتَ فِي حَياتِكَ.

Past tense: You can't mark the jussive mood (مَجْزُومٌ) in a past tense verb. Although the verb is in the past, it conveys the meaning of the future.

2	إِنْ تَجْتَهِدْ فِي عَمَلِكَ تَنْجَحْ.

Present tense: You have to use the jussive mood (مَجْزُومٌ).

3	اِجْتَهِدْ فِي عَمَلِكَ تَنْجَحْ.

Imperative: You use the jussive mood (مَجْزُومٌ). Don't forget to write سُكُون in both verb: the imperative and the jussive mood.

255. What are the essential rules for writing numbers?

There are five essential rules.

Numbers are among the most difficult things in Arabic grammar. There are many rules which do not always follow the usual logic of the language. Let's dig through this mess.

The number 1.

In early times, the Arabs had not distinguished between one or two. They used the dual for two.

Otherwise, it was just one. Thus, you never use a إِضافة-con-struction for *one* or *two*.

For emphasis: use an adjective which always follows the word it describes.

A man came.	جاءَ واحِدُ رَجُلٍ.	wrong
	جاءَ رَجُلٌ.	correct
Two men came.	جاءَ اِثْنا رَجُلٍ.	wrong
	جاءَ رَجُلانِ.	correct

	feminine	masculine
1	واحِدةٌ	واحِدٌ
1ˢᵗ	الأُوْلَى	الأَوَّلُ
11	إحْدَى عَشْرةَ	أَحَدَ عَشَرَ
11ᵗʰ	الْحادِيةَ عَشْرةَ	الْحادِي عَشَرَ
21	إحْدَى وَعِشْرُونَ or واحِدةٌ وَعِشْرُونَ	واحِدٌ وَعِشْرُونَ

When should we use واحِد and when أَحَد؟

واحِدٌ	In English, this would be the **adjective** *one*. In Arabic too, it is used as a صِفةٌ/نَعْتٌ which means it **always comes after the word it describes** and never before! For example: *one word (a single word)*: كَلِمةٌ واحِدةٌ

أَحَدٌ	In English, this would be the **noun** *one*. • Normally, this word is used as the first part of a إِضافة. Meaning: *one of*. • It is often used independently and functions as an in-

> definite pronoun (*anyone, someone*). It is usually part of a negated sentence! See *question #115*.

The number 2.

2	اِثْنَانِ - اِثْنَيْنِ	إِثَانِ - إِثْنَيْنِ
2nd	ثَانِيَةٌ	ثَانٍ
12	اِثْنَا عَشْرةَ - اِثْنَتَيْ عَشْرةَ	اِثْنَا عَشَرَ - اِثْنَيْ عَشَرَ

The numbers from 3 to 10.
The numbers 30, 40, 50, ...

- The numbers from 3 to 10 are **regular**. The feminine form is built by adding ة.

- The numbers 30, 40, 50, ... have only one form, so there is **no feminine form**. For example: 40 (أَرْبَعُونَ).

- Watch out if you have *ten* (عَشر). The vowels may change if you change the gender – see *question #257*.

The numbers 100, 1000, and 1 million

They are nouns which have either a masculine or feminine form – but never both.

	feminine	masculine	plural
100	مِائَةٌ (also مِئَةٌ)	---	مِئَاتٌ
1000	---	أَلْفٌ	أُلُوفٌ or آلَافٌ

	feminine	masculine	plural
1 million	---	مِلْيُونٌ	مَلَايِينُ
1 billion	---	مِلْيَارٌ	مِلْيَارَاتٌ

Remark: Why does *thousand* have two plural forms? → See *question #127*. If you want to know more about the spelling of مائَةٌ, see *Arabic for Nerds 2, question #198*.

Now let us check how to connect numbers (عَدَدٌ) with nouns (e.g., *apples, pens, trees*, etc.). In grammar, we call such words the *counted* or *numbered noun* (مَعْدُودٌ). The مَعْدُود is responsible for the gender of <u>the number</u>.

<u>FIRST STEP:</u>

Check the **singular form** of the مَعْدُودٌ.

Some examples:

meaning	masc. singular	fem. singular	plural
pen	قَلَمٌ	---	أَقْلَامٌ
tree	---	شَجَرَةٌ	أشجَارٌ
Genēh	جُنَيْهٌ	---	جُنَيْهَاتٌ

Remark: *Genēh* is the Egyptian currency. In English, the currency is called *Egyptian pound*. The *guinea* was a gold coin used in Great Britain. The name came from the Guinea region in West Africa, where much of the gold used to make the coins originated.

SECOND STEP:

Find the correct form + agreement for the number

Now, our **five important rules** enter the game.

RULE 1	The number has to <u>agree</u> with the مَعْدُود, and the مَعْدُود has to be <u>singular</u>.

This rule is applied to:

- the numbers 1 and 2
- 11 and 12
- 21, 31, 41, …

I bought (only) one pen.	اِشْتَرَيْتُ قَلَمًا وَاحِدًا.
I bought (only) two pens.	اِشْتَرَيْتُ قَلَمَيْنِ اثْنَيْنِ.
I read (only) one page.	قَرَأْتُ صَفْحَةً وَاحِدَةً.
I read (only) two pages.	قَرَأْتُ صَفْحَتَيْنِ اثْنَتَيْنِ.
11 days have passed.	مَرَّ أَحَدَ عَشَرَ يَوْمًا.
12 days have passed.	مَرَّ اثْنا عَشَرَ يَوْمًا.
I read 11 pages.	قَرَأْتُ إِحْدَى عَشْرَةَ صَفْحةً.
I read 12 pages.	قَرَأْتُ اثْنَتَيْ عَشْرَةَ صَفْحةً.
21 days have passed.	مَرَّ واحِدٌ وَعِشْرُونَ يَوْمًا.
22 days have passed.	مَرَّ اثْنانِ وَعِشْرُونَ يَوْمًا.
I read 21 pages.	قَرَأْتُ إِحْدَى وَعِشْرِينَ صَفْحةً.
I read 22 pages.	قَرَأْتُ اثْنَتَيْنِ وَعِشْرِينَ صَفْحةً.

RULE 2 The number has to <u>disagree</u> with the مَعْدُودٌ, and the مَعْدُودٌ has to be in <u>plural</u>.

This rule is applied to:

- the numbers from 3 to 10.

| I bought 10 books. | اِشْتَرَيْتُ عَشَرَةَ كُتُبٍ. |
| I read 10 pages. | قَرَأْتُ عَشْرَ صَفْحاتٍ. |

Notice that the Arabic word for *ten* in our examples takes different vowels → see *question #257*.

RULE 3 The number has to <u>disagree</u> with the مَعْدُودٌ, and the مَعْدُودٌ has to be <u>singular</u>.

This rule is applied to:

- 13, 14, … 19, and so on.

Let' see some examples where the rules (2 and 3) are applied.

I bought 3 books.	اِشْتَرَيْتُ ثَلاثَةَ كُتُبٍ.
I read 3 pages.	قَرَأْتُ ثَلاثَ صَفْحاتٍ.
14 days have passed.	مَرَّ أَرْبَعَةَ عَشَرَ يَوْمًا.
14 years have passed.	مَرَّتْ أَرْبَعَ عَشْرَةَ سَنةً.
I have 26 books.	عِنْدِي سِتَّةٌ وَعِشْرُونَ كِتابًا.
I read 26 pages.	قَرَأْتُ سِتًّا وَعِشْرِينَ صَفْحةً.

Remark: Theoretically (although rarely used) you could also place the number after the noun. If you do so, you can use the masculine or feminine form. For example:

Three men came.	جاءَ رِجالٌ ثَلاثةٌ or ثَلاثٌ.

RULE 4	Numbers which <u>never change</u> their form.
	→ no agreement

This rule is applied to:

- 20, 30, 40, ...

- 100 (for the spelling of *hundred* – see *question #196* and *Arabic for Nerds 2, question #199*)

- 1000

- 1 million

RULE 5	How to combine *hundred* and *thousand*.

In English, you don't have to worry about the grammar when you say *300 men* and want to correct it to *3000 men*. It is the same. In Arabic, it is a different story.

- In most situations, you use the word for **hundred** in the <u>singular</u> form and the word for **thousand** in the <u>plural</u>.

- The number (e.g., *three*) and the word for **hundred** or **thousand** form a إِضافة-construction.

- In our example, this would mean: ثَلاث is the first part and مِئة or آلاف is the second part of the إِضافة.

Let's now apply rules 4 and 5.

In the room are 20 (masc.) students.	فِي الْغُرْفةِ عِشْرُونَ طالِبًا.
In the room are 20 (fem.) students.	فِي الْغُرْفةِ عِشْرُونَ طالِبةً.
A century has 100 years.	الْقَرْنُ مِئَةُ عامٍ.
I read 100 pages.	قَرَأْتُ مِئَةَ صَفْحَةٍ.
In the faculty are 100 (m.) students.	فِي الْكُلِّيَّةِ مِئَةُ طالِبٍ.
In the faculty are 100 (f.) students.	فِي الْكُلِّيَّةِ مِئَةُ طالِبةٍ.
In the faculty are 300 (m.) students.	فِي الْكُلِّيَّةِ ثَلاثُمِئَةِ طالِبٍ.
In the faculty are 300 (f.) students.	فِي الْكُلِّيَّةِ ثَلاثُمِئَةِ طالِبةٍ.
In the faculty are 3000 (m.) students.	فِي الْكُلِّيَّةِ ثَلاثةُ آلافٍ طالِبٍ.
In the faculty are 3000 (f.) students.	فِي الْكُلِّيَّةِ ثَلاثةُ آلافٍ طالِبةٍ.

256. Are numbers in Arabic nouns (إِسْمٌ)?

Yes, they are.

In principle, numbers (عَدَدٌ) are treated like any other إِسْمٌ which means that a number can serve as a subject or object – and **get cases**. It is already difficult to build the numbers correctly, but there is still something left to think about: the correct case marker. Let us check some examples.

Three days of the month passed.	مَضَتْ ثَلاثةُ أَيّامٍ مِن الشَّهْرِ.	1
I read **three** chapters of the book.	قَرَأْتُ ثَلاثةَ فُصُولٍ مِن الْكِتابِ.	2
The book consists of **three** chap-	يَشْتَمِلُ الْكِتابُ عَلَى ثَلاثةِ	3

ters.	فُصُولٍ.	

Subject (فاعِلٌ) of the verbal sentence; thus, it is in the nominative case (مَرْفُوعٌ).	ثَلاثَةٌ	1
Direct object (مَفْعُولٌ بِهِ); in the accusative case (مَنْصُوبٌ).	ثَلاثَةَ	2
This noun follows a preposition and is dragged into the genitive case (اِسْمٌ مَجْرُورٌ).	ثَلاثَةِ	3

Let's see the rules.

RULE 1	The numbers 20, 30, 40, … → you mark the case by a letter: و or ي. Thus, watch out for the ending: ونَ or ينَ.

20 (fem.) students study in the center.	تَدْرُسُ بِالْمَرْكَزِ عِشْرُونَ طالِبَةً.	1
The center receives **20** (fem.) students.	اِسْتَقْبَلَ الْمَرْكَزُ عِشْرِينَ طالِبَةً.	2
The center welcomes **20** (fem.) students.	رَحَّبَ الْمَرْكَزُ بِعِشْرِينَ طالِبَةً.	3
In the center are **25** (masc.) students.	فِي الْمَرْكَزِ خَمْسَةٌ وَعِشْرُونَ طالِبًا.	4

Subject (فاعِلٌ), nominative case (مَرْفُوعٌ).	عِشْرُونَ	1
Direct object (مَفْعُولٌ بِهِ), accusative case (مَنْصُوبٌ).	عِشْرِينَ	2
After a preposition; genitive case (اِسْمٌ مَجْرُورٌ).	عِشْرِينَ	3
This is a so-called *follower* (نابِعٌ) in Arabic. A follower gets the same case as the preceding word. Responsible for all this is the conjunction وَ (عَطْفٌ). Thus,	عِشْرُونَ	4

عِشْرُونَ gets the same case as خَمْسَةٌ: the nominative case (مَرْفُوعٌ).		

RULE 2	Numbers between 11 and 19 always end in فَتْحَةٌ. They are compound nouns and with both parts being fixed on the vowel "*a*". They are indeclinable (مَبْنِيٌّ عَلَى الْفَتْحِ).

11 (male) students came.	حَضَرَ أَحَدَ عَشَرَ طالِبًا.
I met 11 (male) students.	قابَلْتُ أَحَدَ عَشَرَ طالِبًا.
I met 11 (male) students.	اِلْتَقَيْتُ بِأَحَدَ عَشَرَ طالِبًا.

RULE 3	A special case – the **dual**: Numbers which are combinations of the number *two* are treated like a **dual**.
	If you want to emphasize the number *two*, add the number as an **adjective** – after the main word. As always, adjectives need agreement (مُطابَقَةٌ) → the same case!

Two (masc.) students came.	حَضَرَ طالِبانِ اثْنانِ.	1
Two (fem.) students came.	حَضَرَتْ طالِبَتانِ اثْنَتانِ.	
I met two (masc.) students.	قابَلْتُ طالِبَيْنِ اثْنَيْنِ.	2
I met two (fem.) students.	قابَلْتُ طالِبَتَيْنِ اثْنَتَيْنِ.	
I met two (masc.) students.	اِلْتَقَيْتُ بِطالِبَيْنِ اثْنَيْنِ.	3
I met two (fem.) students.	اِلْتَقَيْتُ بِطالِبَتَيْنِ اثْنَتَيْنِ.	
In the department are two hundred (fem.) students.	فِي الْقِسْمِ مِئَتا طالِبَةٍ	4
In the faculty there are two thousand	فِي الْكُلِّيَّةِ أَلْفا طالِبَةٍ.	

(fem.) students.	

Adjective (نَعْتٌ); nominative case (مَرْفُوعٌ).	اِثْنانِ , اِثْنَتانِ	1
Adjective (نَعْتٌ); accusative case (مَنْصُوبٌ).	اِثْنَيْنِ , اِثْنَتَيْنِ	2
Adjective (نَعْتٌ); genitive case (مَجْرُورٌ).	اِثْنَيْنِ , اِثْنَتَيْنِ	3
Delayed subject (مُبْتَدَأٌ مُؤَخَّرٌ) of the nominal sentence (جُمْلَةٌ اِسْمِيَّةٌ); nominative case (مَرْفُوعٌ).	مِئَتا , أَلْفا	4

257. Why can it be difficult to pronounce *ten* (عشر)?

Because the correct pronunciation depends on the word after.

You may have noticed that the number *ten* (عشر) doesn't always get the same vowels. Hence, it is pronounced differently.

There is a reason for this. In order to find the correct vowel of the **letter ش**, you have to check the gender of the noun to which it refers, i.e., the word which is placed after عشر.

RULE 1	If عشر points to a <u>masculine</u> word, there is a فَتْحة on the letter ش.

I bought 10 pens.	اِشْتَرَيْتُ عَشَرَةَ أَقْلَامٍ.
I bought 13 pens.	اِشْتَرَيْتُ ثلاثةَ عَشَرَ قَلَمًا.
ten days	عَشَرَةَ أَيَّامٍ
ten men	عَشَرَةَ رِجالٍ
ten thousand	عَشَرَةَ آلافٍ

The Prophet said: "Had only ten Jews (amongst their chiefs) believe me, all the Jews would definitely have believed me." *(Sahīh al-Bukhārī 3941)*	قَالَ: لَوْ آمَنَ بِي عَشَرَةٌ مِنَ الْيَهُودِ لَآمَنَ بِي الْيَهُودُ.

RULE 2	If عشر points to a <u>feminine</u> word, there is a سُكُون on the letter ش.

I read 10 pages.	قَرَأْتُ عَشْرَ صَفْحَاتٍ.
I read 13 pages.	قَرَأْتُ ثَلاثَ عَشْرَةَ صَفْحَةً.
ten degrees	عَشْرُ دَرَجَاتٍ
ten women	عَشْرُ فَتَيَاتٍ

The Prophet remained in Mecca for ten years. *(Sahīh al-Bukhārī 4978)*	لَبِثَ النَّبِيُّ بِمَكَّةَ عَشْرَ سِنِينَ.

What about the numbers 13 to 19? You need the word *ten* to form it. In fact, we use rule 1 and 2 to determine the shape.

fifteen years	خَمْسَ عَشْرَةَ سَنَةً	numbered thing is
fifteen nights	خَمْسَ عَشْرَةَ لَيْلَةً	**feminine** (مُؤَنَّثٌ)

fifteen dinar	بِخَمْسَةَ عَشَرَ دِينَارًا	numbered thing is
fifteen days	خَمْسَةَ عَشَرَ يَوْمًا	**masculine** (مُذَكَّرٌ)

258. Does *few* (بِضْع) sometimes change its shape?

Yes, it does.

The word بِضْع is a noun which includes a number from three to nine. It therefore denotes *some, a few, several*. For example, *for a few days; a few hundred*.

بِضْع changes its **gender depending on the word it refers to**. The rules for بِضْع are similar to the rules of numbers from 3 to 10. In other words, you need the **opposite gender** of the numbered word (مَعْدُود). If it is masculine, you need بِضْعَة. If it is feminine, you need بِضْع.

for a few days	You have to use the feminine form of *few* since *day* (يَوْم) is masculine.	لِبِضْعَةِ أَيَّامٍ.
a few years	You use the masculine form of *few* since *year* (سَنَة) is feminine.	بِضْعُ سَنَواتٍ.
There were a few hundreds.	You use the masculine form of *few* since *hundred* (مِئة) is feminine.	كانَ بِضْعُ مِئاتٍ.

twenty and a few dinars.	بِضْعَةٌ وَعِشْرُونَ دِينارًا
a few tens	بِضْعَةَ عَشَرَ

259. What is a *logical subject*?

*It is the topic of the debate whether you should say: many **are**... or many **is**...*

Let's start our discussion with the following sentence: *Many (a lot of) devices support the operating system.*

What is the subject of this sentence? Is it *many* or *devices*?
This is crucial for the correct form of the verb.

	verb refers to	
1	*many* (الْعَدِيدُ)	يُدَعِّمُ الْعَدِيدُ مِن الْأَجْهِزَةِ نِظامَ التَّشْغِيلِ.
2	*devices* (الْأَجْهِزَةِ)	تُدَعِّمُ الْعَدِيدُ مِن الْأَجْهِزَةِ نِظامَ التَّشْغِيلِ.

Does the verb refer to الْعَدِيدُ? Then the verb should be يُدَعِّمُ.
Or does it refer to الْأَجْهِزة? Then the verb should be تُدَعِّمُ? But
may a verb refer to a word as an agent that is, grammatically
speaking, not the subject? In Arabic, a subject needs the nominative case. Thus, theoretically, only one answer is correct.
Only الْعَدِيدُ can be the subject (فاعِلٌ).

The whole topic has to do with what linguists call the <u>logical
subject</u>. The problem with **quantifiers** is whether they should
be treated like real (masculine singular) nouns or ignored in
verbal agreement. In English, you ignore quantifiers: You say
some/a lot of people <u>are</u> here – and not: *<u>is</u> here*.

But in Arabic they are **true nouns** (اِسْمٌ), and form compound إِضافة-constructions with the following اِسْم, so they
should be treated as the main اِسْم. But since semantically they
are not the salient part, people often make the verb agree with
the following word.

What is the solution?

- If you want to be on the **safe side**, you should use يُدَعِّمُ,
  since عَدِيدٌ is technically a masculine noun (اِسْمٌ) and
  serves as the (فاعِلٌ). It is مَرْفُوع and marked by a ضَمّة!

- However, you can use the **logical subject** as well for agreement and use تُدَعَّمُ then. Although it is grammatically semi-correct, you will hear and see it occasionally.

This is similar to كُلٌّ. The word كُلٌّ is a masculine singular noun, verbs and adjectives may (should) agree in the masculine singular.

But it is also common for the verb or adjective (تَعْتُ) to agree with the gender and number of the word governed by كُلّ (i.e., the *logical subject*). Let us look at both options.

Option 1:	Verbs and adjectives agree in the masculine singular since كُلّ is a masculine singular اِسْمُ.
They are all silent.	كُلُّهُمْ صامِتٌ.

Option 2:	The adjective or verb agrees with the gender and number of the logical subject (= second part of the إِضافة).
We all will go.	كُلَّنا سَنَذْهَبُ.

The same is true for the word جَمِيعُ. When it is the first part of a إِضافة, the agreement is usually with the number and gender of the logical subject (= second part of the إِضافة).

You will find more examples in *Arabic for Nerds 2, question #148*.

260. How do you express: emphasis?

Arabic offers an arsenal of possibilities to emphasize something (التَّأْكِيدُ). By the way, did you know that *arsenal* is taken
from Arabic? Its origin may be the expression دارُ الصِّناعةِ
which means *house of manufacture*.

Arabic grammar alone gives you many tools to emphasize a
word. For example: أَنَّ • إِنَّ • the energetic ن in verbs • extra prepositions (بِ and مِنْ) • لِ.

You can also use expressions. Use these forms to emphasize
your statements when you are expressing your opinions, dis-
agreeing, making strong suggestions, expressing annoyance.

There is no doubt that	وَلا شَكَّ فِي أَنَّ
	وَمِمَّا لا شَكَّ فِيهِ أَنَّ
Surely; undoubtedly; no doubt	بِلا شَكَّ = بِلا رَيْبٍ
In fact; matter of fact; indeed	وَفِي واقِعِ الْأَمْرِ
	وَفِي حَقيقةِ الْأَمْرِ
	وَواقِعُ الْأَمْرِ
	وَحَقيقةُ الْأَمْرِ
Things being as they are; there will, no doubt, ...	أَمَّ وَالْأَمْرُ كَذَلِكَ
At first; in the beginning	فِي أَوَّلِ الْأَمْرِ
I totally reject this opinion.	وَإِنِّي أَرْفُضُ هذا الرَّأْيَ بِرُمَّتِهِ.
I am supporting (accepting) this opinion.	وَإِنِّي أَرْتَضِي هذا الرَّأْيَ.
This opinion is not acceptable from	وَلَيْسَ هذا الرَّأْيُ بِمَقْبُولٍ مِن

my point of view.	وِجْهَةِ نَظَرِي.
To a certain degree; to a certain extent	إلَ حَدٍّ ما
Of course; certainly	وَبِالطَّبْعِ
In the same book	وَفِي هٰذا الْكِتابِ نَفْسِهِ
He himself preferred this opinion.	وَقَدْ ذَهَبَ هُوَ نَفْسُهُ إِلَى هٰذا الرَّأْيِ.
The scientists/academics all agree	وَالْعُلَماءُ كُلُّهُمْ مُتَّفِقُونَ عَلَى
This matter is nothing but	وَلَيْسَ هٰذا الْأَمْرُ إِلَّا
Without limitation, we could say	وَما مِنْ حَدٍّ يَسْتَطِيعُ الْقَوْلَ إِنَّ
I (indeed; certainly) think that	وَأَظُنُّ ظَنًّا أَنَّ
And particularly	وَبِخاصَّةٍ
In particular	وَعَلَى وَجْهِ الْخُصُوصِ
Generally	وَعامَّةً
In general	وَبِعامَّةٍ
Boundless; infinite; unlimited	لا حَدَّ لَهُ = بِلا حَدٍّ = إِلَى غَيْرِ حَدٍّ
And the Arabs in general and the Egyptians in particular	وَالْعَرَبُ بِعامَّةٍ وَالْمِصْرِيُّونَ بِخاصَّةٍ
Though it clearly seems that	وَإِنَّ الْأَمْرَ لَيَبْدُو واضِحًا إِذا...
And one should never think that	وَلا يَحْسَبَنَّ أَحَدٌ أَنَّ
It is an opinion that is really worth mentioning.	وَهُوَ رَأْيٌ جَدِيرٌ بِالْقَوْلِ حَقًّا.

261. How do you express: amplification or likeness?

Amplification (التَّوْسِعةُ or التَّشابُهُ) is a rhetorical device writers use to embellish a sentence or statement by adding further information. You use such phrases if you want to highlight the importance of an idea.

Moreover; besides	وَفَضْلًا عَلَى ذٰلِكَ
In addition to that	وَبِالْإِضافةِ إِلَى ذٰلِك
Moreover; and again and once more	ثُمَّ إِنَّ
Moreover; just as; quite as; as on the other hand	كَما أَنَّ
As to, as for, as far as... is concerned; but; yet, however; on the other hand	أَمّا... فَ...
Regarding; concerning	فِيما يَتَعَلَّقُ بِ... فَ...
Perhaps it would be useful to say that	وَلَعَلَّ مِنَ الْمُفِيدِ الْقَوْلَ إِنَّ
Perhaps it is clear that	وَلَعَلَّ مِنَ الْواضِحِ أَنَّ
It is known that	وَمِنَ الْمَعْلُومِ أَنَّ
Notably; it is noticeable that	وَمِنَ الْمُلاحَظِ
And also	وَأَيْضًا
As well as	وَكَذٰلِكَ
A question arises here, which is	وَيَبْرُزُ هُنا سُؤالٌ هُوَ
It should be noted here	وَتَجْدُرُ الْإِشارةُ هُنا إِلَى
It is worth mentioning that	وَجَدِيرٌ بِالذِّكْرِ أَنَّ
	وَالْجَدِيرُ بِالذِّكْرِ أَنَّ

Likewise; similarly	وَعَلَى نَحْوٍ مُمَاثِلٍ
	وَعَلَى نَحْوٍ مُشَابِهٍ
In the same manner; likewise	عَلَى حَدٍّ سَوَاءٍ = عَلَى حَدٍّ سِوَى
It seems that	وَيَبْدُو أَنَّ
It also seems that	وَكَذَلِكَ يَبْدُو أَنَّ
It is strange that	وَمِن الْغَرِيبِ أَنَّ
The strange thing is that	وَالْغَرِيبُ مِن الْأَمْرِ أَنَّ
Not only this, but	لَيْسَ هذا فَحَسْبُ وَلَكِنْ
And that's all; and no more; only	فَحَسْبُ = فَقَطْ

262. How do you express: contrast or concession?

If you want to connect opposing ideas, you need the right words and expressions. We call these ideas contrast or concession. In English, you use *but, although, however, despite.*

| Contrast (الْمُقَابَلَةُ) | I used to live in Alexandria, but now I live in Tunis. |
| Concession (التَّسْلِيمُ) | Even though I live in Alexandria, I work in Cairo. |

But	وَلَكِنَّ	وَلَكِنْ
However	بَيْدَ أَنَّ	إلَّا أَنَّ
However; nevertheless		غَيْرَ أَنَّ

Although	وَعَلَى الرَّغْمِ مِن... فَ...
If it was not for	وَلَوْلا أَنَّ
In contrast to	وَعَلَى النَّقِيضِ مِن ذٰلِك
In contrast to this view	وَفِي مُقَابِلِ هٰذا الرَّأْي
The other opinion is that...	وَيَذْهَبُ رَأْيٌ آخَرُ إِلَى
Nevertheless	وَمَعَ أَنَّ وَمَعَ ذٰلِكَ
On the other hand	وَمِنْ نَاحِيةٍ أُخْرَى
Whilst	فِي حِينٍ يَرَى
One could say that	وَقَدْ يُقَالُ إِنَّ
If we compare this view to	وَإِذا قَارَنَّا هٰذا الرَّأْيَ بِ
After examining this view/opinion, it looks to me that	وَعِنْدَ تَمْحِيصِ هٰذا الرَّأْي يَبْدُو لِي أَنَّ
And if we challenged this	وَإِذا وَضَعْنا هٰذا بِإِزاءِ
It is acknowledged that	وَمِنَ الْمُسَلَّمِ بِهِ أَنَّ
It can't be denied	وَمِمَّا لا يُمْكِنُ إِنْكارُهُ
Whatever the case/matter is	وَمَهْما يَكُنْ مِن أَمْرٍ
Most likely	وَفِي أَغْلَبِ الظَّنِّ
It is likely that	وَمِنَ الْمُرَجَّحِ أَنَّ
Probably; most likely	وَالأَرْجَحُ أَنْ
I agree with this opinion.	وَإِنِّي أَتَّفِقُ مَعَ هٰذا الرَّأْي.
I accept this opinion.	وَإِنِّي أَرْتَضِي هٰذا الرَّأْيَ.
I tend to agree with this opinion.	وَإِنِّي أَمِيلُ إِلَى الأَخْذِ بِهٰذا الرَّأْي.

263. How do you express: to give an example?

How often do you say *for example* in English? It is indeed one of the most important expression. In Arabic, there are sophisticated ways to show that you want to explain something or give an example of something (الْمِثالُ).

For example, as an example	فَمَثَلًا
	فَعَلَى سَبِيلِ الْمِثالِ
An example of this is	وَمِن الْأَمْثِلةِ عَلَى هذا
The clearest example of this	وَأَوْضَحُ مِثالٍ عَلَى هذا
The closest (most tangible) example of this	وَأَقْرَبُ مِثالٍ عَلَى هذا
What shows; illustrates this	وَمِمَّا يُوَضّحُ هذا
What makes this idea clearer	وَمِمَّا يَزِيدُ هذِهِ الْفِكْرةَ وُضوحًا
An example that illustrates my opinion	وَمِن الْأَمْثِلةِ الّتِي تُوَضّحُ رَأْيِي
One example cited/given by the author	وَمِن الْأَمْثِلةِ الّتِي ذَكَرَها الْمُؤَلّفُ
This is similar to; this is like	وَيُشْبِهُ هذا بِ
	وَهذا شَبِيهُ بِ
Like this; similar to this	وَشَبِيهٍ بِهذا
Likewise	وَنَظِيرُ هذا
This is like	وَهذا مِثْلُ

264. How do you express: proof?

People always doubt. If you want to convince people, you need to show them that there is evidence or proof (الدَّلِيلُ) of what you are saying or writing. Here are some expressions that might do the job.

The proof	الدَّلِيلُ = الْحُجَّةُ = الْبُرْهانُ = الْبَيِّنَةُ
The evidence of this	وَالدَّلِيلُ عَلَى هٰذا
The evidence that supports this view	وَالدَّلِيلُ الَّذِي يَدْعَمُ هٰذا الرَّأْيَ
According to his statement; as he asserts; in his own words	عَلَى حَدِّ قَوْلِهِ
To draw conclusions (اِسْتَدَلَّ) from (مِنْ or بِ) with regard to (عَلَى)	اِسْتَدَلَّ
To hold the view; to be of the opinion (إِلَى that)	ذَهَبَ إِلَى
I quote what I am saying from	وَأَسْتَدِلُّ عَلَى ما أَذْهَبُ إِلَيْهِ بِ
What supports my opinion	وَمِمَّا يَدْعَمُ رَأْيِي
I support my opinion with some evidence	وَأَدْعَمُ رَأْيِي بِعِدَّةِ أَدِلَّةٍ
This is conclusive evidence	وَهٰذا دَلِيلٌ قاطِعٌ عَلَى
This is a clear proof of	وَهٰذا بُرْهانٌ ساطِعٌ عَلَى
A proof of this from real life	وَالدَّلِيلُ عَلَى هٰذا مِنْ واقِعِ الْحَياةِ
What confirms this opinion and supports it are the words of... (in-	وَمِمَّا يُؤَكِّدُ هٰذا الرَّأْيَ وَيَدْعَمُهُ قَوْلُ (فُلانٌ)

sert a name of a person)	
Perhaps the best evidence of what (name of a person) said	وَلَعَلَّ خَيْرَ دَلِيلٍ عَلَى هذا ما قالَ (فُلانٌ)
And (name of a person) agrees with me in this opinion	وَيَتَّفِقُ مَعِي فِي هٰذا الرَّأْي (فُلانٌ)
I don't agree with this opinion because it seems to me that	وَلَسْتُ أَتَّفِقُ مع هٰذا الرَّأْي إِذْ يَبْدُو لِي أَنَّ
The clearest evidence of my opinion are the words of (name of a person) in his book "xy" in which he says: "xy"	وَأَوْضَحُ دَلِيلٍ عَلَى ما أَذْهَبُ إِلَيْهِ قَوْلُ (فُلانٌ) فِي كِتابِهِ "xy" حَيْثُ يَقُولُ: "xy"

265. How do you express: cause and effect?

Cause and effect is a common method of organizing and discussing ideas. To determine **causes** (السَّبَبُ), you ask: *Why did this happen?* To identify **effects** (النَّتِيجةُ): *What happened because of this?* Let's see some examples in Arabic.

It is evident that; it is clear that	وَمِنْ هُنا يَتَّضِحُ أَنَّ
Thus, we conclude that	وَمِنْ ثَمَّ نَسْتَنْتِجُ أَنَّ
Hence, it is evident (clear) that	وَهٰكَذا يَتَّضِحُ أَنَّ
It is true to say that	وَعَلَى هٰذا يَصِحُّ أَنْ يُقالَ إِنَّ
This is necessarily a result of	وَيَنْتُجُ مِنْ هٰذا بِالضَّرُورةِ
This necessarily requires	وَ يَقْتَضِي هٰذا بِالضَّرُورةِ
As a result of this	وَنَتِيجةٌ لِهٰذا

For some reason or other	لِأَمْرٍ ما
Though, although, even though	وَإِنْ

Excursus: How do you use وَإِنْ?

If it denotes *although*, it needs to be preceded by وَ. We call this particle إِنْ الْوَصْلِيَّةُ. Usually, you find either (1) a **past tense verb** or (2) لَمْ **plus** verb in the jussive mood (مَجْزُومٌ) after وَإِنْ. The same is true for وَلَوْ which also conveys the meaning of *although*.

Zayd, although he is rich, is stingy.	زَيْدٌ وَإِنْ كَثُرَ مالُهُ بَخِيلٌ.
He has guided you, although before, you were of those astray. *(Sura 2:198)*	هَدَاكُمْ وَإِن كُنتُم مِّن قَبْلِهِ لَمِنَ الضَّالِّينَ.
So invoke Allah [...], although the disbelievers dislike it. *(Sura 40:14)*	فَادْعُوا اللَّهَ ..وَلَوْ كَرِهَ الْكَافِرُونَ.

Accordingly, we can say that	وَعَلَى هٰذا يَصِحُّ الْقَوْلُ إِنَّ
We can conclude from this	وَيُمْكِنُ أَنْ يُسْتَنْتَجَ مِن هٰذا
So	لِذٰلِكَ لِهٰذا لِذا
For this reason we can say that	وَلِهٰذا السَّبَبِ يُمْكِنُ الْقَوْلُ إِنَّ
And the explanation of that	وَتَعْلِيلُ ذٰلِكَ
This goes back to	وَهٰذا راجِعٌ/عائِدٌ إِلَى
Perhaps the reason for this is that	وَلَعَلَّ السَّبَبَ فِي هٰذا أَنَّ

266. How do you express: restatement?

Once you have presented your ideas in a passage, it is often useful to summarize or restate the main thought (إِعادةُ تَقْرِيرِ الْفِكْرةِ). Here are some expressions that might help.

In a summarized form	وَبِعِبارةٍ مُوجَزةٍ
All in all	وَخُلاصَةُ الْقَوْلِ أَنَّ
In short	وَبِعِبارةٍ مُخْتَصَرةٍ
In short, briefly, concisely	وَبِإِيجازٍ
It can be summarized as	وَيُمْكِنُ إِجْمالُ هذا فِي
To summarize this we can say that	وَإِيجازًا لِهذا يُمْكِنُ الْقَوْلُ إِنَّ
In other words	وَبِعِبارةٍ أُخْرى
Briefly, this means	وَيَعْنِي هذا فِي إِيجازٍ
This means	وَمَعْنَى هذا
To explain this idea I say that	وَإِيضاحًا لِهذِهِ الْفِكْرةِ أَقُولُ إِنَّ

267. How do you express: conclusion?

If you have to write an article, these expressions might be useful to express a conclusion – الْخاتِمَةُ

Finally	وَخِتامًا	وَأَخِيرًا
In short	وَجُمْلةُ الْقَوْلِ	
	وَخُلاصةُ الأَمْرِ	

All in all	وَإِجْمالًا لِما سَبَقَ
To sum it up, I say that	وَعَلَى سَبِيلِ الْإِجْمالِ أَقُولُ إِنَّ
In conclusion, I say that	وَفِي الْخاتِمَةِ أَقُولُ إِنَّ
I conclude by saying that this topic	وَأُخْتِمُ هٰذا الْمَوْضُوعَ بِقَوْلِي إِنَّ
So	وَإِذَنْ
And so we can say in conclusion	وَهٰكَذا يُمْكِنُ الْقَوْلُ فِي الْخِتامِ
To conclude this article I say that	وَخِتامًا لِهٰذا الْمَقالِ أَقُولُ إِنَّ
At the end, and to summarize what's above I say that	وَأُوثِرُ فِي الْخِتامِ أَنْ أُوجِزَ ما سَبَقَ فَأَقُولُ إِنَّ

268. How do you express: time or place?

Oftentimes, you need to go back in time or jump virtually into the future to express ideas. If you want to make that clear, you need an indicator of time (الزَّمانُ).

	وَحِينَئِذٍ
And then (see *question #228*)	وَعِنْدَئِذٍ
	وفِي ذٰلِك الْحِينِ
At that time	وَوَقْتَئِذٍ
And then	وَبَعْدَئِذٍ
Previously	وَمِنْ قَبْلُ
Onwards	وَما بَعْدُ

Following that	وَعَقِبَ ذٰلِك
Immediately; right away	وَعَلَى الْفَوْرِ
Since then	وَمُنْذُ ذٰلِكَ الْحِينِ
Later in; at a later stage	وَفِي مَرْحَلَةٍ مُتَأَخِّرَةٍ
At the turn of the century	فِي مَطْلَعِ الْقَرْنِ
Until	إِلَى أَنْ
Until; even	وَحَتَّى
When	وَعِنْدَما
As	وَلَمَّا
As *soon as* this book appeared, the general concept began to change.	وَما إِنْ ظَهَرَ هٰذا الْكِتابُ حَتَّى بَدَأَ الْمَفْهُومُ الْعامُّ يَتَغَيَّرُ.
They promised to help him *as soon as* they could.	وَعَدُوهُ بِالْمُساعَدةِ حالَما يُصْبِحُونَ قادِرِينَ عَلَى ذٰلِك.

Sometimes you need to change the perspective of the narrator and switch positions and places (الْمَكانُ). Here are some examples of how to do that in Arabic.

From a distance it looks like that	وَيَظْهَرُ عَلَى الْبُعْدِ
Up close/far; at a short/long distance	وَعَلَى مَسافةٍ قَرِيبةٍ/بَعِيدةٍ
Taking a closer look at, it seems…; from a very short distance, it seems	وَعَلَى مَسافةٍ أَقْرَب يَبْدُو
If we take a good look	وَإِذا دَقَّقْنا النَّظَرَ
At first glance the place seems	وَيَبْدُو مِنْ خِلالِ النَّظْرةِ الْأُولَى إِلَى الْمَكانِ

And after a closer look, it appears	وَيَبْدُو مِنْ خِلالِ النَّظْرِة الْفاحِصةِ
In the heart of the place	وَفِي صَدْرِ الْمَكانِ
From the front, it appears	وَيَبْدُو فِي الْمَنْظَرِ الْأَمامِيِّ
From the back (to the rear), it appears	وَيَبْدُو إِلَى الْخَلْفِ
From far away, the place appears	وَعَلَى مَسافةٍ أَبْعَدَ يَظْهَرُ الْمَكانُ
The general overview of the place shows that	وَالنَّظْرةُ الْعامَّةُ لِلْمَكانِ تُظْهِرُ أَنَّ

269. How do you start emails and formal letters in Arabic?

Writing letters or emails in Arabic is not that difficult. Once you have started writing letters or emails, you will get used to the standard phrases pretty quickly.

Never forget the most important rule: **try to be polite!**

1. The salutation (الْمُخاطَبَة). The key word is *mister* (سَيِّدٌ) and its plural forms.

plural	sing.	meaning
سَيِّداتٌ	سَيِّدَةٌ	Miss

plural	sing.	meaning
سادةٌ	سَيِّدٌ	Mister, Sir

Ladies and gentlemen!	(أَيُّها) السّادةُ وَالسَّيِّداتُ!

German	English	Arabic
Sehr geehrte Herren	Dear gentlemen	السَّادَةُ الْمُحْتَرَمُونَ جِدًّا
Sehr geehrte Damen und Herren	Dear ladies and gentlemen	السَّيِّداتُ الْمُحْتَرَماتُ وَالسَّادَةُ الْمُحْتَرَمُونَ
Sehr geehrter Herr	Dear Sir	سَيِّدِي الْمُحْتَرَمُ
Sehr geehrter Herr Salem	Dear Mr. Salem	السَّيِّدُ سالِم الْمُحْتَرَمُ جِدًّا
Sehr geehrter Herr Dr. Salem	Dear Dr. Salem	السَّيِّدُ الدُّكْتُورُ سالِم الْمُحْتَرَمُ
Liebe Mama	Dear Mother	أُمِّي الْحَبِيبَةُ
Lieber Hassan	Dear Hassan	عَزِيزِي حَسَن
Liebe Fatima	Dear Fatima	عَزِيزَتِي فاطِمة
Geschätzter Scheich	Esteemed Sheikh	فَضِيلةُ الشَّيْخِ
Herr Vorsitzender (Anrede eines Richters)	Your Honor	حَضْرَةُ الْقاضِي

Note: Also in dialects, people use the word *presence* (حَضْرَة) as a respectful term of address. For example, if you want to address a man, you say حَضْرَتُكَ, which literally means *your presence*.

2. Phrases to start the letter.

German	English	Arabic
Wir danken Ihnen für Ihre Informationen, die wir mit Interesse	We thank you for your information which we found in-	نَحْنُ نَشْكُرُكُمْ عَلَى المَعْلُوماتِ الَّتِي تَهْتَمُّ

zur Kenntnis genommen haben.	teresting.	بِمَعْرِفَتِها.
Wir danken Ihnen für Ihre Bestellung vom 7. August.	We thank you for your order dated 7th August.	نَحْنُ نَشْكُرُكُمْ عَلَى طَلَبِكُمْ 7 أَغُسْطُس.
Herzlichen Dank für Ihr Angebot vom 7. August.	Thank you very much for your offer dated 7th August.	شُكْرًا جَزِيلًا عَلَى الْعَرْض الَّذِي قَدَّمْتُمُوهُ يَوْمَ 7 أَغُسْطُس.
In Antwort auf Ihren Brief sende ich Ihnen...	In response to your letter I hereby send...	رُدًّا عَلَى خِطابِكُمْ, أُرْسِلُ لَكُمْ...
Wir beantworten gerne Ihre Anfrage bezüglich...	We are happy to respond to your inquiry regarding...	تَوَدُّ أَنْ نُجِيبَ عَنْ اِسْتِفْسارِكُمْ بِشَأْنِ
Mangels einer Kontaktadresse wende ich mich an Sie mit der Bitte, diesen Brief an die richtige Stelle weiterzuleiten.	In the absence of a contact address, I turn to you with a request to forward this letter to the right place.	نَظَرًا لِعَدَم وُجُودِ عُنْوانٍ لِلْاتِّصال بِالْمَكانِ الْمَطْلُوبِ, فَإِنِّي أَرْجُوكُمْ أَنْ تَبْعَثُوا بِهذا الْخِطابِ إِلَى الْجِهَةِ الْمُخْتَصَّةِ.
Ich möchte bei Ihnen Folgendes reservieren:	I would like to make the following reservation:	أَوَدُّ أَنْ أَحْجُزَ لَدَيْكُمْ كَما يَلِي:
Bitte teilen Sie uns den Preis für 3 Doppelzimmer mit Bad/WC und Frühstück für die Zeit vom 5. bis 8. August mit.	Please tell us the rate for 3 double rooms with bathroom/WC, breakfast included, for the period of 5th to 8th August.	بِرَجاءِ إِبْلاغِنا بِسِعْرِ 3 غُرَفٍ مُزْدَوِجَةٍ بِالْحَمّام/النَّوالِيتِ وَبِالفَطُورِ فِي الْفَتْرَةِ مِن 5-8 أَغُسْطُس.
Wir danken Ihnen für	We thank you for	نَحْنُ نَتَقَدَّم بِالشُّكْرِ

German	English	Arabic
Ihren Anruf.	your call.	الْجَزِيلِ عَلَى مُكالَمَتِكُمْ.
Mit Bezug auf Ihr Schreiben vom 4. August dieses Jahres müssen wir Ihnen leider mitteilen, dass wir nicht in der Lage sind…	Concerning your letter dated 4th August 2018, we are very sorry to inform you that we are not able to…	بِالإِشارَةِ إِلَى خِطابِكُم الْمُؤَرَّخ 4 أُغُسْطُس لِهذا الْعام يُؤْسِفُنا أَنْ نُبْلِغَ حَضْرَتَكَ أَنَّنا لا نَسْتَطِيعُ أَنْ…-.
Leider muss ich mich über den schlechten Service Ihres Hotels während meines letzten Aufenthalts beschweren.	Unfortunately, I have to complain about the poor service of your hotel during my last stay.	إِنَّهُ يُؤْسِفُنِي أَنْ أَشْكُو لِسِيادَتِكُمْ سُوءَ الْخِدْمَةِ فِي فُنْدُقِكُمْ وَالَّذِي تَعَرَّضْتُ لَهُ خِلالَ فَتْرَةِ إِقامَتِي الْأَخِيرَةِ لِدَيْكُمْ.

270. How do you end emails and formal letters in Arabic?

The conventional ending (الْخِتامُ) in Arabic letters or emails is usually a very polite expression.

1. Sentences and phrases that you might use in the last part of a letter or e-mail.

German	English	Arabic
Könnten Sie mir die diesbezüglichen Formalitäten mitteilen und mir die erforderlichen Formulare zukommen lassen?	Could you inform me about the formalities and provide me with the necessary forms?	هَلْ يُمْكِنُ أَنْ تُمِدُّونِي بِمَعْلُوماتٍ عَنْ شَكْلِيّاتٍ مُحْتَمَلَةٍ، وَأَنْ تُرْسِلُوا لِي الْاِسْتِماراتِ الْمَطْلُوبَةَ كَذَلِكَ؟

Für Ihre diesbezüglichen Informationen wären wir Ihnen äußerst dankbar.	We would be very grateful for your information concerning that matter.	سَنَكُونُ فِي غَايَةِ الْإِمْتِنَانِ لِسِيَادَتِكُم لِلْمَعْلُومَاتِ الْخَاصَّةِ بِهذا الشَّأْنِ.
In der Anlage finden Sie eine Fotokopie des …	Attached you will find a photocopy of …	مُرْفَقٌ بِهذا الْخِطَابِ صُورَةٌ لِ...٠
Ich entschuldige mich noch einmal für die Ihnen verursachten Unannehmlichkeiten und verspreche Ihnen, dass solche Irrtümer nicht wieder vorkommen werden.	I once again apologize for the inconvenience caused to you and promise you that such mistakes will not happen again.	أَنَا أَعْتَذِرُ مَرَّةً أُخْرَى عَنِ الْمُضَايَقَاتِ النَّاجِمَةِ عَن ذلِكَ, وَأَعِدُكُمْ بِأَنَّ هذِهِ الْأَخْطَاءَ لَنْ تَتَكَرَّرَ مَرَّةً أُخْرَى.
Die Frist ist nun abgelaufen und wir erwarten die sofortige Begleichung der oben genannten Rechnung.	The deadline has now expired, and we expect the immediate settlement of the above mentioned invoice/bill.	وَلَقَدْ إِنْتَهَتْ هذِهِ الْمُدَّةُ, وَنَحْنُ نَنْتَظِرُ السَّدَادَ الْفَوْرِيَّ لِلْفَاتُورَةِ الْمَذْكُورَةِ أَعْلاهُ.
Wir sehen Ihrer Antwort gern entgegen.	We are looking forward to your answer.	نَحْنُ نَنْتَظِرُ رَدَّكُمْ بِشَغَفٍ.
Falls Sie Fragen zu diesen Änderungen haben, zögern Sie bitte nicht, uns zu kontaktieren.	If you have any questions about these changes, please do not hesitate to contact us.	إِذَا كَانَ لَدَيْكُمْ أَيُّ إِسْتِفْسَارَاتٍ عَن هذِهِ التَّغْيِيرَاتِ فَلَا تَتَرَدَّدُوا أَنْ تَلْجَأُوا إِلَيْنَا.
Sie erreichen uns unter der Telefonnummer 1234. Ich werde	You can reach us by phone (1234). I will be in your area next	يُمْكِنُكُم الْإِتِّصَالُ بِنَا فِي رَقْمِ التِّلِيفُونِ 1234, إِذْ إِنِّي سَأَكُونُ

German	English	Arabic
kommende Woche in Ihrer Gegend sein und könnte bei dieser Gelegenheit bei Ihnen vorsprechen.	week and could talk with you on this occasion.	فِي الْأُسْبُوعِ الْمُقْبِلِ فِي مِنْطَقَتِكُمْ, وَبِإِمْكَانِي التَّحَدُّثُ مَعَكُمْ.
Wir möchten Sie deshalb ersuchen, die Angelegenheit im Interesse unserer zukünftigen Geschäftsbeziehungen zu klären.	Therefore, we would like to ask you to clarify the matter in the interest of our future business relationships.	وَلِذَلِكَ نَوَدُّ مِنْ سِيَادَتِكُمْ تَوْضِيحًا لِهَذِهِ الظَّاهِرَةِ لِمَصْلَحَةِ عَلَاقَاتِنا التِّجارِيَّةِ الْمُسْتَقْبَلِيَّةِ.
Wir möchten Sie ersuchen, die Angelegenheit so bald wie möglich richtig zu stellen.	We would like to ask you to correct the matter as soon as possible.	وَنَوَدُّ إِصْلاحَ مَوْقِفِكُمْ بِأَسْرَعِ وَقْتٍ مُمْكِنٍ.

2. Conventional ending. That's pretty standard in Arabic.

German	English	Arabic
Mit besten Grüßen; Mit freundlichen Grüßen	Best regards; With kind regards	• مَعَ خالِصٍ • تَحِيّاتِنا مَعَ خالِصِ تَحِيّاتِي • أَرَقُّ تَحِيّاتِنا
In unendlicher Dankbarkeit	With infinite gratitude	وَلَكُمْ مِنِّي جَزِيلُ الشُّكْرِ وَالْإمْتِنانِ
Mit dem aufrichtigsten Ausdruck von Dankbarkeit und Rücksichtnahme	With the most sincere expressions of gratitude and consideration	مَعَ أَخْلَصِ عِبارَاتِ الشُّكْرِ وَالتَّقْدِيرِ

GLOSSARY OF ENGLISH GRAMMAR TERMS

Adjectives	الصِّفةُ, النَّعْتُ	Words that describe: a *nice* girl, the *big* house.
Adverb	الظَّرْفُ	Any word, phrase, or clause that tells you how, when, where, or why: he drove *quickly*; he came *after the appointment*; he entered *smiling*.
		What we call in English an adverb could be in Arabic a: مَفْعُولٌ فِيهِ, مَفْعُولٌ لَهُ, حالٌ, etc.
Apposition	الْبَدَلُ	Two noun phrases next to each, and they refer to the same person or thing. Usually we can reverse the order of the phrases. For example: Michael, their oldest child, is... Their oldest child, Michael, is...
Agreement	الْمُطابَقةُ	Shows that a word hangs together with a particular noun – in English, a word may agree in number and gender (sometimes in person) with another noun. In Arabic, you have to pay attention to "harmonize" the case and definiteness as well.
Clauses	الْعِبارةُ	These are sentences nested inside the larger sentence. There are basically two types: main clauses and subordinate clauses, which are joined by certain grammatical devices such as conjunctions: He said (that) *you are beautiful.* A clause is a group of words that consists of a subject and a verb. A phrase is a collection of words without having a sub-

		ject. What in English would be a clause could be in Arabic a phrase and vice versa.
Comparative (superlative)	اِسْمُ التَّفْضِيلِ	Denotes *more, most; better, best, etc.*
Construct phrase, possessive construction	الْإِضافةُ	Two Arabic words side by side, like English *the teacher's house.* In order to convert an English construction into Arabic, use this formula: English *B's A* = Arabic *A of B.* (teacher's house = house of the teacher = بَيْتُ الْمُدَرِّسِ).
Declension (inflection); declinable; indeclinable	الْإِعْرابُ؛ التَّصْرِيفُ؛ التَّغْيِيرُ فِي الْكَلِمةِ	A process which involves changing the form of a word: of nouns, pronouns, adjectives, adverbs, numerals, and articles to indicate number (singular and plural), case or mood (nominative, genitive, accusative case; indicative, subjunctive, jussive mood), and/or gender. Usually achieved by adding prefixes, suffixes, case markers (not in English).
Definite article	أَداةُ التَّعْرِيفِ	Simply said, it is the word *the* in English.
Demonstratives	اِسْمُ الْإِشارةِ	They single out: *this* book, *that* girl (demonstrative determiners); tell me *this*, what's *that*? (demonstrative pronouns).
Implicitly understood; supposition, assump-	التَّقْدِيرُ تَقْدِيرُالْحَذْفِ	In a way that is not directly expressed; tacitly. It means that a part of the sentence has been omitted because it is implied. In Arabic, we will often use this concept to explain cases, missing words,

tion; ellipsis		etc. But it is also found in English. For example: Question: *Why did you go to Egypt?* Answer: *To study Arabic.* Here, the implied part is: *Because I wanted to study Arabic.* This element is implicitly understood, so we can leave it out and use the infinitive on its own.
Imperative	الْأَمْرُ	A verb form expressing a request or demand: *Stop* that car! *Drink!*
Masculine (feminine)	الْمُذَكَّرُ؛ الْمُؤَّنَّثُ	All Arabic nouns have a certain gender, either masculine or feminine. The gender is not necessarily connected with male or female.
Mood	صِيغةُ الْأَفْعالِ	The mood, or <u>purpose</u>, of a sentence is related to its *form*. Tense is a form as well an idea. The past tense, e.g., can express time or an idea (conditional mood). When a sentence makes a statement, it is in the indicative mood (فَعْلٌ مَرْفُوعٌ) – the normal mood.
Object	الْمَفْعُولُ	The object of a verb is the person or thing undergoing the action. For ex., I wrote *the book.*
Ordinals	الْعَدَدُ التَّرْتِيبِيُّ	Indicate order by number: *first, forth.*
Participles (active and passive)	اِسْمُ الْفاعِلِ؛ اِسْم الْمِفْعُولِ	They are called participle because they "participate" the properties of both a verb and an adjective. Usually you identify them by the ending: -*ing* or -*ed*. The participles of *to write* are *writing* (active

participle) and *written* (passive participle). In English, a participle plays a role similar to an adjective or adverb (a *written* letter). In Arabic, participles can do many jobs in a sentence.

The whole concept is different in English. The past participle is often what we would call the passive participle in Arabic: The food was *eaten*.

Passive voice	صِيغَةُ الْمَبْنِيِّ لِلْمَجْهُولِ	The passive is used to show interest in the person (or thing) that *experiences* an action rather than the person/thing that *performs* the action (active voice). E.g.: My car *was stolen*.
Plural	الْجَمْعُ	Indicates more than one: book vs. *books*
Possessive pronoun	ضَمِيرُ الْمِلْكِيّةِ	Indicates to whom or what something belongs or relates. For example, *my* book.
Prefix	السّابِقةُ	Bits or devices added before a word – future tense prefixes, noun prefixes, ...
Prepositions	حَرْفُ الْجَرِّ	Short words (in Arabic sometimes just letters) indicating an object or when, where, how, etc. For ex.: *to* John, *for* you, *with* Sarah, *under* the tree, *after* that. What we call in English a preposition might be in Arabic an adverb.
Pronouns	الضَّمِيرُ	They stand in for a specific noun: *they, them, this, someone, who, what*. Personal pronouns denote *I, you, he, she,* ...
Quantifiers	الْمُحَدَّدُ الْكَمّيُّ	They indicate quantity: *a lot of, some, all*.

Regent (governor, operator)	الْعَامِلُ	Government in grammar is the control by words over other words. It defines the relationship between words (agent and patient). A regent or operator has the power to govern other words and triggers a specific case or state/mood to describe that relationship.
Reflexive verbs	فِعْلُ الْمُطاوَعةِ	Such verbs denote doing something to oneself: he killed *himself*.
Relative clauses	عِبارةُ الصِّلةِ	They add information about a noun: the book *that I wrote* has 770 pages.
Root	الْجِذْرُ	Arabic words are based on skeletons of consonants (usually three) from which the typical Arabic word is built.
Singular	الْمُفْرَدُ	Indicates one: *book* vs. books.
Subject	الْفاعِلُ or الْمُبْتَدَأُ	Subject of sentences are the nouns doing the action (nouns with which the verbs agree). *The dog* bites the post man.
Suffixes	اللَّاحِقةُ	Bits or devices attached as word endings: dog*s*, mov*able*.
Tenses	الزَّمَنُ	They determine the form of a verb expressing past, present and future **time**.
Verbs	الْفِعْلُ	Verbs indicate actions (rarely states): to eat, to talk, to love.
Vocative	النِّداءُ	A form of direct address to indicate the person or thing addressed. For example, *Have mercy, O Lord!*

ISLAMIC SALUTATIONS AFTER CERTAIN NAMES

After mentioning Allah, Muhammad, Islamic prophets or companions of Muhammad, Muslims are supposed to praise them by uttering specific expressions. I don't use these expressions in the book, however, Muslims are supposed to say them. Here is a list of complimentary phrases that are used after certain names:

ALLAH: After mentioning Allah, Muslims say *"subhānahu wa ta'ālā"* (سُبْحانَهُ وَتَعالَى) which means: *"Glorious and exalted is He (Allah)"*. This is exclusively used with Allah. Abbreviation in English texts: SWT.

MUHAMMAD (مُحَمَّدٌ): After mentioning the Prophet's name, Muslims say *"sallā Allāhu 'alayhi wa sallam(a)"* (صَلَّى اللهُ عَلَيْهِ وَسَلَّمَ). It means: *"Allah bless him and grant him peace."* You may also hear: *"(May) Allah pray for him and save him!"* The abbreviation is, SAAS or SAAW or in its English translation: peace be upon him (PBUH).

MESSENGERS, PROPHETS and ARCHANGELS – in short: people who are unerring according to Islam. After their names, Muslims say: *"'alayhi al-Salām"* (عَلَيْهِ السَّلامُ) which means: *"Peace be upon him"*. It is said after mentioning, e.g. Noah (نُوح) or Gabriel (جِبْرِيل). Abbreviation in English: AS.

COMPANIONS (الصَّحابةُ) **of the Prophet Muhammad:** After mentioning one of Muhammad's companions, Muslims say the wish *"radiya Allāhu 'anhu"* (رَضِيَ اللهُ عَنْهُ). It means: *"May Allah be pleased with them."* This is said for example after Muhammad's father-in-law 'Abū Bakr (أَبُو بَكْر) or Muhammad's wife 'Ā'isha (عائشة بِنْت أَبِي بَكْر). Abbreviation in English: RA.

INDEX

Printed in Poland
by Amazon Fulfillment
Poland Sp. z o.o., Wrocław

60886851R00309